Praise for *Slouching Towards Gomorrah*

"Bork makes some astute points about the politicization (not to mention Balkanization) of American culture and the diminished role that reason and rationality have come to play in our intellec tual discourse."

"A superb new book."

—Rich

"America will ignore Robert Bork's ....age and repentance at its own peril."

—Ernest Lefever, *Books & Culture*

"Judge Bork pulls no punches in describing the past and challenging us to fight for our children's future."

—Dan Quayle,
Forty-fourth Vice President of the United States

"Here is a certain trumpet in the midst of the cacophony of crap flooding and penetrating our ears, eyes, and senses. Read and heed!"

—Alan K. Simpson, former Senator from Wyoming

"*Slouching Towards Gomorrah* is for Americans who are concerned about the hedonistic drift of our nation."

—Alexander M. Haig

"The ideological triumph of liberalism among American elites— far from bringing the individual and social enlightenment it promised—has produced unprecedented moral decay. The principal victims of this decay are the poorest and most vulnerable among us—those most in need of the support of a healthy culture. Bork courageously and boldly states these truths. A judge as wise as Solomon has become a prophet as powerful as Isaiah."

—Robert P. George,
Department of Politics, Princeton University

"A thesis that cannot be ignored. Mr. Bork, one of America's clearest thinkers, uses a variety of current issues of debate to argue that America is on the decline."

—John Cardinal O'Connor, Archbishop of New York

"A tour de force. A must-read for anyone concerned about the state of American society at the close of the twentieth century."

—Ralph Reed, Executive Director, Christian Coalition

"A brilliant blend of passionate conviction and sustained argument. May be the most important book of the '90s."

—Michael Novak, George Frederick Jewett Scholar in Religion and Public Policy, American Enterprise Institute

"With his inimitable combination of outrage and wit, Judge Bork has written the definitive account of an America on the eve of the millennium. Ranging through every aspect of our culture and society—sex and race, crime and welfare, religion and the courts—his book is not only a comprehensive description of our condition; it is a profound analysis of its ideological and historical roots."

—Gertrude Himmelfarb, Professor Emeritus of History, City University of New York

"A must-read for anyone who cares about the future of American society. Presents a provocative, critical, and convincing picture of a culture careening out of control, a culture that must change its ways or face destruction."

—Senator Chuck Grassley (R-Iowa)

SLOUCHING TOWARDS GOMORRAH

Robert H. Bork

SLOUCHING TOWARDS GOMORRAH

MODERN LIBERALISM AND AMERICAN DECLINE

HARPER ● PERENNIAL

NEW YORK ● LONDON ● TORONTO ● SYDNEY

For Mary Ellen, sharer of good days,
comforter on bleak ones

HARPER ● PERENNIAL

Grateful acknowledgment is made to Simon & Schuster for permission to reprint in the U.S. "The Second Coming" from *The Poems of W. B. Yeats: A New Edition*, edited by Richard J. Finneran. Copyright © 1924 by Macmillan Publishing Company; © renewed 1952 by Bertha Georgie Yeats. Reprinted in the U.K. with the permission of A. P. Watt Ltd. on behalf of Michael Yeats.

A hardcover edition of this book was published in 1996 by HarperCollins Publishers, and a paperback edition appeared in 1977.

HarperCollins books may be purchased for educational, business, or sales promotional use. For information, please e-mail the Special Markets Department at SPsales@harpercollins.com.

Revised paperback edition published 2003.

Designed by Alma Orenstein

The Library of Congress has catalogued the hardcover edition as follows:

Bork, Robert H.
    Slouching towards Gomorrah : modern liberalism and American decline / Robert H. Bork.
        p.   cm.
    Includes bibliographical references.
    ISBN 0-06-039163-4
    1. United States—Social conditions—1980–   2. Liberalism—United States.   3. Social values—United States.   I. Title.
HN59.2.B68   1996
306' .0973—dc20   96-31277

ISBN 978-0-06-057311-9

HB 01.03.2024

There is good reason why William Butler Yeats's "The Second Coming" is probably the most quoted poem of our time. The image of a world disintegrating, then to be subjected to a brutal force, speaks to our fears now.

THE SECOND COMING

Turning and turning in the widening gyre
The falcon cannot hear the falconer;
Things fall apart; the centre cannot hold;
Mere anarchy is loosed upon the world,
The blood-dimmed tide is loosed, and everywhere
The ceremony of innocence is drowned;
The best lack all conviction, while the worst
Are full of passionate intensity.

Surely some revelation is at hand;
Surely the Second Coming is at hand.
The Second Coming! Hardly are those words out
When a vast image out of Spiritus Mundi
Troubles my sight: somewhere in sands of the desert
A shape with lion body and the head of a man,
A gaze blank and pitiless as the sun,
Is moving its slow thighs, while all about it
Reel shadows of the indignant desert birds.
The darkness drops again; but now I know
That twenty centuries of stony sleep
Were vexed to nightmare by a rocking cradle,
And what rough beast, its hour come round at last,
Slouches towards Bethlehem to be born?

—WILLIAM BUTLER YEATS

When Yeats wrote that in 1919, he may have foreseen that the twentieth century would experience the "blood-dimmed tide," as indeed it has. But he can hardly have had any conception of just how thoroughly things would fall apart as the center failed to hold in the last third of this century. He can hardly have foreseen that passionate intensity, uncoupled from morality, would shred the fabric of Western culture. The rough beast of decadence, a long time in gestation, having reached its maturity in the last three decades, now sends us slouching towards our new home, not Bethlehem but Gomorrah.

Contents

PART III

Acknowledgments

My first debt is to the late Erwin Glikes, my editor and publisher at The Free Press when I wrote, with his sympathetic guidance, my previous book. We agreed that the next book should deal with American culture. He did not live to see the project underway. His death at the age of 56 was both a great personal and an intellectual loss.

Judith Regan, the publisher of ReganBooks at HarperCollins, has my gratitude for offering me a new home after Erwin's death. She has proved an extraordinarily patient editor-publisher, with just the right amount of impatience to bring what could have been an endless labor to an end.

Midge Decter, the editor of my first book, on antitrust policy, consented to edit this book as well. She proved exceptionally helpful and supportive, not only on questions of tone and approach, but upon details of the argument. I am deeply indebted and grateful to her.

Daniel E. Troy, who was my clerk when I was a judge, took time out from a busy private practice to read the manuscript more than once and make any number of highly intelligent and useful suggestions.

John DiIulio, Professor of Politics and Public Affairs, Princeton University, and Director, Center for Public Management, Brookings Institution, read and greatly improved chapter 9. Charles Krauthammer, columnist and former practitioner of medicine, read and made very useful comments on chapter 10. Irving Kristol read the book and offered some general and well-taken criticisms that I tried to meet. Dianne Irving, Professor of Philosophy, DeSales School of Theology and a research biochemist, educated me about the beginnings of life and abortion. (See, for example, her "Scientific and Philosophical Expertise: An Evaluation of the Arguments on 'Personhood,'" *Linacre Quarterly*, February, 1993, p. 18.) My wife, Mary Ellen, made many suggestions and provided moral support on bleak days.

Jennifer Boeke Caterini conducted research, gave advice, and supervised the interns who assisted with research and the organization of materials. My secretary, Laura Hardy, did everything: typing, copying, dealing with callers and correspondents, finding books, and handling innumerable details of life so that I was free to write.

In the early stages, research assistance was provided by Gregory Maggs, now an Associate Professor of Law at George Washington University, and Joshua Abramowitz.

Robert Barnett, lawyer and literary agent, has now twice led me through the labyrinths of the publishing world and again drafted a contract that pleased everyone involved.

The New Criterion has authorized me to include passages from my article in their series "The Survival of Culture": "Adversary Jurisprudence," Vol. 20, No. 9 (May 2002), p.4.

Chapter 16 is a substantial revision of a chapter of the same name in *Aspects of American Liberty: Philosophical, Material, and Political* (Philadelphia: The American Philosophical Society, 1977), p. 174.

I am grateful to the American Enterprise Institute, which has supported me in this enterprise, and to the John M. Olin Foundation, whose grant makes that support possible. My personal thanks go to Christopher C. DeMuth, the President of AEI, and to William Simon and James Piereson, President and Executive Director, respectively, of the Olin Foundation.

The views expressed in this book are my own and are not necessarily shared by any of the people or organizations I have thanked.

A Word About Structure

Part I of this book begins with two chapters about the Sixties because that decade brought to a climax trends that had long been developing in America and in other nations of the West. It was a politicized decade, one whose activists saw all of culture and life as political. The consequence is that our culture is now politicized. It worked the other way as well: our politics is increasingly (we need such a word) culturized. We have a new and extremely divisive politics of personal identity. We have invented a range of new or newly savage political-cultural battlegrounds. Democrats and Republicans have begun to line up on opposing sides of the war in the culture.

Because my thesis is that these developments have been coming on for a long time and may be inherent in Western civilization, Part I continues with two chapters that examine the themes of liberty and equality, which were celebrated in the Declaration of Independence and are dominant in our culture today. These ideals have been pressed much too far and account for the cultural devastation wrought by modern liberalism. Chapters 5 and 6 discuss the forces that advance the agenda of modern liberalism: the "intellectual" class and that class's enforcement arm, the judiciary, headed by the Supreme Court of the United States.

Part II, consisting of chapters 7 through 15, examines the particular institutions and areas of cultural warfare that result from the twin thrusts of modern liberalism: radical individualism and radical egalitarianism. This part of the book takes up the collapse of popular culture; the case for censorship; crime, illegitimacy, and welfare; abortion and euthanasia; the politics of sex (radical feminism); the dilemmas of race; the decline of intellect; the trouble in religion; and the fragmentation of our society into warring groups.

Part III consists of two chapters examining the prospects for the survival of democratic government and the question of whether America can reverse its decline and avoid becoming Gomorrah.

Introduction

One morning on my way to teach a class at the Yale law school, I found on the sidewalk outside the building heaps of smoldering books that had been burned in the law library. They were a small symbol of what was happening on campuses across the nation: violence, destruction of property, mindless hatred of law, authority, and tradition. I stood there, uncomprehending, as a photograph in the next day's *New York Times* clearly showed. What did they want, these students? What conceivable goals led them to this and to the general havoc they were wreaking on the university? Living in the Sixties, my faculty colleagues and I had no understanding of what it was about, where it came from, or how long the misery would last. It was only much later that a degree of understanding came.

To understand our current plight, we must look back to the tumults of those years, which brought to a crescendo developments in the Fifties and before that most of us had overlooked or misunderstood. We noticed (who could help but notice?) Elvis Presley, rock music, James Dean, the radical sociologist C. Wright Mills, Jack Kerouac and the Beats. We did not understand, however, that far from being isolated curiosities, these were harbingers of a new culture that would shortly burst upon us and sweep us into a different country.

The Fifties were the years of Eisenhower's presidency. Our

domestic world seemed normal and, for the most part, almost placid. The signs were misleading. Politics is a lagging indicator.

Culture eventually makes politics. The cultural seepages of the Fifties strengthened and became a torrent that swept through the nation in the Sixties, only to seem to die away in the Seventies. The election of Ronald Reagan in 1980 and the defeat of several of the most liberal senators seemed a reaffirmation of traditional values and proof that the Sixties were dead. They were not. The spirit of the Sixties revived in the Eighties and brought us at last to Bill and Hillary Clinton, the very personifications of the Sixties generation arrived at early middle age with its ideological baggage intact.

This is a book about American decline. Since American culture is a variant of the cultures of all Western industrialized democracies, it may even, inadvertently, be a book about Western decline. In the United States, at least, that decline and the mounting resistance to it have produced what we now call a culture war. It is impossible to say what the outcome will be, but for the moment our trajectory continues downward. This is not to deny that much in our culture remains healthy, that many families are intact and continue to raise children with strong moral values. American culture is complex and resilient. But it is also not to be denied that there are aspects of almost every branch of our culture that are worse than ever before and that the rot is spreading.

"Culture," as used here, refers to all human behavior and institutions, including popular entertainment, art, religion, education, scholarship, economic activity, science, technology, law, and morality. Of that list, only science, technology, and the economy may be said to be healthy today, and it is problematical how long that will last. Improbable as it may seem, science and technology themselves are increasingly under attack, and it seems highly unlikely that a vigorous economy can be sustained in an enfeebled, hedonistic culture, particularly when that culture distorts incentives by increasingly rejecting personal achievement as the criterion for the distribution of rewards.

With each new evidence of deterioration, we lament for a moment, and then become accustomed to it. We hear one day of the latest rap song calling for killing policemen or the sexual mutilation of women; the next, of coercive left-wing political indoctrination at a prestigious university; then of the latest homicide figures for New York City, Los Angeles, or the District of Columbia; of the collapse of the criminal justice system, which displays an inability to punish adequately and, often enough, an inability even to convict the clearly guilty; of the rising rate of illegitimate births; the uninhibited display of sexuality and the popularization of violence in our entertainment; worsening racial tensions; the angry activists of feminism, homosexuality, environmentalism, animal rights—the list could be extended almost indefinitely.

So unrelenting is the assault on our sensibilities that many of us grow numb, finding resignation to be the rational, adaptive response to an environment that is increasingly polluted and apparently beyond our control. That is what Senator Daniel Patrick Moynihan calls "defining deviancy down."[1] Moynihan cites the "Durkheim constant."[2] Emile Durkheim, a founder of sociology, posited that there is a limit to the amount of deviant behavior any community can "afford to recognize."[3] As behavior worsens, the community adjusts its standards so that conduct once thought reprehensible is no longer deemed so. As behavior improves, the deviancy boundary moves up to encompass conduct previously thought normal. Thus, a community of saints and a community of felons would display very different behavior but about the same amount of recognized deviancy.

But the Durkheim constant is now behaving in a very odd way. While defining deviancy down with respect to crime, illegitimacy, drug use, and the like, our cultural elites are growing intensely moralistic and disapproving about what had always been thought normal behavior, thus accomplishing what columnist Charles Krauthammer terms "defining deviancy up."[4] It is at least an apparent paradox that we are accomplishing both forms of redefining, both down and up, simultaneously. One would suppose that as once normal behavior became viewed as deviant, that would mean that there was less really bad conduct in the society. But that is hardly our case. Instead, we have redefined what we mean by such things as child abuse, rape, and racial or sexual discrimination so that behavior until recently thought quite normal, unremarkable, even benign, is now identified as blameworthy or even criminal. Middle-class life is portrayed as oppressive and shot through with pathologies. "As part of the vast social project of moral leveling," Krauthammer wrote, "it is not enough for the deviant to be normalized. The normal must be found to be deviant."[5] This situation is thoroughly perverse. Underclass values become increasingly acceptable to the middle class, especially their young, and middle-class values become increasingly contemptible to the cultural elites.

That is why there is currently a widespread sense that the distinctive virtues of American life, indeed the distinctive features of Western civilization, are in peril in ways not previously seen. This time the threat is not military—the Soviets and the Nazis are defunct. Nor is it external—the Tartar armies receded from Europe centuries ago. If we slide into a modern, high-tech version of the Dark Ages, we will have done it to ourselves without the assistance of the Germanic tribes that destroyed Roman civilization. This time we face, and seem to be succumbing to, an attack mounted by a force not only within Western civilization but one that is perhaps its legitimate child.

The enemy within is modern liberalism, a corrosive agent carrying a very different mood and agenda than that of classical or traditional liberalism. That the modern variety is intellectually bankrupt diminishes neither its vitality nor the danger it poses. A bankrupt philosophy can reign for centuries and, when its bankruptcy becomes apparent, may well be succeeded by an even less coherent outlook. That is what is happening to us now. Modernity, the child of the Enlightenment, failed when it became apparent that the good society cannot be achieved by unaided reason. The response of liberalism was not to turn to religion, which modernity had seemingly made irrelevant, but to abandon reason. Hence, there have appeared philosophies claiming that words can carry no definite meaning or that there is no reality other than one that is "socially constructed." A reality so constructed, it is thought, can be decisively altered by social or cultural edict, which is a prescription for coercion.

"Modern liberalism" may not be quite the correct name for what I have in mind. I use the phrase merely to mean the latest stage of the liberalism that has been growing in the West for at least two and a half centuries, and probably longer. Nor does this suggest that I think liberalism was always a bad idea. So long as it was tempered by opposing authorities and traditions, it was a splendid idea. It is the collapse of those tempering forces that has brought us to a triumphant modern liberalism with all the cultural and social degradation that follows in its wake. If you do not think "modern liberalism" an appropriate name, substitute "radical liberalism" or "sentimental liberalism" or even, save us, "post-modern liberalism." Whatever name is used, most readers will recognize the species.

The defining characteristics of modern liberalism are radical egalitarianism (the equality of outcomes rather than of opportunities) and radical individualism (the drastic reduction of limits to personal gratification). These may seem an odd pair, for individualism means liberty and liberty produces inequality, while equality of outcomes means coercion and coercion destroys liberty. If they are to operate simultaneously, radical egalitarianism and radical individualism, where they would compete, must be kept apart, must operate in different areas of life. That is precisely what we see in today's culture.

Radical egalitarianism reigns in areas of life and society where superior achievement is possible and would be rewarded but for coercion towards a state of equality. Quotas, affirmative action, and the more extreme versions of feminism are the most obvious examples but, as will be seen, radical egalitarianism is damaging much else in our culture. Radical individualism is demanded when there is no danger that achievement will produce inequality and people wish to be unhindered in the pursuit of pleasure. This finds expression especially in the areas of sexuality and the popular arts.

Sometimes the impulses of radical individualism and radical egalitarianism cooperate. Both, for example, are antagonistic to society's traditional morality—the individualist because his pleasures can be maximized only by freedom from authority, the egalitarian because he resents any distinction among people or forms of behavior that suggests superiority in one or the other. When egalitarianism reinforces individualism, denying the possibility that one culture or moral view can be superior to another, the result is cultural and moral chaos, both prominent and destructive features of our time.

Radical egalitarianism necessarily presses us towards collectivism because a powerful state is required to suppress the differences that freedom produces. That raises the sinister and seemingly paradoxical possibility that radical individualism is the handmaiden of collectivist tyranny. This individualism, it is quite apparent in our time, attacks the authority of family, church, and private association. The family is said to be oppressive, the fount of our miseries. It is denied that the church may legitimately insist upon what it regards as moral behavior in its members. Private associations are routinely denied the autonomy to define their membership for themselves. The upshot is that these institutions, which stand between the state and the individual, are progressively weakened and their functions increasingly dictated or taken over by the state. The individual becomes less of a member of powerful private institutions and more a member of an unstructured mass that is vulnerable to the collectivist coercion of the state. Thus does radical individualism prepare the way for its opposite.

Modern liberalism is very different in content from the liberalism of, say, the 1940s or 1950s, and certainly different from the liberalism of the last century. The sentiments and beliefs that drive it, however, are the same: the ideals of liberty and equality. These ideals produced the great political, social, and cultural achievements of Western civilization, but no ideal, however worthy, can be pressed forever without turning into something else, turning in fact into its opposite. That is what is happening now. Not a single American institution, from popular music to higher education to science, has remained untouched.

In one sense, decline is always with us. To hear each generation of Americans speak of the generation coming along behind it is to learn that our culture is not only deteriorating rapidly today but always has been. Regret for the golden days of the past is probably universal and as old as the human race. No doubt the elders of prehistoric tribes thought the younger generation's cave paintings were not up to the standard they had set. Given this straight-line degeneration for so many millennia, by now our culture should be not merely rubble but dust. Obviously it is not: until recently our artists did better than the cave painters.

Yet if the doomsayers are always with us, it is also true that sometimes they are right. Cultures do decline, and sometimes die. The agenda of liberalism has been and remains what historian Christopher Lasch called an "unremitting onslaught against bourgeois culture [that] was far more lasting in its effects, in the West at least and now probably in the East as well, than the attack on capitalism."[6] Making capitalism the explicit target became an unprofitable tactic when the case for the only alternative, socialism, collapsed in ruins. But capitalism cannot survive without a bourgeois culture; if that culture is brought down, so too will capitalism be replaced with one or another variety of statism presiding over a degenerate society.

Modern liberalism is powerful because it has enlisted our cultural elites, those who man the institutions that manufacture, manipulate, and disseminate ideas, attitudes, and symbols—universities, churches, Hollywood, the national press (print and electronic), foundation staffs, the "public interest" organizations, much of the congressional Democratic Party and some congressional Republicans as well, and large sections of the judiciary, including, all too often, a majority of the Supreme Court.

This, it must be stressed, is not a conspiracy but a syndrome. These are institutions controlled by people who view the world from a common perspective, a perspective not generally shared by the public at large. But so pervasive is the influence of those who occupy the commanding heights of our culture that it is important to understand what modern liberalism is and what its ascendancy means. That is what this book attempts to explain.

The wonder is that the culture of liberalism triumphed over conventional middle-class culture so rapidly. One would have expected rejection of radical individualism and radical egalitarianism by those whose interests would be damaged by them or whose idea of a good society was offended by them. Instead, resistance has been mild, disorganized, and ineffective. This suggests that the supposedly oppressive "Establishment," without realizing it themselves, had already been eaten hollow by the assumptions that flowered into modern liberalism. When the push came in the Sixties, an empty and guilt-ridden Establishment surrendered.

But why now? Liberalism has been with us for centuries; why should it become modern liberalism in the latter half of this century? The desire for self-gratification, which underlies individualism, has been around since the human species appeared; why should it become radical individualism in our time? The desire for equality, in large part rooted in self-pity and envy, is surely not a new emotion; why has it recently become the menace of radical egalitarianism?

The complete answer is surely not simple, but a large part of the answer surely is. Liberalism always had the tendency to become modern liberalism, just as individualism and equality always contained the seeds of their radical modern versions. The difference was that classical liberalism, the glory of the last century, was not simply a form of liberalism but an admixture of liberalism's drives and the forces that opposed those drives. As the opposing or constraining forces weakened and the drives of liberalism increasingly prevailed, we were brought to our present condition, and, it must be feared, will be taken still further, much further, in the same direction. Then a culture whose increasing degradation we observe will have attained ultimate degradation, unless, of course, we can rebuild the constraints that once made liberalism classical liberalism. A consideration of the nature of those constraints and what weakened them is not encouraging.

Men were kept from rootless hedonism, which is the end stage of unconfined individualism, by religion, morality, and law. These are commonly cited. To them I would add the necessity for hard work, usually physical work, and the fear of want. These constraints were progressively undermined by rising affluence. The rage for liberty surfaced violently in the 1960s, but it was ready to break out much earlier and was suppressed only by the accidents of history. It would be possible to make a case that conditions were ripe at the end of the nineteenth century and the beginning of the twentieth but that the trend was delayed by the Great War. The breaking down of restrictions resumed in the Roaring Twenties. But that decade was followed by the Great Depression, which produced a culture whose behavior was remarkably moral and law-abiding. The years of World War II created a sense of national unity far different from the cultural fragmentation of today. The generations that lived through those times of hardship and discipline were not susceptible to extreme hedonism, but they raised a generation that was.

Affluence reappeared in the late 1940s and in the decade of the 1950s and has remained with us since. Despite complaints, often politically motivated, about the economic hardships endured today by the American people, it is blindingly obvious that standards of living, even among the poorest, are far above any previous level in this or any other nation's history. Affluence brings with it boredom. Of itself, it offers little but the ability to consume, and a life centered on consumption will appear, and be, devoid of meaning. Persons so afflicted will seek sensation as a palliative, and that today's culture offers in abundance.

This brings us to the multiple roles rapidly improving technology plays in our culture. America was a nation of farmers, but the advance of technology required fewer and fewer farmers and more and more industrial workers. The continuing advance required fewer industrial workers and more white collar workers, and eventually still more sophisticated workers of a kind that made the term "white collar" seem denigrating. Hard physical work is inconsistent with hedonism; the new work is not. With the time and energy of so many individuals freed from the harder demands of work, the culture turned to consumerism and entertainment. Technology and its entrepreneurs supplied the demand with motion pictures, radio, television, and videocassettes, all increasingly featuring sex and violence. Sensations must be steadily intensified if boredom is to be kept at bay.

A culture obsessed with technology will come to value personal convenience above almost all else, and ours does. That has consequences we will explore. Among those consequences, however, is impatience with anything that interferes with personal convenience. Religion, morality, and law do that, which accounts for the tendency of modern religion to eschew proscriptions and commandments and turn to counseling and therapeutic sermons; of morality to be relativized; and of law, particularly criminal law, to become soft and uncertain. Religion tends to be strongest when life is hard, and the same may be said of morality and law. A person whose main difficulty is not crop failure but video breakdown has less need of the consolations and promises of religion.

The most frightening aspect of the march of technology, however, is the potential for reshaping human beings and their nature through genetic science. No one can predict what the full consequences of that technology will be, but horrifying prospects can easily be imagined. There seems no possibility that this technology can be halted—whatever scientists can do, they feel they must do—and little likelihood that the ability to reshape humans will not be used.

As will be seen, the possibilities of technology in all of these areas—from lightening work to providing ever more degenerate entertainments to reengineering humans—are far from exhausted. And it is impossible to imagine that the rapid advance of technology can be halted or even significantly slowed.

Radical egalitarianism also seems likely to continue to advance, although some of its manifestations are now being resisted politically for the first time in years. The simplistic notion that if social processes were fair, all races and ethnic groups and both sexes would be represented proportionately in all areas of endeavor dies hard. The absence of equality of results is taken to mean that equality of opportunity has been denied and must be remedied with coercive action to produce equality of results. Then, too, the spread and triumph of the democratic ideal leads, irrationally, to the belief that inequalities are unjust so that hierarchical institutions must be democratized. That leads to demands for corporate democracy, for student participation in running universities, and to criticism of the Roman Catholic Church because its doctrines do not conform to whatever it is that a large number of the laity prefer. The idea that democracy and equality are not suited to the virtues of all institutions is a hard sell today.

Demands for greater or complete equality seem to have other sources. Boredom plays a role here as well. It is impossible, for example, to observe radical feminists without thinking that their assertions of oppression and victimization, their never-ending search for fresh grievances, are ways of giving meaning to lives that would otherwise seem sterile to them. Self-pity and envy are also undoubtedly factors, as are the prestige and financial support to be had from pressing their claims, but I tend to think that the search for meaning plays a prominent and perhaps predominant role in many forms of radical egalitarianism.

A crucial factor in the creation of liberalism and its gradual transformation into modern liberalism has yet to be mentioned: the rise of intellectual and artistic classes independent of patrons toward the close of the eighteenth century and their subsequent growth in size and prestige. For reasons to be canvassed in chapter 5, these classes tend to be hostile to traditional culture and to the bourgeois state. They powerfully reinforce and mobilize the forces pressing towards radical individualism and radical egalitarianism.

The fact that resistance to modern liberalism is weakening suggests that we are on the road to cultural disaster because, in their final stages, radical egalitarianism becomes tyranny and radical individualism descends into hedonism. Those translate into a modern version of bread and circuses. Government grows larger and more intrusive in order to direct the distribution of goods and services in an ever more equal fashion while people are coarsened and diverted, led to believe that their freedoms are increasing, by a great variety of entertainments featuring violence and sex.

Having spoken of liberty and equality (in their modern, radical forms), it is time to complete the triad by mentioning fraternity. It is no mere rhetorical device to use the slogan of the French Revolution, for liberty, equality, and fraternity are enduring aspirations, and dilemmas, of humans in society. The desire for fraternity or community is inevitable in a social animal, but that desire is condemned to frustration, to be a wistful hope, anywhere modern liberalism holds sway. Radical individualism, radical egalitarianism, omnipresent and omni-incompetent government, the politicization of the culture, and the battle for advantages through politics shatter a society into fragments of isolated individuals and angry groups. Social peace and cohesion decline as loneliness and alienation rise. Life in such a culture can come close to seeming intolerable.

A fragmented society, one in which a sense of community has disappeared, is necessarily a society with low morale. It displays loss of nerve, which means that it cannot summon the will to suppress public obscenity, punish crime, reform welfare, attach stigma to the bearing of illegitimate children, resist the demands of self-proclaimed victim groups for preferential treatment, or maintain standards of reason and scholarship. That is precisely and increasingly our situation today.

Perversely, modern liberals seek to cure the disease of a politicized culture with the medicine of more politics. More politics means more clashes between interest groups, more anger and division, and more moral assaults upon opponents. The great danger, of course, is that eventually a collectivist solution will be adopted to control social turbulence. Turbulence is not limited to political and cultural warfare; it is increasingly a phenomenon of violence in streets and neighborhoods. If society should reach a chaotic condition of warring groups and individual alienation, a condition in which even personal security is problematic for a majority of its people, authoritarian government may be accepted. Worse, a movement with transcendental principles, not necessarily benign ones, may promise community and ultimately exact a fearful cost.

The encroachments of liberalism upon traditional ways of thinking and acting have created not just a battle here and a skirmish there but a conflict across the entire culture. This is different in kind from the usual piecemeal revisions we have seen in the past. "Now and then," according to literary scholar Lionel Trilling, "it is possible to observe the moral life in the process of revising itself, perhaps by reducing the emphasis it formerly placed upon one or another of its elements, perhaps by inventing and adding to itself a new element, some mode of conduct or of feeling which hitherto it had not regarded as essential to virtue."[7] A nation's moral life is, of course, the foundation of its culture. When Trilling's words were published in 1970, though he had seen the convulsions of the Sixties, he could not have imagined the scope and depth of the "revisions" yet to come. What we experience now is not the subtraction or addition of one or another of the elements of our moral life, but an assault that aims at, and largely accomplishes, sweeping changes across the entire cultural landscape. Large chunks of the moral life of the United States, major features of its culture, have disappeared altogether, and more are in the process of extinction. These are being, or have already been, replaced by new modes of conduct, ways of thought, and standards of morality that are unwelcome to many of us.

Trilling went on: "The news of such an event [a revision in moral life] is often received with a degree of irony or some other sign of resistance."[8] Given the comprehensive scope of the changes in our moral-cultural life, it is not surprising that signs of resistance, though late in appearing, are becoming equally widespread and vigorous. The addition or subtraction of a single virtue may provoke only a degree of irony, but when the changes are across the board, the thrust and the resistance add up to a major conflict. Irony there is in plentiful supply, but also anger, and even a continuing realignment of our political parties along cultural lines. In the future, our political contests will also be cultural struggles.

This book will examine the changes wrought by liberalism in a variety of seemingly disparate areas of life, from popular entertainment to religion to scholarship to constitutional law, from abortion to crime to feminism, and more. It will attempt to answer where modern liberalism came from and why its ideas are pressed so immoderately. Are cultural trends cyclical or is this trend inherent in Western civilization, or even, perhaps, in human nature itself? There is a case for one of the latter answers, and if that argument is correct, the future is probably bleak. No one can be certain of that, however. Cultures in decline have, unpredictably, turned themselves around before. Perhaps ours will too.

I begin with the theory and the practice of the decade of the Sixties, the decade not only of burning law books but of revolutionary nihilism, occupied and terrorized universities, and the Establishment's surrender. The Sixties may be seen in the universities as a mini-French Revolution that seemed to fail, but ultimately did not. The radicals were not defeated by a conservative or traditionally liberal opposition but by their own graduation from the universities. And theirs was merely a temporary defeat. They and their ideology are all around us now. That is the reason for understanding the Sixties.

PART I

PART I

1

"The Vertical Invasion of the Barbarians"

It is important to understand what the Sixties turmoil was about, for the youth culture that became manifest then is the modern liberal culture of today. Where that culture will take us next may be impossible to say, but it is also impossible even to make an informed guess without understanding the forces let loose by the decade that changed America.

Many people attribute the student frenzy, civil disobedience, and violence of the Sixties to the war in Vietnam. That is a comforting thought, for, if true, it would mean that the Sixties pivoted on a single ephemeral issue rather than representing a major, and perhaps permanent, upheaval across all of American culture. Unfortunately, the evidence seems clear that Vietnam was more an occasion for the outbreaks than their cause. The war at most intensified into hatred a contempt for American civilization that was already in place.

During the same period, other countries that had no involvement in the Vietnamese war, notably France, Italy, and Germany, saw serious student rebellions. In France the students came closer to toppling the government than the radicals ever did in the United States. The turmoil seems to have had more to do with attitudes that reached their culmination in a particular generation in Western democracies than with the war.

Contrast the reaction of American youth to the wars in Korea and in Vietnam. Both were wars in Asia, both exacted high prices in Americans killed or disabled, both had only the rationale of containing communism, both soon became unpopular. Yet American youth went willingly, if not gladly, to Korea, while they demonstrated against Vietnam, marched on the Pentagon, threw blood on draft records, fled to Canada and Sweden, and denounced "Amerika." Something in our culture, or at least the culture of our youth, had changed between the two wars. Vietnam was a convenient and powerful metaphor for what was in reality the belief that America's culture, society, economy, and polity were corrupt.

One must not, of course, discount the great reservoir of self-interest that underlay much of the rhetoric of morality. The generation that fought in Korea had not grown up with affluence. Many had served in World War II or grew up during the war. The middle-class youths who were asked to fight in Vietnam were of a pampered generation, one that prized personal convenience above almost all else. The prospect that their comfortable lives might be disrupted, or even endangered, by having to serve their country in Vietnam was for many intolerable. Thus, the student protests wound down when the draft ended.

Yet to this day, many contend that the radicals' protests against the war were honorable. Professor James Miller of the New School for Social Research, for example, argues that there were substantial benefits from the riots at the 1968 Democratic Convention because of the "dissent, confrontation, the passionate expression of moral outrage at a war that was, after all, morally reprehensible and unjust in its brutality, as well as strategically mistaken."[1] Those who speak in this fashion, and there are many, realize that something is still at stake in the argument over Vietnam. Indeed there is. The debate about that war is a contest between two opposed ways of viewing the world, whose current form is the war in the culture. That makes Vietnam worth a word or two.

It may be doubted, to begin with, that a difference of opinion about strategy brought the radicals into the streets. SDS (Students for a Democratic Society) did not arrive at its position on the war through a close study of Clausewitz and Jomini. Nor has anyone persuasively explained why the war was morally reprehensible or unjust in its brutality. It was a time of very worrisome communist expansion by force around the world. The United States had succeeded in saving South Korea by force of arms but had seen China and Cuba fall and was facing an aggressive and heavily armed Soviet Union. Attempting to contain communist dictatorships was hardly an immoral project. It was known at the time that Ho Chi Minh's triumph in the North had resulted in the killing of about 100,000 people, and it was certainly reasonable to anticipate a larger slaughter in the South if we lost the war.

The subsequent fate of the South Vietnamese people ought to convince anyone that the war should have been fought and won. We know of the tortures and murders in the re-education camps, and of the "postwar terror which destroyed the lives of hundreds of thousands of Vietnamese, and which produced over a million refugees."[2] To anyone with the slightest knowledge of communist takeovers in other countries, these things were entirely foreseeable. The almost complete indifference of American antiwar radicals to the terrible fate of the South Vietnamese after the Communists' victory demonstrates that the protests were not motivated by concern for the people of Vietnam. The protests were primarily about the moral superiority of the protesters and their rage against their own country.

What *was* morally reprehensible were the New Left's attempts to ensure the American and South Vietnamese defeat. North Vietnam's resolve was greatly increased by the demonstrations against the war in the United States. Bui Tin, a former colonel on the general staff of the North Vietnamese army who left after the war because he became disillusioned with his country's communism, said in an interview that Hanoi intended to defeat the United States by fighting a long war to break America's will. The American antiwar movement was "essential to our strategy. Support for the war from our rear was completely secure while the American rear was vulnerable. Every day our leadership would listen to world news over the radio at 9 a.m. to follow the growth of the American antiwar movement. Visits to Hanoi by people like Jane Fonda, former Attorney General Ramsey Clark, and various clergy gave us confidence that we should hold on in the face of battlefield reverses. We were elated when Jane Fonda, wearing a red Vietnamese dress, said at a press conference that she was ashamed of American actions in the war and that she would struggle along with us."[3]

Reprehensible as well were the timid strategies of President Lyndon Johnson and Secretary of Defense Robert MacNamara— their refusal to bomb the North, allowing sanctuaries for enemy troops, absurd limitations on the bombing of enemy missile sites, even in the South; and generally fighting a half-hearted war. Bui Tin said that Hanoi could not have won if Johnson had approved General William Westmoreland's requests to enter Laos and block the Ho Chi Minh Trail. Instead, our political leadership ensured that the war could not be won. By the time Richard Nixon came to office, the opportunity to win was gone, and he sought only to get out on honorable terms. But Congress, now cowed and sick of the effort, refused assistance to the South Vietnamese after American troops were brought home. It may or may not have been a mistake to get involved in Vietnam; it was most certainly a mistake, and worse, having gotten involved, not to fight to win. As for brutality, there was no more than is inseparable from any major armed conflict. Accounts of ground combat in the Second World War in Europe and the Pacific, not to mention the destruction of Dresden and Hiroshima, are sufficient to demonstrate that proposition.

The true basis of student opposition, in addition to personal concern for safety and convenience, was that the war was being waged by the United States. That was the major reason radical students did not merely call for our withdrawal but openly hoped for America's defeat. "The common bond between the New Left and the NLF [the National Liberation Front, or Vietcong]," Christopher Jencks wrote, "is not, then, a common dream or a common experience but a common enemy: the US government, the system, the Establishment. The young radicals' admiration for the NLF stems from the feeling that the NLF is resisting the enemy successfully, whereas they are not."[4]

We recently passed the twentieth anniversary of our defeat, and some commentators expressed surprise that the war continues to arouse strong feelings on both sides, that there has not been a more complete "healing." The reason so many still feel anger is not far to seek. It is not merely the number of American lives thrown away in a war that was lost and could have been won. Nor is it simply the memory of the atrocious behavior of the resisters. The reason is that we see at work in today's culture the same attitudes, indeed many of the same people, that undermined America then. Our division over the Vietnam conflict has been called America's second Civil War. "Healing" will not happen until the people who remember have passed from this world.

THE GESTATION OF THE SIXTIES

I have discussed Vietnam only to show that the war does not explain the Sixties. The questions remain: What was the student radicalism about and where did it come from? Why should the brightest, best-educated, most affluent members of the baby boom generation hate the culture that lavished privileges on them? Why did that age cohort turn to dreams of revolution and the destruction of institutions? There are several obvious answers: the very size of the generation; its concentration in the universities; its affluence; the pampering of its parents; new technologies of entertainment; the creation of an industry to cater to youth's discontents; the need to find meaning in life; the liberalism of their elders, which played into the natural romanticism and absolutism of the young; and the abnormal power drives of radical leaders.

Every new generation constitutes a wave of savages who must be civilized by their families, schools, and churches. An exceptionally large generation can swamp the institutions responsible for teaching traditions and standards. This was a problem well before the Sixties generation arrived. Ortega y Gasset in 1930 described the rapid increase in population that occurred in Europe between 1800 and 1914: "a gigantic mass of humanity which, launched like a torrent over the historic area, has inundated it."[5] He was impressed by the "dizzy rapidity" of that increase. "For that rapidity means that heap after heap of human beings have been dumped on to the historic scene at such an accelerated rate, that it has been difficult to saturate them with traditional culture."[6] This was what "Rathenau called 'the vertical invasion of the barbarians.'"[7] The baby boomers were a generation so large that they formed their own culture rather than being assimilated into the existing one. The so-called silent generation, born between 1922 and 1947, numbered 43.6 million. The boomers, by contrast, born between 1946 and 1964, had 79 million persons still living in

1974. The "baby bust" generation, born between 1965 and 1983, had 67.9 million births. The culture the boomers formed was, as is natural for adolescents, opposed to that of their parents.

After World War II, universities expanded and multiplied, fattened by a surge of veterans added to the normal component of students. Though professors were often highly critical of American society, the university culture as a whole was not initially adversarial. The veterans were too mature, too anxious to get on with their careers, for that. But the combined effects of population growth and the new idea that virtually everyone should go to college caused a phenomenal growth in the size of universities. In 1930, as Seymour Martin Lipset noted, there were about 1,000,000 students and 80,000 faculty. By the end of World War II, the comparable numbers were 1,675,000 and 165,000. But in 1970, there were 7,000,000 students and over 500,000 full-time faculty. Thus, in twenty-five years the number of faculty tripled and the number of students quadrupled.[8] Written at a time when the campuses were still in turmoil, Lipset's analysis remains well worth reading.

The university archipelago was now able to create its own cultural enclaves, ones ever more distinct from the surrounding bourgeois culture. When the youths of the Sixties generation got out of their homes, away from their parents, listened to liberal and often leftist faculty members, and were concentrated in unprecedented numbers in the universities, it was inevitable that they would incite one another so that their natural rebelliousness was magnified many times over. Hence, we had our vertical invasion of the barbarians; barbarians they were, and many of them still are. Only now they are tenured barbarians.

The Sixties university students were exceptionally affluent. After the war the United States entered a period of unprecedented prosperity. The effects of affluence were compounded by parents who, having known the hardships of the Depression and World War II, were determined to give their children every comfort they could. One of the SDS leaders wrote later, "Without thinking about it, we all took the fat of the land for granted."[9] Assuming there would always be money, unlike previous generations they did not worry that either lack of study or unacceptable behavior would jeopardize their futures. This freed them for political action. A major strength of the radicals was that they had money to travel from campus to campus, inciting and organizing, and from campuses to rallies around the country.

The absence of economic pressure and the assumption that there would never be want in their futures led the young to boredom. Life stretched before them as a wasteland of suburbia and consumerism. One young idiot later said that "hell is growing up in Scarsdale." Boredom is a much underrated emotion. The young, especially the very intelligent and vigorous, who have not yet found a path in life, are particularly susceptible to boredom's relentless ache. It is an emotion that is dangerous for individuals and for society because a lot of the cures are anti-social: alcohol, narcotics, cruelty, pornography, violence, zealotry in a political cause. Many of the Sixties generation shopped that list. The rhetoric of revolution, which was to be heard on campuses continuously, was, as Peter Berger said, "not so much motivated by sympathy with black people in slums and yellow people in rice paddies as by boredom with Connecticut."[10]

Technology, a new music, and entrepreneurs' feel for a new mass market intensified the rebelliousness of the young. Portable radios became widely available so that youths could choose their music without parental supervision. No longer must they sit in the living room with their parents and siblings to listen to the radio together. The music they listened to now was rock and roll, which their parents hated. It would be difficult to overstate the cultural importance of that music. Visiting Yugoslavia in that era, Irving Kristol learned that the regime banned rock because it was subversive of authority. In a personal communication he remarked that rock and roll is subversive of all authority, that of Western democracies, bourgeois families, schools, and churches as well as communist dictatorships.

Those in the rock business understood very well that the music's subversion of authority was a large part of its appeal to the young. An impresario who developed one star after another was asked how he did it. He said, "I look for someone their parents will hate." As Professor Todd Gitlin notes, the blues had been music for adults, but rock was about teenage problems. Its "incoherence, primitive regression, was indeed part of the music's appeal" to the young.[11] Gerald Howard wrote: "Rock 'n' roll, a raw and powerful new form of music, crystallized all the youthfulness, dynamism and hypersexuality on the loose—the Pied Piper's tune of the new freedoms."[12] An apt metaphor: I have read that the historical Pied Piper led the children into the forest, where he massacred and dismembered them.

Gitlin, once a leader in SDS, stresses many of these factors as shaping his generation, and adds another: the "rock-bottom fact that life ends."[13] To adolescents without religious belief, that realization can be devastating. Radical politics can then become a substitute for a religion, a way to seek meaning in life, and even, one can hope, a form of immortality. To lead or to be part of a movement that changes the world is, perhaps, to be remembered forever. For many, modern liberalism is a religion.

Sixties generation attitudes were also shaped by the severe critiques of America offered by their liberal-to-left elders. If that criticism was taken more seriously than the elders intended, the logical (or emotional) conclusions that followed went well beyond moderate liberalism. Many in the younger generation leaped to those conclusions. A justly celebrated professor at Columbia urged his colleagues not to be hostile to the rampaging students, for "these are our proper children." And he was right. As the title of Midge Decter's book put it, *Liberal Parents, Radical Children*.[14] It wasn't just traditional liberalism. Though admirers of the Sixties prefer to pass over the point, some of the radical core were "red diaper babies," the children of Communist Party members whose radicalism was passed down in the family.[15]

There was, of course, a strong psychological component to student radicalism. Stanley Rothman, professor of government at Smith College, and S. Robert Lichter, co-director of the Center for Media and Public Affairs, studied the New Left and found that radicalism correlated with a personal drive for power. Moreover, while "most student radicals were not authoritarians. . . . we found a larger number of authoritarians among the student radicals than we did in our comparison groups. We believe that these young people exercised an influence far beyond their numbers. . . ."[16] That could be observed during any of the campus disturbances of that era. The condition of the youth culture gave the radicals and authoritarians opportunities they would have been denied in more normal times.

Sympathizers with the New Left said the radicals were a new, healthier, more expressive generation of Americans, in contrast to the authoritarianism and repression of traditional American society. But Rothman and his colleagues, in a series of studies of student and adult radicals, found that "rather than exhibiting the liberating themes, both radical adults and students exhibit marked narcissism and enhanced needs for power."[17] They also showed a higher fear of power than traditionals or nonradicals.

There is another factor in student radicalism that deserves mention, however. At the time, I read that an Israeli visitor to the United States said of those students something to this effect: "Their fathers gave them prosperity and freedom, and so they hate their fathers." It seemed merely a biting comment on the ingratitude of that generation. It was that, but now it seems to have conveyed a deeper insight. In his superb work on envy, sociologist Helmut Schoeck[18] recounts the findings of psychiatrist Robert Seidenberg about a young man whose repressed envy of his hosts and their possessions made him so acutely uncomfortable that any dinner party was an ordeal for him.

"Probably this personality type," Schoeck comments, "can help us to understand the world-wide rebellion of youth since 1966. As the 'envious guest,' Seidenberg's clinical case, these young people lack the maturity to be the 'guests of our affluent society.' The overprivileged youngsters, from California to West Berlin, from Stockholm to Rome, strike out in senseless acts of vandalism as a result of their vague envy of a world of affluence they did not create but enjoyed with a sense of guilt as a matter of course. For years they were urged to compare guiltily their lot with that of the underprivileged abroad and at home. Since the poor will not vanish fast enough for their guilt to subside, they can ease their tensions only by symbolic acts of aggression against all that is thought dear and important to the envied elders."[19]

These factors operating together produced the restless, rebellious Sixties, and what former radicals Peter Collier and David Horowitz aptly called a "destructive generation."[20]

THE BIRTH OF THE SIXTIES

The Sixties were born at a particular time and place: June, 1962, the AFL-CIO camp at Port Huron, Michigan. (There were preliminary stirrings in parts of the civil rights movement and in the

Free Speech movement at Berkeley.) Though most Americans have never heard of the proceedings at Port Huron, they were crucial, for the authentic spirit of Sixties radicalism issued there. That spirit spread and evolved afterwards, but its later malignant stages, including its violence, were implicit in its birth.

Port Huron was an early convention of SDS, then a small group of alienated, left-wing college students. There were fifty-nine delegates from eleven campus chapters. One of them described their mood: "four-square against anti-Communism, eight-square against American culture, twelve-square against sell-out unions, one-hundred-twenty square against an interpretation of the Cold War that saw it as a Soviet plot and identified American policy fondly."[21] In short, they rejected America. Worse, as their statement of principles made clear, they were also four-square against the nature of human beings and features of the world that are unchangeable. That is the utopian impulse. It has produced disasters in the past, just as it was to do with the Sixties generation.

Starting from a draft by Tom Hayden (heavily influenced by the writings of the radical sociologist C. Wright Mills), the convention wrangled out the *Port Huron Statement*,[22†] a lengthy, stupefyingly dull manifesto, setting forth the SDS agenda for changing human beings, the nation, and the world. Like the wider student radicalism that ensued, the document displayed the ignorance and arrogance proper to adolescents. These youths were in a state of euphoria about their own wisdom, moral purity, and power to change everything. They were short on specifics about how they would reform the world, what the end product would look like, and what was to be done if the world proved intractable.

SDS and the *Port Huron Statement* did not create the temper of the Sixties out of nothing. They coalesced the restless discontents of their generation. While most student rebels did not belong to SDS, the *Port Huron Statement* repays attention: it was the most widely circulated document of the Left in that decade, brought

†Reprinted in James Miller's *"Democracy Is in the Streets": From Port Huron to the Siege of Chicago*. Miller's subtitle rather neatly sums up the progression inherent in the manifesto.

SDS to national prominence, and its notions became the common currency of the New Left. The New Left is important because it is still with us in the guise of modern liberalism. What was composed at Port Huron, therefore, is a guide to today's cultural and political debacles.

The pronouncements of the Sixties radicals were intellectually negligible, often farcical. But many of us were naive enough at the time to assess them, and their capacity for destruction, in intellectual terms. Had we known more about past utopian movements, we would have seen that the *Port Huron Statement*, though nonsense, was also a document of ominous mood and aspiration.

"We regard men as infinitely precious and possessed of unfulfilled capacities for reason, freedom, and love," SDS proclaimed. The phrase "unfulfilled capacities" was substituted for the statement in Hayden's draft that man was "infinitely perfectible." (A few religious delegates objected that men cannot achieve perfection on earth.) Hayden's original words, which were not that different from the replacement words, expressed the view, common to totalitarian movements, that human nature is infinitely malleable so that a new, better, and perhaps perfect nature can be produced by the rearrangement of social institutions. Since actual humans resist attempts to remake their natures, coercion and, ultimately, violence will be required. The initial rhetoric of the movement, however, before disillusion set in, was one of peaceful aspiration.

"[H]uman brotherhood must be willed . . . as a condition of future survival and as the most appropriate form of social relations." This is but one of many references to equality of condition throughout the document. The talk of brotherhood, of man's unfulfilled capacities for reason, freedom, and love, and of radical equality was, and proved to be, dangerously unrealistic. Without reference to a supernatural Being, SDS was proposing, largely through politics, to bring their secular vision of the kingdom of God to fruition on earth, now. It is an ideal that the most devout and active Christians have never remotely approximated for any community larger than a monastery, and probably not in any monastery.

SDS' search for a shortcut to heaven was in the spirit of millenarianism, a phenomenon well-known in the history of Christianity. In the Middle Ages, historian Paul Johnson informs us, "The official Church was conventional, orderly, hierarchical, committed to defend Society as it existed, with all its disparities and grievances. But there was also, as it were, an anti-Church, rebellious, egalitarian, revolutionary, which rejected society and its values and threatened to smash it to bits."[23]

The millenarian seizure of Munster in Germany is a case in point. It was a brief reign of communism (all food and valuables taken by the government, housing reallocated on the basis of need), forced polygamy (women who refused were summarily executed), and frequent executions for a long list of infractions, including complaining and disobedience. When the town was retaken, the millenarian leader, I was almost pleased to learn, "was led about like a performing animal until January 1536, when he was publicly tortured to death with red-hot tongs."[24] "It is a tragic but recurrent feature of Christianity that the eager pursuit of reform tends to produce a ruthlessness in dealing with obstacles to it which brings the whole moral superstructure crashing down in ruins."[25] SDS made the same mistakes about the possibility of creating a paradise on earth, ruthlessly attacked the moral superstructure, but did not, some may think unfortunately, suffer similar consequences.

Real human beings do not have any unfulfilled capacity for love, or at least not a large one; they simply do not regard men as infinitely precious, whatever the homilist may say on Sunday; and they lack the boundless energy and selflessness required to will themselves to brotherhood. Any program for society based on such vapors is headed for disaster. The real ideals, perceptions, and interests of humans differ and conflict, and always will. Attempts to suppress aggression entirely and to substitute love, being unnatural, will finally erupt in greater aggression. When utopians are frustrated in the realization of their vision by the real nature of humans, who are then seen as perversely evil, they can turn nasty and violent. Others will engage in moral assault. SDS did both, and other student radicals followed them.

"The goal of man and society should be . . . finding a meaning in life that is personally authentic." How was that to be done? "[P]olitics has the function of bringing people out of isolation and into community, thus being a necessary, though not sufficient, means of finding meaning in personal life." Nowhere is one informed what "meaning in personal life" might be. It is an amorphous concept, held by the SDSers in much the same way as the New England clergyman who said that whenever he tried to imagine God, all he conjured up was a "sort of oblong blur." Nor is it at all clear why politics is necessary to meaning. One supposes that any number of fathers and mothers, religious people, scientists, novelists, philosophers, businessmen, et al. have found meaning in their lives without resort to politics. Note that politics seems to be the only way of escaping isolation and coming into community, a proposition that assumes the only real and significant communities are political.

The search for a "politics of meaning" is a feature of modern liberalism, and reflects the human yearning for the transcendental by persons for whom religion no longer fills that need. But politics as a transcendental value cannot be satisfied by the compromises and partial successes of democratic processes. Transcendental politics requires the absolute, and necessarily moves, as far as circumstances permit, towards authoritarian or totalitarian models. Modern liberalism displays that tendency, which, fortunately, is frustrated by the structure of American government, the party system, and most Americans' distrust of excessive zeal.

The notion that politics is a necessary means of finding meaning in personal life also necessarily leads to the politicization of all areas of life and culture, summed up in the phrase used by feminists and others that "the personal is political and the political is personal." Politics is always and inevitably about power. Personal relationships are, therefore, inevitably power relationships. The radical feminist branch of modern liberalism, to take one example, sees all male-female interactions, including marriage, as power relationships—a view that does not do a lot of good for marriages and families.

The longing for personal authenticity appears to be common in radical movements. "By the height of the [French] Revolution in 1793–94," sociologist Robert Nisbet tells us, "the passion for authenticity was almost uncontrollable among the revolutionaries. The Revolution began to devour its own, keeping the guillotine working overtime in the execution of even high officials like

Robespierre for the crime of 'hypocrisy' or 'inauthenticity.'"[26] As Lionel Trilling wrote, after the spirit of the Sixties generation had become manifest, "'[A]uthenticity'. . . . is a word of ominous import. . . . [It] is implicitly a polemical concept, fulfilling its nature by dealing aggressively with received and habitual opinion, aesthetic opinion in the first instance, social and political opinion in the next."[27] It is a word associated with extreme autonomy as well, but as Trilling also pointed out, one can be certain of one's authenticity only by knowing that one has achieved that state in the opinion of others, which is a contradiction of the extreme autonomy sought. To judge one's own independence through the opinions of others is to forfeit independence.

That is precisely what the Sixties radicals did. They prized individualism so greatly that it turned them into egalitarian conformists. What made them individualists was their rejection of American culture and bourgeois morals. What made them egalitarians was also their rejection of American culture and bourgeois morals. Since none of them aspired to an aristocracy or to asceticism, they had to reject bourgeois hierarchies and morals from the other direction. This translated as foul language, sexual promiscuity, marijuana and hard drugs, and disdain for the military and for conventional success. Since these were the only "authentic" ways to think and behave, the student radicals eagerly became what Harold Rosenberg once characterized as a "herd of independent minds."

"In social change or interchange," said SDS, "we find violence to be abhorrent because it requires generally the transformation of the target, be it a human being or a community of people, into a depersonalized object of hate." This sentiment is particularly poignant in retrospect since some in SDS, within a very few years, became violent. A few years after Port Huron, its organization's offshoot and legitimate heir, the Weathermen, organized the Days of Rage riots in Chicago. At a subsequent "War Council," Tom Hayden led the Weathermen in "a workout of karate jabs and kicks" for a "strenuous fifteen minutes" in preparation for armed struggle.[28] Port Huron's professions of love and brotherhood had, predictably, turned to rage and attack, both physical and moral, when society would not accept brotherhood on SDS's terms.

The relentless message of the *Port Huron Statement* was that

America was corrupt from top to bottom. Grave and critical faults that required sweeping change were found with American foreign policy, corporations, labor unions, old-style liberalism, universities, race relations, economic arrangements, military preparations, government, political parties, the desire for material goods, and much more. People with such a view of their society could not respect its institutions, its leaders, its moral tone, or accept a process of gradual reform.

"The final session [drafting the *Statement*] lasted all night and then the delegates walked down to Lake Huron; some held hands as they watched the sun rise. 'It felt like the dawn of a new age,'" one of them said, "'It was exalting. . . . We thought we knew what had to be done, and that we were going to do it.'"[29]

In the Sixties the spirit and the exaltation expressed at Port Huron played out across the country and produced a massive lurch to the left among university students. SDS grew from 600 members in 1963 to over 100,000 in 1968, but then collapsed in 1969 into hostile factions and in the end consisted only of a small group of Maoists. SDS had been the center of the New Left, but contrary to some accounts,[30] the shattering of SDS did not mean the collapse of the New Left. The New Left was a confused and confusing movement of radicals lacking any fixed center. After 1969, it remained that for several years more. This was simply an uncritically anti-American leftishness, not at all like the disciplined and programmatic older Left, exemplified by the Communist Party. Being unprogrammatic, the New Left's ideas of where they wanted to take the nation ran the gamut of leftist sentiments from amorphous to vaporous. They did not have doctrine; they had youth, self-righteousness, euphoria, and, many of them, ultimately, fury.

The young are naturally romantic and given to moral absolutes that necessarily make the real world of compromises, half-measures, and self-seeking appear corrupt. A youth culture, particularly in times of rapid social change, like the Sixties, is likely to develop a passionate adherence to principle, and the principles for a new age and a better world were at hand in articulations of the liberal elders. But the elders had not taken those principles seriously enough; they had compromised. The Sixties young were, therefore, in opposition not only to the larger society in general but to traditional liberals in particular.[†]

Their politics was expressive of attitudes rather than practical means to a stated goal. They regularly announced a "revolution" but, a few Weathermen terrorists aside, did little more than disrupt, confront, destroy property, paralyze universities, denounce America, and scream obscenities. "Relatively unconcerned with the long-term consequences of their actions, the New Left student movement appeared ready to attack all existing structures, including the university, and to use tactics which alienated the majority, in order to make manifest their contempt, their total rejection of the intolerable world created by their elders."[31] The New Left may have practiced a politics of expression and self-absorption, but that did not mean the politics was innocuous. To the contrary, it did serious, lasting, and perhaps permanent damage to valuable institutions, socially stabilizing attitudes, and essential standards.

The revolt was against the entire American culture. The United States, it was said, was engaged in an immoral war only because the United States itself was deeply immoral, being racist, sexist, authoritarian, and imperialistic. The arrangements of the liberal capitalist order were themselves illegitimate, conferring power where none was deserved and withholding power from the poor and minorities. The bourgeois class, which sustained and benefitted from these societal arrangements, was, therefore, oppressive. It followed that bourgeois morality and standards of excellence were

---

[†] In many ways, I understand the Sixties generation because at that stage of life, I reacted similarly. Suburban, middle-class life seemed stifling. Dixieland jazz was my rock and roll. All night partying was my escape, political radicalism my protest. The superintendent of schools in a heavily Republican suburb had to be brought in to prevent me from running an editorial in the high school newspaper calling for the nationalization of industry. Denunciations of bourgeois values rolled easily off my tongue. Fortunately, mine was not a large generation and very few of my high school classmates—none to be precise—felt the same way. There was no critical mass. By the time I got to the University of Chicago, where there were student radicals, I had been in the Marine Corps, an organization well known for teaching the reality principle to its recruits; and the Chicago school of free market economists educated me out of my dreams of socialism. I was fortunate; the Sixties generation was not. On this disposition of the young, see Lipset (note 8), especially chapter 1, "Sources of Student Activism."

part of the apparatus that supported the status quo and repressed the individual. Destruction was, therefore, the only legitimate response.

That is what I did not understand as I stood over the smoldering books outside the Yale law school.

2

What They Did and Where They Went

Epiphanies: they made the world worthy of us. We searched for them like stargazers. This was part of the decade's transcendental conviction that there was something apocalyptic lurking behind the veil of the ordinary, and that just a little more pressure was needed to pierce the last remaining membrane—of civility, bourgeois consciousness, corporate liberalism, sexual uptightness, or whatever else prevented us all from breaking through to the other side.[1]

That was the authentic voice of adolescent Sixties radicalism—impatient, destructive, nihilistic. Modern liberalism is its mature stage. The temporary abeyance of the Sixties temper was due to the radicals graduating from the universities and becoming invisible until they reached positions of power and influence, as they now have, across the breadth of the culture. They no longer have need for violence or confrontation: since the radicals control the institutions they formerly attacked, the Sixties temper manifests itself in subtler but no less destructive ways.

What the radicals did in the Sixties illuminates their mood and goals today. How the besieged "Establishment" responded tells a great deal about the softness and self-doubt that had come to afflict American cultural leaders even before they were assailed. We are currently being fed revisionist histories that paint student rebellion and hedonism of that time as idealism and excitement. No doubt that is partly due to the nostalgia of the Sixties generation for a time when everything seemed possible. But the revisionism also serves to consolidate the Left's cultural victories of that decade. Rewritten history has always been a weapon in the struggle for control of the present and the future. The true version of what took place is to be consigned to the memory hole. The radicalism of those times, we are informed, was a reaction against the cold war culture of the Fifties by idealistic students who sought to break free of the deadening intellectual conformity, spiritual emptiness, and social injustices of their parents' generation. The truth, as any accurate account of the times makes plain, is otherwise.

One of the more egregious pieces of revisionism appeared, appropriately enough, in a *New York Times* editorial, "In Praise of the Counterculture."[2] The *Times*, whose editorial page and some of its regular columns seem to have been handed over to a group of unregenerate Sixties radicals, remarks of that decade: "Only a few periods in American history have seen such a rich fulfillment of the informing ideals of personal freedom and creativity that lie at the heart of the American intellectual tradition." If that statement is accurate, and it may well be, then, as the state of our current culture attests, the American intellectual tradition has a lot to answer for. The *Times* even manages to say that the decade's "summery, hedonistic ethos then and now reduced modern puritans to fits of twisting discomfort. America is still close enough to the frontier experience of relentless work and danger to view any kind of fun with suspicion." That is an exceedingly odd description of a society positively addicted to fun: television sitcoms, sensational motion pictures, rock and rap music, recreational sex and drugs, spectator and participatory sports, Disneyland vacations. The "fun" viewed with suspicion then and now involved such "summery" pastimes as hard drug use and sexual anarchy. To cap this litany of Sixties-era fatuities, the editorial solemnly pronounces that the counterculture is "part of us, a legacy around which Americans can now unite, rather than allow themselves to be divided." There is no possibility that Americans will unite around that legacy. Those of us who regard the Sixties as a disaster are not "allowing" ourselves to be divided; we *insist* on it. Opposition to the counterculture, the culture that became today's liberalism, is precisely what our culture war is about.

Perhaps more books have been written about the Sixties than

any other decade in American history with the exception of times of war or the decade of the Great Depression. Some of those books have been analytical, some factual, most are admiring. But there is a different story to tell, and that story focuses on the universities, for it was there that the cadres of the new liberalism first appeared.

THE SACKING OF THE UNIVERSITIES

The campus madness may have started at Berkeley, but "it was the Ivy League that was ultimately to set the pace in the retreat of reason."[3] When the first demonstrations broke out at Yale, a visiting professor pointed out that it was organized by a transfer student from Berkeley. At every university, he said, the first eruptions could be traced to a radical who had "come down the Ho Chi Minh Trail from Berkeley." Yale had for years been politically liberal, no department more so than the law school. I was one of two Republicans on a faculty of about forty-five. When it was proposed that we hire a man who might possibly have been a third, he was rejected, one faculty member remarking that he would "tip the balance."

But liberal as it was, Yale was unprepared for the shock when student radicals first appeared in our midst. We knew of the riots at places like Berkeley and Columbia, but that was not the same as seeing irrational fury face to face. The change at the law school began abruptly with the class that entered in 1967. Unlike the traditional liberal students of the second- and third-year classes, whom they frightened as much as they dismayed the faculty, these students were angry, intolerant, highly vocal, and case-hardened against logical argument.

Two decades before their leftist orthodoxy had been given a name, this group developed a rigid "political correctness" of its own. In the first-year course on constitutional law, I led one student through a conventional analysis of an aspect of the Fourteenth Amendment to the Constitution, in which he reached the only coherent and legally non-controversial conclusion possible. (I think it was that the amendment prohibited only official and not private action.) About ten minutes later he raised his hand, was recognized, rose from his front-row seat, turned to his fellow students, and said, "I want to apologize to the class for reaching the conclusion I did.

I must have sounded like Attila the Hun." He resumed his seat and waited for me to proceed with whatever topic was then under discussion. The class showed no sign that anything unusual had happened. Neither then nor afterward did he explain what was wrong with the reasoning that led to the conclusion; the latter was just not acceptable politically, and that was that. When last heard of, he was a professor of law. No doubt he is indoctrinating his students in non-Tatar constitutional theory.

The entry of another politicized class in 1968 gave the radicals effective control of the student body. I was on sabbatical leave that academic year, but upon returning in 1969 I saw the entry of a third such class and a law school becoming an intellectual and pedagogical shambles. At Yale, as elsewhere, part of the faculty began to side with the students. Some professors were radicals themselves, a few were emotionally unstable, some needed student approval and would do whatever was necessary to keep it, others simply withdrew or went into denial. This was characteristic of all the university departments outside the hard sciences. The administration, thoroughly intimidated, refused to get involved. All of which meant that effective faculty resistance was impossible. The results were calamitous.

Turmoil was the order of the day—student strikes, arson in university buildings (three episodes in the law school alone), angry demonstrations, classroom disruptions, rejection of rationality as reactionary, obscenities shouted at faculty members, the usual assortment of barbarities. There were a few compensating amusements. Students would notify the press of a scheduled demonstration, but if the television cameras failed to appear, the protest was promptly canceled. The ferocity of demonstrations was in direct proportion to the number and importance of the news outlets present. CBS News was a great prize, the *New York Times* slightly less valued, and interest in the *New Haven Register* was negligible. Once when the press failed to show up, the law students posted a notice reserving their right to disrupt at a later time, thus nicely combining the fervor of revolutionaries with the caution of legal draftsmen.

Some of the faculty became a bit unbalanced. The admissions committee accepted one meagerly qualified student because, as a radical protest, he had attempted to burn down his college's cafeteria and was, therefore, "interesting." College students disrupted law school classes. (The spokesman for a relatively mild group that invaded my seminar displayed the acuity typical of such students, saying, "We don't want to disrupt. You are teaching antitrust and we are willing to discuss monopoly in America. Why aren't there more day care centers?") We often had to get to our classes through pickets marching in the halls. Faculty, afraid for their safety, no longer returned to their offices in the evening. Most took their research and writing home to avoid the possibility of its destruction. Professors at other universities had suffered losses of years of work. We were probably average in disruptions, suffering less than some universities and more than others.

Most disheartening was the rhetoric which foreclosed argument and rendered the radicals' minds as clouded as drugs did. They seemed to think that "If you're not part of the solution, you're part of the problem" was profound analysis and that institutions such as Yale could be dismissed as "irrelevant." Nobody seemed to have any idea what either the problem or the solution might be or what we were supposed to be relevant to. That is not entirely accurate, since one gathered that the problem was "the system" and that the solution was dismantling it, with no very clear notion of what came next, except that "the people" would come to power. The "system" was not just capitalism but all institutions wielding any authority in American society. These white, upper-middle-class Yale law students saw themselves as the people's vanguard. Judging from the reaction of the non-Yale population of New Haven, "the people" would have liked nothing better than to cane their vanguard's bottoms.

It should not be supposed that all, or even a majority, of the students were radicals. It is customary to refer to the radical students or the hippies of that era as the "Sixties generation," but the great majority of that generation was not radical or hippie, anymore than the majority of them today are modern liberals. In fact, Clinton's age group gave him a lower proportion of its vote than did any other age cohort. But the radicals set the tone and the pace, particularly in the more prestigious universities. One lesson we learned is that a minority of fanatical disposition can effectively control an institution.

The activists organized and acted in concert. Those who did not join them were regarded with contempt as moral inferiors.

Though they spoke of democracy and brotherhood, they were in fact authoritarian and manipulative. These activists had their way because at Yale, as at every other university, the moderate students did not organize. "Moderation" is not a cry that packs auditoriums or brings throngs into the streets. The moderates kept quiet, and tried to live through it with as little discomfort as possible. Students who just wanted to get on with their studies were intimidated by the radicals. The threat of physical violence was always in the air, but the intimidation was primarily moral. It must be remembered that the moderates were youths in their early twenties; most of them had little experience of life outside an academic institution and had no fixed convictions about the morality of America's culture. As they watched the faculty waver and appease, they must have wondered whether the radicals did not have at least a partial truth. In that time, it was true, as Yeats wrote: "The best lack all conviction, while the worst/ Are full of passionate intensity." In the event, the center certainly did not hold.

Shortly before his graduation, one student orator said, "We came here to make the Yale law school fit to survive in America. And we failed." If his and his friends' efforts were any guide, the law school could have been made fit to survive only by destroying its intellectual and professional standards, and they made a pretty decent run at that.

Black law students had a separate grievance. The law school, competing with other schools, had rushed into affirmative action and recruited black students who, having attended very inferior colleges, were in no way prepared for the Yale law school. As economist Thomas Sowell has pointed out, a minority student who is overmatched can react in one of two ways. Either he can accept his inability to meet the standards of the school or he can attack the standards as dishonest, corrupt, and probably racist. In an effort to hold on to self-respect in a bewildering and seemingly hostile environment, many will choose to reject both the standards by which they are judged and the faculty that judges them.

One Saturday I was writing at home when a telegram arrived from the Black Law Students Union announcing that I, along with the rest of the faculty, was "summoned" to appear before the BLSU in the faculty lounge the following week. In a mild panic, the faculty met at the dean's house but could not agree on a course of action. Some denied that the "summons" was an insult. One professor said that it was his custom to accept "invitations." The president of Yale, Kingman Brewster, was present but, already daunted by the radicals, declined to give any advice. I decided not to go. In the end, a little over half the faculty appeared as summoned. The result was a fiasco.

The faculty sat in folding chairs that had been set out for them; the BLSU leaders stood before them like instructors—very angry instructors—before a class. Two large students stood at the door, seeming to prevent any faculty from leaving, and no professor chose to test that proposition. In violently obscene language, the BLSU leaders berated the faculty which sat submissively in their chairs and took it. When the dean, a man who had marched at Selma and had a long and distinguished record of fighting for racial equality, tried to speak, he was told that he must remain silent so long as any black had something to say. But, for some reason, the BLSU leader did recognize the former dean, Eugene Rostow. He, however, refused to speak unless the present dean was given the floor. At that, the students swept angrily out of the room, much to the relief of a very frightened faculty. Probably the students needed a pretext to leave since there was no reason for the gathering except to shout obscenities at the faculty, and, that having been fulsomely accomplished, continuation could only have been anticlimactic. When the BLSU was gone, a prominent member of the faculty turned to Alexander Bickel, from whom I had this account, and said, "Wasn't that wonderful! They were so sincere!" Bickel did not speak to the man for almost a year.

White radicals behaved no better. One of the few favorable developments, from the faculty's point of view, was that the black radicals refused to cooperate with the white radicals. They believed, accurately, that the whites wanted to use them to further the whites' aims. Blacks sat at separate tables in the dining room, sat together in the rear of the classrooms, stood apart at receptions and other functions, demanded and got their own office and television set on the ground that they could not relax with whites. Timid professors cajoled the white radicals, both cajoled the blacks. Neither set of cajolers got anywhere.

Violence and threats of violence occurred on and off campuses across the country. The culmination at Yale, which revealed a great deal about us, came on May Day weekend, 1970. The body of a black male, who had been tortured and then shot in the head and chest, was found in the spring of 1969. Alex Rackley had been a Black Panther and was believed, on the basis of solid evidence, to have been killed in New Haven by other members who suspected him, probably wrongly, of being a police informer. Bobby Seale, a national leader, and other Panthers were indicted. As trial came nearer, agitation among radical groups across the country grew more strident. This was to be a cause célèbre for the Left, a rallying point like the trials of Sacco and Vanzetti and the Rosenbergs.

May Day weekend was chosen for a convergence on New Haven to protest the trial. Some of the groups were known to be violent and the F.B.I. told government officials that there were killers among them. Tension escalated day by day until it was palpable among students and faculty. Though many of the out-of-town groups who were coming did not care if the Panthers were guilty, it was an article of faith among many students that all trials of radicals, and most especially of black radicals, were nothing more than political suppression by a fascistic nation. The Student Senate voted a campus-wide strike in support of the Panthers. Students voted to house and feed the out-of-towners in Yale's residential colleges. Students demanded that Yale pay for the Panthers' defense, but it was illegal to use educational funds for such purposes. Frenzied mass meetings on campus demanded that the trial be canceled. Chanting pickets paraded before the courthouse on the town Green.

As the hysteria on campus mounted, Kingman Brewster emerged from an overheated faculty senate meeting to announce to the press that he was "skeptical of the ability of black revolutionaries to achieve a fair trial anywhere in the United States." He said he was "appalled and ashamed" and that questions about the fairness of such trials had "been created by police actions and prosecutions against the Panthers in many parts of the country. It is also one more inheritance from centuries of racial discrimination and oppression."[4] Yale alumni were not amused—Brewster became a major liability to fund-raising efforts—nor were judges, lawyers, or citizens generally.

We lived in the "faculty ghetto," close enough to the campus and the town Green, where the demonstration was to take place, to be mildly worried. Should a rampage occur, as many thought possible, the faculty homes were not out of reach. Just before the designated weekend, Ralph Winter, a professor of law and a friend of mine, told a reporter: "If 10 percent of the rumors spreading around here are true, there will be no New Haven on Monday." Stores sold out their stocks of fire extinguishers. A surprising number of faculty families found it just the time for out-of-town vacations. So did many students, including some who had voted to open the campus to the demonstrators.

Radicals poured into town in bus loads. Over 13,000 people—students from Yale and other universities mingled with Black Panthers, Weathermen, and other violent groups—in a volatile mass worked up by the usual demagogues. My wife and I sat all day in the backyard with our children to reassure them and to make certain they did not go off to see the excitement. The shouts and chants from the mob and the obscene speeches given over loudspeakers were audible, though most of the words, fortunately, were not clear. Over 4,000 federal troops were stationed nearby as reserves for the New Haven police and Connecticut state troopers. Low overhead, light spotter planes and helicopters circled watching for outbreaks. The only daytime violence occurred when Jerry Rubin said that to free Bobby Seale it was necessary to go to "the court of the streets." Fifteen hundred demonstrators ran from the Yale campus onto the Green where they threw bottles and cans at the police, who regained control with tear gas. Radical leaders began to caution the crowd to remain peaceable, which was not the way they had spoken at the outset. In the end, the presence of the troops damped the radicals' enthusiasm for physical force.

Night came, the town grew quiet, we put the children to bed, and raised our glasses to one another in a toast of satisfaction and relief. The explosion was so loud it seemed to slosh the whiskey in our glasses. More likely, the thud made our hands shake. The Yale hockey rink had been dynamited. Kingman Brewster, the president of Yale, announced the next day, on no evidence he ever cared to disclose, that the sabotage was done by right-wing terrorists. That was a particularly penetrating insight since no one knew of any right-wingers, much less right-wing terrorists, anywhere near New Haven, or Connecticut, or New England. No matter. Known left-wing terrorists, who *were* in town, must not be suspected.

Brewster was defended in his serial capitulations by the Yale establishment. A prime instance was John Hersey's book *A Letter to the Alumni*.[5] Hersey, a novelist who was then the master of one of Yale's residential colleges, capped Brewster by writing that based on his research, "I am skeptical of the ability of any black person to get as fair a trial as any white person in any American court today."[6] He wrote that he feared for the country more because of the older generation that denounced the student radicals than because of the disrupters themselves.

The insanity of the times is difficult to credit a quarter of a century later. That a man had been tortured and murdered was all but forgotten as many Yale students and faculty simply assumed the evil of police, prosecutors, and courts. Outrage was expressed that Black Panther suspects should even be tried. Yet there was no doubt that sufficient evidence to compel a trial connected the Panthers with the crime. As a matter of fact, one Panther was convicted of conspiracy to murder, two others pleaded guilty, and the jury deadlocked as to the charges against the other defendants.

Because there was advance warning and a massing of police and federal troops, and only because of that, Yale's troubles were minor compared to those of other universities and of the wider society. Cornell collapsed under the threats of black and white radicals (the Afro-American Society, soon renamed the Black Liberation Front, and SDS, respectively).[7] The nation was jolted by front-page newspaper photographs of rifle-carrying black students emerging from a university building they had occupied. They came out to sign the surrender that president James A. Perkins and a majority of the faculty had accepted. The surrender was the rescission of the very mild punishments the university had imposed for such actions as trashing a library and occupying a building. Perkins was so reduced to servility that at an angry gathering of over 8,000 students, he publicly embraced the leaders of the AAS and SDS on stage; they mocked him in turn, and then kept him sitting cross-legged on the floor of the stage while they orated. When his turn finally came, Perkins submissively told the crowd that the occupation of the university building and the student pressure was "probably one of the most constructive, positive forces that have been set in motion in the history of Cornell."

Thomas Jones, an AAS leader and one of the rifle brandishers, speaking over the Cornell radio station, identified four administrators and three faculty members as "racists," and said, "they will be dealt with." He stated that the university had only "three hours to live." On the advice of security officials, most of those threatened moved their families to motels and registered under assumed names. One of these was the distinguished political scientist, now my colleague at the American Enterprise Institute, Walter Berns. At a subsequent faculty meeting, "One speaker stressed that Jones had made personal threats against seven Cornell personnel and asked pointblank what would be done about such threats. The President remained silent, and no faculty member offered a motion on the subject." Berns, Allan Bloom, and Allan P. Sindler, the chairman of the government department, soon resigned from Cornell because the university had lost its integrity and abandoned its commitment to academic freedom and scholarly standards.

It was altogether in keeping with the spirit of the capitulation that Cornell *celebrated* the twenty-fifth anniversary of its collapse. Both Perkins and Jones returned, and Jones established a Perkins award to be given annually to a person who had done the most to foster racial harmony on campus. The message appears to be that barbarism and surrender to it are to be viewed as expressions of idealism. In a variant of Marx's maxim, tragedy was remembered in farce.

The U.S. invasion of Cambodia in order to deny the North Vietnamese and Vietcong troops a sanctuary from which to attack our troops in South Vietnam made the spring of the 1969–70 academic year intensely violent. About a thousand demonstrations erupted on more than two hundred campuses. Arson, bombings, and window-smashing wreaked damage in the millions of dollars. Hundreds of students, police, and others were injured, and at least seven students were killed. But it was at Kent State that the inevitable tragedy immanent in the many violent confrontations between radicals and the forces of society was played out. On May 4, 1970, Ohio National Guardsmen fired at student rioters, killing four and wounding ten.

Kent State was hardly a placid campus before the Cambodian operation. The university had 21,000 students, and a sizeable SDS chapter devoted to making trouble. In November, 1968, for example, charges were brought against 250 members of SDS and the Black United Students who had demonstrated against police recruiting on campus. The charges were dropped when about 300 black students left campus demanding amnesty. On April 8, 1969, SDS led a demonstration that resulted in clashes with university police. The demonstrators demanded that the university abolish the Reserve Officers Training Corps, a crime laboratory, and a school for law enforcement training. State police were called in and quelled the disruption. SDS was then banned from campus, thirty-seven students were suspended, and five were charged with assault and battery. Worse was to come.

On the evening of May 1, 1970, a day after Richard Nixon announced an American counter-attack into Cambodia, students rioted in the main street of town, broke windows, set fires, and damaged cars. On May 2, a crowd of about 800 assembled on campus, disrupted a dance in a university hall, smashed the windows of the ROTC building, and threw lighted railroad flares inside. The building burned to the ground. A professor who watched the arson later told the Scranton commission, which investigated the shooting and the events leading up to it, "I have never in my 17 years of teaching seen a group of students as threatening, or as arrogant, or as bent on destruction."[8] When firemen arrived students threw rocks at them, slashed their hoses with machetes, took away hoses and turned them on the firefighters. The police finally stopped the riot with tear gas. The National Guard was called in by the governor on May 2 and student rioters pelted them with rocks, doused trees with gasoline, and set them afire. Students attempted to march into town on May 3 but were stopped by the National Guard, the Kent city police department, the Ohio highway patrol, and the county sheriff's department. The protesters shouted obscenities and threw rocks.

From May 1 to May 4 there were, in addition, riots in the town's main street, looting, the intimidation of passing motorists, stoning of police, directions to local merchants to put antiwar posters in their windows or have their stores trashed, and miscellaneous acts of arson. All of this occurred before the shooting.

On May 4, a Monday, about a thousand students gathered on campus. Guardsmen arrived and, probably unwisely, ordered the crowd to disperse. The order was predictably ignored. The Guard fired tear gas canisters into the crowd. The Guard, consisting of a hundred men surrounded by rioters shouting obscenities and chanting "Kill, kill, kill," were under a constant barrage of rocks, chunks of concrete and cinderblock, and canisters. Fifty-eight Guardsmen were injured by thrown objects. Several of them were knocked to the ground. They had little tear gas left, and the gas had, in any event, been made ineffective by the wind. The Guardsmen retreated up a hill, appearing frightened, and then some of them suddenly turned and fired for thirteen seconds. The firing was apparently spontaneous rather than ordered.

The events of May 4 were viewed differently by a grand jury, which exonerated the Guardsmen as having fired in legitimate fear of their lives, and the Scranton commission appointed to investigate the shootings. The commission, which had the grand jury findings before it, concluded: "The actions of some students were violent and criminal and those of some others were dangerous, reckless and irresponsible. The indiscriminate firing of rifles into a crowd of students and the deaths that followed were unnecessary, unwarranted, and inexcusable."[9] Those conclusions seem appropriate, though it should be remembered that the grand jurors, unlike the commission members, experienced at first-hand the four-day crazed rampage of the students in their town and on the campus. It tends to make a difference if you have lost property and felt fear for yourself, your family, and your neighbors. The grand jury was surely correct in laying a large part of the blame on the university administration, which had progressively surrendered control of the university to radical students and faculty. In that, Kent State behaved like almost all universities at the time.

There is no need to sort out conflicting versions of the event, whether, for example, the Guardsmen had objective reason to fear for their safety. What is undeniable is that on May 2, 3, and 4, these young men faced far greater numbers of students who were screaming threats and engaging in violence. When confrontations of that sort occur again and again, as they did across the country, it is inevitable that sooner or later a tragedy like Kent State will occur.

It should be apparent by now that the campus radicals were not by any stretch of the imagination the idealists they were painted as at the time and continue to be called now. The strong family resemblance of the New Left to German and Italian fascism was described by the sociologist Peter Berger in 1970, when the student revolt was in full swing.[10] Berger was himself opposed to the war in Vietnam, but he could not share the radical's "principle of selectivity in its humanistic rhetoric." There was a complete difference, he was informed, between insurgents torturing a prisoner to death and the same act done by members of counterinsurgency forces. The first was moral, but the second was utterly immoral. The parallel to the views of radical students at Yale is precise. That Black Panthers might have (and had) tortured and murdered Alex Rackley as a suspected informer was not viewed as a serious moral offense. But it was the height of immorality for Connecticut to put the Panthers on trial.

Berger traced a number of parallels between the New Left's ideology and that of the European fascists he had observed first hand in his youth. Both were movements that were without a positive view of the future but were simply against their society— against stability, traditional liberalism, capitalism, and intellectualism. The Nazis, like the New Left, referred to themselves as the "movement" and they hated the "system." Both proclaimed that liberal democracy was a fraud and rationality merely a prop for the evil status quo. "[T]he emotional context within which these negations are proclaimed is one of hatred and rage."

Both fascists and the New Left had faith in the therapeutic value of violence. Watching on television a group of students chanting "The streets belong to the people," Berger felt almost a physical shock as he remembered a verse of the Nazis' "Horst Wessel Lied": "Clear the streets for the brown battalions." There was as well the glorification of youth, which was explicit in the anthem of Mussolini's Italy.

Both the fascists and the New Left dehumanized their enemies. (It is instructive to remember that the *Port Huron Statement* abjured violence because it transformed the target into a "depersonalized object of hate," which is what New Left violence soon did.) The Nazis referred to Jews as "pigs" which is what American radicals called the police. Finally, there was a "mystical elitism" that made the radicals sure they represented a "general will." "This elitism is particularly repulsive in view of the democratic rhetoric" of the new radicals. Despite its democratic rhetoric, the New Left was not only contemptuous of liberal parliamentary democracy, but "fundamentally contemptuous of *any* procedures designed to find out what people want for themselves. . . . What this elitism means in practice can be readily grasped by watching the manipulations of any SDS group on an American campus."[11†]

That was the pattern across the United States in the late 1960s and early 1970s: violent rhetoric and violent action from the fascists of the New Left, followed by the abject moral surrender of academic officials the public had a right to expect would defend the universities and the orderly processes of their governance. University establishments collapsed under moral, and sometimes physical, assault, and often publicly accepted the Left's indictments of themselves and of America. In this, Yale and Cornell were entirely typical. Scenes such as these, and worse, were played out on scores of campuses. Almost nowhere did the faculty and the administration stand firm.[††]

What can account for the abject surrender of the elders? What could account for such craven responses, such self-abasement before barbarians, white and black, such willingness to jettison without struggle academic standards it had taken decades, even centuries, to establish? Fear played a part, for there was usually an implication, and sometimes the explicit threat, of violence. That need not have been a problem. The police were always available. It is true that calling in police often caused more students to join in the disruption and violence, but the issue was who controlled the universities. The price should have been paid. Crime on a campus is not essentially different from crime anywhere else.

[†]Berger noted that two themes of fascism were missing in the student radical movement—nationalism and the authoritarian leadership principle. Yet "the new radicals have shown a considerable capacity for what could be called vicarious nationalism" in uncritical identification with black nationalism, not even shrinking from its anti-Semitic undertones (today, no longer an undertone), and "vicarious solidarity with the virulent nationalisms of the Third World." He thought a charismatic leader, cynically using the democratic rhetoric of the radicals, could overcome their antiauthority stance. If so, we are lucky such a leader did not emerge.

[††]At the University of Chicago, students seized the administration building. After they left, the university empaneled a tribunal and tried a number of them. Those found guilty were expelled. Parents took out newspaper advertisements protesting the draconian punishment visited upon their darlings, thus providing a clue to what had gone wrong with their children.

But universities thought of themselves as divorced from the communities they lived in, indeed divorced from, and superior to, American civilization. It was often psychologically impossible for them to call upon the civil authorities to maintain campus order. Faculties found upper-middle-class student radicals more congenial, on both political and cultural grounds, than working-class policemen. I remember a university official (not at Yale) who described his anguished dilemma when the radicals threatened to burn the school's buildings. Asked what the dilemma was, he said that while the physical destruction of the university would be a great evil, it was almost unthinkable to call in the forces of the outside world.

There was more to it than that, however. There was a predisposition to surrender. Faculties and administrators being overwhelmingly liberal (in the traditional sense) could not help feeling that the radicals were in some sense right about the unworthiness of America. The students had taken seriously the rhetoric of their liberal elders and the faculties were in a poor position to say they really hadn't meant the full implications of what they had said in the past. Not all liberal faculty reacted in this way. Splits developed. Some enthusiastically supported the radicals; some, feeling guilt, could not resist. But others, though not enough, were honest old-style liberals; they meant what they had said about reason, the life of the mind, and openness to ideas reasonably presented. The radicals resented this last group most of all. My friend Alexander Bickel, a constitutional scholar, had a reputation as a liberal, but because he tried to uphold standards of reason and civilized discourse and because he thoroughly disapproved of the mob, he was harassed regularly and hung in effigy in the law school courtyard during alumni weekend. Since nothing good was expected from a conservative, the radicals left me pretty much alone.

Walter Berns captured the emptiness of both the radicals and the Establishment. Members of SDS, he said, are miserable and obsessed, while the Organization Man is content. "Beyond this there is no difference. The Organization Man says SDS should not burn down the universities, but he can provide no reason other than one coming from the law, which is of course no reason at all to SDS. SDS, in turn, says that the Organization Man should feel miserable too and join them in burning down the universities, but they can provide no reason other than one arising out of their idiosyncratic despair, which the Organization Man neither shares nor understands. The only thing that can come out of this confrontation is a test of wills."[12] In a test of wills, a comfortable, liberal, mildly guilty Establishment is no match for angry, nihilistic radicals. Nihilists must be sat upon rather than argued with, but the "oppressive" Establishment lacked the will for that.

In the crunch, the universities proved hollow. The Sixties students did not create the emptiness of the universities; they simply exploited it and made it obvious to the world. They learned that the universities would usually cave in and so their "non-negotiable demands" escalated. The student radicals were flabbergasted. This was no way for oppressors to behave. Even the radicals didn't want enemies who didn't believe anything. Only institutions that were already soft, alienated from the surrounding society, without belief in themselves and the worth of what they did would have surrendered so easily and so completely. The rot was there before the radicals hit.

Nihilism was the order of the decade. It came in two varieties: hedonism and political rage. Some students or dropouts exhibited both. The Hippies rejected middle-class morality for an unprecedented permissiveness. The incessantly repeated slogans were taken seriously: "If it feels good, do it," "Do your own thing," and "It is forbidden to forbid." The symbol of this attitude was, of course, the Woodstock festival, where half a million youths camped in the rain and mud to listen to rock music, take drugs, and engage in sex. That, too, was celebrated by a similar gathering on the twenty-fifth anniversary of the first: this time, farce was repeated as farce.

Radical groups, even as they grew more violent in their effort to destroy the white, bourgeois world, were without any notion of what was to come after. As one of the apostles of violence put it, "The idea was not to create a perfect state operating by the clockwork principles of Marxist law but to promote a chaos that would cripple America and ultimately cast it into a receivership that would be administered by the morally superior third world. . . . [P]eople shouldn't expect the revolution to achieve a Kingdom of Freedom; more likely, it would produce a Dark Ages."[13] It may yet.

The Sixties were, as Robert Nisbet wrote, "a decade of near revolutionary upheaval and of sustained preaching of social nihilism."[14] Except that it was even worse than that. Unlike any previous decade in American experience, the Sixties combined domestic disruption and violence with an explosion of drug use and sexual promiscuity; it was a decade of hedonism and narcissism; it was a decade in which popular culture reached new lows of vulgarity. The Sixties generation combined moral relativism with political absolutism. And it was the decade in which the Establishment not only collapsed but began to endorse the most outrageous behavior and indictments of America by young radicals. It was the decade that saw victories for the civil rights movement, but it was also the decade in which much of America's best educated and most pampered youth refused to serve the country in war, disguising self-indulgence and hatred of the United States as idealism. What W. H. Auden said of the 1930s was even more true of the 1960s: it was "a low, dishonest decade."[15]

*   *   *

The message and the mood of the Sixties did not, of course, remain safely within the universities.

> By the early Seventies, a subtle panic had overtaken the Movement. The revolution that we had awaited so breathlessly was nearing the end of what we now realized would be a dry labor. The monstrous offspring of our fantasies would never be born. People who had gathered for the apocalypse were dropping off into environmentalism and consumerism and fatalism. . . . I watched many of my old comrades apply to graduate school in the universities they had failed to burn down so that they could get advanced degrees and spread the ideas that had been discredited in the streets under an academic cover.[16]

They didn't go just into the universities. The radicals were not likely to go into business or the conventional practice of the professions. They were part of the chattering class, talkers interested in policy, politics, and culture. They went into politics, print and electronic journalism, church bureaucracies, foundation staffs, Hollywood careers, public interest organizations, anywhere attitudes and opinions could be influenced. And they are exerting influence. The view that radical faculties, for example, are not influencing students is the "Goldman Sachs Fallacy." In a question period after I had given a talk, a young man said he had taught at Yale for a brief period and, despite radical faculty members' attempts at indoctrination, most of his students wanted jobs at some place like Goldman Sachs, the investment bankers. He overlooked the fact that he probably did not draw radicals to his course. I pointed out that those graduates who went to Goldman Sachs would play little or no part in shaping the culture. Some of them may continue counter-cultural drug sniffing and sexual promiscuity in their off hours, but that is not the same thing as actively proselytizing for Sixties views. Those who are reached by radical professors would, like those professors, join faculties or take up other culture-shaping careers. It may be that the Left can perpetuate itself forever on our cultural heights by continuing to dominate the universities and indoctrinating its share of the young.

Because of the universities' expansion, this might have occurred in any event, but more slowly. The Sixties compounded the problem. An entire generation of students carried a more virulent form of intellectual class attitudes and cynicism about this society into a range of occupations outside the universities. The transformation of the *New York Times* illustrates what has happened to prestige journalism generally. A newspaper once called "the good, gray lady" is now suffused with Sixties attitudes, which are most explicit, of course, in its editorial and opinion pages, though they can be detected as well in its news pages. Similarly, Hollywood, which once celebrated traditional virtues, has become a propaganda machine for the political outlook and permissive morality of the Sixties generation. If the universities have become permanent enclaves of Sixties culture, and continue feeding converted students into such fields, this may be a permanent feature of our intellectual and artistic communities.

It is commonly said that the New Left of the Sixties collapsed and disappeared. "Has there ever been such politically barren radicalism as that of the Sixties?" Columnist George Will wrote, ". . . The Sixties are dead. Not a moment too soon."[17] Would that it were so, but the truth, alas, is otherwise. The New Left did collapse as a political movement because of its internal incoherence and amorphous program, and because its revolutionary rhetoric and proclivity for violence repelled most Americans. There never was any chance that this collection of frantic youths could become or instigate a popular movement. What we see in modern liberalism, however, may be the ultimate triumph of the New Left.

Its adherents did not go away or change their minds; the New Left shattered into a multitude of single-issue groups. We now have, to name but a few, radical feminists, black extremists, animal rights groups, radical environmentalists, activist homosexual organizations, multiculturalists, and new or freshly radicalized organizations such as People for the American Way, the American Civil Liberties Union, the National Abortion Rights Action League (NARAL), the National Organization for Women (NOW), and Planned Parenthood.

Each of these pursues a piece of the agenda of the cultural and political Left, but they do not announce publicly an overarching program, as the New Left did, that would enable people to see that the separate groups and causes add up to a general radical philosophy. Yet these groups are in touch with one another and often come together in a coalition on specific issues. The splintering of the New Left proved to be an advantage because the movement became less visible and therefore more powerful, its goals more attainable, than was the case in the Sixties.

As the rioting and riotousness died down in the early 1970s and seemingly disappeared altogether in the last half of that decade and in the 1980s, it seemed, at last, that the Sixties were over. They were not. It was a malignant decade that, after a fifteen-year remission, returned in the 1980s to metastasize more devastatingly throughout our culture than it had in the Sixties, not with tumult but quietly, in the moral and political assumptions of those who now control and guide our major cultural institutions. The Sixties radicals are still with us, but now they do not paralyze the universities; they run the universities.

If the problem were only the universities and the chattering classes, there might be reason to be more optimistic. The Sixties have gone further than that, however. "The New Left's anti-institutional outlook and anti-bourgeois value scheme has fed into the 'new liberalism' increasingly held by the upper middle class. Indeed, the 'radical' values and orientations expressed by SNCC [Student Nonviolent Coordinating Committee] and SDS workers in the early sixties have become the conventional wisdom of college-educated urban professionals, especially those under thirty-five. . . . Whatever their other successes and failures, the youthful radicals of that decade propelled a new set of values from the fringes to the very midst of contemporary social conflict."[18] That was written in 1982. It seems even more true today.

Thus, the themes and traits of the New Left have become prominent in today's culture. As will be seen throughout this book, the Sixties generation's fixation on equality has permeated our society and its institutions, much to our disadvantage. Their idea of liberty has now become license in language, popular culture, and sexuality.

The idea that everything is ultimately political has taken hold. We know its current form as "political correctness," a distemper that afflicts the universities in their departments of humanities, social sciences, and law. Works of literature are read for their subtexts, usually existing only in the mind of the politically correct reader, about the oppression of women, Western imperialism, colonialism, and racism. Political correctness is not confined to the enclaves of the academy. It is now to be found in museums, art galleries, seminaries, foundations—all the institutions relating to opinion and attitude formation.

A corollary to the politicization of the culture is the tactic of assaulting one's opponents as not merely wrong but morally evil. That was, of course, a key stratagem of the New Left, and it remains a crucial weapon in modern liberalism's armory. The rioters in the streets did not criticize the universities as in need of reform but as institutions rotten with immorality from top to bottom. Critics of Hillary Clinton's health care plan were not said to be mistaken but were denounced as greedy pharmaceutical companies, doctors, and insurance companies out to protect their illicit profits.

The student radicals' habitual lying is easily enough explained. They were antinomians. Just as those Christian heretics thought themselves freed by God's grace from any obligation to the moral law, so the student radicals, imbued with the political grace of the Left, were freed of the restraints of law and morality. It could not be immoral to lie in a noble cause. For the same reason, it could not be wrong to break laws or heads.

Modern liberals, being in charge of the institutions they once attacked, have no need to break heads and only an occasional need to break laws. They do, however, have a need to lie, and do so abundantly, since many Americans would not like their actual agenda.

One of the New Left's ambitions was to move the Democratic Party further to the left of the American center, to convert it to a more radical stance from the traditional liberal-labor ideology the party had espoused since Franklin Roosevelt built his coalition. Historian Terry H. Anderson, a rather uncritical admirer of the New Left, claims that the Democrats embraced the ideas expressed in the *Port Huron Statement*.[19] There is much truth in that. Certainly student radicals provided the McGovern cadres that took the party left in 1972. Later, as Capitol Hill staffers and elected congressmen, they moved the congressional Democrats well to the left of most Americans who consider themselves Democrats. The parties are aligning themselves along the lines of the war in the culture. Issues such as abortion, flag burning, special homosexual rights, feminism (including women in combat), quotas and affirmative action, the direction of welfare reform, all of these and more already are or are coming to be issues that divide Congress along party lines. The perception that the Democrats are on the wrong side of some of these issues helps to explain the political successes of the Republicans in recent years.

But the primary effect of the Sixties generation is in the realm of culture, as the following chapters seek to demonstrate. Politics may have little effect on elite culture and hence little impact on what is taught in schools and universities or on the reinstitution of the restraints of religion, morality, and law that once gave us classical liberalism instead of the modern variety.

It is troubling to realize that the Sixties merely gave enormous acceleration to trends that had been in place for some time. It may well be that we would ultimately have arrived where we are if the Sixties had never happened. We might, on the other hand, have recognized the problems at a less virulent stage and have been able to deal with them more effectively if the Sixties had not crashed down upon America and overwhelmed us. For those who dislike what we are becoming, the task is not merely to resist but to attack the many manifestations of corruption and restore something of what we once were. That will not be easy: the formulations of the Sixties are now deeply embedded in our opinion-forming institutions and our culture.

In the end, the spirit of Port Huron triumphed: it did change the world. Whether that change is permanent remains to be seen.

3

"We Hold These Truths to Be Self-Evident"

THE RAGE FOR LIBERTY AND THE PURSUIT OF HAPPINESS

For all the decade's lurid brutality and revolutionary upheaval, the Sixties were not a complete break with the spirit of the American past. Rather, those years saw an explosive expansion of certain American (and Western) ideals and a corresponding severe diminution of others. That deserves to be stressed because if modern developments are in the American grain, if they grow from our roots, as there is reason to believe they do, they will be much harder to reverse than it is comfortable to think.

Though the Sixties brought American concepts of liberty and equality to new extremes, that possibility was always inherent in those ideals. Equality and liberty are, of course, what America said it was about from the beginning. The Declaration of Independence drafted by Thomas Jefferson declared: "We hold these truths to be self-evident, that all men are created equal, that they are endowed by their Creator with certain unalienable Rights, that among these are Life, Liberty, and the pursuit of Happiness." It is customary to grow misty-eyed about the elegance and profundity of that formulation. It speaks in the vocabulary of natural rights, which many Americans find congenial, though without examining the full implications of that vocabulary.

It was indeed stirring rhetoric, entirely appropriate for the purpose of rallying the colonists and justifying their rebellion to the world. But some caution is in order. The ringing phrases are hardly useful, indeed may be pernicious, if taken, as they commonly are, as a guide to action, governmental or private. Then the words press eventually towards extremes of liberty and the pursuit of happiness that court personal license and social disorder. The necessary qualifications assumed by Jefferson and the signers of the Declaration were not expressed in the document. It would rather have spoiled the effect to have added "up to a point" or "within reason" to Jefferson's resounding generalities.

The signers of the Declaration took the moral order they had inherited for granted. It never occurred to them that the document's rhetorical flourishes might be dangerous if that moral order weakened. When they had won their independence and got down to the actual business of governing a nation, the Founders were not so lyrical. The "unalienable Rights" of the Declaration turned out, of course, frequently to be alienable. The Fifth Amendment to the Constitution, for example, explicitly assumes that a criminal may be punished by depriving him of life or liberty, which certainly tends to interfere with his pursuit of happiness.

The tension between the rhetoric of the Declaration and the practicalities expressed in the Constitution is instructive. The former articulates a confident liberalism, while the latter assumes that there will be restraints on that liberalism. To note this is not to adopt the old canard that the Constitution was the instrument of a conservative reaction against the liberalism of the Declaration. To the contrary, the Constitution and the laws it permitted expressed the constraints on liberty assumed by those who signed and welcomed the spirit of the Declaration. But these assumptions and restraints are passive and proved ineffective to halt the aggressive march of liberalism to its present condition.

Liberalism does not vary; it is always the twin thrusts of liberty and equality, and these never change. What distinguishes apparently different stages of liberalism—classical liberalism from modern liberalism, for example—is not any difference in liberalisms but a difference in the admixture of other elements that modify or oppose it. Liberalism itself (putting aside, for the moment, its egalitarian element) is nothing but an effort to struggle free of restraints on the individual.

Jefferson was a man of the Enlightenment, and the Declaration of Independence is an Enlightenment document. That means not only faith in the power of reason to build a just and stable social order, but also emphasis on the individual as the building block of society. The Enlightenment optimists made a serious mistake about the nature of the individual human in whom they placed so much faith. Robert Nisbet notes that the men who laid down the principles of liberalism—Locke, Montesquieu, Adam Smith, and Jefferson, for instance—thought "such traits as sovereign reason, stability, security, and indestructible motivations toward freedom and order" constituted the nature of man, that man was "inherently self-sufficing, equipped by nature with both the instincts and the reason that could make him autonomous."[1]

> What we can now see with the advantage of hindsight is that, unconsciously, the founders of liberalism abstracted certain moral and psychological attributes from a *social organization* and considered these the timeless, natural qualities of the *individual*, who was regarded as independent of the influences of any historically developed social organization. . . . A free society. . . . would be composed, in short, of socially and morally *separated* individuals. Order in society would be the product of a natural equilibrium of economic and political forces.[2]

The American Founders shared those sentiments. Jefferson said, "the Creator would indeed have been a bungling artist, had he intended man for a social animal, without planting in him social dispositions. . . ." Gordon Wood comments that "Americans, like others in those years, . . . posit[ed] this natural social disposition, a moral instinct, a sense of sympathy, in each human being. . . . It made benevolence and indeed moral society possible."[3]

Men with such views of human nature would naturally continually emphasize liberty. Though they surely did not envision a society resembling ours, they set in motion a tendency that, carried far enough, could and often did eventually free the individual from almost all moral and legal constraints. (Again, I am speaking of areas of life where radical egalitarianism does not hold sway.) The tendency is forwarded by persons for whom that prospect is attractive. This form of liberalism was powerfully stated and carried to what may seem its logical conclusion in 1859 with the publication of John Stuart Mill's *On Liberty*. Mill advanced "one very simple principle": "the sole end for which mankind are warranted, individually or collectively, in interfering with the liberty of action of any of their number, is self-protection. . . . The only part of the conduct of any one, for which he is amenable to society, is that which concerns others. In the part which merely concerns himself, his independence is, of right, absolute."[4] The individual is to be free both of legal penalties and the "moral coercion of public opinion."

Gertrude Himmelfarb points out that Mill contradicted his own principle in other, far less libertarian writings both before and after *On Liberty*, though he did so without mentioning the contradictions.[5] Although in *On Liberty* he argued that every idea was to be examined and opposed in order to approach truth, elsewhere Mill wrote that it is essential to the stability of society that some fundamental principles of the system of social union be held sacred and above discussion. Although *On Liberty* called for freedom of action, individuality, even eccentricity, for the discovery of new practices, new modes of living, what some today might call "alternative lifestyles," elsewhere Mill praised restraining discipline and the subordination of the individual's impulses and aims to the ends of society.

It is instructive of the temper of our times that it is the Mill of *On Liberty* who is widely known and admired while the non-libertarian writings of the man Ms. Himmelfarb calls the "other Mill" are far less often read or cited. It is typical that a law school casebook designed for the study of the first amendment is dedicated to James Madison, Thomas Jefferson, and John Stuart Mill. I don't think the author was saluting the "other Mill."

Mill's "one very simple principle" is, of course, both impossible and empty. Impossible, because the complex relations of the individual and his society cannot be reduced to a single rule. If that could be done, we should have arranged our society in conformance with the best rule, or at least some single rule, long ago, but all of human history shows that is not the way any real society has ever operated. The principle is empty, because, as stated, it does not really tell us much. Mill thought he knew what conduct of a man concerns others, but the others will often have quite different ideas about what concerns them, and there is no reason why their opinions on that subject are not as valid as, or entitled to more weight than, Mill's.

Depending on how the harm is defined, so that the right of self-protection is triggered, the principle can lead either to tyranny or license or any condition in between: tyranny if a community defines harm as encompassing even Anthony Comstock's psychological anguish at not being certain that private immorality is not taking place; license if only physical or material injury counts as harm. In the first case, the television lenses of the Comstockian moral police would peer everywhere. We would live in Orwell's *Nineteen Eighty-Four.* In the second case, there could be no laws or even moral coercion, for example, about prostitution, indecent exposure, public drunkenness, obscenity, and the like. There is no reason whatever why a community should not decide that there are moral and aesthetic pollutions it wishes to prohibit. Though Mill elsewhere assumed standards of decency—the restraints of law, religion, and morality—that would make his principle less dangerous, this passage contains no such explicit safeguards, and events have proved that standards of decency erode rather quickly. It is difficult not to agree with the man Ms. Himmelfarb calls the "other Mill" rather than with the one who devised "one very simple principle" that underlies today's rage for liberty, or what our forefathers more accurately called license.

Nevertheless, Mill's influence remains pervasive, a testament to the power of an idea that has been repeatedly refuted to continue to dominate the sentiments of men and hence a culture. Perhaps, Ms. Himmelfarb suggests, that is because "'One very simple principle' is always more seductive than a complicated, nuanced set of principles. And this particular principle is all the more appealing because it conforms to the image of the modern, liberated, autonomous, 'authentic' individual."[6] There is a popular notion that expanding the sphere of liberty is always a net gain. That is, quite obviously, wrong. If it were true, our ultimate goal should be the elimination of all law and all the restraints imposed by social disapproval. That condition of moral anarchy seems to be one we are constantly approaching but can never finally reach.

Perhaps the immediate popularity of *On Liberty* was entirely due to its simplicity, but it is also possible to think that we tend to overrate the power of social philosophers to change the direction of a culture. Perhaps Mill was influential while British legal scholar James Fitzjames Stephen's contemporary rebuttal[7] dropped from sight—until recently it had long been out of print—because the culture was moving towards Mill's liberalism semiconsciously and gradually adopted this articulation of its inchoate mood. That speculation may be reinforced by the fact that while Mill's principle became widely known at once, "By a kind of cultural lag the practical implications of Mill's idea of liberty did not make themselves felt until long after the idea itself had become thoroughly familiar, so familiar that we have almost lost sight of its origin. Only now are we experiencing its full impact."[8] This suggests, perhaps, that the culture created the status of *On Liberty* as much as the book created the culture. The culture had been moving in the direction of Mill's principle at least since the Enlightenment. Ms. Himmelfarb notes that Mill's essay "points to a radical disjunction between the individual and society—indeed, an adversarial relationship."[9] That is precisely what is to be expected of the socially and morally separated individuals the Enlightenment liberals contemplated.

The idea of liberty has continuous change built into it, precisely because it is hostile to constraints. Men seek the removal of the constraint nearest them. But when that one falls, men are brought against the next constraint, which is now felt to be equally irksome. That is why the agenda of liberalism is in constant motion and liberals of different eras would hardly recognize one another as deserving the same label. Harry Truman would have hated the Sixties, and, because his liberalism contained more powerful constraints on individualism, he was not a liberal in the same sense that Bill Clinton is. The perpetual motion of liberalism was described by T. S. Eliot half a century ago: "That Liberalism may be a tendency towards something very different from itself, is a possibility in its nature. . . . It is a movement not so much defined by its end, as by its starting point; away from, rather than towards something definite."[10] What liberalism has constantly moved away from are the constraints on personal liberty imposed by religion, morality, law, family, and community.

Liberalism moves, therefore, toward radical individualism and the corruption of standards that movement entails. "By destroying traditional social habits of the people, by dissolving their natural collective consciousness into individual constituents, by licensing the opinions of the most foolish, by substituting instruction for education, by encouraging cleverness rather than wisdom, the upstart rather than the qualified ... Liberalism can prepare the way for that which is its own negation: the artificial, mechanised or brutalised control which is a desperate remedy for its chaos."[11]

Chaos, which only government can control, results when other sources of authority are denigrated and diminished. Pierre Manent remarks that liberalism is based on two ideas, one of which is representative government. "The idea of representation postulates that the only legitimate power is founded on the consent of those subject to power. In such a regime, all powers within civil society born from the spontaneous interplay of economic and social life or from traditions come to seem essentially illegitimate since they are not representative. Hence they are slowly but surely eroded."[12] The family is not representative, nor are business organizations, the Catholic Church, or universities. All have been attacked precisely on that ground. If freedom is to be limited in any way, it is argued, that should only be done by the votes or expressed desires of those affected. It also seems apparent that the authority of these institutions has, in varying degrees, been eroded and that of the state, which represents everyone, has been correspondingly enhanced. We already have reason to regret both developments.

Since liberalism is a movement away from, an impulse, not a stable agenda, it continually revises the agenda it has at any particular moment. That accounts for the gradual transformation of the older or classical liberalism into the radical individualist component of today's liberalism. Because the desire for and achievement of liberty has moved on in the last half century, Eliot's version of our decline now seems too optimistic. Many of us would gladly settle for what he regarded as degradation. If our society has abandoned education, in the larger sense in which Eliot meant it, that is probably irreversible in a democratized culture, but he did not foresee that we would then abandon even instruction for self-esteem and multiculturalism. If only we could recover mere instruction in an era when SAT scores decline and the solution is not improved instruction but raising all scores so that students seem more accomplished than they actually are.

I once made the entirely unoriginal observation that there is an emptiness at the heart of the American ideology, democratic capitalism, and a colleague said that was incorrect, that meaning is given by the idea of the "pursuit of happiness." But the liberty to pursue happiness means that each of us pursues whatever it is he may desire. We are to move away from restraints in pursuit of we know not what. Such a person leads a precarious existence, for as W. H. Auden said: "Emancipated from the traditional beliefs of a closed society, he can no longer believe simply because his forefathers did and he cannot imagine not believing—he has found no source or principle of direction to replace them. . . . Liberalism is at a loss to know how to handle him, for the only thing liberalism knows to offer is more freedom, and it is precisely freedom in the sense of lack of necessity that is his trouble."[13]

The mistake the Enlightenment founders of liberalism made about human nature has brought us to this—an increasing number of alienated, restless individuals, individuals without strong ties to others, except in the pursuit of ever more degraded distractions and sensations. And liberalism has no corrective within itself; all it can do is endorse more liberty and demand more rights. Persons capable of high achievement in one field or another may find meaning in work, may find community among colleagues, and may not particularly mind social and moral separation otherwise. Such people are unlikely to need the more sordid distractions that popular culture now offers. But very large segments of the population do not fall into that category. For them, the drives of liberalism are catastrophic.

The consequences of liberalism, liberty, and the pursuit of happiness pushed too far are now apparent. Irving Kristol writes of "the clear signs of rot and decadence germinating within American society—a rot and decadence that was no longer the consequence of liberalism but was the actual agenda of contemporary liberalism. . . . [S]ector after sector of American life has been ruthlessly corrupted by the liberal ethos. It is an ethos that aims simultaneously at political and social collectivism on the one hand, and moral anarchy on the other."[14] I would add only that current liberalism's rot and decadence is merely what liberalism has been moving towards for better than two centuries.

We can now see the tendency of the Enlightenment, the Declaration of Independence, and *On Liberty*. Each insisted on the expanding liberty of the individual and each assumed that order was not a serious problem and could be left, pretty much, to take care of itself. And, for a time, order did seem to take care of itself. But that was because the institutions—family, church, school, neighborhood, inherited morality—remained strong. The constant underestimation of their value and the continual pressure for more individual autonomy necessarily weakened the restraints on individuals. The ideal slowly became the autonomous individual who stood in an adversarial relationship to any institution or group that attempted to set limits to acceptable thought and behavior.

That process continues today, and hence we have an increasingly disorderly society. The street predator of the underclass may be the natural outcome of the mistake the founders of liberalism made. They would have done better had they remembered original sin. Or had they taken Edmund Burke seriously. Mill wrote: "Liberty consists in doing what one desires."[15] That might have been said by a man who was both a libertine and an anarchist; Mill was neither, but his rhetoric encouraged those who would be either or both. Burke had it right earlier: "The only liberty I mean is a liberty connected with order; that not only exists along with order and virtue, but which cannot exist at all without them."[16] "The effect of liberty to individuals is, that they may do what they please: We ought to see what it will please them to do, before we risque congratulations, which may soon be turned into complaints."[17] Burke, unlike the Mill of *On Liberty*, had a true understanding of the nature of men, and balanced liberty with restraint and order, which are, in truth, essential to the preservation of liberty.

The classical liberalism of the nineteenth century is widely and correctly admired, but we can now see that it was inevitably a transitional phase. The tendencies inherent in individualism were kept within bounds by the health of institutions other than the state, a common moral culture, and the strength of religion. Liberalism drained the power from the institutions. We no longer have a common moral culture and our religion, while pervasive, seems increasingly unable to affect actual behavior.

Modern liberalism is one branch of the rupture that occurred in liberalism in the last century. The other branch is today called conservatism. American conservatism, neo or otherwise, in fact represents the older classical liberal tradition. Conservatism of the American variety is simply liberalism that accepts the constraints that a clear view of reality, including a recognition of the nature of human beings, places upon the main thrusts of liberalism—liberty and equality. The difference, it has been said, is that between a hard-headed and a sentimental liberalism. Sentimental liberalism, with its sweet view of human nature, naturally evolves into the disaster of modern liberalism.

"During the past 30 years," William Bennett writes, "we have witnessed a profound shift in public attitudes." He cites polls showing that "we Americans now place less value on what we owe others as a matter of moral obligation; less value on sacrifice as a moral good, on social conformity, respectability, and observing the rules; less value on correctness and restraint in matters of physical pleasure and sexuality—and correlatively greater value on things like self-expression, individualism, self-realization, and personal choice."[18] Though I think the shift in public attitudes merely accelerated in the past thirty years, having been silently eroding our culture for much longer, it is clear that our current set of values is inhospitable to the self-discipline required for such institutions as marriage and education and hospitable to no-fault divorce and self-esteem training.

Our modern, virtually unqualified, enthusiasm for liberty forgets that liberty can only be "the space between the walls," the walls of morality and law based upon morality. It is sensible to argue about how far apart the walls should be set, but it is cultural suicide to demand all space and no walls.

4

"We Hold These Truths to Be Self-Evident"

THE PASSION FOR EQUALITY

Despite its rhetorical vagueness, or because of it, the Declaration of Independence profoundly moved Americans at the time, and does still. The proposition that all men are created equal said what the colonists already believed, and so, as Gordon Wood put it, equality became "the single most powerful and radical ideological force in all of American history."[1] That is true and, though it verges on heresy to say so, it is also profoundly unfortunate.

The deep emotional, indeed religious, appeal of equality is not, of course, a peculiarly American phenomenon; the ideal informs all of the West. Besides being a matter for regret, the appeal of equality, outside the context of political and legal rights, is puzzling. Neither of those thoughts is new; in fact, they are trite. Writer after writer has demonstrated the pernicious effects of our passion for equality and the lack of any intellectual foundation for that passion. If there is anything new in this book, it is the demonstration of the ill effects of the passion in a variety of contemporary social and cultural fields.

The Declaration's pronouncement of equality was sweeping but sufficiently ambiguous so that even slave holders, of whom Jefferson was one, subscribed to it. That ambiguity was dangerous because it invited the continual expansion of the concept and its requirements. The Declaration was not, clearly, a document that was understood at the time to promise equality of condition, not even among white male Americans. The meaning of equality was heavily modified by the American idea of reward according to individual achievement and reverence for private property. But those modifications are hostile to the egalitarian impulse, which constantly expands the areas in which equality is thought desirable or even mandatory. Hence they, like the constraints on the ideas of liberty and the pursuit of happiness, gradually give way before the active principle, in this case ever greater equality.

The idea of equality began to undergo considerable and worrisome change soon after its enshrinement in the Declaration. Alexis de Tocqueville, who observed the United States for nine months in 1831–32, remarked that Americans loved equality more than freedom. Though Tocqueville found that ominous, it was not until the twentieth century that equality became a serious threat to freedom. The great political upsurge of equality occurred with Franklin Roosevelt's New Deal and Harry Truman's Fair Deal. The names suggest that the cards have been unfairly stacked, that there are inequalities that must be rectified. Since these were sentiments expressed in the political arena, the message was that inequality must be cured by government. No other institution is sufficiently powerful and sufficiently comprehensive in its jurisdiction to undertake the task, which means that the egalitarian passion must always lead to greater centralized power and coercion. Lyndon Johnson's Great Society carried forward what Roosevelt and Truman had begun and accomplished the most thorough-going redistribution of wealth and status in the name of equality that this country had ever experienced. Whether the political movements produced the passion for equality or reflected it—probably the two reinforced one another—is, for the moment, unimportant. The fact is that antihierarchical, egalitarian sentiments were on the rise in political movements, whose tendencies were, therefore, towards collectivism and centralization, with a concomitant decline in the freedoms of business organizations, private associations, families, and individuals. We have come further along that path since the Great Society.

The general subject of equality may be approached through

the topic of economic inequality. It is an almost universal assumption among cultural elites, particularly intellectuals, that inequalities of wealth or income pose a serious problem that the political nation should address. Christopher Lasch, to take but one of many examples, asserted that "economic inequality is intrinsically undesirable. . . . Luxury is morally repugnant, and its incompatibility with democratic ideals, moreover, has been consistently recognized in the traditions that shape our political culture. . . . [A] moral condemnation of great wealth must inform any defense of the free market, and that moral condemnation must be backed up with effective political action."[2]

As an empirical matter, Lasch is no doubt correct in saying that many of our political traditions find economic inequality incompatible with democratic ideals. That is merely a way of saying that if you extend the idea of democracy far enough, you arrive at socialism: "one person, one vote" extended to the economic realm. But why anybody should agree with Lasch that such a situation would be desirable is not readily apparent; the basis for his proposition seems no more than a reflexive egalitarianism. If economic inequality is "intrinsically" bad, then it is bad regardless of any consequences, good or bad, such as increases in freedom and productivity or, on the other hand, the social unrest it may be thought to produce.

What then can be the moral basis for objecting to economic inequality and asserting that condemnation of great wealth, backed up with political action, is essential to any defense of the free market? The obvious candidate is envy. It is impossible to see any objective harm done to the less wealthy by another's greater wealth. It is not, after all, the case that the richer man's income is extracted from the poorer man. Vacationing at the shore, I see a large yacht at anchor in the harbor. Though I may wish I had one, it is quite clear that I do not lack a yacht because another man has one. The economy is not a zero/sum game. A Rockefeller's or a Bill Gates's or a Michael Jackson's wealth does not diminish my wealth or anybody else's. (It is irrelevant to the present point to note that political action to deprive such folks of their luxuries would, because of its adverse effects on incentives, make the rest of us poorer.)

Nor is it at all clear why luxury should be morally repugnant.

If luxury is inconsistent with the democratic ideals that have shaped our political culture, that means only that some of our democratic "ideals" are the product of envy. Envy has been said to be pure evil because it wishes to deprive others even though we gain nothing for ourselves. That is not quite the case. The political action Lasch called for results in redistribution. It may be that academic intellectuals would gain only the satisfaction of seeing the better off lessened, but there are many classes of people who will receive income that is transferred to them from the wealthy through government. For such folks, the emotion of envy is reinforced by cupidity. Much of the wealth will accrue to the bureaucrats who accomplish the redistribution but who would otherwise be employed in the private sector. (We are not discussing here the case of redistributions to persons who would otherwise fall below a subsistence level. Such redistributions result from compassion rather than envy.)

Envy certainly has shaped and continues to shape our political culture. That is probably why it is front-page news in the *New York Times* that the United States displays greater inequality in wealth than other industrialized nations.[3] The unstated assumption that makes this worthy of the front page is that there is something morally wrong, even shameful, in having greater wealth inequalities than other societies. The problem allegedly posed is not about an inequality between those who do and do not have enough money to subsist or to lead a life free of want. The problem raised is the inequality between persons or families that are above that line.

It would be possible to argue that the measurement of inequalities used is dubious as a factual matter,[4] but it is more to the present point to accept the story's assertion as true and ask why it is even worth mentioning. The answer is not obvious. We have seen that nobody has less wealth *because* others have more. What, then, is the problem? Sometimes the egalitarian appeals to an undefined, and undefinable, notion of "social justice." Thus, our current president justifies higher tax rates on those with higher incomes because they are "not paying their fair share." He does not, of course, specify how one knows what a fair share would be. Egalitarians never tell you that; they never specify how much reduction of inequality would be enough. They cannot do that since there is no objective criterion to specify the stopping place between the present situation and complete equality. They content themselves with saying that present inequalities are too great, and they will go on saying that so long as any inequality remains. Irving Kristol, as editor of the *Public Interest*, wrote to professors who had expressed great discontent with inequalities in the distribution of income in the United States, asking them to write articles about what a "fair" distribution would be. He was never able to get that article and has concluded, no doubt correctly, that he will never get it.[5] It has often been observed that the more inequalities are reduced, the greater is the resentment of any remaining inequalities.

The primary tool for reducing inequalities of income is redistribution through the progressive income tax. The intellectual case for the fairness of any progressive income tax was fatally undermined years ago by Walter J. Blum and Harry Kalven, Jr., professors at the University of Chicago school of law.[6] They examined and found seriously wanting the various theoretical supports for progression. Their discussion of theoretical economic rationales is beside the point here, but they also examine "the possible rationale for desiring to lessen economic inequalities within the confines of a private enterprise and market system." They begin by asking whether, if the wealth of the society tripled overnight without any changes in the relative distribution among individuals, the issue of inequality would be any less urgent. Since there have been enormous increases in wealth, even among the poorest, and the issue of equality has grown more disturbing, the answer cannot be in the affirmative. Thus: "It initially appears that what is involved is envy, the dissatisfaction produced in men not by what they lack but by what others have." I think that is what finally appears as well, though it would be impolitic for a supporter of progression to say so. "No proponent of progression has rested his case for doing something about economic inequality on the grounds of mitigating greed and envy."

Two other lines of argument are advanced instead. The first contends that improvements in the general welfare will result from greater economic equality. The second contends that permitting the existing degree of inequality works injustices between individuals. Blum and Kalven found these contentions weak. I find them weaker still.

To the first, the authors advance a technical objection, which is nonetheless important, but then object: "The general welfare is stated in deceptively simple terms." One may grant the assumption that lessening inequality would produce a net increase in the aggregate happiness of the community. "No matter how the case is put, it is still true that all that has happened is that the welfare of one group in the society has been increased at the expense of the welfare of a different group. Stated this way there is no 'general' welfare; there is only the welfare of the two groups and the wealthy receive no counterbalancing benefits for their surrender of income or wealth. . . . If the wealthy have otherwise valid claims to their income, there is little reason for subordinating those claims to this narrow version of general welfare."

As for the argument that the government or the less wealthy would spend the money in more desirable ways than the rich, the authors attribute its appeal not to the way the less wealthy are spending the money but to the fact that they, rather than the wealthier, are spending it. Nor does the contention stand up that the workings of democracy are impeded if there is too great a disparity in the wealth of the citizens. There are many avenues to political power and wealth is not the most significant.

In order to address the argument about justice as between individuals, Blum and Kalven examined the claims of the more wealthy to the income that is to be taken from them by progressive taxation. There is, they concede, a large amount of "undeserved" income—due to factors like monopoly, fraud, duress, and chance—but this does not establish a case for redistribution. That would require a correlation between such income and the rates of progression, which would further require that there be some general relationship between total income and undeserved income and that the undeserved component increase more rapidly than total income. They point out that almost nothing is known about the distribution of undeserved income, and guesses about it "seem to be a most precarious base on which to rest the tax structure." They might have added that, to make progression just, we would have to assume not only these things but that all persons with large incomes had the same proportion of undeserved income. That is extremely improbable.

It would unduly lengthen this discussion to take up all of the arguments for greater economic equality. The authors noted, however, that "it is quite difficult to sponsor progression on the basis of economic equality without calling into question either the meaningfulness of personal responsibility [in achieving success] or the fairness with which the market distributes rewards. Progression, when offered on these grounds, is an unsettling idea." It will be seen, I believe, that most demands for equality, even those outside the subject of income equality, also involve questioning the meaningfulness of personal responsibility and the fairness with which (non-economic) rewards are distributed.

But if the intellectual case for lessening income inequalities fails, the political appeal of the idea remains. James Q. Wilson has analyzed the concept of fairness, which children understand at a very early age.[7] He attributes that to the sociability of children, who want to win approval, initiate play, or maintain contact. The idea of fairness is, then, built into humans as social animals. Wilson says the concept has one or more of three meanings, the relevant one for our present purpose being equity. "In modern equity theory, a division of something between two people is fair if the ratio between the first person's worth (his effort, skill, or deeds) and that person's gains (his earnings, benefits, or rewards) is the same as the ratio between the second person's worth and gains."[8] But "severe inequalities [of wealth] distort the evaluation of contributions by both the advantaged and the disadvantaged, leading to outcomes that are unfair as judged by the natural standards of equity that develop in the household."[9] The problem, therefore, is not the inequality itself, but that the severity of the difference makes it difficult to know whether the same ratio of inputs to outputs exists between the advantaged and the disadvantaged. This uncertainty leads, in turn, to a suspicion that the ratio is skewed and hence unfair.

While that is no doubt true, it is inadequate to explain current levels of taxation. (Wilson was not attempting such an explanation.) Progression today sets in for a married couple at an income of $38,000, and the next higher bracket begins at $91,850. Those incomes are certainly not large enough to distort the evaluation of inputs between such couples and couples making $25,000. The difficulty of assessing the ratio between inputs and outputs does not exist. The ratio assessment problem cannot account for even more dramatic examples of progression. A family with a $500,000 income pays $154,000 in taxes while a family with an income of $45,000 pays $3,800. "With eleven times the income, the rich[er] family pays 40 times the taxes."[10] Something besides a suspicion of skewed ratios is obviously in play. Even if a discrepancy in wealth or income were great enough to make ratio assessment difficult, the presumption Wilson describes favors denying that the inputs of the richer person can really be great enough to justify his rewards. Why that presumption? Why not a presumption that the richer person has in fact merited his wealth? The presumption Wilson describes is not explained by the difficulty of comparing inputs and outputs. If difficulty of assessment does not explain current rates of progression in the tax code, the only remaining explanation seems to be envy. The United States tolerates much greater income disparities than other industrialized democracies. Sweden is the extreme example of taxation for egalitarian purposes. Given the non-existent case for income equalization, it is not that America is odd compared to Sweden, but that Sweden is odd compared to us, and that we are odd compared to a rational, nonenvious view of income distribution.

President Clinton at one point proposed raising taxes on the rich although it did not appear that it would increase the tax revenues received from them. A substantial proportion of the public said they favored higher taxes on high-income earners even if that did not increase the total taxes such people paid. The effect would not be to help anyone else but merely to pull down the better off. The motivation can only be envy, and it is surprising that so many people would admit harboring that emotion. Helmut Schoeck states:

> Since the end of the Second World War, however, a new "ethic" has, astonishingly, come into being, according to which the envious man is altogether acceptable. Progressively fewer individuals and groups are ashamed of their envy, but instead make out that its existence in their temperaments axiomatically proves the existence of "social injustice," which must be eliminated for their benefit. Suddenly it has become possible to say, without loss of public credibility and trust, "I envy you. Give me what you've got." This public self-justification of envy is something entirely new. In this sense it is possible to speak of the age of envy.[11]

The admission of envy is even more surprising when one considers who "the rich" are and how they got that way. We are not talking about South American plutocrats living on million-acre estates that have been in their families for generations while peasants scrabble for a living on tiny plots of land. In America "the rich" are overwhelmingly people—entrepreneurs, small businessmen, corporate executives, doctors, lawyers, etc.—who have gained their higher incomes through intelligence, imagination, and hard work. The desire to deprive them of the rewards they have earned, with no tangible benefit to oneself, is pure envy, and it is an ugly emotion. Yet it is the basis for progression in our tax system, as it is the basis for much else in our culture and social policies.

Envy is not simply about inequality, however. It is, as Bertrand de Jouvenel points out, about who is unequal: "During the whole range of commercial society, from the end of the Middle Ages to our day, the wealth of the rich merchant has been resented far more than the pomp of rulers. The ungrateful brutality of kings towards the financiers who helped them has always won popular applause. . . . The film star or the crooner is not grudged the income that is grudged to the oil magnate. . . . [The people] want to feel that exceptional income is their gift and they demand that beneficiaries thereof shall make a gallant spectacle."[12] Were he writing today, observing many of our entertainers, Jouvenel might want to drop the word "gallant" from the last sentence.

There may, however, be an additional reason why the wealth of merchants and oil magnates, and even that of mid-level doctors and engineers, is resented far more than that of kings or film stars. People accept that they cannot be kings or film stars. But in an increasingly meritocratic society, they are asked to accept as well that there is justice in the standards by which others have outpaced them. The comparison between their incomes and those of the most successful businessmen is thus felt to be invidious. This may be one reason the merit principle, reward according to achievement, is today under attack.

The desire for equality of incomes or wealth is, of course, but one aspect of a more general desire for equality in such matters as social and cultural status. "The essence of the moral idea of socialism," historian Martin Malia wrote, "is that human equality is the supreme value in life."[13] Socialism is thus merely the manifestation in the field of economic organization of a more general yearning that operates across the entire culture.

The French scholar Pierre Manent, discussing Tocqueville's views on equality, remarks that every man naturally wants to believe that he is just as good as anybody else. In a democracy, the law adds its authority, proving his equality by giving him an equal share in the governing of the nation. "But what his heart whispers to him, and the law proclaims, the society around him incessantly denies: certain people are richer, more powerful than he, others are reputed to be wiser or more intelligent. The contradiction between social reality and the combined wishes of his heart and the law, therefore incites and nourishes a devouring passion in everyone: the passion for equality. It will never cease until social reality is made to conform with his and the law's wishes."[14]

The usual strategy for coping with the discomfort of knowing that others are superior in some way is to try to reduce the inequalities by bringing the more fortunate down or by preventing him from being more fortunate. This is the strategy of envy.

The apparent difficulty of requiring equality of wisdom and intelligence was solved in a satirical story by Kurt Vonnegut in 1961, even before the plethora of civil rights laws seeking equality by race, ethnicity, sex, age, disability, and so on and on.[15] Americans would achieve perfect equality by forcing persons of superior intelligence to wear mental handicap radios that emit unsettling noises every twenty seconds to keep them from taking unfair advantage of their brains, persons of superior strength or grace were to be burdened with weights, and those of uncommon beauty must wear masks. Thus, social reality can be made to conform with the envious man's and the law's wishes.

The unwillingness to admit inherent individual differences is astounding. One night, shortly after I became a federal judge, I spoke informally to a gathering of Yale law school alumni in Washington. Someone asked how I found the quality of briefs and oral arguments, and I replied that some were quite good but a great many were poor, some sadly so. The question was then put, why should that be so? I said that many areas of law and procedure had now become so complex that the gene pool was inadequate to operate the system. Afterwards, my clerks gathered around me and said, urgently: "Never say anything like that again." They said a shock had run through the audience at the suggestion that talents differed and that the differences might be largely inherited. They did not deny that it was true, but were adamant that it was not a politic thing to say.

The advance of this "cultural socialism" was under way well before the Sixties. Our leveling instincts are so developed that men and women are allowed celebrity, but, outside the realms of entertainment and sports, rarely are they permitted superiority. Great men are no longer admired, unless they learn how to disguise their greatness. Otherwise, they will be faced with the fatal charge of "elitism." Even to speak of "great men" now has an old-fashioned, even reactionary, sound about it.

The contrast between the popularity of Douglas MacArthur in the First and Second World Wars and of MacArthur and Dwight Eisenhower during World War II illustrates the rise of cultural socialism or radical egalitarianism in the twentieth century. William Manchester writes: "Egalitarianism did not become the triumphant passion of Western society until about the middle of this century. . . . Veterans of World War I and World War II saw MacArthur very differently. Doughboys were proud to have fought under the General. GIs weren't; by the 1940s antiauthoritarianism had become dominant."[16]

Mid-twentieth century seems to be when envy and egalitarianism became rampant together: "Since about the middle of this century a quite remarkable irresolution and weakness toward the envious have manifested themselves in a significantly greater number of people than hitherto. . . . The mere expression of envy, whether in a political speech or caricature, or in a satirical song etc., is now enough to convince such people that an objective infringement of justice exists. . . . [W]e meet with an insufficiently reasoned reaction which accepts all forms of envy as justified in the light of the idea of equality."[17]

One American general noted the contrast between the singing armies of World War I and the wisecracking armies of World War II. That difference reflects a massive cultural shift. A singing army expresses an element of romanticism, of poetry. Such an army would be capable of admiring courage and ability, even distinction, all of which MacArthur displayed. The wisecrack, however, is a leveler, a means of bringing down the person at whom it is directed. The San, African bushmen who foraged widely, were egalitarian out of necessity, but "Culture reinforced necessity: the San engaged in ritual joking designed to deflate any claims to status or prowess."[18]

MacArthur's grand manner aroused intense dislike and made him the butt of countless jokes in World War II. Eisenhower designed a blousy battle jacket that bespoke informality, and he cultivated the troops with a regular-guy manner. There was no doubt who was more popular. The troops spoke affectionately of "Ike," but referred sarcastically to "Dugout Doug" (who actually took more chances with his life than most of his men did). The change between wars was not in MacArthur but in America.

Why egalitarianism should have become an obsession between the two world wars is difficult to say, but that it did cannot be doubted. The ground was thus prepared for the Sixties generation which grew up in the grip of the "triumphant passion." The Sixties rebels attacked hierarchies and lines of authority resulting from merit and achievement. They wanted parity with the faculty, an end to grading, admissions on the basis of race, and the right to participate in the governance and alteration of academic institutions they did not understand and would be in for only a few years. Allan Bloom wrote at the time, "[I]t is almost inconceivable to them that there can be a theoretical questioning of the principle of equality, let alone a practical doubt about it. . . . Student participation is the catchword in all talk of university reform. The goals to be achieved by student participation are never explicitly defined. It is enough to refer to the democratic view: everyone has the right to vote."[19]

In a seminar we taught together, Alexander Bickel got into just this argument with the students (who were not particularly radical). To illustrate his point, Bickel asked them to suppose a group of a dozen people trying to decide whether to picnic at the beach or in the mountains. It turns out that five of the group are utterly indifferent but want to vote on the question anyway. Bickel contended that they should not be allowed to vote, that the outcome should not be determined, whimsically, by people who have no interest in it. But many, perhaps most, of the students thought the right to vote was more important than the desires of those who cared about the location of the picnic. This feeling explains efforts, such as the Motor-Voter Act, to make voters out of people who don't care about elections. Nor was it just the right to vote; the students wanted an end to status. One student said to me that the faculty and the students would get along if we conceded that neither side knew anything. I was willing to concede half his proposition. When they moved out to the wider society, those students did not know a great deal more than when they entered the universities, but they had many more targets for their egalitarianism. They carried with them the belief that hierarchies are presumptively illegitimate, and very nearly conclusively so. From there it is a short step to the rejection of the achievement principle since differing achievements create hierarchies.

Karl Mannheim, a German sociologist, saw this coming at least as early as 1940. He proposed that three principles for the selection of elites—blood, property, and achievement—have marked different historical periods.[20] Aristocratic society chose elites primarily on the blood principle; bourgeois society on the property principle; modern democracy has stressed the achievement principle. These were never entirely pure principles; achievement, for instance, could lift one into the elite even when one of the other two principles was dominant. Of more interest to our current situation is that Mannheim also wrote: "The real threat of contemporary mass society [is] . . . that it has recently shown a tendency to renounce the principle of achievement as a factor in the struggle of certain groups for power, and has suddenly established blood and other criteria as the major factors to the far-reaching exclusion of the achievement principle."[21] If we recognize reward according to race, ethnicity, and sex as aspects or analogues of the blood principle, it is obvious how far the achievement principle has been discarded in America today in the name of equality.

The rise in hostility to inequalities of status or condition seems a very peculiar phenomenon. It is easy enough to understand dislike of inequalities in legal and political rights. Equality in those respects is a guard against tyranny and irrationality, which is a form of tyranny. A statute or judicial decision providing that left-handed drunk drivers must be imprisoned but right-handed ones will merely be fined would violate equality because the distinction bears no conceivable relationship to the purpose of the law. When the distinction is rational—for example, between drunk and sober drivers, the inequality of legal consequences is considered just. A perception of this sort was the original basis for the civil rights laws. Once it was agreed that the sex or race of a job applicant had no rational relationship to job performance, non-discrimination was thought a proper goal for the law to pursue. It is true that the discrimination was not the command of government but the choice of individuals and private organizations. But it was believed to be so widespread as to have almost the force of law.

What is harder to understand is the radical egalitarian notion that equality must be imposed even when very rational distinctions militate against it. That notion caused the prompt skewing of the non-discrimination laws by the bureaucrats and courts into whose care the implementation of the policy was given. Non-discrimination became discrimination, but against different people: white males. The new discrimination did not violate the tenets of radical egalitarianism, because modern liberals, who control these policies, do not think in terms of individuals but in terms of groups. Thus, proportional representation of groups in the work-place, on faculties, and in student bodies looks like non-discrimination to them. That is the rationale for affirmative action.

The passion for equality is especially virulent among intellectuals, or at least academics, two groups that are by no means identical. Though the theme of equality runs everywhere in the writings and teachings of professors of law, sociology, political science, history, the humanities, etc., the most celebrated and influential work is that of John Rawls.[22] For many years, Rawls has worked assiduously and with high intelligence to develop the principles of a just social order. Yet because he was determined to establish equality as one fundamental requirement, the results are most unhappy. One of the principles he develops is that, to be just, social and economic inequalities must "be to the greatest benefit of the least advantaged members of society."[23] He does not consider the enormous bureaucratic despotism that would be required to enforce that principle (or, rather, to attempt its enforcement, since the requirement is clearly unadministrable).

Rawls and his admirers would probably not think that a valid objection since the object of his enterprise can be seen as devising criteria by which existing societies can be compared and judged. It is necessary, therefore, to address the principle on those terms, and on those terms it clearly fails. What reason is there to think that justice requires such a principle? There is none. A social or economic inequality will almost certainly have no effect on the "least advantaged." The millionaire's wealth does not cause the pauper's poverty. The millionaire's investments may make it possible for the pauper to find a job, though he will be less benefitted by those investments than is the millionaire, so that Rawls' requirement is not met. The intellectual's or the socialite's social status does not cause the social status that anyone else possesses. Why in either case is it just to condemn the inequality? Rawls' condition could only be met by bringing everyone down to the economic and social condition of the least advantaged. It is difficult to imagine any reason for that other than envy or the flaunting of moral superiority. The envy and display of moral superiority, however, is not that of the pauper or the sewer worker; it is that of the modern liberal.[†]

The condition Rawls demands is pernicious because it condemns all actual societies, including that of the United States, by setting a requirement that can never be satisfied. This legitimates, from a left-liberal perspective, a ground for perpetual attacks upon and hostility towards the hierarchies and lines of authority of this society as it is, or even as it could possibly become. Whatever Rawls' own intentions may be, such demands for extreme equality are typically weapons in the hands of the liberal-left, which is why Rawls' work is acclaimed in academia.

Rawls has the burden of proof backward. A free society produces inequalities of all sorts. No vital society can exist without

---

[†]Richard Grenier records a conversation with the late novelist Mary McCarthy. "'Wouldn't it be wonderful if everyone in the world were absolutely equal,' she said. 'What do you mean "equal,"' I said, always picky. 'I mean *equal*,' she replied with some impatience. 'Everyone living in exactly the same material circumstances.'" Grenier knew that McCarthy was a Vassar graduate and had been living in Paris rather luxuriously. "'Well, you'd have to give up a lot, Mary,' I said, thinking of the descent from quails' eggs served on silver platters to the life of a Chinese peasant. 'But it would be worth it for the intellectual excitement!' Miss McCarthy exclaimed enthusiastically." She could, Grenier says, "babble this nonsense of hers all day and all night without changing her life by an iota—while gaining in her own eyes, it was evident, a distinct moral superiority to those selfishly unwilling to live like Chinese peasants."[24]

inequalities. Yet when a demand is made for greater equality than freedom produces, the defender of rewards according to achievement is thrown on the defensive and expected to justify the inequality. It would be more sensible to demand that the proponent of greater equality show that that would produce a greater general benefit than does freedom to achieve.

It is obvious that a society attempting to implement Rawls' principles would have to submit to despotism. Radical egalitarianism cannot be implemented by individuals, families, or any group other than government. As government taxes more and subsidizes more, a greater portion of society's wealth passes through its hands. Individuals and families have less income to dispose of as they see fit, which is why Jouvenel said that "redistribution is in effect far less a redistribution of free income from the richer to the poorer, as we imagined, than a redistribution of power from the individual to the State."[25] The same thing is true of redistributions of jobs, educational opportunities, access to credit, etc., through government action. All of this requires centralization, larger government, and a vastly increased apparatus of bureaucratic coercion.

Wood and Manchester are right. Equality is "the single most powerful and radical ideological force in all of American history" and egalitarianism became our "triumphant passion" in this century. This is having, and will continue to have, very unpleasant consequences. As the late political scientist Aaron Wildavsky wrote: "[R]ising egalitarianism will lower our standard of living, decrease our health, debase public discourse, lower the quality of public officials, weaken democracy, make people more suspicious of one another, and (if it be possible) worse. Worse is the constant denigration of American life—our polity, economy, and society— with no viable alternative to take its place."[26] We will see the truth of those propositions throughout this book.

Once more, none of this is new. Tocqueville sounded the warning well over a century ago: the principle of equality prepares men for government that "covers the surface of society with a network of small complicated rules, minute and uniform, through which the most original minds and the most energetic characters cannot penetrate, to rise above the crowd. The will of man is not shattered, but softened, bent, and guided. . . . Such a power . . . stupefies a people, till each nation is reduced to nothing better than a flock of timid and industrious animals, of which the government is the shepherd."[27] This "servitude of the regular, quiet, and gentle kind"[28] he saw was not at all incompatible with the sovereignty of the people; it is just that the ability to elect representatives from time to time becomes less and less important. "The evils that extreme equality may produce are slowly disclosed; they creep gradually into the social frame; they are seen only at intervals; and at the moment at which they become most violent, habit already causes them to be no longer felt."[29]

Power in the "new despotism" will be gentle because government will try to protect its citizens from every occasion for suffering, physical or moral. Democratic man, thinking that others are like himself, identifies with anyone who suffers.[30] This compassion born of the passion for equality leads to the power of claiming victim status. We have become what Charles J. Sykes called a nation of victims.[31] The list of victim groups—minorities, women, homosexuals, the disabled, the obese, the young, the old—is virtually endless, including at one time everybody but ordinary white males. Now, however, there is even a men's movement claiming victim status. Putative victims stress their pain as a way of demanding special treatment from others, and they often get it. If there is power in claiming to feel pain as a victim, there is also power to be gained by the politician who assures us that "I feel your pain."

The last line of *Democracy in America* reads: "The nations of our time cannot prevent the conditions of men from becoming equal, but it depends upon themselves whether the principle of equality is to lead them to servitude or freedom, to knowledge or barbarism, to prosperity or wretchedness."[32]

5

"Intellectuals" and Modern Liberalism

In tracing the progression of liberty and equality to their present corrupt states of moral anarchy and despotic egalitarianism, the influence of the "intellectual" class must be noticed. Intellectual is in quotes to indicate that most of that class is not involved with serious mental work. Its members are generally critical of, if not actively hostile to, bourgeois society and culture. They are, moreover, susceptible to utopian fantasies. As Friedrich Hayek, a Nobel laureate in economics, observed: "The mood of [the West's] intellectual leaders has long been characterized by disillusionment with its principles, disparagement of its achievements, and exclusive concern with the creation of 'better worlds.'"[1]

The economist Joseph Schumpeter defined the class of intellectuals and saw qualities in them that may explain both their hostility and their fantasizing:

> Intellectuals are in fact people who wield the power of the spoken and the written word, and one of the touches that distinguish them from other people who do the same is the absence

of direct responsibility for practical affairs. This touch in general accounts for another—the absence of that first-hand knowledge of them which only actual experience can give.[2]

Schumpeter's acidic view of intellectuals is understandable enough: he was on the Harvard faculty. Intellectuals in Schumpeter's sense are often referred to as the "chattering class," people who spend their time, and usually make their livings, by producing or distributing, at wholesale or retail, ideas and symbols. They need not be, and often are not, very good at dealing with ideas. They may not even be very intelligent or sensible.

The intellectual class, then, is composed of people whose mindset is very like that of the student radicals of the Sixties: hostility to this culture and society coupled with millenarian dreams. Those students, like Schumpeter's intellectuals, had no direct responsibility for practical affairs, no first-hand knowledge of the world's workings, and hence were free to demand that reality be something other than what it was or could be. People so constituted are, in today's circumstances, necessarily of the Left.

Intellectuals may be intellectually negligible, but they are an important cultural force nonetheless. Because they wield the power of language and symbols, their values and ideas are broadcast by the press, movies, television, universities, primary and secondary schools, books and magazines, philanthropies, foundations, and many churches. Thus, intellectuals are influential out of all proportion to their numbers. Worse, it may well be that their leftist political and cultural attitudes are permanent, beyond the reach of rational argument.

That somber thought is suggested by Max Weber's analysis of the psychology of intellectuals, an analysis that fits well with what we observe in the intellectuals who drive modern liberalism:

The salvation sought by the intellectual is always based on inner need, and hence it is at once more remote from life, more theoretical and more systematic than salvation from external distress, the quest for which is characteristic of nonprivileged classes. The intellectual seeks in various ways . . . to endow his life with a pervasive meaning, and thus to find unity with himself, with his fellow men, and with the cosmos. . . . As a consequence, there is a growing demand that the world and the total pattern of life be subject to an order that is significant and meaningful.[3]

The inner need for pervasive meaning was satisfied through most of history in Western civilization by religion. But as religious faith began a retreat, beginning in the eighteenth century and proceeding apace in the nineteenth and twentieth, the intellectual's need for meaning did not decline but remained urgent. Now, however, meaning must be found in a secular belief system. It is difficult to think of anything that would fit this specification for most intellectuals other than politics. For a few, meaning might be found in devotion to a field like scientific inquiry, but for the vast majority of intellectuals, for whom no such levels of achievement are possible, politics must be the answer. To be a civil religion, however, this politics cannot be the politics of mundane clashes of material interests and compromises; it must be a politics of ideology.

In our time that means left-wing politics, which offers a comprehensive world view and a promise of ultimate salvation in a utopia that conventional politics cannot offer. The religious impulse underlying left radicalism has often been noted. Weber remarked that when certain types of German intellectualism turned against religion, there occurred "the rise of the economic, eschatological faith of socialism."[4] Not only communism but fascism and Naziism were faith systems of the Left, offering transcendental meaning to their adherents.

It requires extraordinary circumstances for fascism or communism to come to power openly as a mass movement, but, even in relatively stable societies, devotion by any significant number of people to radical politics can be enormously damaging. It is well to recall Peter Berger's comparison of the New Left of the Sixties with the European fascists. Modern liberalism, the descendant and spiritual heir of the New Left, is what fascism looks like when it has captured significant institutions, most notably the universities, but has no possibility of becoming a mass movement or of gaining power over government or the broader society through force or the threat of force. Power must then be sought in increments and by indirection. There are, of course, shades of modern liberalism, just as there were of fascism. The more extreme varieties are likely to be found these days on campuses or in public interest organizations, but there are many more people who vaguely share many of the assumptions of modern liberalism and thereby lend it a power the extremists could not muster on their own.

Weber even identified the groups who would be subject to the yearnings for transcendence that produce modern liberals. Richard Grenier, a commentator on culture, capsulates Weber's prediction:

> Among intellectuals of high social and economic standing most subject to longings for meaning, Max Weber listed, prophetically: university professors, clergymen, government officials, certain nobles, "coupon-clippers," and, at the time farther down on the social scale, journalists, school teachers, "wandering poets," and some self-taught proletarians. . . . Drawn up a full half-century before the shock waves of political radicalism that swept through many of these exact social classes in America in the 1960s and early 1970s, this is a remarkable list.[5]

By "coupon clippers" Weber undoubtedly meant those who live on inherited wealth, a fact that explains, for example, why the great foundations established by wealthy conservatives often turn left when the second or third generation takes over. "Wandering poets," the artistic class, could be translated today as Robert Redford, Jane Fonda, Gore Vidal, and those of similar ilk.

There was an eerie confirmation of Weber's thesis in Hillary Rodham Clinton's musings about a "politics of meaning." Neither she nor others who took up the phrase can begin to explain what that politics might be, but it is clearly the mood of politics as religion, the mood, therefore, of Sixties student radicalism. In 1969, Hillary Rodham gave the student commencement address at Wellesley in which, speaking for her class, she said that "for too long our leaders have used politics as the art of the possible. And the challenge now is to practice politics as the art of making what appears to be impossible, possible. . . . We're not interested in social reconstruction; it's human reconstruction." She said her class had "feelings that our prevailing, acquisitive, and competitive corporate life, including tragically the universities, is not the way of life for us. We're searching for more immediate, ecstatic and penetrating mode[s] of living." She spoke of dissent and protest as "unabashedly an attempt to forge an identity in this particular age."[6] The themes of the *Port Huron Statement* are there: a politics that accomplishes the impossible (i.e., creates utopia); the remaking of human nature; opposition to capitalism; flight from the mundane; and dissent as a means of finding an (authentic) identity.

A lot of people, and not just students, talked that way back then. It would be unjust to criticize a person today for speaking the nonsensical language of political religiosity that was typical of that generation. Twenty-four years later, however, speaking at the University of Texas, and now the wife of the President of the United States, Hillary Rodham Clinton said that "remolding society certainly in the West is one of the great challenges facing all of us." She mentioned alienation, despair, and hopelessness, and said we are "in a crisis of meaning." She called for "a new politics of meaning" that would answer questions such as "What do our governmental institutions mean? What do our lives in today's world mean? . . . What do all of our institutions mean? What does it mean to be educated? What does it mean to be a journalist? What does it mean in today's world to pursue not only vocations, to be part of institutions, but to be human?" She wanted "a society that fills us up again and makes us feel that we are part of something bigger than ourselves."[7] Nobody knew what that sort of blather meant in the Sixties and nobody knows now. We do know what it is about, however; it is about self and the attempt to give life meaning through the quest for a vaguely imagined utopia. The religious impulse is obvious, but it is only an impulse, a religious feeling without structure.

According to journalist Michael Kelly, Ms. Clinton agrees that she is searching for a "unified-field theory of life."[8] He notes that her Wellesley and Texas speeches "share all the same traits: vaulting ambition, didactic moralizing, intellectual incoherence and the adolescent assumption that the past does not exist and the present needs only your guiding hand to create the glorious future."[9]

There is in the politics of meaning, at least as expressed by the inventor of the phrase, Rabbi Michael Lerner, a tinge of totalitarianism. Lerner, editor of the liberal Jewish magazine *Tikkun*, as a student headed the Berkeley chapter of Students for a Democratic Society, roomed with Jerry Rubin, became part of a network of young activists that included Tom Hayden. Lerner now says things like: "For any of his [Clinton's] programs to work, he must explicitly and consciously confront the ethos of selfishness that has been dominating this country in the 1980s and generate in its place an ethos of caring, an ethos of social responsibility, an ethos of community, an ethos of connectedness to each other. That view of the world must replace the old ethos."[10] The "ethos" Lerner describes is consistent with his youthful radicalism's coercive phase. Lerner has suggested such things as having the Labor Department order "[e]very workplace" in America "to create a mission statement explaining its function and what conception of the common good it is serving and how it is doing so."[11] No doubt self-criticism sessions in every workplace will follow.

Ms. Clinton is by no means unique. She is discussed here because in 1969 she was representative of the Sixties generation just as today she is typical of the intellectuals of modern liberalism, and because she is a highly visible illustration of Weber's thesis.

If Ms. Clinton shares one other characteristic of modern liberalism—hostility to bourgeois culture and society—she has not said so recently, though it often seems implicit in her words. Modern liberalism forms what Lionel Trilling called an "adversary culture." The components of that culture, according to Stanley Rothman and his coauthors, are alienation from the American system and lack of concern about threats to the regime.[12] "Radical egalitarians are likely to take a more relaxed view of foreign adversaries and crime than are adherents to other political cultures. It is not that they necessarily regard the threats as less significant. Rather, given their hostility to the system, such threats do not concern them."[13] They may even welcome them.

What I have called radical individualism, Rothman calls "expressive individualism": "In the 1920s, expressive individualism became the ideology of the American intellectual, serving as a debunking tool for disassembling the status quo. . . . Part and parcel of the good life for the intellectual strata thus became the free expression of individual desires and pursuit of individual passions. The core of this concept is the priority given to free, unfettered expression of impulses, assumed to be good in and of themselves."[14] I suggest that the attitude described went back well before the Roaring Twenties, probably into the 1890s, and that its explosion in the Sixties was delayed only by two world wars, the Great Depression, and the smaller size of the academic community prior to the Second World War.

Rothman documents with answers to questionnaires, tests, and extensive interviewing the attitudes he reports, such as that "American intellectuals, however, are overwhelmingly adversarial towards the American system. The dominant institutions that transmit their values are predominantly liberal, and often also adversarial. In any case, conservatives in these occupations are vastly outnumbered."[15] Hatred of America and the West is seen most clearly in American universities, which, as sociologist Paul Hollander remarks, "have since the 1960s become the major resources or reservoirs of the adversary culture."[16] When Yale proposed a program for the study of Western civilization, a professor of English exploded: "Western Civilization? Why not a chair for colonialism, slavery, empire, and poverty?" while a history professor said: "The major export of Western Civilization is violence."[17] Their opposition prevailed. In order to defeat the remaining traditional values in today's culture, it is necessary to attack the roots of those values in the history of Western civilization.

The stories about hostility to America in the universities are legion, but universities are by no means unique. That same hostility is to be found wherever intellectual modern liberals go—into museums, art galleries, publishing houses, Hollywood, all of the places where ideas and symbols are manufactured and manipulated. Moreover, all intellectuals are aware of their affinity with all others. Frederick Lewis Allen, the popular historian of the 1920s, referred to "[A] newly class-conscious group. The intellectuals of the country. . . . Few in numbers though they were, they were highly vocal, and their influence not merely dominated American literature but filtered down to affect by slow degrees the thought of the entire country."[18]

This "filtering down" is not a mechanical process in which ideas of intellectuals just happen to come to the attention of the general public. It is instead a conscious effort on the part of intellectuals to alter Americans' perceptions of the world and of themselves, an effort, among other things, to weaken or destroy Americans' attachment to their country and to Western civilization. A major weapon employed in that attack on Western civilization is the fantasizing of past utopias destroyed by whites. Thus, the myth of the noble native Americans who lived peacefully and in harmony with nature but who were corrupted and destroyed by

Europeans is everywhere about us today. (Actually, there are no native Americans. The Indians are immigrants who simply arrived well before the Europeans did. A better name for them might be senior Americans.) This version of utopia may sometimes be merely sentimental nonsense; more often it is a weapon in the moral assault on this society and its institutions.

Not too long ago the Smithsonian Institution mounted an impressive display of paintings and sculptures depicting America's western expansion. The title gave a warning: "The West as America: Reinterpreting Images of the Frontier, 1820–1920." The texts that accompanied the art were an extended diatribe about the greed and evil of whites. For example, Frederic Remington's painting *The Fight for the Water Hole*, showing five cowboys defending a water hole against Indians, must be interpreted according to the world of those who purchased such paintings, "wealthy industrialists uneasy about social change in the urban East. The industrial era they had created required the importation of foreign labor, which frequently reacted to miserable living and working conditions by challenging the owners of industry. Substitute immigrants or laborers for Indians in *Fight for the Water Hole* and one has revealed a very different kind of frontier than the one these paintings have been thought to represent."

The bashing of whites, capitalism, and American history was so relentless that historian and former librarian of Congress Daniel J. Boorstin wrote in the guestbook, "A perverse, historically inaccurate, destructive exhibit. No credit to the Smithsonian."[19] There was so much adverse commentary that the museum arranged a panel discussion of the exhibit. The participants were almost all art historians from universities, which is a little like asking Damon for an evaluation of Pythias. Their view was that the commentary was justified. One of them said, "This was a war between two cultures and the inferior culture won."

Political correctness is rampant at the Smithsonian. It planned to mark the fiftieth anniversary of the atom bombing of Hiroshima that brought the Pacific war to an end by displaying the *Enola Gay*, the plane that dropped the bomb. But the commentary to accompany the exhibit said, "For most Americans . . . it was a war of vengeance. For most Japanese, it was a war to defend their unique culture against Western imperialism." No doubt that explained, to the satisfaction of the museum's staff of social historians, why Japan had been waging a bloody war of aggression against China for years before its surprise attack on the American naval base at Pearl Harbor on December 7, 1941. There was no mention of Japanese atrocities in China, the Philippines, and elsewhere. The commentary was scrapped when congressional hearings were planned, but the two episodes revealed the degree to which the corruption of the universities has moved into other institutions dominated by intellectuals.

The Persian Gulf War brought into view the anti-Americanism of church intellectuals. Many church leaders and their organizations opposed the use of American troops to force Iraq out of Kuwait and, not so incidentally, prevent Saddam Hussein from controlling a large fraction of the world's oil. Some of this might have been religious pacifism, but that fails to explain why so many religious leaders remained silent about Iraq's use of force to conquer another nation but condemned the U.S. use of force in response. Distrust of U.S. power and intentions are shown as well by the frequent call to put our armed forces under United Nations command rather than under American control. The preference for the United Nations over the U.S. is characteristic of modern liberals. That is probably today's manifestation of the Sixties belief in the moral superiority of the Third World.

Mainline churches often display double standards. Paul Hollander notes that the concern churches expressed for Third World nations and groups allegedly harmed or threatened by the United States is to be contrasted with "the relative indifference these activist and globally involved churches have shown toward Afghanistan and the suffering of its people [under Soviet attack], perhaps because those sufferings did not offer possibilities for holding the United States, the West, capitalism, or the multinational corporations responsible."[20]

It may be objected that many or even most persons on university faculties or other intellectual class institutions do not hold the views or display the fanaticisms described. But for liberalism to do its work and win its victories it is not necessary that they should. Institutions are regularly politicized by minorities within them. "Morson's Law," framed by Slavic scholar Gary Saul Morson, puts the tipping point at no more than 20 percent.[21] Activists are willing to spend much more time and energy politicizing than others are willing to spend resisting, and much of the faculty will "fall in line with the activists out of sheer conformist fear of being deemed retrograde."

So uniform is the antagonism of the intellectual class to the United States and the West that it calls for explanation. Intellectuals, after all, have not always expressed hostility to the societies in which they lived. This fact is sometimes taken to mean that something in the nature of intellectuals has changed, that the sheer perversity of modern intellectuals is to be contrasted with the healthy integration of past intellectuals into their societies. That may not be the correct interpretation. It may be in the nature of intellectuals to oppose, but prior to the closing decades of the eighteenth century, open opposition was often not safe and certainly not prudent. Schumpeter makes the point that prior to the Enlightenment intellectuals were few in number and dependent upon the support of the Church or some great patron: "the typical intellectual did not relish the idea of the stake which still awaited the heretic." They preferred honors and comfort which could be had only from "princes, temporal or spiritual."[22] What freed them was the invention of the printing press and the rise of the bourgeoisie, which enabled intellectuals to find support from a new patron, the mass audience. Schumpeter places the decline of the importance of the individual patron in the last quarter of the eighteenth century.[23] James Gardner, art editor for the *National Review,* says that artists began to direct their anger at the bourgeois state three generations after the French Revolution.[24] The modern universities, foundations, museums, etc. have provided patrons for tens of thousands of disaffected intellectuals. Perhaps, then, intellectuals were always potentially hostile to the social order in which they lived but were held in check by self-interest until the public relieved them of their dependence on private patrons and the bourgeois state lost the will to suppress.

It is notable that today intellectual and moral attack on the bourgeois state and culture comes almost entirely from the left. Sociologist Seymour Martin Lipset states that over time the political and cultural stances of intellectuals have shifted. Much of intellectual criticism in the last decades of the nineteenth century was aimed at crude materialism and the vulgar taste of a democratic society. "Increasingly, however, during the twentieth century, the critical stance of the intellectuals, including first the social scientists and later the humanists within the university, took the form of a predominant sympathy for antiestablishment, liberal–left positions. . . . They have lent disproportionate support to atheistic, antiwar, civil rights, civil liberties for deviants, liberal Democratic, and third party causes."[25]

There are several more or less plausible explanations for that shift. One is, of course, that the steady progress of the egalitarian passion eroded what was essentially an aristocratic disdain for this society so that it became more comfortable to attack the bourgeoisie from the left. Equality is always the cry of the Left. It must also have become increasingly obvious that an aristocratic pose would cost intellectuals any possibility of widespread influence or popularity and, undoubtedly, would diminish material rewards. An assault from an egalitarian position would be far more acceptable.

Schoeck thinks the intellectual's leftism is often due to envy avoidance. Not only do people feel envy, they fear being envied. The more distinguished a man is, the more reason he has to fear envy, which may account for the number of intellectuals and artists who have been not only leftist but have dallied with communism. The substitute for religion is apparent.

> As in a Christian world where all shared the same belief, anyone, regardless of his worldly status or position, could regard himself as connected with his neighbor and reconciled with him through the transcendent God, and, furthermore he might not even envy him because to do so would reflect on God's wisdom; so the agnostic twentieth-century intellectual seeks a new god, promising the same protection as the Christian God's against the next man's envy (often only suspected) and the same freedom from the consuming sense of guilt engendered by his personal superiority. This substitute god is progressivist ideology or, more precisely, the utopia of a perfectly egalitarian society. It may never come true, but a mere mental pose of being in its favour helps to bear the guilt of being unequal.[26]

Intellectuals will not like that explanation of their liberalism, just as they will not like any of the others offered here. That may be the reason, Schoeck suggests, that envy is so little mentioned in the social science of this century, particularly in the United States. He thinks that blind spot is not accidental, and he notes the common resentment of this society by social scientists.

> The common denominator for this discontent, this unrest, is the egalitarian impulse; most of the problems experienced or imagined by such minds would theoretically be solved in a society of absolute equals. Hence the constant and strangely tenacious preoccupation of Anglo-Saxon social science with models and programmes for a society of absolute equals. The utopian desire for an egalitarian society cannot, however, have sprung from any other motive than that of an inability to come to terms with one's own envy, and/or with the supposed envy of one's less well-off fellow men.[27]

There are other possibilities, of course. Perhaps the movement to the left was due to a combination of the intellectuals' hostility to bourgeois society and their well-known tendency to admire power and even brutality. We tend to forget that there was burgeoning sympathy for fascism of both the Italian and German varieties among intellectuals until that became a dangerous sentiment to express during World War II. The most powerful influence on intellectuals came earlier and lasted longer. The Russian Revolution of 1917 exemplified brutal power attacking traditional and capitalistic societies from the left. Communism being the only effective enemy of bourgeois society, and being utopian and egalitarian into the bargain, intellectuals moved left. That many of them became not merely sympathizers or fellow travelers but Party members, a few even spies for the Soviet Union, testifies to the enormous pull of the rhetoric and ideals of the left upon intellectuals. That phase is over but we still face the active hostility of much of the intellectual class to traditional culture. The results of that hostility are partially spelled out in the remainder of this book.

Writers on the baleful influence of certain ideas commonly exonerate those who advance the ideas from blame for the results. Thus, James Q. Wilson, writing of the public philosophy that flows from the Enlightenment, says that "Most of us will continue to enjoy [its] benefits for centuries to come. But some will know only the costs, costs imposed on them by well-meaning people who want only to do the right thing."[28] Myron Magnet, of *Fortune Magazine* and the Manhattan Institute, similarly absolves many people of anything worse than misguided efforts to help.[29] Surely a number of such people want to do the right thing, are well-intentioned, but just as surely some do not act from creditable intentions. Some of our elites—professors, journalists, makers of motion pictures and television entertainment, et al.—delight in nihilism and destruction as much as do the random killers in our cities. Their weapons are just different. But who, familiar with the academic world, to take a single instance, has not seen destructive ideas spread by men and women, not because they mean well but because they want notoriety, influence, power, or just because they enjoy laying waste the structures built by others? There is no particular reason to think that people with Ph.D.s are more well-intentioned than people who dropped out of high school.

It will be extremely difficult to defend traditional values against intellectual class onslaught. Not only do the intellectuals occupy the commanding heights of the culture and the means by which values and ideas are created and transmitted, they control the most authoritarian institution of American government, the federal and state judiciaries, headed by the Supreme Court of the United States. The courts have increasingly usurped the power to make our cultural decisions for us, and it is not apparent that we have any means of redress. We turn to that next.

6

The Supreme Court as an Agent of Modern Liberalism

It is arguable that the American judiciary—the Supreme Court, abetted by the lower federal courts and many state courts—is the single most powerful force shaping our culture. There are other claimants to the title, to be sure, but the judges' preeminence seems clear. I will focus here primarily on the Supreme Court. The Court today is, as it always has been, a legal institution, but it also undertakes to decide hot button questions of culture and politics that are, strictly speaking, none of its business.

In its cultural-political role, the Court almost invariably advances the agenda of modern liberalism. That is to say, the Justices, or a majority of them, are responsible in no small measure for the spread of both radical individualism and radical egalitarianism. The Court chose this path before the spirit of the Sixties became evident, which is another sign that the Sixties radicals did not originate but accentuated trends that were already active.

"Over and over again," observes Robert Nisbet, "constitutional history in America is one of conflict between those insisting upon maximization of *individual* rights and those insisting upon the autonomies of the *corporate* rights of states and local communities."[1] The Court in modern times has regularly maximized individual rights against the corporate rights of all intermediate institutions. In the adversarial relationship between the individual and society posited by Mill's "one very simple principle," the Court in matters of morality and social discipline has sided with Mill far more often than the actual Constitution warrants. But when government imposes egalitarianism, the Court has ratified that choice. When liberty and equality come into conflict, the Court almost always prefers equality, even in its modern, corrupt, egalitarian form.

This is a philosophy, or mood, that cannot be derived from the Constitution. It is approved, however, by a group we have just discussed, the intellectual class. That class has distinctive attitudes, well to the left of the American center, and their command of the avenues for the dissemination of facts (whether true or false) and attitudes, their capacity to make and unmake reputations, makes them a powerful cultural force, a force to which some judges respond and others cater. It will not have escaped the reader's notice that judges belong to that class and so absorb its viewpoints and predilections naturally.

It is instructive that in the United Kingdom, the primary proponents of adopting a written constitution and the power of judicial review of legislation are the Labor Party and intellectuals. The reasons are obvious. That development would shift a great deal of power from the British electorate to judges who would better reflect the leftish agendas of Labor and intellectuals. Cultural and political victories would then be achieved in the courts that could not be achieved in Parliament. The British proponents of judicial supremacy have learned from the American experience.

The pure version of intellectual class leftishness, to the point of being a parody of modern liberalism, exists in institutionalized form in the American Civil Liberties Union, which has had, through litigation and lobbying, a very considerable effect upon American law and culture. William A. Donohue, a long-time student of the organization, says that the ACLU "fixes its eyes exclusively on individual rights and is deterred from its atomistic vision only when the competing issue of group equality emerges."[2] Thus, the ACLU argues on the one hand for rights to abortion, to practice prostitution, to homosexual marriage, to produce and consume pornography, and much more. Its individualism is so radical that it contends nude dancing is constitutionally protected free speech and it opposes metal detectors in airports as an intrusion upon individual autonomy. But when equality comes into play, the ACLU is for affirmative action and generally for more government limitations on the freedoms of business owners and managers, such as the power to discharge an employee for unsatisfactory performance. The ACLU is the premier litigating and lobbying arm of modern liberalism, and it has been extremely successful. Our primary concern here, however, is with the judiciary rather than the ACLU's influence upon the course of adjudication.

First of all, there is the Supreme Court's constitutionalizing of radical individualism. In this area, we have arrived where Mill pointed, at an increasing disjunction between the individual and the society. The result is the "adversary culture." Though it is neither logical nor legitimate as a matter of constitutional interpretation, there is a psychological basis in our Constitution for judicial radical individualism. One of the prices we pay for our Bill of Rights is an emphasis on personal freedom that is not balanced in the document by a Bill of Personal Responsibilities or a recognition, as in the constitutions of other countries, of limits set by community welfare. It is perhaps understandable, though certainly not excusable, that judges began to inflate enumerated rights and to create new rights, which they enforce against democratic decisions. Given the way the Court's decisions are reported—as victories for attitudes or moral positions rather than as legal determinations—those decisions resonate throughout our culture with powerful effects on public attitudes.

The unqualified language of the Bill of Rights and the Declaration of Independence, reflected in the continual expansion of individual rights by the judiciary, feed our national obsession about "rights." That obsession, as Harvard law professor Mary Ann Glendon has pointed out,[3] impoverishes cultural, political, and judicial discourse. There is no more sterile form of "argument" than the bald assertion of rights. But bald assertion, unaccompanied by analysis or reasons, is the common form of discourse in these matters.

The jurisprudence of the First Amendment is a case in point. That amendment is a central concern of modern liberal intellectuals, dealing as it does with speech and religion. The difference in the Court's treatment of those two subjects flows naturally from radical individualism. Modern liberals value speech, which they have now expanded to include non-verbal expression, while their attitude toward religion ranges from indifference to hostility. It is not surprising, then, that the Court's decisions expand the area of protected non-religious expression beyond reason in the interest of the utmost individual freedom. Simultaneously, and largely in the interest of individual autonomy, the Court has drastically limited the public expression of religion beyond anything the ratifiers intended.[4]

The freedom of speech guaranteed by the amendment was long thought by the Court to be speech about ideas, but that is not the Court's view today. Today, the Court reads the speech clause as a protection of self-expression, personal autonomy, or individual gratification. Perhaps the best known instance is *Cohen v. California*,[5] which conferred First Amendment protection on a young man who refused to remove a jacket with the words "F . . . the Draft" (without the ellipsis) that he wore in a courthouse corridor. Saying that the state could not convict Cohen of disorderly conduct, the Court majority observed: "[T]he principle contended for by the State seems inherently boundless. How is one to distinguish this from any other offensive word?"[6] The Court went on to offer as the decisive consideration: "[O]ne man's vulgarity is another's lyric."[7] Moral relativism, which the Court endorsed, is necessary to radical individualism. But it must, of course, be confined to areas such as speech and sexuality. It would never do to reverse a conviction for assault on the ground that one man's battery is another's sparring practice.

The same impulse was on show in the flag-burning case, *Texas v. Johnson*.[8] Forty-eight states and the federal government had enacted laws prohibiting the physical desecration or defilement of the American flag. Johnson and his companions burned a flag while chanting "America, the red, white, and blue, we spit on you." Texas indicted and convicted him for burning the flag, not for his speech. But five Justices gave two reasons why Johnson's conviction could not stand. Neither reason bears examination.

The majority's first reason was that enforcement of the statute violated the "bedrock principle underlying the First Amendment," that being: "the government may not prohibit the expression of an idea simply because society finds the idea itself offensive or disagreeable."[9] That certainly is a bedrock principle, and it had absolutely no relevance to the case. Texas did not prosecute because Johnson's idea was offensive but because his mode of expression was. There were dozens or hundreds of ways for Johnson to express his offensive sentiments with the complete protection of the First Amendment. Nor is it unusual for the First Amendment to permit the banning of particular modes of expression. One supposes (though one is no longer quite sure) that government could still prohibit the telecasting of political views in obscenities or the expression of them by loudspeaker at three in the morning in a residential neighborhood. The Court got itself into this particular intellectual quagmire because its responsiveness to the claims of individualism led it to decide previously that an amendment protecting only the freedom of "speech" somehow protects conduct if it is "expressive."

That brings us to the second reason the Court majority offered:

> To conclude that the government may permit designated symbols to be used to communicate only a limited set of messages would be to enter territory having no discernible or defensible boundaries. Could the government, on this theory, prohibit the burning of state flags? Of copies of the Presidential seal? Of the Constitution? In evaluating these choices under the First Amendment, how would we decide which symbols were sufficiently special to warrant this unique status? To do so, we would be forced to consult our own political preferences, and impose them on the citizenry, in the very way that the First Amendment forbids us to do.[10]

There are so many answers to that it is hard to know where to begin. The most obvious has been mentioned: burning a flag is not speech and should not fall under First Amendment protection. Beyond that, the Court's claim that it cannot make distinctions without forcing its political views on us is specious. The customs and practices of Americans make the very distinction the Court says it cannot. Our national flag is entirely different from other symbols. Nobody pledges allegiance to the presidential seal or salutes when it appears. Marines did not fight their way up Mount

Suribachi to raise a copy of the Constitution on a length of pipe. Nor did forty-eight states and the United States enact laws to protect these symbols from desecration.

Symbols are necessary to community. As columnist Paul Greenberg put it: "[I]f a nation lives by its symbols, it also dies with them. . . . There are some so rooted in history and custom, and in the heroic imagination of a nation, that they transcend the merely symbolic; they become presences. . . . Today's strange arguments from our best-and-brightest against protecting the national emblem are not symptomatic of any kind of treason-of-the-intellectuals, but of a different malady: an isolating intellectualism cut off from a sense of reverence, and so from the historical memory and heroic imagination that determines the fate of any nation."[11] But the denigration of unifying symbols advances the cultural and social dissolution that radical individualism seeks. To realize how far the Court's "isolating intellectualism" has progressed in recent years, it is necessary only to recall, as the dissenting opinion in *Johnson* did, that Chief Justice Earl Warren and Justices Hugo Black and Abe Fortas, a trio unlikely to be enshrined in any conservative pantheon, had said that, of course, the Constitution did not bar the states and the federal government from prohibiting the desecration of the American flag.[12] The Justices in the *Johnson* majority were not unintelligent people. They could see the flaws in their argument as well as anyone. But it is no longer necessary to construct or be guided by a logical argument. What matters is that the result be consonant with the modern liberal mood. One can only hope that some day the Court will have occasion to review a conviction of a man who protested the sodomy laws of his state by engaging in indecent exposure. Would the Court hold that the state could not punish him because he was expressing an offensive or disagreeable idea? Would the Justices decide that they could not distinguish between different parts of the anatomy used as symbols without imposing their psycho-social views on the citizenry? I am not sure of the answer, but the oral argument should be high comedy.

The same judicial mood is on show in the rules devised by the Court for speech advocating violence and law violation. The Court has wobbled about on these questions for some time. In a case involving advocacy of violent revolution to impose a proletarian dictatorship, Justice Holmes, joined by Justice Brandeis, contended that "the only meaning of free speech" is that such ideas should be given their chance to have their way. Constitutional scholar Walter Berns summed up that position: "The only meaning of free speech turns out to mean that it is worse to suppress the advocacy of Stalinism or Hitlerism than to be ruled by Stalin or Hitler. The reasons for this are not, one might say, readily apparent."[13] At least in 1925 Holmes and Brandeis were in dissent. But by 1969 a unanimous Court could dash off a short, unsigned opinion in *Brandenburg* v. *Ohio*: "[T]he constitutional guarantees of free speech and free press did not permit a state to forbid or proscribe advocacy of the use of force or of law violation except where such advocacy was directed to inciting or producing imminent lawless action and was likely to incite or produce such action."[14]

There is no reason whatever to throw constitutional protection around such speech except to protect the enjoyment of the individuals speaking or hearing the words. In a republic, where the polls are open and elected representatives make the law, there can be no value in speech advocating the closing of the polls or nullifying the effect of laws democratically made. There is, moreover, no idea that cannot be expressed without advocating violence or law violation—except the idea that the audience should engage in violence or law violation. That idea can hardly be said to have any social benefit in a democracy dedicated to operating under the rule of law.

The Court's treatment of religion is of a piece. Under the First Amendment's prohibition of the establishment of religion, the Court has steadily made religion a matter for the private individual by driving it out of the public arena. *Lee* v. *Weisman*[15] held, for example, that a short, bland, non-sectarian prayer at a public-school commencement amounted to a forbidden establishment of religion. Government coercion of Deborah Weisman was seen by the Court in the possibility that she might feel "peer pressure" to stand or, if not that, to maintain respectful silence during the prayer. While the Court's insistence on driving religion and religious symbolism from the public arena has often been justified because of the alleged dangers of allowing religion and government to come close together, a closeness that is not within light years of establishing a theocracy, the Court frequently emphasizes the harm to an individual's sensibilities of seeing religious expression with which he disagrees.

Radical individualism is the only explanation for the Supreme Court's creation, out of thin air, of a general and undefined right of privacy. The Court used the invented right, allegedly to protect the sanctity of the marital bedroom, to strike down a dormant Connecticut statute prohibiting the use of contraceptives.[16] But marital privacy was shortly transformed into individual autonomy when the Court invalidated a Massachusetts law restricting access to contraceptives by single persons.[17] That in turn led to *Roe* v. *Wade*[18] and the right to abortion. Whatever one's feelings about abortion, the decision has no constitutional foundation, and the Court offered no constitutional reasoning.[19] *Roe* is nothing more than the decision of a Court majority to enlist on one side of the culture war.

The extra-constitutional individualism that undergirds the "constitutional" right to abortion was made clearest in the joint opinion of three Justices in *Planned Parenthood* v. *Casey*.[20] These Justices, whose votes created a majority to sustain most of *Roe*, invented a heretofore unheard-of constitutional right to "personal dignity and autonomy." They attempted to explain the appearance of this previously unsuspected right by saying: "At the heart of liberty is the right to define one's own concept of existence, of meaning, of the universe, and of the mystery of human life."[21] Beliefs about such matters were said to define "personhood," which is to be protected from state compulsion. It is not recorded that any American government, from the founding on, has ever thought it worthwhile to compel anyone's concept of meaning or of the mystery of human life. What this judicial grandiloquence means, aside from a right to have an abortion, nobody knows. But then hymns to radical individualism are necessarily murky and obscure. This particular one is known in the trade as "the mystery passage."

The language of the four dissenters in *Bowers* v. *Hardwick*—the case deciding, five to four, that homosexual sodomy is not a constitutional right—is clearer but even more dismaying. (After he retired, Justice Lewis Powell stated that he regretted not voting with the four, thus making a majority for their position.) The dissent would have found a constitutional right to engage in homosexual sodomy by invoking the right of privacy once more: "[The Court] has recognized a privacy interest with reference to certain decisions that are properly for the individual to make."[22] The word "properly" signifies that not all decisions are for the individual to make, just those the Court, as opposed to the legislature, approves of. The majority, which ruled against Hardwick, tried to limit the reach of the right of privacy by saying that the cases decided under that heading had related to the protection of the family. The dissenters made an astonishing response: "We protect those rights not because they contribute, in some direct and material way, to the general public welfare, but because they form so central a part of an individual's life."[23] So much for the family as the basic unit of society. The family's value is measured by its contribution to individual gratification. That is a major theme of modern liberalism, particularly of its feminist component, which views the family as oppressive to individuals.

Apparently not satisfied, the four dissenters immediately made things worse: "'[T]he concept of privacy embodies the "moral fact" that a person belongs to himself and not others nor to society as a whole.'"[24] There are "moral facts," but that is certainly not one of them. It would mean that no one has any obligations as a family member or as a citizen, no obligations to anyone or anything outside his own skin. Radical individualism can't be taken any further. The Justices did not really mean what they said, of course, for their proposition would make society impossible. But the fact that they could say such a thing, however thoughtlessly, shows how strongly they lean toward radical individualism.

It would unduly prolong this chapter to rehearse in detail what the Court has done in criminal law and in education. The rights of criminals have been steadily expanded and those of the community contracted. The exclusionary rule bars probative evidence that the police are judged, often on the sheerest technicality, to have obtained improperly. Every television viewer is familiar with the *Miranda* warnings ("You have the right to remain silent," etc.) that the Court imposed, which have made law enforcement more difficult.

The same thing is true of public schools, where the power to discipline has been severely circumscribed and the power to expel virtually amputated. No more the paddle for students who disrupt study hall; no more the expulsion or segregation of students who make learning next to impossible for others. It is not a matter for wonder that the home schooling movement and private schools are growing. In their solicitude for aberrant individuals, courts have seriously infringed what once were the rights of other individuals by weakening the powers of the institutions that protected those rights.

Judicial radical individualism weakens or destroys the authority of what sociologists call "intermediate institutions"—families, schools, business organizations, private associations, mayors, city councils, governors, state legislatures—that stand between the individual and the national government and its bureaucracies. All of this has happened within the lifetimes of many Americans. We are worse off because of it, and none of it was commanded or contemplated by the Constitution.

The Court's commitment to radical egalitarianism has been equally strong. Equality, the dominant theme of the Warren Court, made a sensational appearance soon after Earl Warren became Chief Justice in 1953. In 1954, *Brown* v. *Board of Education*[25] held that racial segregation in public schools violated the equal protection clause of the Fourteenth Amendment. I have argued elsewhere that, though the decision was correct and could have been supported by an analysis that took into account the original understanding of the amendment's meaning by those who wrote and ratified it, the Court's weak and disingenuous opinion, by the Chief Justice, indicates that the Justices believed they were departing from the Constitution in order to promote a desirable equality.[26] The unfortunate result was that the Justices were encouraged to more adventures in egalitarianism that, unlike *Brown*, really did depart from the Constitution.

In *Harper* v. *Virginia State Board of Elections*,[27] for example, the Court struck down an annual poll tax of $1.50 under the equal protection clause of the Fourteenth Amendment, thus overruling its own decisions that such taxes were entirely constitutional if not used for purposes of racial discrimination. The reason offered was that "notions" of equality "*do* change." The notions that changed were the Justices', not the legislators', and they certainly had changed as modern liberalism took hold in the judiciary.

The Warren Court's obsession with equality was such that in

Reynolds v. *Sims*[28] it ordered state legislatures restructured to produce absolute equality of voters. Most states, like the federal government, elected senators from geographic districts, which meant that the senators often represented constituencies of very different sizes, as is also true of United States senators. The theory was that different geographic areas often have different interests so that it was appropriate to give some of those interests a voice larger than their population alone would suggest. That was a structural arrangement designed—like federalism, the separation of powers, and the Bill of Rights—to moderate pure majoritarianism. The other house of a state legislature was typically based on population so that representatives' constituencies were approximately equal. Seizing upon the equal protection clause, the Court adopted a formula of one person, one vote, which meant that both houses of state legislatures had to be based on population. There is a good deal wrong with this as political theory; everything was wrong with it as constitutional law. There is no reason in political theory why regional minorities may not be protected, as they are in the federal Constitution by giving two senators to each state. State after state had gained admission to the union with senates based on the federal model, and nobody had suggested that the arrangement violated the Constitution. The representation formula the Court required in order to produce equality had not been the American practice from colonial days to the day of the *Reynolds* decision. The Court ordered that state legislatures be transformed on the basis of an abstract, and simplistic, theory of equality.

It was in the areas of race and sex, however, that radical egalitarianism proved most potent. So strong was the impulse that, in a masterpiece of statutory deconstruction, the Court overrode the explicit text and legislative history of the 1964 Civil Rights Act (that it is unlawful for an employer "to discriminate against any individual . . . because of such individual's race, color, religion, sex, or national origin") in order to allow preferences in hiring and promotion for blacks[29] and women.[30] The Court usually argued that the preferences were remedies for past discrimination. This makes no sense, since the person now being preferred is not the person discriminated against in the past. Even the requirement of past discrimination was dropped when, in *Metro Broadcasting, Inc.* v. *FCC*,[31] the Court allowed racial preference in the grant of station licenses by the Federal Communications Commission despite the lack of any evidence that such grants had ever been tainted by discrimination. These cases all approved what is today known as "affirmative action."

The list of egalitarian decisions not warranted by law could be extended almost indefinitely as the Court, entranced with equality, extended the reach of the equal protection clause of the Fourteenth Amendment far beyond any conceivable intention of those who made the amendment law and far beyond anything previous Courts had been willing to do.

Almost as instructive about the nature of modern liberalism is the Court's recent, partial, and very tentative retreat from its approval of governmental attempts to require equality of condition according to race, ethnicity, and sex. One such program required federal agency contracts to give a prime contractor monetary rewards for hiring subcontractors certified as small businesses controlled by socially and economically disadvantaged individuals. These included minorities or any individuals the Small Business Administration found to be disadvantaged.† A prime contractor on a highway project awarded a subcontract to a firm owned by an Hispanic despite the fact that a white-owned firm had submitted a bid at a lower price. (Though many Hispanics are white, the law in its impartiality treats them as though they were not.)

The Supreme Court, in a five-to-four decision, found that the preference constituted discrimination and violated the equal protection component of the due process clause of the Constitution.[32] The result was correct, and a welcome relief from the discrimination against white males practiced, egregiously, in the name of equality. It is too soon, however, to say that the Court has abandoned its extreme egalitarianism, under which racial, ethnic, and sexual groups must be proportionally represented in each field of endeavor. The vote was by the narrowest majority, and at least one member of that majority indicated the possibility of voting the other way in the future. Seven members of the Court, moreover, said that discrimination against white males was acceptable to

---

†So valuable had the status of being "disadvantaged" become that when the Hasidim were so certified, a Reagan administration official traveled to New York City and congratulated them on having "made it in America."

"remedy past discrimination." That is an unprincipled compromise: it is impossible to remedy past discrimination against Jones by preferring Smith today and discriminating against Brown in the process. The most likely result of this judicial desire not to appear insensitive is that the industry already devoted to proving past discrimination statistically will now experience new growth and prosperity.

The Court continues to use equal protection to take basic cultural decisions out of the hands of the people. Culture is made by the fiat of a majority of nine lawyers and forced upon the nation. No more egregious example can be found than the decision in *United States v. Virginia*[33] that the Virginia Military Institute, the state's only single-sex school, must now admit women. VMI was, and now has been for 157 years, an all-male military college whose mission was to produce "citizen soldiers." The majority held that it was the denial of equal protection for Virginia to offer this education only to men. As George Will wrote, "The Supreme Court gave [women] the right to enroll in an educational institution which, the moment they enter it, will essentially cease to exist."[34] Women will have gained little as a proud tradition and a valuable asset are destroyed by the sterile abstractions of a uni-sex Court.

Justice Scalia was the sole dissenter (Justice Thomas took himself out of the case because his son attended another all-male military college, The Citadel, which is now also destroyed). Of the majority opinion's denigration of prior generations of Americans for having insufficiently enlightened views about the role of women, Scalia observed: "The virtue of the democratic system with a First Amendment is that it readily enables the people, over time, to be persuaded that what they took for granted is not so, and to change their laws accordingly. That system is destroyed if the smug assurances of each age are removed from the democratic process and written into the Constitution. So to counterbalance the Court's criticism of our ancestors, let me say a word in their praise: they left us free to change. The same cannot be said of this most illiberal Court, which has embarked on a course of inscribing one after another of the current preferences of the society (and in some cases only the counter-majoritarian preferences of the society's law-trained elite) into our basic law."[35]

The judicial adoption of the tenets of modern liberalism has produced a crisis of legitimacy. Contrary to the plan of the American government, the Supreme Court has usurped the powers of the people and their elected representatives. We are no longer free to make our own fundamental moral and cultural decisions because the Court oversees all such matters, when and as it chooses. The crisis of legitimacy occurs because the political nation has no way of responding. The Founders built into our government a system of checks and balances, carefully giving to the national legislature and the executive powers to check each other so as to avoid either executive or legislative tyranny. The Founders had no idea that a Court armed with a written Constitution and the power of judicial review could become not only the supreme legislature of the land but a legislature beyond the reach of the ballot box. Thinking of the Court as a minor institution, they provided no safeguards against its assumption of powers not legitimately its own and its consistent abuse of those powers. Congress and the President check and balance one another, but neither of them can stop the Court's adventures in making and enforcing left-wing policy.

The effects on law and democracy have been horrendous. It is impossible for a Court that views itself as a political and cultural institution as much as a legal institution to make reasoned decisions whose principles it will adhere to in the future. The Court will change the Constitution as politics and culture change. The reasons given in one opinion are often little indication of what will happen in the next case. Since a cultural Court acts without guidance from the historic Constitution, the Justices could produce a coherent jurisprudence of individual rights only if they could construct and agree upon a systematic moral philosophy. Moral philosophers have been unable to agree on such a philosophy; it is preposterous to suppose that a committee of lawyers could. One result is that the Court's opinions, when it is engaged in the enterprise of creating rights, defy logical parsing. The decisions are diktats embedded in lofty but irrelevant rhetoric.

Those diktats, moreover, are almost entirely governed by the agenda of liberalism at the moment. Within the last three or four decades that agenda has shifted considerably and the Court has followed suit. The Court headed by Earl Warren was left-wing in every area of the law. Not only were constitutional rulings uniformly left–liberal but so were decisions across the board. Antitrust defendants never won before the Warren Court, no matter what the facts, the law, or the rulings of the courts below. The government always prevailed over taxpayers, patents were routinely declared invalid, government regulations were upheld regardless of their rationality.

But liberalism has changed. With the exception of certain new fields that have become trendy, such as environmentalism, the Left is no longer terribly interested in economic matters. Today, therefore, the Supreme Court affords a fair hearing to the antitrust defendant, the taxpayer, and the patent holder. In such fields, the Justices comport themselves as good lawyers, paying attention to the law and the facts. But modern liberals have shifted their focus to the war in the culture, and the Court has shifted with them. Today the Court has lined up with the cultural elite and against the majority of the electorate. The same thing is true in many of the lower courts, federal and state.

Quite recently, two federal courts, a state court, and the Supreme Court demonstrated their powers, their contempt for the electorate, the direction in which they intend to drive the country, and why the abuse of judicial power has become intolerable.

The Ninth Circuit Court of Appeals found a right to assisted suicide in the federal Constitution. The fascination with death as a right began elsewhere in the culture but swiftly found allies in a modern liberal judiciary. The decision in *Compassion in Dying* v. *State of Washington*[36] is instructive not only about our intellectually corrupted judiciary but about what is happening to the broader culture. The state enacted a statute making it criminal knowingly to aid another person in attempting suicide. The statute was challenged in court as a violation of the liberty and of the equal protection of the laws guaranteed by the Fourteenth Amendment to the Constitution.

The district court ruled for the plaintiffs on both grounds. The Court of Appeals for the Ninth Circuit reversed, sensibly finding that the right to assisted suicide, whose presence in the Constitution had never been suspected in over two hundred years, did not exist. The Court of Appeals, however, decided to rehear the case *en banc*, eleven judges sitting to decide the law of the circuit. The majority opinion is a model of judicial lawlessness partially hidden by obfuscation. The court began by noting "the compelling similarities between right-to-die cases and abortion cases."[37] It need hardly have gone on, wasting dozens and dozens of pages. When a liberal says something is like abortion, we know that something, whatever it is, is protected by the Constitution. In fact, this opinion, in its intellectual dishonesty, its pretense that what it is saying relates to law, bears an uncanny resemblance to *Roe* v. *Wade*. Like *Roe*, it undertakes a survey of historical attitudes, in this case towards suicide. We learn about the Greeks, the Romans, the early Christians, English common law, the American states—none of it of the slightest relevance to the case. We are then informed about polling data and current social attitudes, again of no relevance to the meaning of the Constitution.

Eventually, we get to the interest in liberty under *Casey*. Here the Ninth Circuit repeats and relies upon the fatuities of the joint opinion there: "[T]he most intimate and personal choices a person may make in a lifetime, choices central to personal dignity and autonomy, are central to the liberty protected by the Fourteenth Amendment." If that seems fog-filled, vapid rhetoric intended to put the reader's mind to sleep, the court at once brought its notion of intellectual rigor to bear: "At the heart of liberty is the right to define one's own concept of existence, of meaning, of the universe, and of the mystery of human life." Oh, that explains it. One would think that grown men and women, purporting to practice an intellectual profession, would themselves choose to die with dignity, right in the courtroom, before writing sentences like those. They mean nothing and were intended to mean nothing. They were intended, through grandiose rhetoric, to appeal to a free-floating spirit of radical autonomy. Those words illustrate the anti-intellectualism that suffuses constitutional law as a consequence of modern liberalism. Being a mood rather than a philosophy, modern liberalism cannot be other than anti-intellectual.

In a subsequent case, the Second Circuit Court of Appeals found a right to die under the equal protection clause, reasoning that since terminally ill patients had a right to refuse treatment, which is effectively suicide, there is no sufficient state interest to prevent a terminally ill patient, who is not on treatment whose withdrawal would be fatal, from obtaining drugs to terminate life.[38]

Meanwhile, the Supreme Court of Hawaii ruled under the equal protection guarantee of the state constitution that Hawaii's statute restricting marriage to the union of a man and a woman "is presumed to be unconstitutional."[39] This presumption can be overcome, the court said, only if the state can show that the statute "is justified by compelling state interests." Statutes almost never survive that test, and it seems only a matter of time before the Hawaii court creates a right to same-sex marriage. Since a ruling of unconstitutionality would be based on state law, no federal court would have jurisdiction to review it.

Though a large majority of Hawaiians as well as citizens of other states oppose homosexual marriage, the likely outcome of the Hawaii case may very well become the law of every state in the union. Article IV, Section 1 of the United States Constitution states: "Full Faith and Credit shall be given in each State to the public Acts, Records, and judicial Proceedings of every other State; and the Congress may by general Laws prescribe the Manner in which such Acts, Records and Proceedings shall be proved, and the Effect thereof."

The first part of that sentence almost certainly means that, if the Hawaii court rules as expected, other states must accept marriages between homosexuals performed in Hawaii. The Supreme Court has previously held that a state must accept a divorce performed in another state although the law and the policy of the objecting state prohibited such divorces. Homosexuals presumably could marry in Hawaii and settle in Utah as spouses no matter what the citizens of either Hawaii or Utah thought about the matter. The only way of avoiding this outcome lies in the second part of the sentence which says that Congress may prescribe the effect of a state's acts, records, and proceedings. The Supreme Court might uphold congressional legislation stating that a Hawaiian same-sex marriage does not require other states to accord that marriage legitimacy in their territories. The Court's response is in some doubt because it has recently shown a tendency to view homosexuality as a matter of required moral indifference under the Constitution.

In *Romer* v. *Evans*[40] the United States Supreme Court struck down, six to three, the Colorado constitution's provision that homosexual, lesbian (which is homosexual), or bisexual status should not entitle any person to claim quota preferences, protected status, or discrimination. This meant only that, notwithstanding local ordinances prohibiting discrimination on the basis of sexual orientation, private persons and institutions remained free to find homosexuality morally objectionable. Thus, a woman with a room to rent could refuse to let it to a pair of homosexual men, or a church whose religion prohibited homosexual conduct could deny a practicing homosexual a position on its staff. No jurisdiction within Colorado could require that homosexuals be given the protection from private discrimination that racial minorities are afforded. The Supreme Court held, nevertheless, that the state's decision to withdraw this special protection, which it was not required to give in the first place, was motivated only by "animus" and so could not stand under the rationale of the equal protection clause. Homosexuals were, the Court said, uniquely disfavored because they could not win protected status through local elections unless they first won a statewide election to remove the constitutional provision in question.

That is a very odd rationale, or rather it is no rationale. Moral objection to homosexual practices is not the same thing as animus, unless all disapprovals based on morality are to be disallowed as mere animus. Modern liberalism tends to classify all moral distinctions it does not accept as hateful and invalid. Moral views about sexual practices are particularly suspect. As for the claim that homosexuals are uniquely burdened because they cannot pass the laws they want without changing the Colorado constitution, that burden is imposed on various groups by every constitutional guarantee of freedom. Those who want to prohibit speech advocating law violation or violence cannot attain their end without amending the First Amendment. The First Amendment also stands in the way of those who would like to vote for an established church in their home state. All constitutional prohibitions of certain types of laws are subject to the same attack the Supreme Court levelled at Colorado's provision. The majority did not even mention its prior decision that homosexual conduct is not a constitutional right, but it is well on the way to holding that it is. If homosexuality may not be discouraged by state constitutions, it is difficult to see how the provisions of various state constitutions banning polygamy can stand. They can't as a logical matter, but the Court (like modern liberal culture) is not as solicitous of polygamy as it is of homosexuality.

There is no logical or constitutional foundation for the majority's decision in *Romer* v. *Evans*. The decision is an unsupported victory for homosexual activists, with whom the Court evidently sympathizes. As Justice Scalia said in dissent, the Colorado constitutional provision was merely a "rather modest attempt by seemingly tolerant Coloradans to preserve traditional sexual mores against the efforts of a politically powerful minority to revise those mores through the use of the laws. . . . [The Court's decision] places the prestige of this institution behind the proposition that opposition to homosexuality is as reprehensible as racial or religious bias."[41] He concluded with the just observation that the Colorado provision "was an entirely reasonable provision which does not even disfavor homosexuals in any substantive sense, but merely denies them preferential treatment. [It] is designed to prevent piecemeal deterioration of the sexual morality favored by a majority of Coloradans, and is not only an appropriate means to that legitimate end, but a means that Americans have employed before. Striking it down is an act, not of judicial judgment, but of political will."[42] That is just what the dissent said of the majority's decision in *Roe* v. *Wade*, and the condemnation was correct in both cases, as it would be in dozens of other decisions in which the Court, without authority in the Constitution or any law, has forced Americans to adopt the Court's view of morality rather than their own.

As Lino Graglia, a professor of law at the University of Texas, put the matter, "the thing to know to fully understand contemporary constitutional law is that, almost without exception, the effect of rulings of unconstitutionality over the past four decades has been to enact the policy preferences of the cultural elite on the far left of the American political spectrum."[43] That is exactly right, and the question is what, if anything, can be done about it.

Graglia points out that changing the behavior of the Court through appointments is a failed tactic. Republican presidents have appointed Justice after Justice with the avowed intention of changing the Court's direction. That has not worked. Most of those appointed turn out not to be restrained or start that way but then, having no firm judicial philosophy, migrate to the left. Presidents

Reagan and Bush, who quite deliberately tried to bring the Court back to a judicial rather than a political role, had five appointments, three of whom voted to retain *Roe* v. *Wade*. Now that Bill Clinton has made two appointments, the Court is certain to be activist on the cultural left well into the next century.

Any more serious efforts to limit the powers of the courts will run into the familiar refrain that this would threaten our liberties. To the contrary, it is now clear that it is the courts that threaten our liberty—the liberty to govern ourselves—more profoundly than does any legislature. Any reform effort must contend with the sanctity the courts have attained, not least through their own rhetoric. A federal district judge suppressed evidence and allowed drug dealers to go free on the theory that flight was a rational response to the sight of the police since the residents in that neighborhood view the police as "corrupt, abusive and violent." The evidence of guilt that the judge suppressed was overwhelming. When political leaders denounced the ruling and the judge, four members of the court of appeals issued a statement saying that political attacks on the ruling "threaten to weaken the constitutional structure of this nation," and "These attacks do a grave disservice to the principle of an independent judiciary and, more significantly, mislead the public as to the role of judges in a constitutional democracy."[44] For sheer chutzpah that is hard to beat. It is the judiciary's assumption of power not rightfully its own that has weakened, indeed severely damaged, the constitutional structure of the nation. It has been the judiciary, and not its critics, that has misled the public as to the role of judges in a constitutional democracy. Harsh criticism by political leaders of outrageous judicial decisions is a legitimate and necessary response. That will not be enough, however, to restore the proper balance between the branches of government and between the states and the federal courts.

Conservatives often argue that the situation can be cured by Congress removing the jurisdiction of the federal courts in classes of cases where the courts have clearly exceeded their legitimate powers. There is no comfort to be found in that response, however. Article III, Section 1 of the Constitution leaves it to the discretion of Congress whether to create any courts below the Supreme Court. It is usually thought that congressional discretion to create or not create inferior courts means that Congress could deprive those courts of all jurisdiction or of jurisdiction over particular classes of cases. That would solve nothing, however, since such cases would continue to reach the Supreme Court on appeal from state courts. The argument then turns to the statement in Section 2 that, as to most types of cases, the Supreme Court "shall have appellate Jurisdiction . . . with such Exceptions, and under such Regulations as the Congress shall make." Surely, it is argued, this means that Congress can deprive the Court of jurisdiction over cases involving abortion or flag desecration or assisted suicide or whatever else Congress deems necessary to rein in a runaway judicial branch.

The matter is not that easy. The power to make "Exceptions" is probably a housekeeping power, a power to control the appellate jurisdiction in the interest of efficiency and convenience as circumstances change. It was certainly not a power to assert democratic supremacy over the judiciary. That can be seen from the results that would follow from making exceptions to the Supreme Court's jurisdiction. If Congress deprived the Court of jurisdiction over abortion cases, for example, those cases would simply be decided by state courts, and neither Congress nor the state legislatures could remove that jurisdiction. Article VI states: "This Constitution, and the Laws of the United States which shall be made in Pursuance thereof; and all Treaties made, or which shall be made, under the Authority of the United States, shall be the supreme Law of the Land; and the Judges in every State shall be bound thereby, any Thing in the Constitution or Laws of any State to the Contrary notwithstanding."

Two things follow. Article VI thus lodges jurisdiction to decide federal constitutional issues in state courts, and there is no power in any legislature to make exceptions. The framers almost certainly did not intend that the exceptions power be used to control the Supreme Court. If they had so intended, they would not have devised a scheme that, instead of restoring democratic authority, merely shifted final disposition of issues to another set of judges. It is not at all certain, therefore, that the Court would acquiesce in the removal of its jurisdiction. If it ruled the statute making an exception to its jurisdiction unconstitutional, that would be the end of the matter.

But even if the Court accepted the statute, the fact that the

Constitution places jurisdiction to decide constitutional questions in the state courts would frustrate the congressional purpose. The state courts, at least most of them, would certainly follow existing Supreme Court precedent. A few years back, when there was considerable talk of taking away Supreme Court jurisdiction, the conference of state Chief Justices unanimously adopted a resolution promising to adhere to the Supreme Court's past rulings. Any plan to curb the judiciary by first removing the jurisdiction of the lower federal courts and the Supreme Court and then bullying the state courts is too extravagant to be contemplated.

There appears to be only one means by which the federal courts, including the Supreme Court, can be brought back to constitutional legitimacy. That would be a constitutional amendment making any federal or state court decision subject to being overruled by a majority vote of each House of Congress. The mere suggestion of such a remedy is certain to bring down cries that this would endanger our freedoms. To the contrary, as already noted, it is the courts that are not merely endangering our freedoms but actually depriving us of them, particularly our most precious freedom, the freedom to govern ourselves democratically unless the Constitution actually says otherwise. The United Kingdom has devloped and retained freedom without judicial review.

Consider what the effects of such an amendment would be. This is a civilized nation; there is no reason to suppose that the citizens of some benighted town would suddenly become fascists and return to a regime of racial segregation. The Court would strike down any such laws and Congress would support the Court. What might be in danger would be the Court's cultural drive to the left. There is no reason to suppose that representatives and senators would be skilled interpreters of the Constitution, but then the Court isn't either—or rather chooses not to be. If constitutional jurisprudence remained a mess, at least it would be a mess arrived at democratically. There is no reason to regard this proposal as at odds with constitutionalism. When Congress proposed the original Constitution and the various amendments, it did so by laying them before the states for democratic decision. The Supreme Court changes the Constitution without any such ratifying process. The clearest equivalent would be laying judicial changes of the Constitution before Congress for ratification or rejection.

It will be said that this suggestion is "extremist." I think not. It is part of a long tradition of seeking ways to tame judicial power so that it achieves democratic legitimacy. Robert LaFollette, if I recall correctly, proposed amending the Constitution to allow the Senate by a two-thirds vote to override Supreme Court decisions. Learned Hand, considered to be America's premier appellate judge, was nearly apoplectic at the Supreme Court of his day. In 1914, Hand wrote to Felix Frankfurter denouncing "the fatuous floundering of the Supreme Court which goes by the name of Constitutional Law. Am I perverted that I alone of those who touch it have acquired such a contempt for the subject? I can scarcely think of a matter to which the human mind has been applied with less credit to itself than that." He referred to the Court and its constitutional rulings as "that solemn farce."[45]

The Court legislated, as it does today, through the due process clauses of the Fifth and Fourteenth Amendments. (The potential for judicial legislation through the equal protection clause had not yet been discovered.) Hand ultimately came to the conclusion that these clauses should be repealed, certainly an "extreme" position, then as now. Gerald Gunther, from whose biography of Hand I have been quoting, summarized Hand's view on judicial power in a democracy:

> At the root of the evil, Hand insisted, was "the fatuity of the system which grants such powers to men it insists shall be independent of popular control!" If the courts were to retain their legislative power under the guise of interpreting the due-process clauses, they must either "abdicate their exercise except on rare visitations," or "submit to a popular control which they rightly enough resent." Judicial self-restraint and popular control of the judiciary were the only two possibilities consistent with democracy: "One or the other is a condition of democracy; it is a condition of anything but ceremonial dancing before the ark of the covenant."[46]

Hand was speaking of a Court that was then activist in conservative causes. There is no reason to suppose that he would have been kinder to later Courts whose "fatuous floundering" was in the service of modern liberal causes. Perhaps the real lesson to be derived from both the conservative and modern liberal eras is that judges cannot be trusted with a written constitution and an unlimited and uncheckable power of judicial review. Most men and women, given final power, will prove unable to subordinate their personal sympathies and passions to the legitimate range of meanings that a dispassionate mind can find in the Constitution.

The Court is obviously not responsible for all that has gone wrong in our culture, but it is responsible in no small measure. Some of its results are described in the following chapters. Those results include the declining legitimacy of democratic institutions, the promotion of anarchy and license in the moral order, and advancing tyranny in the social order. The upshot is that the democratic nation is helpless before an antidemocratic, indeed a despotic, judiciary. The American people seem, at the moment, to be submissive and without the political will to reclaim the liberty that is rightfully theirs.

PART II

PART II

7

The Collapse of
Popular Culture

The distance and direction popular culture has travelled in less than one lifetime is shown by the contrast between best-selling records. A performer of the 1930s hit "The Way You Look Tonight" sang these words to romantic music:

Oh, but you're lovely, / With your smile so warm, / And your cheek so soft, / There is nothing for me but to love you, / Just the way you look tonight.

In our time, Snoop Doggy Dogg's song "Horny" proclaims to "music" without melody:

I called you up for some sexual healing. / I'm callin' again so let me come get it. / Bring the lotion so I can rub you. / Assume the position so I can f . . . you.

Then there is Nine Inch Nails' song, "Big Man with a Gun." Even the expurgated version published by the *Washington Post* gives some idea of how rapidly popular culture is sinking into barbarism:

I am a big man (yes I am). And I have a big gun. Got me a big old
[expletive] and I, I like to have fun. Held against your forehead, I'll
make you suck it. Maybe I'll put a hole in your head. . . . I can
reduce it if you want. I can devour. I'm hard as [expletive] steel and
I've got the power. . . . Shoot, shoot, shoot, shoot, shoot. I'm going to
come all over you. . . . me and my [expletive] gun, me and my
[expletive] gun.

The obscenity of thought and word is staggering, but also notable is the deliberate rejection of any attempt to achieve artistic distinction or even mediocrity. The music is generally little more than noise with a beat, the singing is an unmelodic chant, the lyrics often range from the perverse to the mercifully unintelligible. It is difficult to convey just how debased rap is. Not even printing the words adequately expresses that. There have, however, been some noteworthy attempts to get the point across. The music industry, Michael Bywater writes as part of an extended piece of masterful vituperation, "has somehow reduced humanity's greatest achievement—a near-universal language of pure transcendence—into a knuckle-dragging sub-pidgin of grunts and snarls, capable of fully expressing only the more pointless forms of violence and the more brutal forms of sex." He contrasts this with the remarkably subtle and emotionally precise popular music of only a few decades ago: "If Bach is the sound of God thinking, then perhaps Gershwin is, at least, the sound of St. Anthony of Padua whistling as he works."[1]

The difference between the music produced by Tin Pan Alley and rap is so stark that it is misleading to call them both music. Rock and rap are utterly impoverished by comparison with swing or jazz or any pre–World War II music, impoverished emotionally, aesthetically, and intellectually. Rap is simply unable to express tenderness, gentleness, or love. Neither rock nor rap can begin to approach the complicated melodies of George Gershwin, Irving Berlin, or Cole Porter. Nor do their lyrics display any of the wit of Ira Gershwin, Porter, Fats Waller, or Johnny Mercer. The bands that play this music lack even a trace of the musicianship of the bands led by Benny Goodman, Duke Ellington, and many others of that era.

Rap songs like "Horny" and "Big Man with a Gun" are not, as

one might hope, culturally marginal; they produce best selling records. Nor is this "black music." Some of the worst rappers are white, and by far the largest number of records are sold to white suburban adolescents. What is one to make of these facts? One obvious answer has been mentioned: bored, affluent people in a society that no longer possesses the disciplinary tools of shame and stigma will indulge the most primitive human emotions. Sex, violence, and domination qualify.

Beyond that, it is possible to think these songs reflect a generalized rage, particularly rage against social authority. That seems to be the theme, expressed in obscene language and mixed with the celebration of violence in records like Ice-T's "Cop Killers." There is continuity with the Sixties hatred of authority and in particular of the police, expressed in the phrase "Off the pigs." That may also explain the fury directed at women in this music. In that part of the black community where men are absent from the home, women are often figures of considerable power. White adolescents, with similar rebellious impulses, may resent the authority figures of mothers and female teachers, and the domineering whining feminists. The songs can be heard as paeans of revenge. No doubt the young have always chafed under authority; the difference now is that obscene assaults on authority have become culturally acceptable.

In keeping with the progress of liberalism, popular entertainment generally—and the worst of it in particular—celebrates the unconstrained self, and savages those who would constrain. People who consume these diversions are, it would appear, fascinated with self, which must be autonomous to be authentic. Protests and threatened boycotts caused Calvin Klein to cancel his semipornographic ad campaign showing teenagers in sexually provocative poses—a girl of 13 or 14 for instance, on her back, skirt lifted to show her panties. Columnist John Leo of *U.S. News & World Report* called the ads "decadent." But a spokesman for Klein said that the ads were perfect for today's independent generation: "people who do only what they want to do." That is a good working definition of decadence. It is also the definition John Stuart Mill gave of liberty. Would that he could see where it led.

There are words to describe the Klein attitude. One, obviously, is narcissism; the other is nihilism. One who is absorbed in himself and his sensations, believing in few or no moral or religious principles, in nothing transcendental, is a nihilist. A culture that preaches narcissistic nihilism is asking for trouble.

Klein's sleaze set off an uproar primarily because it was impossible to avoid; the ad thrust the offensive pictiures in our faces. Even those of us who try to avoid the more repellant aspects of popular culture know about it through a sort of peripheral vision. The rap beat blasts out of the car waiting beside you at a red light; blatant sexuality, often of a perverse nature, assualts the reader in magazine advertisements; carnage is promised in newspaper motion picture advertisments. Popular entertainment sells sex, pornography, violence, vulgarity, attacks on traditional forms of authority, and outright perversion more copiously and more insistently than ever before in our history. It is no answer to point out that much of popular culture is harmless or even benign. The culture has changed, is changing, and the change is for the worse. The worst is the leading edge.

The fixation on self first became obvious with rock 'n' roll, which evolved into "hard" rock. "The extrovert, the hedonist, the madman, the criminal, the suicide, or the exhibitionist can rise to heroic stature in rock for the same reasons that Byron or Raskolnikov became Romantic heroes—profligacy and murder are expressions of an emotional intensity that defies the limits imposed by nature and society."[2] Now we have moved on to rap, which is even less constrained. Its performers don't just sing about criminals; some of them are criminals. Which does not seem to diminish their popularity.

What we hear in rap is paralleled elsewhere in popular culture in varying degrees. That the movies feature sex, violence, and vile language is not news. Car chases ending in flaming crashes, the machine gunning of masses of people, explosions of helicopters, the liberal production of corpses, language previously not heard even in semipolite society, these are now standard fare. It is no doubt true that Hollywood is appealing to profitable adolescent audiences, which appear to think that dismemberments and obscenities are an excellent evening's entertainment. But there is probably more to these developments than that. Many in Hollywood insist upon a liberal lacing of foul language in their films because they regard brutality and obscenity as signs of "authenticity," the polemical idea whose nature, Trilling told us, is to deal aggressively with traditional aesthetic opinion and then with traditional social and political opinion.

Television, not surprisingly, displays the same traits as the movies and music, though because it is viewed by families in the home, not to the same degree. Television viewing still resembles a bit the days when the family sat around the radio console, and that places a few restrictions on the medium. Still, things have changed here, too. Language is increasingly vulgar. A major study of changes in program content over the life of television finds, as might have been expected of a medium that has recently come under the influence of the Sixties generation, that "[B]eginning from a relatively apolitical and traditional perspective on the social order, TV has meandered and lurched uncertainly along paths forged by the politics of the populist Left."[3] That has dictated changes in the way sex, social and cultural authority, and the personifications of good and evil are presented. Recreational sex, for example, is pervasive and is presented as acceptable about six times as often as it is rejected. Homosexuals and prostitutes are shown as social victims. Television takes a neutral attitude towards adultery, prostitution, and pornography. It "warns against the dangers of imposing the majority's restrictive sexual morality on these practices. The villains in TV's moralist plays are not deviants and libertines but Puritans and prudes."[4] The moral relativism of the Sixties is now television's public morality.

Though it cannot begin to match rap, TV undermines authority in gentler ways. Families are relatively egalitarian; at work, subordinates ridicule their bosses and usually prevail over them. Businessmen are depicted negatively: they were three times more likely to commit crimes and five times as likely to be motivated by pure greed as people in most other occupations. Politicians fare no better. The military suffered a great fall in prestige beginning in the Sixties. Law enforcement officials are now shown as corrupt and as likely to commit crimes as anyone else, but criminals are portrayed sympathetically. This has begun to change. Police and prosecutors are now more often seen as heroes, which, it has been suggested, may be due to the widespread and justified fear of crime in this society.

Perhaps popular culture is inevitably vulgar but today's is more vulgar than at any time in the past. Sex in sitcoms, previously pervasive, has recently exploded. A Super Bowl halftime show staged an elaborate sequence in which the central feature was Michael Jackson writhing and clutching his private parts for the edification of family audiences. But the television talk shows are perhaps the most astonishing. There are about twenty-five hosts competing for audiences and they generate about a hundred hours of programs weekly. I learned from a Montel Williams show about the institution of shore parties: people take vacations, engage in as much random sex as possible, and keep the score on a paper fastened to the refrigerator door. There was a show on women who marry their rapists and another about mothers and daughters having affairs with the same man. "In one Richard Bey outing last week," wrote Walter Goodman, "I met Karen, who admitted that she had offered her husband to Donna as a sleeping companion; Carolyn, who said her brother had slept with her boyfriend, and Geena, who said she had slept with an old friend's fiancé. . . . Geena presented her old friend with a birthday cake on stage before confessing to her, and got the cake back in her face. The audience whooped."[5]

The question is asked, where do the shows find people willing to appear and reveal their most tawdry intimacies.[6] A better question might be, where do the networks find an estimated audience of 50 million people per week who want to watch such things as a 13-year-old boy bragging about having sex with twenty-six women and then being confronted on camera by his mother. But this is merely blatant vulgarity. There is worse.

Television becomes the equivalent of rap and movies on Music Television Videos and some of the pay channels. MTV is the more pernicious because it is usually part of the basic package that subscribers get automatically. They pay nothing extra and, unless the parents are vigilant, children will watch it. A rap song, for example, is accompanied by a video that may or may not illustrate the words of the song. Images often follow one another at breakneck speed, images of guns, killings, police baiting, and sex. Like the movies, MTV is all the more dangerous because it is brilliantly produced.

One evening at a hotel in New York I flipped around the television channels. Suddenly there on the public access channel was a voluptuous young woman, naked, her body oiled, writhing on the floor while fondling herself intimately. Meanwhile, a man's voice and a print on the screen informed the viewer of the telephone number and limousine service that would acquaint him with young women of similar charms and proclivities. I watched for some time—riveted by the sociological significance of it all. Shortly after that, men only slightly less nude advertised homosexual prostitutes.

Art, by adopting many of the techniques and much of the content of popular entertainment, is becoming popular entertainment. And popular art, paintings of tomato cans, is taken as high art. James Gardner notes the incongruity that art has never been more admired, more adulated, than it is now, that it draws larger crowds and attracts more money than ever before, and yet the art itself is impoverished.[7] Here, as in popular music and television entertainment, it is not that there is no genuinely serious art at all; it is that there is so much that is meaningless, uninspired, untalented, or perverse. Perhaps the Sixties brought in a fascination with the perverted, but lack of meaning was evident well before that decade. In a prestigious New York museum in the early 1950s, a piece of black burlap nailed to a board was presented as art. In a London museum, I thought I had come upon leftovers from a carpet laying: strips of brown felt in a heap in the middle of the room. Then I saw that the pile had a title. I asked a sculptor on the Yale faculty what his sculpture, which looked like a half-melted tree stump, represented. He said quite seriously: "Whatever you want it to be." Yale was willing to support a man whose idea of art was a three-dimensional Rorschach test. It is thus no cause for surprise that our great universities now offer courses on comic books.

These may be taken as manifestations of an individualism barren of substance, expressions of selves that are empty. But what are we to make of art that is both popular and perverted? For instance: a plastic puddle of vomit; piles of papier-mâché excrement; jars of the artist's actual excrement; a painting entitled *Shit Faith* in which "crudely drawn excrement emerges from four abutting anuses."[8] We are informed that a "reinvigorated London art scene. . . . began to be the envy of the contemporary art world in the late 1980's" with such offerings as a dead fourteen-foot shark floating in a tank of formaldehyde, a portrait bust of the artist in his own frozen blood, and "Everyone I've Ever Slept With: 1963–1993," which is a small tent "whose interior is lovingly appliqued with the names of [her] past loves and bedmates."[9] The object as always, one supposes, is to shock the bourgeoisie, but the bourgeoisie eagerly buy it. As we will see shortly, fascination with such materials as urine and excrement seems to be characteristic of today's bourgeoisie, if that is any longer the proper term for such people.

The hostility to traditional culture was manifest in the arts long before the Sixties. "Anyone who thinks that fatuousness, nonsense, and obscenity in the arts are wholly recent, NEA-sponsored affairs," Roger Kimball, managing editor of *The New Criterion*, writes, "should look back for a moment at some of the numerous avant-garde movements that captured headlines in Europe from the turn of the century through the 1920s."[10] Reviewing a book that praised the Dadaist movement for subverting the values of bourgeois society, Kimball remarks: "Consistent with its attack on 'bourgeois values' (e.g., order, reason, honesty, propriety) is its fascination with violence, the scatological, and the obscene. This it shares with its close cousin, surrealism."[11] While this is undoubtedly true—Gardner says that art began to direct its anger at the bourgeois state in the last quarter of the eighteenth century—it does appear that the proportion of art that assaults bourgeois values is far higher today than in the days of Dadaism and surrealism. When the object is to attack bourgeois culture by delivering shocks to its standards, and when that culture keeps revising its standards by assimilating each new outrage, it is necessary to keep upping the ante by being ever more shocking. It seems clear, however, that large sections of the bourgeoisie, like drug-resistant bacteria, are approaching a state of being unshockable.

There is resistance in the public to the downward spiral we are riding. But it was not until the critic John Leo called Time Warner "our leading cultural polluter"[12] that the process of galvanizing public opinion really got under way. Senator Robert Dole found political capital in denouncing the more outrageous motion pictures and forms of rap music. But the most instructive episode was the behavior of the management of Time Warner when C. DeLores Tucker, a Democrat and head of the National Political

Congress of Black Women, and William Bennett, former secretary of education and drug czar, met with the top Time Warner executives to protest the filth they were putting on the market. Tucker passed copies of the lyrics of Nine Inch Nails' "Big Man with a Gun" to the Time Warner executives and asked them to read the words aloud. None of them would. One of the Tucker-Bennett party did read out the words and asked if the executives found the lyrics offensive. The discussion included such modern liberal gems from Time Warner as "Art is difficult to interpret," "What is art?," and "Who decides what is pornography and what isn't?" The answers are simple: to the first question: "Big Man with a Gun" is as easy to interpret as an obscenity scrawled in a public lavatory; to the second: whatever art may be, this isn't it; and to the third: the public acting through its designated representatives can decide.

The executives talked about finding the "root causes" of crime and violence. That is the standard liberal diversion when anybody suggests doing something serious about an obvious problem. They said Tucker and Bennett were talking about symptoms. Of course, because it is the symptoms and not the root causes that kill, physicians treat the symptoms. My favorite Time Warner response was: "Elvis was more controversial in his day than some rap lyrics are today."[13] That is less a justification of today's music than a measure of how far our culture has fallen. The very fact that we have gone from Elvis to Snoop Doggy Dogg is the heart of the case for censorship.

Bennett asked the executives "whether there was anything so low, so bad, that you will not sell it." There was a long silence. But when Bennett said "baloney" a couple of times to the vapid responses he was getting, Time Warner's chairman, Gerald M. Levin, in a sudden onrush of sensitivity about words, objected to such language and walked out of the meeting.

The industry's responses to the criticism were even more instructive. Michael Fuchs, then chairman of Time Warner Music Group, shot back that offensive lyrics are "the price you pay for freedom of expression."[14] But obscenity in word and thought is a price that should not be paid simply so we can say there are no limits to what may be said. Fuchs might as well have said that crack addicts are the price you pay for a free market. Danny Goldberg, chairman of Warner Bros. Records, said: "Nine Inch Nails is a Grammy Award-winning, critically acclaimed artist [sic] who millions of people love. Why should a corporation listen to a bunch of middle-aged people who don't like the music and don't listen to it, and ignore the people who do love it and who do buy it?"[15] The reason the corporation should listen to those middle-aged people is that they are attempting to uphold some standard of decency for the protection, among others, of those who love and buy the filth. It says something frightening about this culture that lyrics like "Big Man with a Gun" win Grammy Awards, critical acclaim, and the love of millions.

The industry rallied round Time Warner with a rolling barrage of witless platitudes. Mark Canton, chairman of the Columbia TriStar Motion Picture Group, said: "The issue here is creative rights. We have to retain the right to make creative choices with diversity and freedom."[16] The industry's chieftains have apparently lost touch with both logic and morality. To speak of songs about ripping vaginas and licking anuses as necessary to retain the right to make creative choices is a rhetorical obscenity that almost matches what is on the records. There has to be a limit somewhere to what a culture can tolerate and still retain not just creative choice but a vestige of decency. That limit is now behind us.

Though there certainly is a simmering dissatisfaction with popular culture, that apparently does not portend any effective action. The Tucker-Bennett episode was entertaining, but Time Warner, apparently embarrassed, sold the unit that produced gangsta rap. The beat apparently goes on as before under new management. In any case, the confrontation tactic had such success as it did because it was new. Attempts to repeat it will have less and less impact, and the music executives will begin to refuse to meet with critics. Popular culture remains just that, popular. The American public watches, listens to, and makes profitable art forms it agrees are debased. That is an important point. The entertainment industry is not forcing depravity on an unwilling American public. The demand for decadence is there. That fact does not excuse those who sell such degraded material any more than the demand for crack cocaine excuses the crack dealer. But we must be reminded that the fault is in ourselves, in human nature not constrained by external forces. If that were not so, the problem would not be so dangerous and difficult to solve.

The casual acceptance and rationalization of this culture by people, intellectuals in particular, who reached maturity before the Sixties hit, is not, I suppose, surprising. The theme of radical individualism was in the air long before the Sixties and, in any event, intellectuals are attracted to modern liberalism. A few years back, the American Enterprise Institute held a conference planned and moderated by Ben Wattenberg to discuss "The New Global Popular Culture," which is increasingly an exported American popular culture. The discussants, a large and quite distinguished group, seemed, by and large, quite sanguine about where we are and where we are headed. One stated that the "core of American ideology is a uniquely insistent and far-reaching individualism—a view of the individual person which gives unprecedented weight to his or her choices, interests, and claims."[17] He said that Americans are distinctively attached to the same values of individualism that Tocqueville, Bryce, and Chesterton saw in us.

No doubt that observation is true, but it is true only semantically. Individualism does not have the same meaning and content today as it had when Tocqueville, Bryce, and Chesterton described us. The individualistic component of liberalism incessantly presses against the limits set by a culture's sense of decency and shame. In America, and perhaps in the nations of the West generally, the limits have been stretched to, and perhaps beyond, the breaking point. What was seen as American individualism a century or more ago becomes a quality different in kind: an absorption in unrestrained hedonism and personal license that is reflected in and magnified by popular culture. Only a modern intellectual could imagine that Tocqueville, Bryce, and Chesterton would recognize rap lyrics as just another manifestation of the individualism they saw in the Americans of their time. They would call it by its proper name: depravity.

The conferees sought to account for the enormous popularity around the world of American pop culture. And our popular culture is everywhere: when the American sociologist Peter Berger, who is completely bald, walked through a remote Indonesian village, the children ran after him shouting "Kojak, Kojak." American rock music can be heard on the radio almost anywhere in the world. Foreign television carries our sitcoms and movies. Why should this be? One participant struck a note of optimism that was echoed by most of the others: "the more straitened or shut-off a culture, the more urgent its hunger for all the qualities it associates with America: freedom and wealth and modernity."[18] The other and more accurate description of what American popular culture increasingly offers to "straitened" cultures is the opportunity for unlimited self-gratification.

At another conference, I referred, not approvingly, to Michael Jackson's crotch-clutching performance at the Super Bowl. Another panelist tartly informed me that it was precisely the desire to enjoy such manifestations of American culture that had brought down the Berlin wall. That seems as good an argument as any for putting the wall back up again. If my informant was right, though I prefer not to believe it, radical individualism expressed in hedonism may be the wave of the future everywhere.

It is remarkable how vigorously the modern intellectual defends the descent of popular culture not merely into vulgarity but into obscenity. At the AEI conference, several of us expressed dismay at the more profane manifestations of popular culture and said that we would favor censorship, were it not already too late: standards can be reinforced by censorship but perhaps not reinstated once they have been abandoned. Most of those present hastened to distance themselves from such reactionary heresy. An eminent scholar expressed horror that anyone would attempt to interfere with the direction of culture. "American culture," he protested with some passion, "is a culture constantly in quest of itself."[19] He liked the image so much that he repeated it twice. And, indeed, questing has a romantic ring to it. It conjures up the image of a knight of the round table travelling in an endless search for the Holy Grail. But the sentiment seems less enchanting if the quest ends in a sewer. Right now, the sewer seems the likely destination.

So far, one low point has been followed by another even lower. It is hardly surprising that rock was followed by such delightful art forms as punk rock, heavy metal, speed metal, death metal, rap, gangsta rap, and grunge. And it is hardly to be doubted, as Martha Bayles says, that these have effects on their "vulnerable target: angry, troubled adolescents."[20] "Only a fool would argue that music—especially music combined with gut-wrenching spectacle—has no impact on audiences. Yet this is exactly what the defenders of heavy metal do when they suggest that a steady diet of gleeful sadism does no harm."[21] The music industry executives are most assuredly not fools, but they must think the rest of us are.

The tastes cultivated by gleeful sadism may be the reason we have now come to "hate rock," which the *New York Times* reviewer John J. O'Connor calls "a racism-and-violence virus in pop music that has become an international infection." (Since O'Connor wrote this review, the egregious Michael Jackson put out a record with anti-Semitic lyrics that caused such an uproar that Jackson had to rerecord at least one song.) Reviewing an MTV documentary on the subject, O'Connor says that MTV straddles the fence: "Should these rockers be silenced? No. Should they be monitored carefully? 'According to what we learned,' says MTV, 'absolutely.'" O'Connor asks, "And then what?"[22]

It is a question we all must soon ask, and not just about the racism and violence of hate rock, the violently obscene and brutal lyrics of rap music, and the obscenities and wild violence of motion pictures. Technology is now bringing worse material than we have ever seen or imagined, and, as technology develops further, the material will become still worse. The Internet now provides users access to what Simon Winchester calls "an untrammelled, uncontrolled, wholly liberated ocean of information."[23] He thought it wonderful. Then one day he came upon a category called alt.sex, which has fifty-five groups including alt.sex.anal, alt.sex.intergen (intergenerational: the pedophile bulletin board), alt.sex.snuff (the killing of the victim) which includes subcategories for bestiality, torture, bloodletting, and sadistic injury.

The first category Winchester tried was alt.sex.stories, which contained a story about the kidnapping of two children. The castration of the 6-year-old boy is "reported in loving detail" and occurs before he is shot. The 7-year-old girl is then repeatedly raped by nine men before having her nipples cut off and her throat slashed. There were 200 such stories and the number was growing daily. "You want tales of fathers sodomising their three-year-old daughters, or of mothers performing fellatio on their pre-pubescent sons, or of girls coupling with horses, or of the giving of enemas to child virgins? Then you need do no more than visit the newsgroup that is named 'alt.sex.stories' and all will reliably be there, 24 hours a day, for everyone with a computer and a telephone, anywhere on (or above) the face of the earth."[24] The stories are written by pseudonymous authors and are filtered through two or three computers so that the authors and the points of origin are not known. The material is not only disgusting, it is a dangerous incitement. There is, for example: "A long and graphic account of exactly how and at what hour you wait outside a girls' school, how best to bundle a seven-year-old into your van, whether to tell her at the start of her ordeal that she is going to be killed at the end of it . . . how best to tie her down, which aperture to approach first, and with what—such things can only tempt those who verge on such acts to take a greater interest in them."[25]

Users can download pornographic pictures as well as prose from the Internet. And there is a lot of both available. The demand, moreover, is for material that can't be easily found elsewhere—pedophilia, sadomasochism, eroticized urination, defecation, and vaginal and rectal fisting. Among the most popular are sex acts with a wide variety of animals, nude children, and incest. The adult bulletin board service describes videos for sale and also provides over 25,000 pictures. The material is too obscene to be quoted here, but it involves girls defecating, girls eating feces (in both cases far more obscene language is used), oral sex with animals. One video is described as "Rape, torture, pussy nailed to table." It is impossible in short compass to give an adequate idea of the depravity that is being sold, apparently profitably.

The Internet, Stephen Bates informs us, offers plans for making bombs, instructions for painless suicide, the anti-Semitic forgery *Protocols of the Elders of Zion* (compressed for faster downloading), and racist diatribes, along with sexual perversion. There are certain to be offline harms from this material. "Pedophiles will abuse children they first met online, kids will blow off fingers with Net's bomb recipes, despondent teens will poison themselves using recipes from *alt.suicide.holiday*. Maybe all these tragedies would have occurred without the Net, but that's tough to prove."[26] It would be even tougher to prove that this material has any social value. Only the most radical individualism imaginable could countenance these uses of the Internet.

What Winchester says of the alt.sex.stories he read is true of these other categories of prose and images: "Surely such essays tell the thinker of forbidden thoughts that there exists somewhere out there a like-minded group of men for whom such things are really not so bad, the enjoyment of which, if no one is so ill-starred as to get caught, can be limitless. Surely it is naive folly—or, the other end of the spectrum, gross irresponsibility—to suppose otherwise."[27]

But the situation is likely to get still worse than this. The pornographic video industry is now doing billions of dollars worth of business and volume is increasing rapidly.[28] Companies are acquiring inventories of videos for cable television, and a nationwide chain of pornographic video retail stores is in the works. This may, however, be only a transitional phase. George Gilder predicts that computers will soon replace television, allowing viewers to call up digital films and files of whatever they may desire from around the world. He discounts the idea that "liberated children [will] rush away from the network nurse, chasing Pied Piper pederasts, snuff-film sadists, and other trolls of cyberspace."[29] (The "network nurse," as a matter of fact, looks increasingly like a lady of the evening.) The computer will give everyone his own channel to do with as he wishes, and Gilder predicts a spectacular proliferation of programs on specialized cultural, scientific, and practical subjects.

That will certainly happen, but the presence of wholesome films and files does not rule out the presence of the corrupt and even diabolical. The Internet is proving that. The more private viewing becomes, the more likely it is that salacious and perverted tastes will be indulged. That proposition is demonstrated by the explosion of pornographic films and profits when videocassettes enabled customers to avoid the embarrassment of entering "adult" theaters. An even greater surge in the demand for perverted sex with violence will certainly occur when customers don't even have to check cassettes out of a store. Calling up films in their own homes, they will not have to face a clerk or let other customers see them browsing through x-rated films.

When digital films become available for viewing on home computers, we are likely to discover that Gilder's "trolls of cyberspace" are very real, very popular, and a very great menace. Imagine Internet's alt.sex.stories on digital film available on home computers anywhere in the world. The dramatization, in living color with lurid special effects, of men castrating and then shooting a 6-year-old boy, then gang raping and killing a 7-year-old girl, is certain to trigger imitations by borderline perverts. Don't think such films won't be made; they will. Don't think that they will not be defended on First Amendment grounds; they will. And don't suppose it will not be said that the solution is simple: if you don't like it, don't watch it. That, too, will be argued.

A great many people are willing to deplore such material but unwilling to take or allow action to stop its distribution. When the Senate Commerce Committee approved a proposal to impose criminal penalties on anyone who transmits on Internet material that is "obscene, lewd, lascivious, filthy, or indecent," ferocious opposition immediately developed from a coalition of business and civil liberties organizations. The wording of the bill leaves much to be desired, but that is not the primary objection these groups have. They do not want restrictions, period, no matter how carefully drawn. The coalition includes, of course, the ACLU and the ubiquitous Time Warner, which John Leo has said is "associated one way or another with most of the high-profile, high-profit acts, black and white, that are pumping nihilism into the culture. . . . We are living through a cultural collapse, and major corporations are presiding over that collapse and grabbing everything they can on the way down."[30]

We are still on the way down and they are still grabbing. I do not suppose for a moment that Time Warner would produce films of the material to be found on the Internet's alt.sex. Nor would any major entertainment corporation. Not today or tomorrow, but as we grow accustomed to brutal and perverted sex, inhibitions will be lowered still further. Some businesses will make such films and some civil libertarians will deplore them, adding, of course, that they should not be banned. In the absence of restraints of some sort, however, everything that can be imagined, and some things that can't, yet, will eventually be produced and shown.

Reflecting on where we have come, Maggie Gallagher wrote: "Sex was remade in the image of Hugh Hefner; Eros demoted from a god to a buffoon. Over the last thirty years, America transformed itself into a pornographic culture."[31] Gallagher accepted Angela Carter's definition, stated in somewhat more basic Anglo-Saxon, that pornography is basically propaganda for fornication, and offered a definition of her own: "[A] pornographic culture is not one in which pornographic materials are published and distributed. A pornographic culture is one which accepts the ideas about sex on which pornography is based."[32]

That is quite right, as far as it goes, but our popular culture has gone far beyond propagandizing for fornication. That seems almost innocent nowadays. What America increasingly produces and distributes is now propaganda for every perversion and obscenity imaginable. If many of us accept the assumptions on which that is based, and apparently many do, then we are well on our way to an obscene culture. The upshot is that American popular culture is in a free fall, with the bottom not yet in sight. This is what the liberal view of human nature has brought us to. The idea that men are naturally rational, moral creatures without the need for strong external restraints has been exploded by experience. There is an eager and growing market for depravity, and profitable industries devoted to supplying it. Much of such resistance as there is comes from people living on the moral capital accumulated by prior generations. That capital may be expected to dwindle further—cultures do not unravel everywhere all at once. Unless there is vigorous counterattack, which must, I think, resort to legal as well as moral sanctions, the prospects are for a chaotic and unhappy society, followed, perhaps, by an authoritarian and unhappy society.

The question is whether we are really content to accept that.

8

The Case for Censorship

The destruction of standards is inherent in radical individualism, but it could hardly have been accomplished so rapidly or so completely without the assistance of the American judiciary. Wielding a false modern liberal version of the First Amendment, the courts have destroyed laws that created pockets of resistance to vulgarity and obscenity.

Sooner or later censorship is going to have to be considered as popular culture continues plunging to ever more sickening lows. The alternative to censorship, legal and moral, will be a brutalized and chaotic culture, with all that that entails for our society, economy, politics, and physical safety. It is important to be clear about the topic. I am *not* suggesting that censorship should, or constitutionally could, be employed to counter the liberal political and cultural propagandizing of movies, television, network news, and music. They are protected, and properly so, by the First Amendment's guarantees of freedom of speech and of the press. I *am* suggesting that censorship be considered for the most violent and sexually explicit material now on offer, starting with the obscene prose and pictures available on the Internet, motion pictures that are mere rhapsodies to violence, and the more degenerate lyrics of rap music.

Censorship is a subject that few people want to discuss, not because it has been tried and found dangerous or oppressive but because the ethos of modern liberalism has made any interference with the individual's self-gratification seem shamefully reactionary. Dole, Bennett, Tucker, and Leo, while denouncing some of the worst aspects of popular culture, were all quick to protest that they were not for censorship. That may be a tactical necessity, at least at this stage of the debate, since it has become virtually a condition of intellectual and social respectability to make that disclaimer. And it is true that there are a variety of actions short of censorship that should be tried. One is to organize boycotts of the other products sold by corporations that market filth. But what happens if a corporation decides it prefers the bottom line to responsibility? What happens if the company does not market other products that can be boycotted? So long as there exists a lucrative market for obscenity, somebody will supply it. That brings us back to "And then what?"

Is censorship really as unthinkable as we all seem to assume? That it is unthinkable is a very recent conceit. From the earliest colonies on this continent over 300 hundred years ago, and for about 175 years of our existence as a nation, we endorsed and lived with censorship. We do not have to imagine what censorship might be like; we know from experience. Some of it was formal, written in statutes or city ordinances; some of it was informal, as in the movie producers' agreement to abide by the rulings of the Hayes office. Some of it was inevitably silly—the rule that the movies could not show even a husband and wife fully dressed on a bed unless each had one foot on the floor—and some of it was no doubt pernicious. The period of Hayes office censorship was also, perhaps not coincidentally, the golden age of the movies.

The questions to be considered are whether such material has harmful effects, whether it is constitutionally possible to censor it, and whether technology may put some of it beyond society's capacity to control it.

It is possible to argue for censorship, as Stanley Brubaker, a professor of political science, does,[1] on the ground that in a republican form of government where the people rule, it is crucial that the character of the citizenry not be debased. By now we should have gotten over the liberal notion that its citizens' characters are none of the business of government. The government ought not try to impose virtue, but it can deter incitements to vice. "Liberals have always taken the position," the late Christopher Lasch wrote, "that democracy can dispense with civic virtue. According to this way of thinking, it is liberal institutions, not the character of citizens, that make democracy work."[2] He cited India and Latin America as proof that formally democratic institutions are not enough for a workable social order, a proof that is disheartening as the conditions in parts of large American cities approach those of the Third World.

Lasch stressed "the degree to which liberal democracy has lived off the borrowed capital of moral and religious traditions antedating the rise of liberalism."[3] Certainly, the great religions of the West—Christianity and Judaism—taught moral truths about respect for others, honesty, sexual fidelity, truth-speaking, the value of work, respect for the property of others, and self-restraint. With the decline of religious influence, the moral lessons attenuate as well. Morality is an essential soil for free and democratic governments. A people addicted to instant gratification through the vicarious (and sometimes not so vicarious) enjoyment of mindless violence and brutal sex is unlikely to provide such a soil. A population whose mental faculties are coarsened and blunted, whose emotions are few and simple, is unlikely to be able to make the distinctions and engage in the discourse that democratic government requires.

I find Brubaker and Lasch persuasive. We tend to think of virtue as a personal matter, each of us to choose which virtues to practice or not practice—the privatization of morality, or, if you will, the "pursuit of happiness," as each of us defines happiness. But only a public morality, in which trust, truth-telling, and self-control are prominent features, can long sustain a decent social order and hence a stable and just democratic order. If the social order continues to unravel, we may respond with a more authoritarian government that is capable of providing at least personal safety.

There is, of course, more to the case for censorship than the need to preserve a viable democracy. We need also to avoid the social devastation wrought by pornography and endless incitements to murder and mayhem. Whatever the effects upon our capacity to govern ourselves, living in a culture that saturates us with pictures of sex and violence is aesthetically ugly, emotionally flattening, and physically dangerous.

There are, no doubt, complex causes for illegitimacy and violence in today's society, but it seems impossible to deny that one cause is the messages popular culture insistently presses on us. Asked about how to diminish illegitimacy, a woman who worked with unmarried teenage mothers replied tersely: "Shoot Madonna." That may be carrying censorship a bit far, but one sees her point. Madonna's forte is sexual incitement. We live in a sex-drenched culture. The forms of sexual entertainment rampant in our time are overwhelming to the young, who would, even without such stimulations, have difficulty enough resisting the song their hormones sing. There was a time, coinciding with the era of censorship, when most did resist.

Young males, who are more prone to violence than females or older males, witness so many gory depictions of killing that they are bound to become desensitized to it. We now have teenagers and even subteenagers who shoot if they feel they have been "dissed" (shown disrespect). Indeed, the newspapers bring us stories of murders done for simple pleasure, the killing of a stranger simply because the youth felt like killing someone, anyone. That is why, for the first time in American history, you are more likely to be murdered by a complete stranger than by someone you know. That is why our prisons contain convicted killers who show absolutely no remorse and frequently cannot even remember the names of the persons they killed.

One response of the entertainment industry to criticisms has been that Hollywood and the music business did not create violence or sexual chaos in America. Of course not. But they contribute to it. They are one of the "root causes" they want us to seek elsewhere and leave them alone. The denial that what the young see and hear has any effect on their behavior is the last line of the modern liberal defense of decadence, and it is willfully specious. Accusing Senator Dole of "pandering to the right" in his speech deploring obscene and violent entertainment, the *New York Times* argued: "There is much in the movies and in hard-core rap music that is disturbing and demeaning to many Americans. Rap music, which often reaches the top of the charts, is also the music in which women are degraded and men seem to murder each other for sport. But no one has ever dropped dead from viewing 'Natural Born Killers,' or listening to gangster rap records."[4] To which George Will replied: "No one ever dropped dead reading 'Der Sturmer,' the Nazi anti-Semitic newspaper, but the culture it served caused six million Jews to drop dead."[5]

Those who oppose any form of restraint, including self-restraint, on what is produced insist that there is no connection between what people watch and hear and their behavior. It is clear why people who sell gangsta rap make that claim, but it is less clear why anyone should believe them. Studies show that the evidence of the causal connection between popular culture's violence and violent behavior is overwhelming.[6] A recent study, *Sex and the Mass Media*, asked: "Does the talk about and images of love, sex and relationships promote irresponsible sexual behavior? Do they encourage unplanned and unwanted pregnancy? Are the media responsible for teenagers having sex earlier, more frequently and outside of marriage?" The researchers concluded: "The answer to all these questions is a qualified 'yes'."[7] The answer was qualified because not enough research has as yet been done on the effects of sexual images. The authors relied in part on the analogous question of media depictions of violence and their effect on aggressive behavior, which would appear to be a parallel situation. Some of the studies found positive but relatively small effects, between 5 and 15 percent. "One of the most compelling of the naturalistic studies . . . found that the homicide rates in three countries (U.S., Canada, and South Africa) increased dramatically 10–15 years after the introduction of television." That study "estimated that exposure to television violence is a causal factor in about half of the 21,000 homicides per year in the United States and perhaps half of all rapes and assaults."[8]

The studies confirm what seems obvious. Common sense and experience are sufficient to reach the same conclusions. Music, for example, is used everywhere to create attitudes—armies use martial music, couples listen to romantic music, churches use organs, choirs, and hymns. How can anyone suppose that music (plus the images of television, movies, and advertisements) about sex and violence has no effect?

Indeed, Hollywood's writers, producers, and executives think popular entertainment affects behavior. It is not merely that they sell billions of dollars of advertising on television on the premise that they can influence behavior; they also think that the content of their programs can reform society in a liberal direction. They understand that no single program will change attitudes much, but they rely upon the cumulative impact of years of television indoctrination.[9] Why should we listen to the same people saying that their programs and music have no effect on behavior? That argument is over. The depravity sold by Hollywood and the record companies is feeding the depravity we see around us.

The television industry, under considerable political pressure, has agreed to a ratings system for its programs. Since assigning ratings to every program—including every episode in a series—will be much more difficult than assigning ratings to motion pictures, it is doubtful that the television rating system will add much except confusion and rancor. The movie ratings have not prevented underage children from freely seeing movies they were not meant to see. No doubt the same will be true of television ratings. The vaunted V chip will prove no solution. Aside from the fact that many parents simply will not bother with it, the V chip will likely lead to even more degrading programming by providing producers with the excuse that the chip adequately safeguards children, though it does not. And the chip certainly does nothing to prevent adults from enjoying the increasingly salacious and even perverted material that is on the way.

The debate about censorship, insofar as there can be said to be a debate, usually centers on the issue of keeping children away from pornography. There is, of course, a good deal of merit to that, but it makes the issue sound like one of child rearing, which most people would like the government to butt out of. Opponents say parents can protect their children by using control features offered by many services. Both sides are missing a major point. Aside from the fact that many parents will not use control features, censorship is also crucial to protect children—and the rest of us—from men encouraged to act by a steady diet of computerized pedophilia, murder, rape, and sado-masochism. No one supposes that every addict of such material will act out his fantasies, but it is willfully blind to think that none will. The pleasures the viewers of such material get from watching a thousand rape scenes or child kidnappings is not worth one actual rape or kidnapping.

There are those who say that the only solution is to rebuild a stable public culture. How one does that when the institutions we have long relied on to maintain and transmit such a culture—the two-parent family, schools, churches, and popular entertainment itself—are all themselves in decline it is not easy to say. Nevertheless, there is something to the point. Determined individuals and groups may be able to revitalize some of those institutions. For much that afflicts us, that is the only acceptable course. Law cannot be the answer in all or even most areas. And there are signs not just of resistance but of positive action against the forces of decadence. For the very worst manifestations of the culture, however, more directly coercive responses may be required. Whether as a society we any longer have the will to make such responses is very much in question.

Arguments that society may properly set limits to what may be shown, said, and sung run directly counter to the mood of our cultural elites in general, and in particular the attitude (it is hardly more than that) of our judges, many of whom, most unfortunately, are members in good standing of that elite. As constitutional law now stands, censorship would be extremely difficult, if not impossible. In *Miller* v. *California*,[10] the Supreme Court laid down a three-part test that must be met if sexually explicit material is to be banned. It must be shown that: (1) the average person, applying contemporary community standards, would find that the work, taken as a whole, appeals to the prurient interest; (2) the work depicts or describes, in a patently offensive way, sexual conduct specifically defined by the applicable state law; and (3) the work, taken as a whole, lacks serious literary, artistic, political, or scientific value.

The first two prongs of the test become increasingly difficult to satisfy as contemporary community standards decline and as fewer and fewer descriptions of sexual conduct are regarded as patently offensive. But it is the third part that poses the most difficulty. There is apparently nothing that a flummery of professors will not testify has "serious value." When Cincinnati prosecuted the museum that displayed Mapplethorpe's photographs, the jury deferred to defense witnesses who said the pictures were art and hence could not be obscene. Cincinnati was widely ridiculed and portrayed as benighted for even attempting to punish obscenity.

One typical cartoon showed a furtive figure stepping out of an alley in the city to offer "feelthy pictures" to a surprised passerby. The picture was a reproduction of a Michelangelo. It is typical of our collapse of standards that Mapplethorpe's grotesqueries can be compared even in a cartoon to Michelangelo's art.

It is difficult to see merit in the serious value test. Serious literary, artistic, political, or scientific value can certainly be achieved without including descriptions of "patently offensive" sexual conduct. This third criterion serves merely as an escape hatch for pornographers whose "experts" can overbear juries. No doubt professors of literature can be found to testify to the serious literary value of the prose found in alt.sex.stories. Some of them are said to be very well written.

Without censorship, it has proved impossible to maintain any standards of decency. "[O]nly a deeply confused society," George Will wrote, "is more concerned about protecting lungs than minds, trout than black women. We legislate against smoking in restaurants; singing 'Me So Horny' is a constitutional right. Secondary smoke is carcinogenic; celebration of torn vaginas is 'mere words.'"[11] The massive confusion Will describes is in large measure a confusion that first enveloped the courts, which they then imposed on us.

It will be said that to propose banning anything that can be called "expression" is an attempt to "take away our constitutional rights." A radio talk show host said that the proposal to censor obscenities on the Internet was a denial of the First Amendment rights of teenagers. Such reactions reveal a profound ignorance of the history of the First Amendment. Until quite recently, nobody even raised the question of that amendment in prosecutions of pornographers; it was not thought relevant even by the pornographers. As late as 1942, in the *Chaplinsky* decision, a unanimous Supreme Court could agree:

> There are certain well-defined and narrowly limited classes of speech, the prevention and punishment of which have never been thought to raise any Constitutional problem. These include the lewd and obscene, the profane, the libelous, and the insulting or "fighting" words—those which by their very utterance inflict injury or tend to incite an immediate breach of the

peace. It has been well observed that such utterances are no essential part of any exposition of ideas, and are of such slight social value as a step to truth that any benefit that may be derived from them is clearly outweighed by the social interest in order and morality.[12]

Under today's constitutional doctrine, it would be difficult to impossible to prohibit or punish the lewd and obscene, or the profane. First Amendment jurisprudence has shifted from the protection of the exposition of ideas towards the protection of self-expression—however lewd, obscene, or profane. Time Warner, citing the authority of a 1992 statute, proposed to scramble sexually explicit programs on a New York cable channel (the channel, I believe, on which I watched the writhing, oily young woman mentioned earlier). Those who wanted the shows with strippers, excerpts from pornographic movies, and advertisements for phone sex and "escort" services would have to send in cards to the cable operator. A federal district judge in New York, disagreeing with the federal court of appeals in Washington, D.C., granted a preliminary injunction against Time Warner, saying that the statute probably violated the First Amendment. The plaintiffs who produce these shows said the scrambling would hurt their ability to reach their audience and stigmatize viewers who tune in to the shows. Both are results that would have been considered laudable rather than forbidden under the First Amendment not many years ago.

Yet it is clear that if there is something special about speech, something that warrants a constitutional guarantee, it is the capacity of speech to communicate ideas. There is no other distinction between speech and other human activities that go unprotected by the Constitution. That is the point the *Chaplinsky* Court grasped. Non-speech activities can give as much pleasure as speech, develop as many human faculties, and contribute to personal and social well-being. The only difference between speech and other behavior is speech's capacity to communicate ideas in the effort to reach varieties of truth. Celebration in song of the ripping of vaginas or forced oral sex or stories depicting the kidnapping, mutilation, raping, and murder of children do not, to anyone with a degree of common sense, qualify as ideas. And when something worthy of being called an idea is involved, there is no reason to protect its expression in lewd, obscene, or profane language. Such language adds nothing to the idea but, instead, detracts from it.

Today's Court majority would have difficulty understanding *Chaplinsky's* statement that an utterance could inflict an injury to morality. Morality itself has become relativized in our constitutional jurisprudence, so that the Court no longer has the vocabulary to say that something is immoral and, for that reason, may be banned by the legislature. As Walter Berns wrote:

> The Court decontrolled the arts, so to speak, and the impact of that has been profound. It not only permitted the publication of sex but it *caused* the publication of sex—or, to coin a word, the "publification" of sex. . . . The immediate and obvious consequence of [the end of censorship] is that sex is now being made into the measure of existence, and such uniquely human qualities as modesty, fidelity, abstinence, chastity, delicacy, and shame, qualities that formerly provided the constraints on sexual activity and the setting within which the erotic passion was enjoyed, discussed, and evaluated, are today ridiculed as merely arbitrary interferences "with the health of the sexual parts."[13]

Berns wrote that in 1976, when he could have had no idea just how far the publification of sex would be carried. We may not know that even now. Our experience after the end of censorship suggests that there are few or no limits to depravity.

It may be too much to ask that the Supreme Court, as presently constituted, revisit and revise its First Amendment jurisprudence. Most people think of the Court as a legal institution because its pronouncements have the force of law. But the perception is flawed. The Court is also a cultural institution, one whose pronouncements are significantly guided not by the historical meaning of the Constitution but by the values of the class that is dominant in our culture. In our day, that means the cultural elite: academics, clergy, journalists, entertainers, foundation staffs, "public interest" groups, and the like. The First Amendment is central to the concerns of such folk because they are chatterers by profession, and their attitudes are relativistic and permissive. The mention of censorship, even of the most worthless and harmful materials, causes apoplexy in the members of that class.

The truth is that the judiciary's view of pornographic sex and pornographic violence will not change until the culture to which the Court responds changes. There is no sign that that will occur any time soon. The public debate in the area of the "arts" is not encouraging. Mapplethorpe's homoerotic photos and Serrano's "Piss Christ" were displayed with grants from the National Endowment for the Arts. So intimidating has the culture of modern liberalism become that cultural conservatives were reduced to complaining that works like these should not be subsidized with "taxpayers' dollars," as if taxpayers should never be required to subsidize things they don't like. If that were the case, government would have to close down altogether. Both spending and taxation would be at zero. To complain about the source of the dollars involved is to cheapen a moral position. The photographs would be just as offensive if their display were financed by a scatter-brained billionaire. We seem too timid to state that Mapplethorpe's and Serrano's pictures should not be shown in public, whoever pays for them. We are going to have to overcome that timidity if our culture is not to decline still further.

Libertarians join forces with modern liberals in opposing censorship, though libertarians are far from being modern liberals in other respects. For one thing, libertarians do not like the coercion that necessarily accompanies radical egalitarianism. But because both libertarians and modern liberals are oblivious to social reality, both demand radical personal autonomy in expression. That is one reason libertarians are not to be confused, as they often are, with conservatives. They are quasi- or semiconservatives. Nor are they to be confused with classical liberals, who considered restraints on individual autonomy to be essential.

The nature of the liberal and libertarian errors is easily seen in discussions of pornography. The leader of the explosion of pornographic videos, described admiringly by a competitor as the Ted Turner of the business, offers the usual defenses of decadence: "Adults have a right to see [pornography] if they want to. If it offends you, don't buy it."[14] Those statements neatly sum up both the errors and the (unintended) perniciousness of the alliance between libertarians and modern liberals with respect to popular culture.

Modern liberals employ the rhetoric of "rights" incessantly, not only to delegitimate the idea of restraints on individuals by communities but to prevent discussion of the topic. Once something is announced, usually flatly and stridently, to be a right—whether pornography or abortion or what have you—discussion becomes difficult to impossible. Rights inhere in the person, are claimed to be absolute, and cannot be diminished or taken away by reason; in fact, reason that suggests the non-existence of an asserted right is viewed as a moral evil by the claimant. If there is to be anything that can be called a community, rather than an agglomeration of hedonists, the case for previously unrecognized individual freedoms (as well as some that have been previously recognized) must be thought through and argued, and "rights" cannot win every time. Why there is a right for adults to enjoy pornography remains unexplained and unexplainable.

The second bit of advice—"If it offends you, don't buy it"—is both lulling and destructive. Whether you buy it or not, you will be greatly affected by those who do. The aesthetic and moral environment in which you and your family live will be coarsened and degraded. Economists call the effects an activity has on others "externalities"; why so many of them do not understand the externalities here is a mystery. They understand quite well that a person who decides not to run a smelter will nevertheless be seriously affected if someone else runs one nearby.

Free market economists are particularly vulnerable to the libertarian virus. They know that free economic exchanges usually benefit both parties to them. But they mistake that general rule for a universal rule. Benefits do not invariably result from free market exchanges. When it comes to pornography or addictive drugs, libertarians all too often confuse the idea that markets should be free with the idea that everything should be available on the market. The first of those ideas rests on the efficiency of the free market in satisfying wants. The second ignores the question of which wants it is moral to satisfy. That is a question of an entirely different nature. I have heard economists say that, as economists, they do not deal with questions of morality. Quite right. But nobody is just an economist. Economists are also fathers or mothers, husbands or wives, voters, citizens, members of communities. In these latter roles, they cannot avoid questions of morality.

The externalities of depictions of violence and pornography

are clear. To complaints about those products being on the market, libertarians respond with something like "Just hit the remote control and change channels on your TV set." But, like the person who chooses not to run a smelter while others do, you, your family, and your neighbors will be affected by the people who do not change the channel, who do rent the pornographic videos, who do read alt.sex.stories. As film critic Michael Medved put it: "To say that if you don't like the popular culture, then turn it off, is like saying if you don't like the smog, stop breathing. . . . There are Amish kids in Pennsylvania who know about Madonna."[15] And their parents can do nothing about it.

Can there be any doubt that as pornography and depictions of violence become increasingly popular and increasingly accessible, attitudes about marriage, fidelity, divorce, obligations to children, the use of force, and permissible public behavior and language will change? Or that with the changes in attitudes will come changes in conduct, both public and private? We have seen those changes already and they are continuing. Advocates of liberal arts education assure us that those studies improve character. Can it be that only uplifting reading affects character and the most degrading reading has no effects whatever? "Don't buy it" and "Change the channel," however intended, are effectively advice to accept a degenerating culture and its consequences.

The obstacles to censorship of pornographic and violence-filled materials are, of course, enormous. Radical individualism in such matters is now pervasive even among sedate, upper middle-class people. At a dinner I sat next to a retired Army general who was now a senior corporate executive. The subject of Robert Mapplethorpe's photographs came up. This most conventional of dinner companions said casually that people ought to be allowed to see whatever they wanted to see. It would seem to follow that others ought to be allowed to do whatever some want to see.

The entertainment industry will battle ferociously against restraints, one segment of it because its economic interests would be directly threatened, the rest because, to avoid thinking, they have become absolutists about First Amendment freedoms. Then there are the First Amendment voluptuaries. The ACLU is to the First Amendment what the National Rifle Association is to the Second Amendment and the right to bear arms. The head of the

ACLU announced in a panel discussion that the Supreme Court's failure to throw protection around nude dancing in night clubs was a terrible blow to our freedom of speech. Some years back, when I suggested to a law school audience that the courts had gone too far in preventing communities from prohibiting pornography, the then president of the organization compared me to Salazar of Portugal and the Greek colonels. Afterward he said he had called me a fascist. It is fascinating that when one calls for greater democratic control and less governance by a judicial oligarchy, one is immediately called a fascist. The ACLU seems to think democracy is tyranny and government by judges is freedom. That is a proposition that in the last half of this century our judiciary has all too readily accepted. Any serious attempt to root out the worst in our popular culture may be doomed unless the judiciary comes to understand that the First Amendment was adopted for good reasons, and those reasons did not include the furtherance of radical personal autonomy.

It is not clear how effective censorship of the Internet or of digital films on home computers can be. Perhaps it is true, as has been said, that technology is on the side of anarchy. Violence and pornography can be supplied from all over the world, and it can be wireless, further complicating the problem of barring it. We may soon be at the mercy of a combination of technology and perversion. It's enough to make one a Luddite. But there are methods of presentation that can be censored. Lyrics, motion pictures, television, and printed material are candidates.

What we see in popular culture, from "Big Man with a Gun" to alt.sex.stories, is the product, though not, it is to be feared, the final product, of liberalism's constant thrust. Doing anything to curb the spreading rot would violate liberalism's central tenet, John Stuart Mill's "one very simple principle." Mill himself would be horrified at what we have become; he never intended this; but he bequeathed us the principle that modern liberals embrace and that makes it possible. We have learned that the founders of liberalism were wrong. Unconstrained human nature will seek degeneracy often enough to create a disorderly, hedonistic, and dangerous society. Modern liberalism and popular culture are creating that society.

9

The Rise of Crime, Illegitimacy, and Welfare

The United States has surely never before experienced the social chaos and the accompanying personal tragedies that have become routine today: high rates of crime and low rates of punishment, high rates of illegitimate births subsidized by welfare, and high rates of family dissolution through no-fault divorce. These pathologies are recent, and it is now widely accepted that they are related to one another.

The proximate cause of these pathologies is the infatuation of modern liberalism with the individual's right to self-gratification along with the kind of egalitarianism, largely based on guilt, that inhibits judgment and reform. These pathologies were easy to fall into and will be very difficult to climb out of. There is, in fact, no agreement about how to cure them. It may be, in fact, that a democratic nation will be unable to take the measures necessary, once we know what those measures are.

If radical individualism and egalitarianism are the causes, we should expect to see their various effects produced at about the same time as one another. And that is what we do see. During the same years that popular culture was becoming ever more sordid, the pathologies of divorce, illegitimacy, and crime exploded. The story is well documented and may be quickly summarized. The more difficult question, particularly about illegitimacy and welfare, is how to escape what we have done.

Rates of illegitimate births and the commission of serious crimes began rising together and did so at the same time in both the United States and England.[1] National illegitimacy statistics were first gathered in the United States in 1920. Illegitimate births then constituted 3 percent of all births. The proportion slowly went up to just over 5 percent in 1960, and then shot up to 11 percent in 1970, above 18 percent in 1980, and 30 percent by 1991. These are figures for the entire population. Black illegitimacy started from a higher base than white and skyrocketed sooner, reaching 68 percent in 1991. White illegitimacy had reached a little over 2 percent by 1960 and then shot up to 6 percent in 1970, 11 percent in 1980, and just under 22 percent in 1991. Combined black and white illegitimacy in 1992 was 32 percent. These are national averages; illegitimacy is much higher in lower-income communities and neighborhoods.

Crime displays the same pattern. National records about violent crime in the United States were first kept in 1960. The number of violent crimes in that year was just under 1,900 per 100,000 people; the number doubled within ten years, and more than tripled to almost 6,000 by 1980. After a brief decline, the crime rate began rising again and had reached almost 5,700 by 1992. It is thus apparent that crime and illegitimacy trends began rising at almost the same time and then rose together.

The figures suggest two things. One is that the social pathologies they reflect did not originate in the Sixties. Crime and illegitimacy began rising in 1960. The men and women (or boys and girls) responsible must have been born not much later than 1945, and the culture that influenced them was that of the Forties and Fifties. The moral chaos of the universities did not become manifest until the mid-1960s. That chaos and the rhetoric and violence that went with it surely contributed to the social breakdown the crime and illegitimacy figures reflect, but they could not have caused it. This suggests further that rising crime, illegitimacy, and student rebellion had a common cause. While the middle-class student radicals turned to dreams of revolution and the destruction of institutions, some of the lower classes turned to crime and sexual license, and probably for the same reasons. That fact bodes ill because it suggests a long-developing weakening of cultural constraints, constraints it will be very hard to put back in place.

A general cultural decline is also suggested by the fact that crime and illegitimacy began to surge at the same time. That means that rising illegitimacy was not then the cause of rising crime. The children born out of wedlock in 1960, no matter how precocious, could hardly have begun committing serious crimes in the same year. That fact does not by any means rule out the inference that, as these processes proceeded, illegitimacy became a major, probably the major, contributor to criminality. But the initial relation of the two reminds us that humans do not respond solely to economic incentives and that a crime wave and a sexual revolution, though perhaps of lesser proportions, were on the way, with or without welfare payments.

Increases in crime are often associated with sudden increases in population, and the baby boom affected all levels of society. The jump in the population of lower-class youths was also a "vertical invasion of the barbarians" that the institutions of the culture—family, school, church—were not fully able to tame. These youths, as much as those destined for prestige universities, had available the new technologies of entertainment, and that entertainment was one of increasingly unbridled emotion and sexuality. The industry that produced such entertainment catered to adolescent fears and discontents, which are as abundant in one social class as another. The factors already discussed as contributing to student radicalism apply in this context as well. Though the trends that made the Sixties were in place long before that decade, the special factors (technology, affluence, etc.) that came together after World War II gave free rein and added impetus to the spirit that had been building.

While they were not influenced to the same extent as the white college students by liberal parents and professors, black youths heard the incessant liberal civil rights rhetoric which insisted then, as it often does now, that the black population's difficulties were entirely due to racism. That message, endlessly repeated, can lead not only to civil rights laws but to fatalism, the aimless search for pleasure—since accomplishment is, by definition, blocked off—and to anger and violence. It should have been possible to campaign for civil rights laws without rhetoric so false and incendiary.

There is no longer any doubt that communities with many single parents, whether because of divorce or out-of-wedlock births, display much higher rates of crime, drug use, school dropouts, voluntary unemployment, etc. Nor is there any doubt that the absence of a father is damaging not only to the unwed mother but to the prospects of the children.

[T]he presence of a decent father helps a male child learn to control aggression; his absence impedes it. . . . When the mother in a mother-only family is also a teenager, or at least a teenager living in urban America, the consequences for the child are even grimmer. The most authoritative survey of what we know about the offspring of adolescent mothers concluded that the children suffer increasingly serious cognitive deficits and display a greater degree of hyperactivity, hostility, and poorly controlled aggression than is true of children born to older mothers of the same race, and this is especially true of the boys.[2]

Add to this the fact that these boys, who have a great deal of time free of oversight, are heavy consumers of the images of violence and sex in television, movies, and rap music, live in neighborhoods where violence and sexual predation are regarded as signs of manhood, and gangs fill the void created by a father's absence. The wonder is that any of these youths avoid underclass behavior. The correlation of illegitimate births and crime has been well documented. The birth rate for unmarried women aged 15 to 19 increased threefold between 1960 and 1992, while the percentage of all babies born to unmarried teenagers went from 15 to 70 percent.[3] It is not surprising then that between 1985 and 1993, murders committed by 18- to 24-year-olds increased by 65 percent, and those committed by 14- to 17-year-olds increased by a staggering 165 percent.[4]

For a long time many people were under the misimpression that divorce does not have effects on children comparable to the effects of illegitimacy. According to this view, children were better off if the divorce was managed well than they would have been if they continued living with parents who had ceased to love one another. We now know better. "Poverty is one of the most easily measured effects of unmarriage as well as one of the most predictable. But it is not necessarily the most destructive to mother, child, or the nation. The evidence is now overwhelming that the collapse of marriage is creating a whole generation of children less happy, less physically and mentally healthy, less equipped to deal with life or produce at work, and more dangerous to themselves and others."[5] The adverse effects of divorce on children and society may not be as devastating as the teenage pregnancies of inner-city welfare mothers, but they are significant nonetheless.

White Americans tend to think of these problems as pretty much confined to the black underclass of the inner cities, but that is not the case, or it will not be the case for long. Charles Murray, a political scientist, and others point out that black trendlines—of crime, dropout from the labor force, and illegitimacy—all moved sharply upward when the black illegitimacy rate passed 25 percent, which suggests that the tipping point is somewhere around that number. Black illegitimacy now stands at 68 percent of births.

By 1991, however, 22 percent of white births were illegitimate and, Murray notes, the figures get much worse when viewed in terms of economic class.[6] For white women below the poverty line in the year prior to giving birth, 44 percent of births were illegitimate, while only 6 percent have been illegitimate for women above the poverty line. This is primarily a lower-class phenomenon, though increasingly women with good educations and income choose to have a child without having a husband. If the tipping point theory is correct, the white lower class is on the verge of becoming an underclass.

Just as the link between illegitimacy and crime is well known, so the association of illegitimacy with the welfare system is increasingly recognized. At a time when the institution of marriage is under attack in the popular culture and in government policy, it is madness to offer an apartment of her own and a steady income to an unmarried young woman or girl if she will only have a baby while remaining unmarried. As she has additional children, her income rises. The availability of welfare relieves the father of any responsibility that perhaps he might have felt.

No one supposes that the relationship between welfare and illegitimacy is unaffected by non-economic factors. James Q. Wilson points out that increases in illegitimate births were strongly correlated with increases in welfare from the early 1960s to about

1980. At that point, however, the value of the welfare package in real dollars flattened out for almost a decade, but the illegitimacy rate continued to rise. (This could be, in part, because the provision of welfare for illegitimacy up to 1980 had drastically weakened the social stigma previously attached to this behavior so that illegitimacy continued to rise even though the economic benefits did not.) There are, moreover, great differences in illegitimacy rates across ethnic groups facing similar circumstances. Mexican-American children, for example, are much more likely to grow up in two-parent families than are black children, and are one-fifth as likely to be on welfare, even though poor. Black illegitimacy is rather low in states such as Idaho, Montana, Maine, and New Hampshire, even though they have rather generous welfare payments, and the rate is quite high in many parts of the Deep South, even though these states have rather low welfare payments.

It is also possible that other factors are pressing toward earlier and more frequent sexual activity, so that even a thorough-going welfare reform, while it would help, would probably not return illegitimacy rates to pre–1960 levels. The attitudes of sexual liberation continue to influence teenage behavior through television, films, popular music, and magazine advertisements. Those attitudes are made all the more potent because boys and girls mature sexually at much earlier ages than they once did. Thus, there is a much longer period of intense sexual desire before marriage would be emotionally or financially appropriate.

Sex education in the schools appears to operate more as an incitement to sexual activity than as a heeded caution. Chelmsford (Massachusetts) High School employed Suzanne Landolphi of Hot, Sexy and Safer Productions to give two performances for students in the ninth through twelfth grades in which she gave sexually explicit monologues and discussed penis and breast size and advocated oral sex, masturbation, and homosexual activity among minors. Parents were not told in advance and students were not permitted to opt out. Some parents and students sued, so far without success. Stories like this abound, but even when the advocacy is less open, the message that the students are expected to engage in sex is always there. Opportunites for teenagers to engage in sex are also more frequent than previously: much of it takes place in homes that are now empty because the mothers are working. The modern liberal devotion to sex education is an ideological commitment rather than a policy of prudence. But even if we could abolish that counterproductive policy, the other factors remain as stubborn facts.

Whatever our dilemmas in these respects, it is clear that the welfare system makes matters far worse than they need to be. This is not a recent insight. I was startled to discover that the point was made in a 1971 article by Irving Kristol,[7] and even more startled to learn from that article that Alexis de Tocqueville made the same point in his *Essay on Pauperism* in 1835. We appear to be slow learners.

An obvious line of attack, then, is the drastic restructuring of welfare. That will be difficult for several reasons. For one, there is a major constituency opposed to any change—any change, that is, other than an increase in welfare benefits. This constituency is made up not just of welfare recipients; its most vociferous component is modern liberals of the welfare-is-a-right-not-a-privilege persuasion. The left wing of the Democratic Party finds it profitable to resist any welfare reform on the stated ground that they are protecting poor children from Republican rapacity that would have those children sleeping on the grates.

Political disingenuousness aside, even those who realize that reform is imperative are far from agreement on what it should look like or how best to accomplish it. A Brookings Institution Occasional Paper shows the range and complexity of the issues to be studied: entitlements versus block grants; family caps on benefits; teenage mother exclusions; work requirements, work support, and participation requirements. About some of these questions social science apparently provides varying degrees of guidance, so that much remains in doubt. Unfortunately, debates over welfare frequently seem less informed by research than by ideology.[8] For the moment, all one can unhesitatingly recommend is experimentation, and experimentation means allowing states greater freedom to innovate. The one certainty is that federal control is not working. Reform at the federal level would produce a single solution for the entire nation, which would almost certainly be the wrong solution. A diversity of programs would not only respond to very different local conditions but would constitute experiments that could, if successful, be adopted by other states or localities, and if failures, be avoided by them. When the best social scientists admit to uncertainty about what will work, decentralization is the rational course. There is no guarantee that a workable solution, if there is one, may not prove more expensive, perhaps much more expensive, than existing welfare programs. But the object is not to save money—existing welfare programs are not that expensive. The object is to save children, and thereby save a civilization.

What should the states do? Charles Murray makes a strong case for adopting a policy that no welfare will be given to support an illegitimate child conceived after the policy has been announced. A welfare mother with illegitimate children would realize that having more would lower her and their standard of living. A young woman or teenager would understand that having a first child out of wedlock would not give her an apartment at public expense or a welfare check. Presumably, these realizations would operate as strong deterrents. It might also, Murray thinks, involve her family in the girl's support, thus encouraging the family to teach and monitor better behavior. John DiIulio, a political scientist at Princeton University and the Brookings Institution, doubts, however, that ending welfare would bring the unwed mother's family back into the picture in enough cases. Many of those families, even if they consist of more than an unwed mother of the unwed mother, are so dysfunctional that the children would most likely experience terrible squalor and malnutrition.

Murray recognizes these problems, of course. That is why he, DiIulio, and Wilson favor a strategy of altering the inner-city ethos by means of private redemptive movements, supported by a system of shelters or group homes in which at-risk children and their young mothers can be given familial care and adult supervision in safe and drug-free settings. Living there would be a condition of receiving public assistance. Boarding schools might be provided for children of mothers who, because of drug addiction or for other reasons, cannot cope. No one knows if this would work, if large programs can do what some small programs have accomplished, or if even the best programs, whose successes pre-dated the arrival of crack cocaine, can salvage people from that drug.

Myron Magnet suggests that welfare payments not be raised to mothers who have a second welfare child, and that out-of-wedlock pregnancies be made much less attractive by refusing to set up unmarried mothers in their own apartments. Instead, they would have to live in group shelters with rules of behavior and work requirements. Resident single mothers would have to attend daily workshops on child care and rearing. Many welfare single mothers are abysmally ignorant of such matters. Pre-school children would be in the shelter's day care center during working hours, where a program like Head Start would give them values and knowledge that underclass children do not adequately acquire. If welfare mothers chose not to participate and failed to support their children, the state will take the children away as it does now.[9] A further question needs to be answered, however. After the child is taken away, what is to be done about the mother, now presumably without support and also likely to produce more children? Giving her welfare to keep her alive would put us right back in the old system; not keeping her alive or letting her sink into utter misery is unthinkable.

For those who distrust the states' response to the welfare problem, there is already a record of how the states behave when they are freed of federal control through a waiver process that has been in place since 1992. Douglas Besharov, a scholar at the American Enterprise Institute, summarizes the most common features of the various state programs.[10] These are: requiring recipients to look for work, which reduces welfare caseloads; allowing recipients to keep more of their earnings (the common policy of reducing welfare by one dollar for every dollar earned provides a strong disincentive to work); making it easier for married couples to receive benefits instead of penalizing two-parent families and so providing a disincentive to stable relationships; requiring welfare mothers to take better care of their children by, for example, reducing welfare payments when parents do not send their children to school.

No one can be sure what will and will not work. In fact, no one should be sure that anything will work. Our policies have produced a large class of people, mostly female, who are dependent on welfare and whose lives, perhaps, cannot now be greatly altered. Proposals to train single mothers for jobs or to require them to take additional schooling have great public appeal, but such programs may produce only meager results. The children will have to be cared for while the mothers are occupied, which probably means an enormous expansion of day care centers. But the main drawback is that these are mostly young women of substandard intelligence, self-discipline, and motivation; otherwise they would not be in the predicament they are. They will not be easy to train and are unlikely to make good employees. Had welfare not seduced them into the lives they lead, they probably would have entered the job market much earlier in life and by now would have learned the habits and attitudes that employers require.

We may have to accept the fact that welfare has produced more than one lost generation. There is probably nothing society or government can do for existing welfare-dependent unwed mothers except keep them on some form of welfare. The question for public policy is what to do about their children and about women who have not yet become single mothers but are very likely to do so. The urgent problem is keeping future generations out of the welfare-illegitimacy-drugs-crime trap.

Fortunately, approaches are being tried that hold promise. For the most part, such approaches involve bringing a stable relationship with an adult into a child's life. Public/Private Ventures (P/PV), a not-for-profit corporation, reported on the effects of mentoring programs at the local affiliates of Big Brothers/Big Sisters of America (BB/BS).[11] BB/BS maintains 75,000 matches between an adult and a youngster. Over an eighteen-month period, P/PV studied 959 10- to 16-year-olds who applied to BB/BS programs, assigning half to a treatment group for which matches with adult volunteers were made or attempted and assigning the other half to a waiting list as a control group. The results showed dramatic differences between the two groups in initiating drug and alcohol use, physical violence, skipping school, the quality of relationships with parents and peers. In all these categories, the treatment group showed superior results. Little Brothers and Little Sisters, for example, were 46 percent less likely than those in the control group to start using drugs. These improvements occurred although the contact between the adult and the child typically consisted of three meetings a month for four hours per meeting.

It is an open question whether programs like BB/BS can be greatly expanded. There is, for instance, the question of whether an adequate supply of suitable adult volunteers can be recruited and whether the cost (about $1000 per match) can be met. P/PV expresses doubt about funding a greatly expanded program entirely with private funds but does not seem adequately aware of the perils of accepting public funding. If the government decided to help, it is entirely predictable that costs and bureaucratic interference would rise and effectiveness would decline.

An additional promising approach, already underway in a few cities, is the mobilization of black churches to carry out youth and community development plans. John DiIulio has announced that he has decided to give over most of the rest of his professional life to working with a coalition of inner-city black Christian clergy to accomplish such a mobilization. He thinks that empowering these ministers is a key to resolving the nation's violent crime problem. That empowerment should be accomplished not with government programs and funds but with "voluntary efforts, with private contributions, and with our respect and prayers."[12]

The benefits of successful welfare reform will be long-term, but we face an urgent short-term problem. Even if we assume that welfare can be reformed and rates of illegitimacy brought down to levels that do not threaten the stability of the social order, the extremely unpleasant fact remains that, for some years ahead, we are in for high, and probably ever increasing, levels of violent crime. The immediate question is how we can protect ourselves. The dimensions of the crime problem are clearly set out in a report, "The State of Violent Crime in America,"[13] in Ben Wattenberg's book *Values Matter Most*,[14] and in DiIulio's Bradley Lecture "Violent Crime and Representative Government" at the American Enterprise Institute. Most of the factual material that follows is drawn from those sources.

One reason crime has increased is that the likelihood and severity of punishment has drastically declined. The United States has adopted a system of revolving-door justice for adults and juveniles alike. A distinctive feature of modern liberalism is its unwillingness to deal with crime with the rigor it deserves and that the general public wants. Paul Johnson argues that this unwillingness calls into question our claim to be a working democracy: "In both Britain and the U.S., a permanent working alliance exists between, on the one hand, liberals in academia and the media, and, on the other, their counterparts in government and its agencies, in private and trade union lobbies, in the courts and in law firms."[15] This alliance opposes severe punishments and opposes, most especially, capital punishment. Stanley Rothman and his colleagues have found that those I have been calling modern liberals see groups, such as criminals, that stand outside society's moral consensus as not constituting a serious threat.[16] The public wants much harder treatment of violent criminals than liberals are willing to give them, in legislation, in court trials and sentencing, and in parole and probation procedures. Our system immediately puts back on the streets 63 percent of all pretrial violent felony defendants, fails to incarcerate 47 percent of those convicted of violent crimes, and releases those convicted of violence and sent to prison before they have served even half their time.

There is, as DiIulio says, an anti-incarceration lobby and as well an antipunishment coalition. These people are difficult to understand. Some years back I met a lawyer who is moderately well known in Washington. He mentioned that he was contemplating a lawsuit to close a nearby prison on the constitutional ground of "cruel and unusual punishment." I asked if the punishment was cruel and unusual because of overcrowding. He said no, it was because people are imprisoned.

Crime rates in a number of areas have stopped rising and in some places have begun to decline. It is possible that the rate of violent crimes has gone down in the nation as a whole. This appears to be partially due to better policing, slightly higher rates of incarceration, and a decline in the number of young males, who are almost entirely responsible for violent crime though more and more women are taking up the practice. But, as the Council on Crime report puts it: "Recent drops in serious crime are but the lull before the coming crime storm."[17] That is because the population of young males in the age groups that commit violent crime is about to increase rapidly, producing more violence than we know at present. It is also likely that the coming young felons will commit more serious crimes than today's juvenile offenders do. According to the report, the literature indicates that "each generation of crime-prone boys is several times more dangerous than the one before it, and that over 80 percent of the most serious and frequent offenders escape detection and arrest."

As for the coming storm, Wattenberg reproduces charts showing that the violent crime rate went up sixfold from 1957 to 1993 and that the punishment expected by criminals for crimes of violence and burglary declined precipitously from 1950 to 1970. The criminals' expectations reflected the reality. The Council on Crime report notes that the American justice system imprisons barely one criminal for every one hundred violent crimes, and that millions of convicted criminals with histories of violence end up on probation and parole rather than behind bars. That holds true even for the most violent repeat offenders. There are far more persons convicted of violent crimes who are on probation and parole than in prison. Many of those "under supervision" commit even more violent crimes.

As the carnage continues, the public is offered such false panaceas as "midnight basketball"—that is, providing nighttime sports facilities to keep young men off the streets—and gun control. Neither is a serious response. Both may be seen as following from the egalitarians' unwillingness to punish. Hence alternatives are sought that must be tried before or in lieu of punishment. Midnight basketball is so obviously a frivolous notion that it need not be discussed. Gun control, though advanced with religious fervor and harrowing tales of loved ones shot to death, is no less frivolous. The real argument against severe gun control is one of policy, not constitutionality.†

As law professor Daniel Polsby demonstrates, "the conventional wisdom about guns and violence is mistaken. Guns don't increase national rates of crime and violence—but the continued proliferation of gun control laws almost certainly does."[18] Gun

---

†The Second Amendment states somewhat ambiguously: "A well-regulated militia, being necessary to the security of a free State, the right of the people to keep and bear Arms, shall not be infringed." The first part of the Amendment supports proponents of gun control by seeming to make the possession of firearms contingent upon being a member of a state-regulated militia. The next part is cited by opponents of gun control as a guarantee of the individual's right to possess such weapons, since he can always be called to militia service. The Supreme Court has consistently ruled that there is no individual right to own a firearm. The Second Amendment was designed to allow states to defend themselves against a possibly tyrannical national government. Now that the federal government has stealth bombers and nuclear weapons, it is hard to imagine what people would need to keep in the garage to serve that purpose.

control laws raise the cost of obtaining a firearm. This is a cost the criminal will willingly pay because a gun is essential to the business he is in. He probably will not have to pay the increased cost, because illicit markets adapt to overcome difficulties. There are, moreover, nearly 200,000,000 firearms in the United States now, many of them unregistered, and it is easy to smuggle guns in or to make them in basements and garages. A gun need not be state of the art to serve a criminal's purpose. Criminals will never have difficulty getting guns. The citizen who wants a firearm for self-defense will not have access to illicit markets and will be deterred by the higher costs charged in legal transactions. The result is a steady supply of guns for criminal aggression and a diminished supply for self-defense.

"It is easy to count the bodies of those who have been killed or wounded with guns," Polsby remarks, "but not easy to count the people who have avoided harm because they had access to weapons. . . . [P]eople who are armed make comparatively unattractive victims. A criminal might not know if any one civilian is armed, but if it becomes known that a large number of civilians do carry weapons, criminals will become warier."[19] Gun control shifts the equation in favor of the criminal. Gun control proposals are nothing more than a modern liberal suggestion that government, which is unable to protect its citizens, make sure those citizens cannot defend themselves.

Like gun control, the idea of life imprisonment for criminals convicted of three crimes of physical violence is probably a false panacea. "Three strikes and you're out" may sound like baseball, and hence be congenial to the American mind, but as a prescription for crime control it is seriously overrated. Washington State adopted such a law in 1993 and reported murders down 10 percent, rapes down 18 percent, and assaults down 4 percent in the first six months.[20] This a hopeful sign, though experience with the law has been too short to be sure. Some offenders are said to be leaving the state, which is good for Washington but may not be so happy for other states. Washington may be enjoying a drop in crime rates because it is exporting its criminals. We would have a better understanding of the policy's effects if every state adopted it.

But there is a more serious problem with "three strikes and you're out." Violent crimes are almost entirely committed by young men. (This may be changing. In an unexpected development, the rate of growth of violent crime perpetrated by women now exceeds that of men.) When a male reaches the age of, say, forty, he almost always ceases to be dangerous. The implications are clear: by the time we have arrested and convicted a violent felon three times and sentenced him to life imprisonment, we may be accomplishing nothing more than warehousing men who have, in all probability, ceased to be a threat.

A problem still more serious is that crimes will be committed by those who are caught and convicted one or two times but not caught for subsequent violence, or who are convicted three times but are free much of the time between their first and third convictions. The problem is even worse than that because in most jurisdictions juveniles who commit violent crimes are not even fingerprinted and their records as juveniles are not available to prosecutors or courts when they commit further crimes as adults. Thus, the third offense as an adult may in fact be the fourth, fifth, or sixth violent crime.

Quite aside from these issues, inadequate prison terms have become a major problem. A Brookings Institution study finds that, on average, the serious criminal commits twelve serious crimes a year.[21] That means that a criminal sentenced to ten years and let out in four will, on average, commit seventy-two violent crimes during the time he should have been in prison. Other studies put the number of violent crimes per year per criminal even higher. Newspapers routinely tell of murders committed by men out on probation, parole, or released early for good behavior. According to John DiIulio, "About three of every four convicted criminals (more than three million people) are on the streets without meaningful probation or parole supervision."[22]

A better response than "three strikes" would be to impose a stiff first sentence and make the offender serve all of it. Imprisonment serves several functions, and one is incapacitating the criminal. A violent man in prison will not shoot you, rape you, or crack your skull. There is no reason to be sentimental about a person who commits even one violent or serious crime. Violence is not inflicted through negligence or inadvertence. If the man who was sentenced to ten years served ten years, at least seventy-two people would be spared death, rape, or other serious injury.

The last-ditch argument, as DiIulio calls it, of the anti-incarceration lobby is that prisons cost too much to permit imprisonment of violent offenders for all or most of their terms. But, as he points out, "barely a half cent of every government dollar (federal, state, and local) goes to keeping convicted criminals behind bars. . . . [and we spend] 12 times more on public welfare programs." It "costs society about twice as much to let a criminal roam the streets as it does to keep him behind bars." And that cost does not include the fear and suffering of victims and their friends or the fear of those who do not become victims but are concerned that they may.

We clearly have need of drastic reform of our criminal justice system, which must begin with a public discussion about restraining violent criminals, adult and juvenile. As the Council on Crime report says:

> Before such a discourse can proceed, however, it must become unacceptable in elite circles to deny, discount, or disparage the public's legitimate desire to slow or stop revolving-door justice. In the 1960's and 70's, prisoners' rights activists and anti-incarceration analysts called for moratoria on prison construction ("Tear down the walls!"). Today many of these same people, flanked by various national media commentators, are battling—sometimes openly, but as often behind the scenes— to eliminate mandatory minimum laws, abolish or subvert truth-in-sentencing laws, and block any species of three strike laws. They freely publicize and propagandize about the social costs of incarceration while choking off public discussion of its considerable social benefits. They lobby to expand the capacity of activist judges to impose prison caps which trigger the release of dangerous felons. In short, they achieve through junk science, administrative discretion, or judicial fiat what could not be achieved through democratic debate and legislative action.[23]

The co-chairs of the Council that issued the report containing that excellent passage are Griffin B. Bell, former federal judge and U.S. Attorney General, and William J. Bennett, former Secretary of Education and "drug czar." The "elite circles" they speak of with anger and frustration are the people I have been calling modern liberals. These are the people Stanley Rothman and his colleagues studied and found that an attitude of non-punitiveness toward criminals correlates with alienation from the American system. The policies and attitudes promulgated by these "elite circles" are the reason that the probability of a violent criminal, even a repeater, going to prison and serving most of his time is now only about one-fifth of what it was in the early 1960s.

These modern liberal elites are the same people who block any significant welfare reform despite the obvious connection between welfare and the explosion of illegitimacy and crime rates. Charles Murray contends that "illegitimacy is the single most important social problem of our time—more important than crime, drugs, poverty, illiteracy, welfare, or homelessness because it drives everything else."[24] The control of the "elite circles" over the making and implementation of policy is the reason we face a highly problematic future. What is a possible cure for crime and illegitimacy at unprecedented and probably still rising levels? One possible answer is that there may be no cure, or none that we can employ against the will of modern liberals. We may go on much as we have, at least until the welfare state collapses and society is engulfed in a hurricane of violence.[25]

When physical safety becomes a major problem even for the middle classes, we must of necessity become a heavily policed, authoritarian society, a society in which the middle classes live in gated and walled communities and make their places of work hardened targets. After the Oklahoma City bombing, there were serious proposals in Washington to use the Army to provide security. The mayor of Washington, D.C., proposed using the National Guard to supplement the police in that drug-ridden and murder-racked city. Whites tend to dismiss the violence of the inner cities as a black problem. As the killing and the drugs spread to white neighborhoods and suburbs, as they are doing, the response will be far more repressive. Both the fear of crime and the escalating harshness of the response to it will sharply reduce Americans' freedom of movement and peace of mind. Ours will become a most unpleasant society in which to live. Murray poses our alternatives: "Either we reverse the current trends in illegitimacy—especially white illegitimacy—or America must, willy-nilly, become an unrecognizably authoritarian, socially segregated, centralized state."[26]

If we would avoid that, we must beat modern liberalism in elections and place the machinery of the state in the hands of people willing to reform welfare and punish crime.

10

Killing for Convenience

ABORTION, ASSISTED SUICIDE, AND EUTHANASIA

Judging from the evidence, Americans do not view human life as sacrosanct. We engage in a variety of activities, from driving automobiles to constructing buildings, that we know will cause deaths. But the deliberate taking of the life of an individual has never been regarded as a matter of moral indifference. We debate the death penalty, for example, endlessly. It seems an anomaly, therefore, that we have so easily accepted practices that are the deliberate taking of identifiable individual lives. We have turned abortion into a constitutional right; one state has made assisted suicide a statutory right, and two federal circuit courts, not to be outdone, have made it a constitutional right; campaigns to legalize euthanasia are underway. It is entirely predictable that many of the elderly, ill, and infirm will be killed, and often without their consent. This is where radical individualism has taken us.

When a society revises its attitude towards life and death, we can see the direction of its moral movement. For that reason, it is necessary to examine the morality of such practices as abortion, assisted suicide, and euthanasia and to try to determine where they are likely to lead.

ABORTION

The necessity for reflection about abortion does not depend on, but is certainly made dramatic by, the fact that there are approximately a million and a half abortions annually in the United States. To put it another way, since the Supreme Court's 1973 decision in *Roe* v. *Wade*, there have been perhaps over 30 million abortions in the United States. Three out of ten conceptions today end in the destruction of the fetus. These facts, standing alone, do not decide the issue of morality, but they do mean that the issue is hugely significant.

The issue is also heated, polarizing, and often debated on both sides in angry, moralistic terms. I will refrain from such rhetoric because for most of my life I held a position on the subject very different from the one I now take. For years I adopted, without bothering to think, the attitude common among secular, affluent, university-educated people who took the propriety of abortion for granted, even when it was illegal. The practice's illegality, like that of drinking alcohol during Prohibition, was thought to reflect merely unenlightened prejudice or religious conviction, the two being regarded as much the same. From time to time, someone would say that it was a difficult moral problem, but there was rarely any doubt how the problem should be resolved. I remember a woman at Yale saying, without any disagreement from those around her, that "The fetus isn't nothing, but I am for the mother's right to abort it." I probably nodded. Most of us had a vague and unexamined notion that while the fetus wasn't nothing, it was also not fully human. The slightest reflection would have suggested that non-human or semi-human blobs of tissue do not magically turn into human beings.

I objected to *Roe* v. *Wade* the moment it was decided, not because of any doubts about abortion, but because the decision was a radical deformation of the Constitution. The Constitution has nothing to say about abortion, leaving it, like most subjects, to the judgment and moral sense of the American people and their elected representatives. *Roe* and the decisions reaffirming it are equal in their audacity and abuse of judicial office to *Dred Scott* v. *Sandford*. Just as *Dred Scott* forced a southern pro-slavery position on the nation, *Roe* is nothing more than the Supreme Court's imposition on us of the morality of our cultural elites.

Qualms about abortion began to arise when I first read about fetal pain. There is no doubt that, after its nervous system has developed to a degree, the fetus being dismembered or poisoned in the womb feels excruciating pain. For that reason, many people would confine abortion to the early stages of pregnancy but have no objection to it then. There are, on the other hand, people who oppose abortion at any stage and those who regard it as a right at any stage up to the moment of birth. I will discuss here the question of abortion at any stage from conception to birth.

In thinking about abortion, it is necessary to address two questions. Is abortion always the killing of a human being? If it is, is that killing done simply for convenience? I think there can be no doubt that the answer to the first question is yes; and the answer to the second is almost always. For many people, these answers will be dispositive, but for others, they will not. It will be necessary, therefore, to discuss some of the justifications given by pro-abortion thinkers who accept those answers but do not regard them as decisive.

In discussing abortion I will not address instances where most people, however they might ultimately decide the issue, would feel genuine moral anguish; cases, for example, where it is known that the child will be born with severe deformities. My purpose is not to solve all moral issues but simply to address the major ones. Abortions in cases of deformity, etc., are a very small fraction of the total and, because they introduce special factors, do not cast light on the direction of our culture as do abortions of healthy pre-borns performed for convenience.

The question of whether abortion is the termination of a human life is a relatively simple one. It has been described as a question requiring no more than a knowledge of high school biology. There may be doubt that high school biology courses are clear on the subject these days, but consider what we know. The male sperm and the female egg each contains twenty-three chromosomes. Upon fertilization, a single cell results containing forty-six chromosomes, which is what all humans have, including, of course, the mother and the father. But the new organism's forty-six chromosomes are in a different combination from those of either parent; the new organism is unique. It is not an organ of the mother's body but a different individual. This cell produces specifically human proteins and enzymes from the beginning. Its chromosomes will heavily influence its destiny until the day of its death, whether that death is at the age of ninety or one month after conception.

The cell will multiply and develop, in accordance with its individual chromosomes, and, when it enters the world, will be recognizably a human baby. From single-cell fertilized egg to baby to teenager to adult to old age to death is a single process of one individual, not a series of different individuals replacing each other. It is impossible to draw a line anywhere after the moment of fertilization and say that before this point the creature is not human but after this point it is. It has all the attributes of a human from the beginning, and those attributes were in the forty-six chromosomes with which it began. Francis Crick, the Nobel laureate and biophysicist, is quoted as having estimated that "the amount of information contained in the chromosomes of a single fertilized human egg is equivalent to about a thousand printed volumes of books, each as large as a volume of the *Encyclopaedia Britannica*."[1] Such a creature is not a blob of tissue or, as the *Roe* opinion so infelicitously put it, a "potential life." As someone has said, it is a life with potential.

It is impossible to say that the killing of the organism at any moment after it originated is not the killing of a human being. Yet there are those who say just that by redefining what a human being is. Redefining what it means to be a human being will prove dangerous in contexts other than abortion. One of the more primitive arguments put forward is that in the embryonic stage, which lasts about two months after conception, the creature does not look human. One man said to me: "Have you ever seen an embryo? It looks like a guppy." A writer whose work I greatly respect refers to "the patently inhuman fetus of four weeks." A cartoonist made fun of a well-known anti-abortion doctor by showing him pointing to the microscopic dot that is the zygote and saying, "We'll call him Timmy." It is difficult to know what the appearance of Timmy (or Theresa) has to do with the humanity of the fetus. I suspect that appearance is made an issue because the more recognizably a baby the fetus becomes, the more our emotions reject the idea of destroying it. But those are uninstructed emotions, not emotions based on a recognition of what the fetus is from the beginning.

Other common arguments are that the embryo or fetus is not fully sentient, or that it cannot live outside the mother's womb, or that the fetus is not fully a person unless it is valued by its mother. These seem utterly insubstantial arguments. A newborn is not fully sentient, nor is a person in an advanced stage of Alzheimer's disease. There are people who would allow the killing of the newborn and the senile, but I doubt that is a view with general acceptance. At least not yet. We will see that our culture may be on the road to accepting such killings. Equally irrelevant to the discussion is the fact that the fetus cannot survive outside the womb. Neither can a baby survive without the nurture of others, usually the parents. Why dependency, which lasts for years after birth, should justify terminating life is unexplainable. No more apparent is the logic of the statement that a fetus is a person only if the mother values its life. That is a tautology: an abortion is justified if the mother wants an abortion.

My wife dealt with a hypothetical in a way that to me seems decisively to rebut all of these abortion justifications. In discussing abortion, James Q. Wilson wrote: "The moral debate over abortion centers on the point in the development of the fertilized ovum when it has acquired those characteristics that entitle it to moral respect."[2] He did not, apparently, think the cell resulting from conception was so entitled. Wilson used an example of when moral respect persists in difficult circumstances: "An elderly man who has been a devoted husband and father but who now lies comatose in a vegetative state barely seems to be alive, . . . yet we experience great moral anguish in deciding whether to withdraw his life support."[3] My wife was moved to observe: "But suppose the doctor told us that in eight months the man would recover, be fully human, and live a normal life as a unique individual. Is it even conceivable that we would remove his life-support system on the ground that his existence, like that of the fetus, is highly inconvenient to us and that he does not look human at the moment? There would be no moral anguish but instead a certainty that such an act would be a grave moral wrong."[4]

It is certainly more likely that a woman or a man would refuse to countenance an abortion if a sonogram showed a recognizable human being than if only a tiny, guppylike being appeared. But that is an instinctive reaction and instinctive reactions are not always the best guide to moral choice. Intellect must play a role as well. What if biology convinces us that the guppylike creature or the microscopic fertilized egg has exactly the same future, the same capacity to live a full human life, as does the fetus at three months or at seven months or the infant at birth? "It is difficult to see that the decision in the imagined case of the comatose elderly man who in time will recover is different from the abortion deci-sion."[5] The elderly man in this condition may not look human (if necessary, we could add other details to his appearance to make that even clearer). He is not sentient, and could not live without artificial life support. If we alter the hypothetical so that he has not been a devoted husband and father but rather a philanderer who refused to support his children, I don't think our answer changes. Killing him would still be a moral wrong. The embryo or fetus, like the comatose man in this hypothetical, will soon be recogniz-able to the eye as a human being, will be fully sentient, and will be able to live outside the womb. In both cases, it is only a matter of time. The difference is that the death of the elderly man would deprive him of a few years of life while the aborted embryo or fetus loses an entire lifetime.

The issue is not, I think, one of appearance, sentience, or any-thing other than the prospective life that is denied the individual by abortion. There used to be a question put: If you could obtain a hundred million dollars by pressing a button that would kill an elderly Chinese mandarin whom you had never seen, and if nobody would know what you had done, would you press the button? That seems to me the same issue as the abortion decision, except that the unborn child has a great deal longer to live, if you don't press that particular button. Most of us, I suspect, would like to think we would not kill the mandarin. The characteristics of appearance, sentience, ability to live without assistance, and being valued by others cannot be the characteristics that entitle you to sufficient moral respect to be allowed to go on living. What char-acteristic does, then? It must lie in the fact that you are alive with the prospect of years of life ahead. That characteristic the unborn child has.

That seems to me an adequate ground on which to reject Professor Peter Singer's argument that supports not only abortion but infanticide.[6] He writes that it is doubtful that a fetus becomes conscious until well after the time most abortions are performed, and even if he or she is conscious, that would not put the fetus at a level of awareness comparable to that of "a dog, let alone a chimpanzee. If on the other hand it is self-awareness, rather than mere consciousness, that grounds a right to life, that does not arise in a human being until some time after birth."

Aware that this line leaves out of account the potential of the child for a full human life, he responds that "in a world that is already over-populated, and in which the regulation of fertility is universally accepted, the argument that we should bring all potential people into existence is not persuasive." That is disingenuous. If overpopulation were a fact, that would hardly justify killing humans. If overpopulation were taken to be a justification, it would allow the killing of any helpless population, preferably without the infliction of pain.

The regulation of fertility through most methods of contraception does not raise the same moral issue as abortion, because they do not permit the joining of the sperm and the egg. Until the sperm and the egg unite, there is no human being. Singer goes on to make the unsubstantiated claim that "just as the human being develops gradually in a physical sense, so too does its moral significance gradually increase." That contention is closely allied to the physical appearance argument and is subject to the same rebuttal. One wonders at measuring moral significance by physique. If a person gradually degenerated physically, would his moral significance gradually decline?

Many who favor the abortion right understand that humans are being killed. Certainly the doctors who perform and nurses who assist at abortions know that. So do non-professionals. Otherwise abortion would not be smothered in euphemisms. Thus, we hear the language of "choice," "reproductive rights," and "medical procedures." Those are oddly inadequate terms to describe the right to end the life of a human being. It has been remarked that "pro-choice" is an odd term since the individual whose life is at stake has no choice in the matter. These are ways of talking around the point that hide the truth from others and, perhaps, from one's self. President Clinton speaks of keeping abortion "safe, legal, and rare." Why rare, if it is merely a choice, a medical procedure without moral problems?

That there are severe moral problems is becoming clear even to many who favor abortion. That is probably why, as Candace C. Crandall observes, in the last half of 1995 "the morale of the pro-choice side of the abortion stalemate has visibly collapsed."[7] The reason: "Proponents of abortion rights overcame Americans' qualms about the procedure with a long series of claims about the benefits of unrestricted abortion on demand. Without exception, those claims have proven false." The pro-abortion side claimed that *Roe* v. *Wade* rescued women from death during unsafe, back-alley abortions, but it was the availability of antibiotics beginning in the 1940s and improved medical techniques that made abortion safe well before *Roe*. It was argued that abortion on demand would guarantee that every child was a wanted child, would keep children from being born into poverty, reduce illegitimacy rates, and help end child abuse. Child poverty rates, illegitimacy rates, and child abuse have all soared. We heard that abortion should be a decision between a woman and her doctor. The idea of a woman and her personal physician deliberating about the choice is a fantasy: women are going to specialized abortion clinics that offer little support or counseling. (Crandall does not address the point, but it is difficult to see that bringing a doctor in for consultation would change the nature of the decision about taking human life.) She does note, however, that many women use abortion for birth control.

Crandall says she sympathizes with abortion-rights advocates. But on her own showing, it is difficult to see why. No anti-abortion advocate could make it clearer that human lives are being destroyed at the rate of 1.5 million a year for convenience.

The author Naomi Wolf, who favors the right to abort, has challenged the feminists whose rhetoric seeks to disguise the truth that a human being is killed by abortion.[8] She asks for "an abortion-rights movement willing publicly to mourn the evil—necessary evil though it may be—that is abortion." But she asks a question and gives an answer about her support for abortion rights that is troublesome: "But how, one might ask, can I square a recognition of the humanity of the fetus, and the moral gravity of destroying it, with a pro-choice position? The answer can only be found in the context of a paradigm abandoned by the left and misused by the right: the paradigm of sin and redemption." That seems an odd paradigm for this problem. It is one thing to have sinned, atoned, and sought redemption. It seems quite another to justify planning to sin on the ground that you also plan to seek redemption afterward. That justification seems even stranger for repeat abortions, which she says are at least 43 percent of the total. Sin plus redemption falls short as a resolution of Ms. Wolf's dilemma. If that were an adequate resolution, it would seem to follow, given the humanity of the fetus, that infanticide, the killing of the elderly, indeed any killing for convenience, would be licensed if atonement and redemption were planned in advance.

Nor is it clear why the evil is necessary. It is undeniable that bearing and rearing a child sometimes places a great burden on a woman or a family. That fact does not, however, answer the question of whether the burden justifies destroying a human life. In most other contexts, we would say that such a burden is not sufficient justification. The fact is, in any event, that the burden need not be borne. Putting the child up for adoption is an alternative. The only drawback is that others will know the woman is pregnant. If that is the reason to choose abortion, then the killing really is for convenience.

But it is clear, in any event, that the vast majority of all abortions are for convenience. In those cases, abortion is used as merely one more technique of birth control. A 1987 survey of the reasons given by women for having abortions, made by researchers with the Alan Guttmacher Institute, which is very much pro-abortion, demonstrated this fact. The following table shows the percentage of women who gave the listed reasons.[9]

Reason	Total
Woman is concerned about how having a baby could change her life	76
Woman can't afford baby now	68
Woman has problems with relationship or wants to avoid single parenthood	51
Woman is unready for responsibility	31
Woman doesn't want others to know she has had sex or is pregnant	31
Woman is not mature enough, or is too young to have a child	30
Woman has all the children she wanted, or has all grown-up children	26

Reason	Total
Husband or partner wants woman to have abortion	23
Fetus has possible health problem	13
Woman has health problem	7
Woman's parents want her to have abortion	7
Woman was victim of rape or incest	1
Other	6

The first eight and the eleventh reasons given fall into the category of birth control for convenience. It is clear that the overwhelming number of abortions were for birth control unrelated to the health of the fetus or the woman. Moreover, of those who were concerned about a possible health problem of the fetus, only 8 percent said that a physician had told them that the fetus had a defect or was abnormal. The rest were worried because they had taken medication, drugs, or alcohol before realizing they were pregnant, but did not apparently obtain a medical confirmation of any problem. Of those aborting because of their own health, 53 percent said a doctor had told them their condition would be made worse by being pregnant. Some of the rest cited physical problems, and 11 percent gave a mental or emotional problem as the reason. Only 1 percent cited rape or incest.

"Some 77 percent of women with incomes under 100 percent or between 100 and 149 percent of the poverty level [in 1987, the federally designated poverty level for a nonfarm family of four was $11,200] said they were having an abortion because they could not afford to have a child, compared with 69 percent of those with incomes between 150 and 199 percent and 60 percent of those with incomes at or above 200 percent of the poverty level."[10] The can't-afford category thus included a great many women who, by most reckonings, could afford to have a baby and certainly could have put the baby up for adoption.

This demonstration that abortion is almost always a birth control technique rather than a response to a serious problem with the mother's or the fetus's health must have been a considerable embarrassment to the pro-abortion forces. Perhaps for that reason no survey by them seems to have been reported since. More recent statistics by anti-abortion groups, however, bear out the conclusions to be drawn from the Guttmacher Institute study. The reasons most women give for having an abortion are "social": a baby would affect their educations, jobs, lives, or they felt unable to handle it economically, their partners did not want babies, etc.[11]

Perhaps the most instructive episode demonstrating the brutalization of our culture by abortion was the fight over "partial birth abortions." These abortions are performed late in the pregnancy. The baby is delivered feet first until only the head remains within the mother. The aborting physician inserts scissors into the back of the infant's skull and opens the blades to produce a hole. The child's brains are then vacuumed out, the skull collapses, and the rest of the newly-made corpse is removed. If the head had been allowed to come out of the mother, killing the baby then would be the criminal act of infanticide.

When it was proposed to outlaw this hideous procedure, which obviously causes extreme pain to the baby, the pro-abortion forces in Congress and elsewhere made false statements to fend off the legislation or to justify an anticipated presidential veto. Planned Parenthood and the National Abortion and Reproductive Rights Action League stated that the general anaesthesia given the mother killed the fetus so that there is no such thing as a partial birth abortion. Physicians promptly rebutted the claim. Local anaesthesia, which is most often used in these abortions, has no effect on the baby, and general anaesthesia not only does not kill the baby, it provides little or no pain-killing effect to the baby. The vice president of the Society for Obstetric Anesthesia and Perinatology said that the claim was "crazy" and that "Anesthesia does not kill an infant if you don't kill the mother."[12] Two doctors who perform partial birth abortions stated that the majority of fetuses aborted in this fashion are alive until the end of the procedure.[13]

Other opponents of a ban on partial birth abortions claimed that it was used only when necessary to protect the mother's life. Unfortunately for that argument, the physician who is the best-known practitioner of these abortions stated in 1993 that 80 percent of them are "purely elective," not necessary to save the mother's life or health.[14] Partial birth understates the matter. The baby is outside the mother except for its head, which is kept in the mother only to avoid a charge of infanticide. Full birth is inches away and could easily be accomplished.

President Clinton did, in fact, veto the bill banning partial birth abortions, demanding a vague exception for health that would have amounted to a ratification of almost all such abortions. His veto and the feminist demand for what is, in truth, infanticide underscore the casual brutality born of nihilism that is an ever more prominent feature of our culture.

No amount of discussion, no citation of evidence, can alter the opinions of radical feminists about abortion. One evening I naively remarked in a talk that those who favor the right to abort would likely change their minds if they could be convinced that a human being was being killed. I was startled at the anger that statement provoked in several women present. One of them informed me in no uncertain terms that the issue had nothing to do with the humanity of the fetus but was entirely about the woman's freedom. It is here that radical egalitarianism reinforces radical individualism in supporting the abortion right. Justice Harry Blackmun, who wrote *Roe* and who never offered the slightest constitutional defense of it, simply remarked that the decision was a landmark on women's march to equality. Equality, in this view, means that if men do not bear children, women should not have to either. Abortion is seen as a way for women to escape the idea that biology is destiny, and from the tyranny of the family role.

The attitude towards human life that abortion fosters affects the debate about other matters as well. Tissue from fetuses is used for medical research and in treating certain disorders, such as Parkinson's disease. The difficulty is that fetal tissue is far more valuable if the fetus is alive when the tissue is removed. Partial birth abortions, for example, produce brain tissue from a living child. The next step has been proposed. Science can create human life outside the mother's body. A panel appointed by the National Institutes of Health recommended that human embryos be created in the laboratory so that they may be subjected to experiments that will kill them. One's first thought might be that the panel consisted of technocrats oblivious to moral considerations, but that is not at all the case. Their report and the sources upon which it relies offer a philosophy to justify what they recommend. The embryos they would create may be human but, the panel said, are not entitled to a "personhood" that requires respect. Personhood is determined by our decision to bestow it. That decision determines whether or not the life involved is protectable. According to the report, an embryo that does not have "potential for further development" is not protectable, and the embryos they would create lack such potential.

The argument is breathtaking for, as Father Richard John Neuhaus observes: "Here the reasoning is utterly circular: An embryo is not protectable because it has no potential for further development, and it has no potential for further development because, having determined that it is not protectable, researchers will not permit it to develop further."[15] The separation of humanity from personhood in this fashion is, as already mentioned, an argument used by pro-abortionists: personhood is conferred when the fetus can live outside the womb or if the mother values the life she carries, etc. The philosophical separation of humanity and personhood carries ominous overtones for the very ill, the very old, the senile, and perhaps for others.

A similar progression may be underway with respect to organ transplants. The "dead donor" rule protects those who have agreed to give their organs for transplantation after death from the possibility of being killed by the removal of their organs while they are still alive. An exception to the rule is now proposed, however. The exception would apply only to anencephalics, children born without the thinking part of the brain. These unfortunates will usually live only a few days and when they die their organs are useless as transplants. The American Medical Association's Council on Ethical and Judicial Affairs recommends the removal of anencephalics' organs before they die. The members seek a change in the current law, which forbids removal of organs from living persons. The Council's report assures us: "Because anencephalic neonates lack functioning cerebral hemispheres, they never experience any degree of consciousness. They never have thoughts, feelings, sensations, desires or emotions."[16] The Council takes this position even though it concedes that these babies "may be able to breathe, suck, engage in spontaneous movements of their eyes, arms, and legs, respond to noxious stimuli with crying or avoidance maneuvers, and exhibit facial expressions typical of healthy infants."[17] Charles Krauthammer reports that they can also exhibit complex behaviors such as consolability, conditioning, and irritability, and some even distinguish their mothers from other people. It is, he says, simply unknown and unknowable whether anencephalics possess consciousness.[18]

It is proposed, nonetheless, that anencephalics' organs be taken while they are alive. If that line is crossed, it may not be a long step to removing the organs of normal dying persons while they are still alive. As Krauthammer says, "The heart, say, from a person not-quite-dead might be less deteriorated and thus more useful for transplantation." The Council recognizes this fear, which it deals with under the label "Slippery Slope Concerns": "[M]any fear that individuals who are in a persistent vegetative state, infants with profound neurological injury, and elderly adults with severe dementia would be considered acceptable sources of organs." To reassure us that this particular slope is not all that slippery, the Council offers analogies: "When patients requested permission to reject life-sustaining treatment, opponents argued that granting such permission would open the way to euthanasia." That remark is not terribly comforting, since a society grown accustomed to the removal of life-sustaining treatment is now moving towards assisted suicide, and very probably from there to euthanasia. It will certainly occur to someone that a person seeking assisted suicide or euthanasia could be rendered unconscious and his or her organs "harvested" while the person is alive. The person's wish would be carried out and the organs would be in better condition than if death had occurred before the organ removal. Doctors will make the same case the AMA's Council makes for removing the organs of living anencephalics: there are "important, unmet social needs" and the donor is not really harmed. And a further step is likely to be taken: patients who have not requested euthanasia will be subjected to it nonetheless. There is, after all, a very great unmet social need for organs. This may be dismissed as wholly unrealistic fear-mongering. I do not think it should be.

ASSISTED SUICIDE AND EUTHANASIA

Decisions about life and death in one area influence such decisions in others. Despite assurances that the abortion decisions did not start us down a slippery and very steep slope, that is clearly where we are, and gathering speed. The movement to make assisting suicides legal was made virtually inevitable by the Supreme Court's creation of a right to abortion. The power of the abortion right to influence opinion about assisted suicide, and soon, euthanasia, arises from the fact that by now we have all come to realize, despite the philosophical fog the pro-abortionists throw up, that abortions destroy human lives for the convenience of others. So long as we permitted ourselves to think that the embryo or the fetus was an undifferentiated piece of tissue, abortion had no implications for other takings of life. But now we know better. The result is that a moral line has been crossed and we are on our way to assisted suicide and euthanasia. Modern liberalism's obsession with the autonomy of the individual is taking us to a culture of death. Ironically, the freedom of the individual to choose death has made it far easier for others to choose his death. The autonomy is often theirs, not his.

The attack on the statutes banning assisted suicide derives its emotional power from the picture painted by the partisans of the right-to-die movement: a terminally ill patient with nothing but intense suffering between him and death. The picture is, in large measure, false. There are ways of managing pain in most of the terminally ill. Something other than pure compassion must be in play. There are, moreover, many people who are in constant discomfort, physical or emotional, but who are not terminally ill. Why should they be denied the relief of assisted suicide? There are 31,000 suicides annually in the United States, and only 2 to 4 percent of those are by people who are terminally ill.[19] Many people have an urgent desire to be released from life. Dr. Jack Kevorkian, whose macabre trade of helping people out of this world elicits considerable public approval, does not confine his "practice" to the terminally ill, and a large percentage of his "patients" are not in that condition. It is telling, however, that he presents himself as one who aids the suffering and dying.

It is, in any event, curious that there should be a demand by those not helpless for assistance in committing suicide. The thing is not all that difficult. There is an abundant supply of high buildings and bridges. If the candidate lives where there are none, or shrinks from the pain of an abrupt landing, there is the gas oven in the kitchen, carbon monoxide from the automobile in the garage, an overdose of sleeping pills, and a variety of other painless ways of shuffling off. For many would-be suicides, however, these are apparently not sufficient. They would be if all that were involved was the individual's assertion of his or her personal autonomy. "Yet," as Elizabeth Kristol writes, "the 'right to choose' is precisely what assisted suicide is not about. The unique service offered by professional suicide assistants is actually an escape from the burden of autonomous choice. . . . [T]he ultimate responsibility for taking one's life . . . can be validated by a doctor, an expert we have come to entrust with a wide range of decisions regarding our well-being."[20]

Kristol perhaps understates the role physicians will sometimes play. They may well initiate and urge the idea of suicide or euthanasia. As Judge John Noonan observed in a Ninth Circuit panel opinion subsequently overturned by the *en banc court*: "Physician neutrality and patient autonomy, independent of their physician's advice, are largely myths. Most patients do what their doctors recommend. As an eminent commission concluded, 'Once the physician suggests suicide or euthanasia, some patients will feel that they have few, if any, alternatives but to accept the recommendation.'"[21]

This reality puts assisted suicide in a somewhat more sinister light, as it does euthanasia. Euthanasia, in which the doctor does the actual killing, is only a half step beyond assisted suicide. It is sure to arrive as accepted practice if assisted suicide is accepted. The courts that have found assisted suicide to be a right have not specified the safeguards that must be followed. We can see the difficulties that will attend any effort to provide safeguards by looking at the conditions required by Oregon's Death With Dignity Act, adopted in 1994. The patient must, for example, make three requests for assistance with suicide (the third one witnessed, transcribed, and signed), and two physicians must determine that the patient has six months or less to live. A physician may then prescribe a lethal dose of medication.

This sounds simpler and safer than it will be. Determinations of life expectancy for the terminally ill can be very wrong. When my first wife was diagnosed with cancer, the doctor told me she would live only six months to two years. She lived nine and a half years, and those were good years, for her, for me, for our children, and for her friends. Mistakes of that nature, and some of that magnitude, are certain to be made under any assisted suicide regime.

Mistakes do not express the full pathos, and evil, that will certainly attend assisted suicides. The patient who is a candidate for medical termination of his life will be in a greatly weakened physical condition, probably frightened or in despair, which means that his will and his capacity for independent thought will also be weakened. He will be flat on his back with his relatives and the authority figure of the doctor looking down at him. There can be few better subjects and settings for subtle or not-so-subtle psychological coercion. The patient will know, and probably will be informed, that prolonging his existence, which the physician says will be brief, places an enormous emotional and financial burden on his family. A great many people in this position are likely to accept premature death under coercion. That can hardly be called death with dignity.

Even when the patient requests aid in committing suicide, that will not always be instance of personal autonomy. Herbert Hendin, a professor of psychiatry, says that chronically ill and dependent people who ask help in committing suicide are not always exercising free choice. "The request can be a way of begging for support. . . . A patient requesting assisted suicide is often ambivalent. The request may cloak a cry for reassurance that one is loved and valued despite physical decline. If the family and the doctor don't wish to listen, the patient may become trapped by the request and feel that he or she has no choice."[22] In fact, many hard-pressed or even not-so-hard-pressed families will prefer to be rid of the encumbrance, and the physician will almost always go along with them. What a wonderful way for an elderly, ill person, who has begged for reassurance, to depart this life and those he or she had hoped were loved ones.

Assisted suicide will certainly lead to euthanasia. "It has been reported that roughly one quarter of assisted suicides fail," writes Doctor Edmund D. Pellegrino. That would spell disaster for any assisted suicide program. "For this law to be effective requires the next step, i.e., authorization of the physician 'to administer the *coup de grace* if necessary.' However, this is the very step the proponents of the law said would never come."[23]

Quite aside from the practical necessity of euthanasia to complete botched suicides, public acceptance of assisted suicide will certainly lead to acceptance of the morally indistinguishable practice of euthanasia. Then we will really be racing down a slippery slope. Because proponents of euthanasia routinely point to the experience of the Netherlands to demonstrate that the practice is humane and not subject to abuse, I offer the contrary views of those who have studied it.

Author Michael Fumento cites the Netherlands' experience to oppose euthanasia, to show what it, probably inevitably, becomes.[24] Until fairly recently, the Dutch law, like Oregon's, forbade any medical killing unless a dying patient requested it. That has changed. The evolution was accomplished by Dutch courts and ratified by the legislature in 1995. In 1973, a doctor killed her terminally ill mother, was convicted, but given only a suspended sentence of one week in jail. The next step was to dispense with convictions and absolve doctors who killed patients with terminal illnesses. Then the Dutch High Court held that killing was permissible if the patient's disability, although not fatal, was incurable. Thus, a doctor who killed a young girl with multiple sclerosis went free.

Next, the requirement that the patient request euthanasia was dropped. Doctors killed babies born with diseases such as spina bifida that were disabling but not fatal, as well as patients in persistive vegetative states. By 1990, about 11,800 deaths (9 percent of all deaths) were inflicted by doctors, about half of them without the patient's consent. Some critics think that a socialized health care system lends itself to rationing resources by killing the sick.

The Dutch experience has also been studied by Carlos F. Gomez, a physician at the University of Virginia School of Medicine.[25] He argues that what began as an exercise in patient autonomy has become something altogether different, that the Dutch experience shows that the practice cannot be regulated, and that if the practice is transplanted to the United States, our experience will be no better and perhaps a good deal worse.

Though the public theory is patient empowerment, the private practice has come to encompass a range of activities and of patients that the original proponents said would clearly be beyond acceptable limits. Gomez found, for example, that a 2-day-old child with Down's syndrome and duodenal atresia was killed with the tacit consent of his parents. A 70-year-old man who had had a stroke was killed without being able to consent (or dissent) because the doctor thought no one would want to live that way, although the patient was only five days into his potential recovery. Euthanasia now extends to incompetent and unconsenting patients. In a substantial number of cases, euthanasia is a unilateral decision by the physician.

Gomez calculates that euthanasia accounts for about 7 percent of all deaths in the Netherlands. If the United States had a similar rate, there would be about 140,000 cases annually. If Fumento's 9 percent figure is correct, the United States number would be 180,000. And if it is correct that half of the Dutch euthanasias are unconsented, applying that proportion here would mean that the number of physician-inflicted unconsented deaths in this country would be between 70,000 and 90,000 annually. In fact, matters might be much worse. The Dutch practice is virtually unregulated despite the guidelines laid down by the courts. The cause of death is often misleadingly reported as something other than euthanasia—cardiac arrest, for example. We will probably never know the number of persons killed by doctors in the Netherlands or the number killed without their consent. The same ignorance will surely prevail if euthanasia comes to the United States.

In fact, Gomez thinks the U.S euthanasia rate would be higher than that in the Netherlands. Given that the rapidly rising cost of health care cannot be sustained at its current rate, it would be dangerous to introduce a license to kill. Those most in danger would be those who now overpopulate the public hospitals and clinics because private institutions will not take care of them—patients with AIDS, minorities, the demented, and those just this side of dementia.

David C. Thomasma also compares the Dutch experience and the likely American experience of euthanasia.[26] He points out that terminal care in the Netherlands is part of a comprehensive national health plan so that the terminally ill need not worry that their care will bankrupt their relatives. That is not so in the United States, where the expense of caring for the terminally ill or the merely aged falls in large measure on the family. The Dutch tend to die at home, while Americans tend to die in hospitals or nursing homes. Thus, in the Dutch case there are no financial or institutional urgencies, while in the American situation there are. These, and perhaps other factors, would press towards euthanasia more urgently in the United States than in the Netherlands.

Thomasma does not rule out the relevance of the Nazi experience. The comparison is extravagant, but there are some similarities in the progression. Hitler signed into law permission for designated physicians to kill patients judged "incurably sick by medical examination." This was billed as merciful. But the practice soon focussed on the retarded and mentally ill, then moved on to include the elimination of Jews, gypsies, and socialists. In the United States, while we will never adopt genocide, we are already discussing euthanizing the demented elderly. There is, moreover, a coming crisis in health care created by an increasingly elderly population. Persons over 85 years of age will increase fivefold in the next fifty years, from 3 million to 15 million. There will be fewer of middle age to bear the heavy costs. "The phenomenon of the elderly (seventy to eighty-five years of age) caring for the 'old old' (those over eighty-five) has already begun."[27]

The proponents of euthanasia and assisted suicide offer a few case histories to show how free the choice is and how compassionate is the process. We have already seen that the claim of free choice is given the lie by the frequency in the Netherlands of unconsented euthanasia. There is no reason to think such killings will be less frequent here. But even where consent is in some sense given, the claim of autonomy is dubious. Hendin says that even the selected model cases proffered by proponents show the discrepancy between theory and practice.[28] He watched a 1994 film shown on Dutch television in which a patient, Cees van Wendel, who had amyotrophic lateral sclerosis (Lou Gehrig's disease), was put to death. He expressed a wish for euthanasia after his disease was diagnosed. Severe muscular weakness confined him to a wheelchair and his speech was barely audible. When this segment was shown on *Prime Time Live*, Sam Donaldson called it "a story of courage and love." Hendin says it is that "[o]nly for the most gullible viewer." The doctor is the primary figure. "The patient is nearly invisible." In the doctor's two house calls, it becomes apparent that Cees's wife, Antoinette, wants her husband to die.

The wife appears repelled by her husband's illness, never touches him during their conversation, and never permits Cees to answer any question the doctor asks. She "translates" for him, although Cees is intelligible, able to communicate verbally although slowly, and able to type out messages on his computer. The doctor asks him if he wants euthanasia, but his wife replies. When Cees begins to cry, the doctor moves sympathetically towards him to touch his arm, but his wife tells the doctor to move away and says it is better to let him cry alone. During his weeping she continues to talk to the doctor. The doctor at no time asks to speak to Cees alone; neither does he ask if anything would make it easier for him to communicate or if additional help in his care would make him want to live. Cees keeps putting off the date of the euthanasia, and his wife becomes impatient. Finally, he is given the lethal injection.

Was this the affirmation of the autonomy of the patient that euthanasia supporters insist is their object? "From the beginning, the loneliness and isolation of the husband haunts the film. Only because he is treated from the start as an object does his death seem inevitable."[29] If this was selected as a model case, it must be true that many such deaths at the hands of doctors are even less stirring examples of patient autonomy.

The systematic killing of unborn children in huge numbers is part of a general disregard for human life that has been growing for some time. Abortion by itself did not cause that disregard, but it certainly deepens and legitimates the nihilism that is spreading in our culture and finds killing for convenience acceptable. We are crossing lines, at first slowly and now with rapidity: killing unborn children for convenience; removing tissue from live fetuses; contemplating creating embryos for destruction in research; considering taking organs from living anencephalic babies; experimenting with assisted suicide; and contemplating euthanasia. Abortion has coarsened us. If it is permissible to kill the unborn human for convenience, it is surely permissible to kill those thought to be soon to die for the same reason. And it is inevitable that many who are not in danger of imminent death will be killed to relieve their families of burdens. Convenience is becoming the theme of our culture. Humans tend to be inconvenient at both ends of their lives.

11

The Politics of Sex

RADICAL FEMINISM'S ASSAULT ON AMERICAN CULTURE

Isaac Newton's *Principia Mathematica* is a "rape manual" because "science is a male rape of female nature"; Beethoven's Ninth Symphony expresses the "throttling murderous rage of a rapist incapable of attaining release."[1] These and other ludicrous pronouncements may incline sensible people to dismiss today's feminism as a mildly amusing but utterly inconsequential fit of hysterics. That would be a mistake.

Radical feminism is the most destructive and fanatical movement to come down to us from the Sixties. This is a revolutionary, not a reformist, movement, and it is meeting with considerable success. Totalitarian in spirit, it is deeply antagonistic to traditional Western culture and proposes the complete restructuring of society, morality, and human nature. Radical feminism is today's female counterpart of Sixties radicalism. The feminist program is in its main features the same as that of the disastrous *Port Huron Statement*,[2] modified to accommodate the belief that the oppressors, the source of all evil, are men, the "patriarchy" rather than the "Establishment." All else remains the same. "Feminism rode into our cultural life on the coattails of the New Left but by now it certainly deserves its own place in the halls of intellectual barbarisms."[3]

America has seen women's movements before, reform movements seeking for women the political and cultural privileges held by men. They represented what best-selling author and professor of philosophy Christina Hoff Sommers calls "equity feminism" to distinguish them from "gender feminism," the radical variety. She identifies herself as an equity feminist.[4] It would be better, I think, to drop the word "feminism" altogether since the movement no longer has a constructive role to play; its work is done. There are no artificial barriers left to women's achievement. That fact does not mollify the radicals in the slightest. Revolutions, it is commonly observed, often break out not when circumstances are next to intolerable but when conditions begin rapidly to improve. There are now more female than male students in universities, and women are entering business, the professions, and the academy in large numbers. Yet this seems only to fuel the rage of the feminists.

Indeed, Midge Decter thinks improvement is precisely the problem. She asks "why there should have been an explosion of angry demand on the part of women who as a group were the freest, healthiest, wealthiest, longest-lived, and most comfortably situated people the world had yet laid eyes on."[5] She answers that "It is a freedom that frightens her [today's woman] and disorients her and burdens her terribly. . . . The appeal to her of the women's movement is that in her fear and disorientation, the movement offers her the momentary escape contained in the idea that she is not free at all; that she is, on the contrary, the victim of an age-old conspiracy that everything troubling to her has been imposed on her by others." Decter has a profound point. A woman who formerly had a constricted range of choices "must now decide everything essential to her." Whether to be serious about a career, whether to marry, whether to divorce, whether to bear children. Everything is in her hands "to a degree possibly unprecedented in the history of mankind, a degree experienced by her as bordering on the intolerable." The responsibility is too much, the choices too many.

The radical feminist movement not only explains that any dissatisfaction she may experience is the fault of others, namely men, but also comforts her with a sense of solidarity and common purpose in the way that some men find the battalion a welcome relief from the freedom of civilian life. There is probably more to it than that, however. Radical feminism is not merely a way of discovering that a woman is not free. It is also a cause that creates an orientation and a meaning in her life that unstructured freedom destroys. Radical feminism is thus similar to causes such as the identity politics of the racial and ethnic programs on campuses.

FEMINISMS PAST AND PRESENT

Some of today's feminist dissatisfaction is due to the lack of adequate recognition of the immense contribution women have made to Western culture. That is changing, but, oddly enough, it is the feminists who continue to denigrate the role women played in the past.

There was a time, of course, when feminism had real tasks to accomplish, real inequities to overcome. Feminism achieved major victories in the last century and the first part of this one. Though they take the credit, feminists, radical or otherwise, actually had little to do with the progress of women in the latter half of this century. The trends that would of themselves produce today's results were in place at least by the early 1960s. Once such things as the right to vote and the right of wives to hold property in their own names had been won, the difference in the opportunities open to women has been largely due to technology. I am old enough to remember my grandmother washing work clothes on a scrub board, mashing potatoes by hand, and emptying the water tray from the bottom of the ice box. There was simply no possibility that she could have had both a family and a career. Were she young today, she would find that shopping, food preparation, laundering and much else have been made dramatically easier so that she could, if she wished, become a lawyer or a doctor or virtually anything that appealed to her.

Many people suppose that feminism today is a continuation of the reform movement of the past. They occasionally notice a ranting Bella Abzug or an icy Gloria Steinem but imagine them to be merely the froth of extremism on an otherwise sensible movement. That is not the case; the extremists *are* the movement. What the moderate academic feminists Daphne Patai and Noretta

Koertge write about radical feminism in the universities is true of the movement as a whole. Today's radical feminism is

> not merely about equal rights for women. . . . Feminism aspires to be much more than this. It bids to be a totalizing scheme resting on a grand theory, one that is as all-inclusive as Marxism, as assured of its ability to unmask hidden meanings as Freudian psychology, and as fervent in its condemnation of apostates as evangelical fundamentalism. Feminist theory provides a doctrine of original sin: The world's evils originate in male supremacy.[6]

Carol Iannone was drawn into feminism in graduate school in the mid-Seventies. "I enjoyed, reveled in the utterly systematic property feminism takes on when used as a tool of analysis, especially when to the exclusion of all others. Like Marxism, feminism can explain everything from advertising to religion by following its single thread, the oppression of women."[7]

Feminists call their grand theory the "gender perspective." "Gender" is a code word in the feminist lexicon. The enormous importance the radicals place on that term became apparent during the preparation for and conduct of the United Nations' Fourth World Conference on Women in Beijing in September, 1995. (The Beijing conference will be mentioned frequently because it demonstrated most of feminism's least attractive features and its worldwide aspirations.) The object was to debate and adopt a set of proposals relating to women (the Platform for Action), which the various nations would, presumably, be under a moral duty to implement. Each nation sent an official delegation, and many nongovernmental organizations (NGOs), accredited by the United Nations to lobby the delegates, were present. The Beijing conference revealed the political and cultural agenda of the movement as a whole. At a preparatory session in New York, Bella Abzug, the head of a major NGO, denounced "retrogressive" developments:

> The current attempt by several Member States to expunge the word "gender" from the Platform for Action and to replace it with the word "sex" is an insulting and demeaning attempt to reverse the gains made by women, to intimidate us and to block further progress.

We will not be forced back into the "biology is destiny" concept that seeks to define, confine and reduce women and girls to their physical sexual characteristics.[8]

This heated oratory may seem puzzling—referring to men and women as sexes would not seem to "reduce" either to their "physical sexual characteristics." What seemed to be nitpicking, however, is part of a larger feminist strategy. In feminist jargon, "sex" is merely biological while "gender" refers to roles and is claimed to be "socially constructed," which means that everything about men and women, other than their reproductive organs, can be altered by changes in the social and cultural environment. One of the major implications of this view is that human sexuality has no natural form but is culturally conditioned. Radical feminists concede that there are two sexes, but they usually claim there are five genders. Though the list varies somewhat, a common classification is men, women, lesbians, gays, and bisexuals. Thus, heterosexuality, being socially constructed, is no more "natural" or desirable than homosexuality. It is not surprising, then, that one of the most active groups preparing for Beijing was the Lesbian Caucus.

Changes in the social and cultural environment to make the roles of men and women identical are what the feminists intend. This explains the Platform's incessant harping on "gender." While I am not sure of the final count, at one point there were 216 references to it. Unfortunately, many people who would dislike the radical feminists' project assume that "gender" and "sex" have the same meaning. They do not. Their attempt at Beijing was to incorporate the "gender perspective" into an internationally accepted document that would impose at least moral obligations on the governments of the world.

The gender perspective of radical feminism is easy to ridicule but it must be taken seriously. It attacks not only men but the institution of the family, it is hostile to traditional religion, it demands quotas in every field for women, and it engages in serious misrepresentations of facts. Worst of all, it inflicts great damage on persons and essential institutions in a reckless attempt to remake human beings and create a world that can never exist. As we will see, among the institutions being severely damaged by radical feminism are the American educational system and the American military.

THE INTELLECTUAL COLLAPSE OF
RADICAL FEMINISM

Perhaps the first thing to point out, however, is that radical feminism in its largest aspirations is doomed to failure. That makes the harms it inflicts on people and institutions in pursuit of its unattainable ends all the more inexcusable. Radical feminism shares the most destructive idea in the original draft of the *Port Huron Statement*: human nature is infinitely malleable and hence infinitely perfectible. This idea, encrypted in the substitution of "gender" for "sex," is essential to the feminist enterprise of removing all differences between men and women in the roles they play in society. If certain talents are predominantly male and others predominantly female by nature, that enterprise is defeated. Hence, feminists insist that the differing roles of the sexes have nothing to do with biology. What a society's culture can construct, it can deconstruct. Culture is everything and culture can be changed so that all male-female differences, other than in their reproductive organs, will disappear. Women will then appear in every profession and occupation in proportion to their representation in the population at large. The statistical imbalances we see today are merely the results of conditioning and discrimination.

Even if this feminist contention were correct, its totalitarian implications are obvious. Culture is a stubborn opponent. To defeat it requires the coercion of humans. The Soviet Union attempted to create the New Soviet Man with gulags, psychiatric hospitals, and firing squads for seventy years and succeeded only in producing a more corrupt culture. The feminists are having a similarly corrupting effect on our culture with only the weapon of moral intimidation. The contention that underneath their cultural conditioning men and women are identical is absurd to anyone not blinded by ideological fantasy.

Males are almost always larger, stronger, and faster. Females are almost always the primary carers for the young. It must be counted as curious that, starting, as feminists suppose, from a condition of complete equality in all matters, males always became the "oppressors" in every human society. What is true of human societies is almost always true in non-human species, from animals to insects. The feminist case for female physical equality or dominance would have to rest, rather uncomfortably one would think, upon such examples as the black widow spider, the praying mantis, and the hyena pack.

The ineradicable differences between the sexes are not merely physical. "Men are more aggressive than women," James Q. Wilson writes. "Though child-rearing practices may intensify or moderate this difference, the difference will persist and almost surely rests on biological factors. In every known society, men are more likely than women to play roughly, drive recklessly, fight physically, and assault ruthlessly, and these differences appear early in life. . . . As they grow up, men are much more likely than women to cause trouble in school, to be alcoholics or drug addicts, and to commit crimes."[9]

The early kibbutz movement in Israel had the same ideology as today's radical feminists: sexual equality meant sexual identity, and sexual differentiation was inequality. For a brief period, the ideologues attempted to raise children apart from their families and to raise boys and girls in ways that would destroy sex roles. The program was as extreme as the most radical feminist could want. But it collapsed within a very few years. Boys and girls returned to different sex roles. The American sociologist Melford Spiro, who studied the kibbutz, wrote that he had wanted to "observe the influence of culture on human nature or, more accurately, to discover how a new culture produces a new human nature." He "found (against my own intentions) that I was observing the influence of human nature on culture."[10]

It should be unnecessary to say (but with feminists at large one cannot be too careful) that male-female differences do not suggest positions of superiority and inferiority. Occupations such as professional football aside, women compete successfully with men almost everywhere. But the evidence does mean that equality must not be confused with identity: there will continue to be statistical disparities in men's and women's presence in various activities and endeavors. Those disparities will come about through the free choices of men and women about the kinds of work they want to do.

The evidence also means that the enterprise of remaking humans in the preferred feminist image is doomed. (So disheartening is that message that some feminists have actually said that research on sexual differences should not be done.) That does not mean that the feminists' attempt to recreate real humans in their image and likeness has not caused, and will not continue to cause, a great deal of institutional damage and human suffering.

THE POLITICS AND MOOD OF RADICAL FEMINISM

The political complexion of feminism ranges from very liberal to hard left. Some of it, though vicious, is mildly amusing, at least if you are not the target. Feminists will not, for instance, recognize the accomplishments of conservative women. They frequently even refuse to accept them as women. Jeane Kirkpatrick has repeatedly been denied status as a woman because of her political views. One critic wrote that she is "without a uterus," an odd remark about a woman married for thirty-nine years with three children. But sex is now a matter of politics, not biology. Although, as our Ambassador to the United Nations in the Reagan administration, she was the highest-ranking woman in the history of American foreign policy at the time, Kirkpatrick was dismissed by a female professor, in the keynote speech at a conference on the history of women, as "not someone I want to represent feminine accomplishment."[11] One wonders why not. At the United Nations, Ms. Kirkpatrick was a forceful defender of United States interests and ideals. That is probably why not.

During the battle over my confirmation, the Brinkley Sunday morning television show scheduled a discussion of the subject. The program's scheduler called a prominent feminist to ask if she might be available. She said yes, but when she heard nothing further, she called and asked why. Told that the panel was filled, she said, "But you have to have a woman." Brinkley's scheduler replied, "We do. Carla Hills." The feminist shot back, "She's not a woman." Ms. Hills was Secretary of the Department of Housing and Urban Development in the Ford administration and United States Trade Representative in the Reagan administration. In addition to five genders, radical feminists apparently recognize three sexes: men, women, and people who might otherwise have qualified as women but have chosen to be Republicans instead.

In keeping with its progenitor, the New Left of the Sixties, feminism is fiercely anti-capitalist and pro-socialist. That, too, was on display at Beijing. It was not merely that capitalism was routinely denounced in the meetings. The Platform claims that every economic and social ill falls most heavily on women and demands that governments act to alleviate their difficulties. Government control over human activity would then be nearly limitless. The document complains of governments' inadequate control of economic development, which is said especially to harm women. The same claim was made of environmental policies, education, health care, poverty, unemployment, and so on and on. Even war is said to be especially harmful to women. Governments are to rectify all of these asserted special problems of women. The prescription, then, is for an enormous increase in the size of government, its powers, and its centralization.

Given its aspiration to remake humanity, radical feminism could not be anything but totalitarian in spirit. Patai and Koertge note "feminism's explicit assault not only on hierarchies generally but also on the boundaries between the public and private, the emotional and the intellectual."[12] Radical egalitarians necessarily hate hierarchies. They attack institutions that are hierarchical by nature. That is why feminists are, as we will see, anti-bourgeois, anti-capitalist, anti-family, anti-religion, and anti-intellectual.

Erasing the line between the public and private is essential to politicizing the culture. Radical feminism is totalitarian because it denies the individual a private space; every private thought and action is public and, therefore, political. The party or the movement claims the right to control every aspect of life. Radical feminists must regard it as unfortunate that they lack the power and mechanisms of the state to enforce their control over thoughts as well as behavior. As we will see, however, the movement is gradually gaining that coercive power in both private and public institutions.

The reason for insisting that the boundary between the emotional and the intellectual be obliterated is, as it was with the New Left and the European fascists, the realization that intellectual analysis would reveal that radical feminism is false. The convert must not be brought to doubt by logical argument. When the evidence and the logic are both against you, it is necessary to claim that evidence and logic are counterrevolutionary props of the status quo. In the feminist case, facts and rationality, when inconvenient, as they usually are, may be dismissed as "patriarchal constructions of knowledge." (A college student rejected criticisms of her paper on the ground that the criteria applied were "masculinist.") Intellect imposes hierarchies. The way out "is to feel and think everything all at once, without any hierarchical ordering. This mulligan stew approach to life is seen as the Answer To It All."[13] Emotion must be allowed to trump intellect if the whole enterprise is not to be revealed as the hoax it is.

Even the language of the movement mirrors the mood of fascism. The apocalyptic and hate-filled rhetoric of radical feminists expresses their eagerness to inflict harm. A radical magazine, using the acronym for the National Organization for Women (NOW), declared on its cover:

> NOW is the time to take back control of our lives. NOW is the time to make reproductive freedom for wimmin of all classes, cultures, ages and sexual orientations a reality. NOW is not the time to assimilate to bureaucratic puppeteers who want to control, degrade, torture, kill and rape our bodies. NOW is the time to drop a boot heel in the groin of patriarchy. NOW IS THE TIME TO FIGHT BACK. NO GOD, NO MASTER, NO LAWS.[14]

That short paragraph expresses the rage, the nihilism, and the incoherence of feminism today. "Wimmin" (a word ending in "men" must be avoided) have lost control of their lives, though it is not stated when they had control and how they lost it. "Reproductive freedom" means abortion on demand for heterosexuals and artificial insemination for lesbians who want to bear and raise children. Then comes the standard feminist tactic of raising up male straw monsters. Nobody has ever come across the "bureaucratic puppeteers" of this fantasy, for the very good reason that such men simply do not exist. Nor does anybody know, and most of us would prefer not to find out, what it means to drop a boot heel in the groin of the patriarchy. The exclamation "no God" presumably refers to the feminist illusion that religion was invented by men to control women. The message is utterly disconnected from any recognizable reality. The rage is a ritual, an institutionalized version of a child's tantrum.

Christina Hoff Sommers tells of attending a feminist conference at which the speakers, female professors tenured at good universities, were each introduced as "enraged." Nothing in their professional situations would seem to explain why women so fortunately placed are furious, but that is a requirement for membership in the radical sisterhood. It is precisely the disconnection between reality and feminist claims that requires constant rage and hatred to keep the movement viable. And rage must be stoked with falsehoods and irrationality. Try to imagine writing a reasoned statement about bureaucrats who want to torture, kill, and rape women's bodies. It cannot be done. Attempting to construct such a statement would reveal the sentiments for the childish shams they are.

Sometimes feminist rage is served with a large dollop of self-pity. Thus, Anne Wilson Schaef writes of the "Original Sin of Being Born Female": "To be born female in this culture means that you are born 'tainted,' that there is something intrinsically wrong with you that you can never change, that your birthright is one of innate inferiority."[15] This is a literary version of Karen Finley's "performance art." Before an audience, she would strip to the waist, smear her body with chocolate (to represent excrement) and sprouts (sperm), and wail about what men have done to women. The fact that this was supported by grants from the National Endowment for the Arts illustrates the corruption feminism, and political correctness generally, have introduced in our cultural institutions.

Finley's self-pity is common among feminists. It is, indeed, common among humans, but the feminist version is particularly destructive because it comes as part of an ideology and a program. It is inane to attribute victimhood and low self-esteem to all women and it is vicious to preach it to young, impressionable women. That may prevent them from maturing into the strong, self-confident women we see in business, the professions, and the academy. Rage and self-pity are much easier than accomplishment, of course, but they can hardly be satisfactory as a career.

FEMINISM VS. FAMILY AND RELIGION

Many feminists are particularly hostile to the traditional family. Martha Nussbaum, a much-touted classical scholar, writes:

It is in families . . . that the cruelest discrimination against women takes place. . . . [T]he patterns of family life limit their opportunities in many ways: by assigning them to unpaid work with low prestige; by denying them equal opportunities to outside jobs and education; by insisting they do most or all of the housework and child care even when they are also earning wages. Especially troubling are ways that women may suffer from the altruism of marriage itself . . . [A] woman who accepts the traditional tasks of housekeeping and provides support for her husband's work is not likely to be well prepared to look after herself and her family in the event (which is increasingly likely) of a divorce or an accident that leaves her alone.[16]

It would be foolish to deny that there is some truth in Nussbaum's argument, though it is inaccurate to depict the family as denying women equal opportunities to outside work and education. The question is what to do about the problems she describes, particularly those arising from the altruism of marriage. Feminists have cooperated in creating the problem by establishing no-fault divorce, and, in their celebration of female autonomy, can hardly agree to make divorce difficult once more. This is one instance of many where feminists have done damage to women. There is no apparent solution to the problems of divorce and widowhood other than denying women the right to choose a traditional family role. The feminist solution is: All women must work.

That was the position taken by the *ur*-feminist Simone de Beauvoir in her interview with Betty Friedan: "No woman should be authorized to stay at home and raise her children. Society should be totally different. Women should not have that choice, precisely because if there is such a choice, too many women will make that one."[17] Feminism is not about giving women freedom to choose; it is about taking away choices of which feminists disapprove. And one choice they disapprove is participation in a conventional family.

In *The Hite Report on the Family*, Shere Hite calls for a "democratic revolution in the family."[18] That involves, among other things, "[c]hildren brought up with choice about whether to accept their parents' power." The extreme aggression in society is brought about, she says, by a family structure in which "in order to receive love, most children have to humiliate themselves, over and over again, before power." Most social scientists seem to have overlooked this cause of our crime wave. Giving children the choice of whether to accept their parents' power will move the crime wave off the streets and into the family. Hite claims that since the personal and political go together, political democracy cannot flourish without a democratic personal life. The family is a political institution created so that a man could "own" a woman and thus be sure that the children were "his."

Before the patriarchy took over about 3,000 years ago, Hite contends in a burst of bogus history, mother-child societies existed. (Feminists find it useful to fictionalize the past; for example, that pre-historic Europe was a peaceful, egalitarian, matriarchal society that worshipped the goddess, but patriarchy was forced upon these societies by conquering horsemen from the east.) She seems pleased that there are a large number of fatherless families today because, contradicting all the social science evidence, she thinks males raised without fathers will treat women better. The family is not a religious institution and there is no need to "show respect and reverence for a 'religious' tradition which has as its basic principle, at its heart, the political will of men to dominate women[.] This is not religion, this is politics." She continues with the basic feminist fallacy: "There is no such thing as fixed 'human nature.' Rather, it is a psychological structure that is carefully implanted in our minds as we learn the love and power equations of the family—for life. Fortunately the family is a human institution: humans made it and humans can change it."

These attitudes are not merely the personal idiosyncrasies of these writers. At the Beijing conference, for instance, the word "family" was not to appear in the Platform. Instead, the word "household" was used. The significance of this is to be found in the feminist insistence upon use of the word "gender." There being five genders, unions or marriages involving any gender or genders are legitimate. These unions can be called households. The traditional family is then presented as a household, just one form of living arrangement, not superior to any other. Indeed, since feminists view the family as a system of oppression, and since feminism contains a large lesbian component, the marriages of men and women are often seen as morally inferior to unions involving the other three genders.

The hostility towards the traditional family goes hand in hand with the feminists' hostility towards traditional religion. They see religion as a male invention designed to control women. The final version of the Platform for Action ran to 180 pages. Earlier drafts mentioned religion only when warning against "religious extremism." Due to pressure from traditional believers, a paragraph was finally added in Beijing defending freedom of religion and acknowledging that religion can contribute to women's lives. The feminists in Beijing opposed even that. Diane Knippers, president of the Institute on Religion and Democracy, reports that in Beijing feminists built a shrine to the Goddesses out of red ribbons in the shape of a Christmas tree decorated with paper dolls representing the goddesses.[19] Women were invited to make and add their own goddesses. The organization headed by Bella Abzug (a former member of the United States House of Representatives) held daily programs, each one dedicated to a different goddess— Songi, Athena, Tara, Pasowee, Ishtar, Ixmucane, Aditi, and Nashe.

FEMINISM VS. FACTS

There is a great deal of reckless disregard for the truth in radical feminism. Some of it is so blatant that it certainly deserves to be called lying, but some of it appears to reflect the delusions of paranoia. What is worrisome is that so much serious misrepresentation passes into the realm of "truth." One might think that misrepresentations about checkable facts could not survive long in an open society, but they can and do, probably because the press and the academy are very pro-feminist. When a sensational report about the amount of domestic violence against women appears, newspapers, magazines, and even textbooks relay the news, and it quickly becomes established folklore. The attitudes formed as a result are embedded in the culture. Yet the facts, for those who care about them, indicate that these reports are wild exaggerations or flat misrepresentations.

Many people believe and repeat that there are 150,000 female deaths annually from anorexia nervosa because women starve themselves to be attractive to men. The real number turns out to be less than one hundred and the imputed motivation is to be doubted. Domestic violence against pregnant women was, falsely, alleged to be responsible for more birth defects than all other causes. The major news media trumpeted the fact that more women were the subject of domestic violence on Super Bowl Sunday than on any other day of the year. The theory was that the violence of the game incited men to attack their wives. The story was without any foundation. Ken Ringle of the *Washington Post* and one or two others checked and prevented the wife-beating of Super Bowl Sunday from passing into the vast realm of myths that everybody knows to be true.

Journalist Susan Faludi, whose book *Backlash: The Undeclared War Against American Women*[20] was an enormous best-seller, provides an example of the sort of misrepresentations that are largely accepted in our culture. She argued that the culture of the 1980s attempted to take back all the gains women had made in the 1970s. The counterattack, she said, was especially insidious because it was not organized but diffuse, was invisible to almost all people, and operated most effectively by influencing women's minds so that they enforced the backlash on themselves. "Taken as a whole, however, these codes and cajolings, these whispers and threats and myths, move overwhelmingly in one direction: they try to push women back into their 'acceptable' roles—whether as Daddy's girl or fluttery romantic, active nester or passive love object."[21]

How anyone could believe such nonsense is difficult to explain. No one who had any experience with women in the '70s, '80s, or '90s could recognize this picture. The 1980s were a time of rapidly increasing female earnings, participation in the economy and in the academy. If there was an attempt, apparently largely subconscious, to push women back into being Daddy's girl, etc., it was a dismal failure, the most pathetic excuse for a counterattack ever mounted. Perhaps recognizing the implausibility of her thesis, Faludi takes care to say that the conspiracy or counterattack was so subtle that few people were even aware of it. That takes care of all the inconvenient facts that contradict her argument.[22] For some people, there can be no surer evidence of a conspiracy than the fact that no conspiracy is apparent. After all, a really effective conspiracy would be invisible. Feminists' ideology is a fantasy of persecution. It is breathtaking that so dishonest and intellectually vacuous a book as *Backlash* could receive book awards, achieve a mass readership, and receive favorable reviews. That alone tells a very sad story about the politics of sex and the decline of rationality in our culture.

Carolyn Heilbrun, recently retired professor at Columbia and author of an admiring biography of Gloria Steinem, remarks that "In life, as in fiction, women who speak out usually end up punished or dead."[23] Susan Cheever, reviewing a book by Norma McCorvey, the plaintiff "Roe" in *Roe* v. *Wade*, concludes, Faludi-like, with the matter-of-fact assertion that this is a "country where the rights of women and children are still under attack."[24] Cheever must have been disappointed when McCorvey subsequently announced that she had experienced a conversion and is now pro-life, unless, of course, that can be rationalized as a successful attack on McCorvey's rights.

These were certainly the views of most of the Western women in Beijing. The official delegations and most of the non-governmental organizations from the United States, Canada, and the European Union were firmly in the feminist camp. The U.S. delegation was, of course, appointed by the Clinton administration. These Western radicals were opposed by representatives from Islamic countries, from many Catholic countries, and from the Vatican. This constellation of forces prompts the somber thought that radical feminism and the movement of which it is a part, modern liberalism, may be the wave of the future as countries develop economically.

RADICAL FEMINISM VS. EDUCATION

There are now more than 600 undergraduate and several dozen graduate programs in Women's Studies in American colleges and universities. At first sight that might seem odd since so much of feminism is utterly inconsistent with intellectual seriousness. In many universities today, however, intellectual integrity comes in a distant second to political correctness. It is thus only an apparent paradox that institutions which, because of their professed devotion to reason and knowledge, should be feminism's sworn enemies are instead the centers of its power.

There are also, of course, programs in African-American Studies, Hispanic Studies, Gay and Lesbian Studies, and more. Nothing could make clearer the politicization of higher education. These so-called disciplines vie with one another in claiming victimhood, but feminism is by far the strongest and most imperialistic, its influence suffusing the most traditional academic departments and university administrations. Feminists are revising and radicalizing textbooks and curricula in the humanities and the social sciences. They have a major say in faculty recruitment. Feminists increasingly control what is taught in high schools and elementary schools as well. Speech codes and "sensitivity" training severely limit what can be said on campus. The feminists have not only done harm to the intellectual function of universities and schools, they have made campuses extremely unpleasant, especially for white males, who are subject to harassment and demands that they toe the feminist cultural and political line.

The incongruity of feminism as an academic subject is heightened by another development. Though most feminists reject the idea of difference between men and women, more recently a coterie has appeared that insists upon, and celebrates, just such difference. These women claim that rationality, sometimes called "linear thinking," is a coercive tool of the oppressive patriarchy. That may be because they have noticed that evidence and logic are running heavily against the no-difference position. It is necessary, therefore, to identify evidence and logic with the enemy and to exalt intuitive and emotional "women's ways of knowing." These "difference feminists" claim to perceive all of reality through the "sex/gender lens." Judging from their reports of what they see, that must be like peering at the world through the thick glass of a bottle bottom.

Thus, we now have what Patai and Koertge call "TOTAL REJ (total rejection) feminists" whose creed is that "Our culture, including all that we are taught in schools and universities, is so infused with patriarchal thinking that it must be torn up root and branch if genuine change is to occur. Everything must go — even the allegedly universal disciplines of logic, mathematics, and science, and the intellectual values of objectivity, clarity, and precision on which the former depend."[25] If acceptance of logic and standards of evidentiary proof are causing radical feminists to lose arguments, it is clear that they must be discarded if the feminist enterprise is not to be abandoned. But if logic and evidence are jettisoned, it follows that all of the disciplines built up on logic and evidence cannot remain intact. In the place of these oppressive disciplines and values there are to be constructed feminist alternative versions. Nobody seems to have the faintest idea, for example, what a feminist physics would look like, but the total rejectionists are sure one is out there somewhere. It seems to be assumed that a feminist physics, though different, would work as well as the version we now have. Feminist rocket scientists, apparently, could place satellites in orbit without using any of the laws of motion that are now employed.

Needless to say, there is so far not a single axiom or proposition of feminist science that explains or predicts anything or is capable of being tested empirically. When that unhappy fact is brought to a feminist's attention, the reply is often that the patriarchy has had over 3,000 years to build its mathematics, logic, and science whereas women have just started. Thus, the absence of anything but oratory about the wrong-headedness of science as it is must not be viewed as an embarrassment. But there is no shortage of oratory.

Anne Wilson Schaef, for example, denounces what she calls the "White Male System" (WMS) of rationality. Schaef says this system consists of four myths. First, the WMS is the only system that exists. Second, the WMS is innately superior. Third, the WMS knows and understands everything. Fourth, the WMS believes that it is possible to be totally logical, rational, and objective. To be sure, no one with any sense has ever claimed anything like all this. The virtue of the scientific method is precisely that mistakes made are corrected by others and that one investigator's results must be replicable by others in order to be accepted. The people involved do not think they are totally logical, rational, and objective. They know that no human is.

Radical feminist inanities about science, rationality, linear thinking, etc., rest on the allegation that knowledge and modes of reasoning are socially constructed; that is, that there are no objective truths and no single valid method of reasoning. That is a very convenient position for someone making irrational assertions. It would be rather difficult to hold an intelligent, or even an intelligible, discussion with someone holding that position, and it would be impossible to win an argument with her. That, of course, is the point of the exercise.

Take women's studies themselves. On the evidence proffered by Sommers, Patai and Koertge, and others, women's studies programs and courses are abysmal swamps of irrational dogma and hatred. The feminist classroom is an arena for emotions rather than intellect or analysis. Agreement with the ideology is mandatory.

A feminist professor can have enormous influence with immature young women in a forum where there are no intellectual constraints. In such a classroom emotion and opinion rule. The students are expected to recount personal experiences of suffering and oppression. Since feminists insist that the oppression of women by men is universal and unrelenting, a failure to have instances ready at hand for recitation is taken as insufficient understanding of the subject. The students are at an age when, male or female, they are uncertain about life, susceptible to absolutisms, and easy to persuade that they are being treated badly. The result is that young women pour out their emotions in uncontrolled fashion. It is dangerous to inflame young women's capacities for anger and self-pity; severe emotional harm can be done. In some classes, the woman may state in advance that she does not want any of her testimony repeated outside the classroom and the others agree to honor that request. No respectable academic discipline would keep classroom discussions secret.

Feminist bias in scholarship seems indomitable. The sociologist Steven Goldberg states that on numerous occasions Margaret Mead denied in writing that her research disproved the existence of sex differences.[26] Indeed, in reviewing Goldberg's book, *The Inevitability of Patriarchy*, Mead wrote: "It is true, as Professor Goldberg points out, that all the claims so glibly made about societies ruled by women are nonsense. We have no reason to believe that they ever existed. . . . Men have always been the leaders in public affairs and the final authorities at home."[27] But when Goldberg examined introductory sociology books, he found that thirty-six of thirty-eight began their sex-roles chapters with a discussion of Mead's work as demonstrating the environmental nature of male and female behavior. These books misrepresented Mead because "[t]hey, like the discipline whose work they represent, have an ideological commitment to denying that masculine and feminine behaviors and emotions are rooted in male and female physiologies and that all social systems conform to the limits imposed by this reality."

Feminists are transforming mainstream college curricula, they claim, in order to "make knowledge broader," but also to fight against prejudice.[28] "There is," said a professor attending a National Women's Studies Association conference, "a correlation between groups excluded from the curriculum and hate violence aimed at groups." She said most "inclusion" work has focused on blacks, Hispanics, Asian-Americans, and American Indians. But in order to "fight the hatreds and 'isms' in the world, we have to include education about more groups than those four." Other groups whose achievements should be taught, she said, include lesbians, gays, bisexuals, and transsexuals, and issues of social class and disability should be included. "Some argue that there are different cultures of disability, like deaf culture."

Students subjected to propaganda in the name of history will graduate with no clear comprehension of what took place and what was important. Students whose instruction is in fighting "isms" and giving recognition to different sexual groups and cultures of disability are unlikely to graduate with any knowledge that would qualify them for positions other than as sensitivity counselors. As part of their campaign to convert higher education into a propaganda tool, feminists are deforming literary studies by seeking to discover classical allusions to feminism. George Will recorded a few of the choicer items:

> Shakespeare's "Tempest" reflects the imperialistic rape of the Third World. Emily Dickinson's poetic references to peas and flower buds are encoded messages of feminist rage, exulting clitoral masturbation to protest the prison of patriarchal sex roles. Jane Austen's supposed serenity masks boiling fury about male domination, expressed in the nastiness of minor characters who are "really" not minor. In "Wuthering Heights," Emily Bronte, a subtle subversive, has Catherine bitten by a *male* bull-dog. Melville's white whale? Probably a penis. Grab a harpoon.[29]

Radical feminists, then, are contributing more than their share to the dumbing of America. And not just America. Oxford University Press has announced *Ideologies of Desire*, "a startling new series in the cultural study of sex, gender, sexuality and power: redefining the meaning of erotics and politics!" The Press informs us that sex is not a matter of physiology but of culture. "The aim of the series is to illuminate both the play of desire in the workings of ideology and the play of ideological forces in the formation of sexual experiences—and, ultimately, to map more precisely the available avenues of cultural resistance to the contemporary institutional and discursive regulation of sex."

That the object of these courses is to indoctrinate students with an all-inclusive condemnation of American or Western culture is shown by the frequent expansion of the feminist accusation from the victimization of females to a charge of general oppression. One feminist professor argues, "All students suffer when the more volatile issues central to feminist analysis . . . [such as] racism, poverty, incest and rape, battering, lesbianism, and reproductive freedom . . . are dropped from a woman's studies course."[30] It seems odd at first glance, given this wide-ranging list of complaints, that the programs are not changed from women's studies to oppression studies. Perhaps it is not so odd, however. If faculty representing all of the oppressed were brought in, feminists might lose control of the curriculum and the funds. Yet it is in keeping with feminism's revolutionary neo-Marxism that the movement attacks bourgeois culture on many fronts.

As one might suspect from their hostility to men, marriage, and family, radical feminists are very much in favor of lesbianism. This involves more than the demand that lesbianism be accepted by society as just another "lifestyle." They want not only lawful lesbian marriages but "reproductive rights" for lesbians. That means the right to bear children through artificial insemination and the right to adopt one's lesbian partner's child. Since sperm is sold freely in the United States, much more freely than in other nations, there are lesbian couples raising children. It takes little imagination to know how the children will be indoctrinated.

In its effort to transform the curriculum, a National Women's Studies Association conference, attended by about 700 administrators, teachers, and students, gave major consideration to including lesbian issues in feminist programs.[31] The Lesbian Caucus was one of the largest contingents at the conference. Among the presentations were "Teaching Queer: Incorporating Gay and Lesbian Perspectives Into Introductory Courses"; "War on Lesbians"; "Lesbian Perspectives on/in Literature"; "Lesbian Theory in Poetry"; and "Dykeotomy." Not surprisingly, there is in women's studies programs a good deal of proselytizing for lesbianism. At the University of Washington, a women's studies instructor showed the class how to masturbate, stating that "the preferable tool is a tongue, a woman's tongue."[32]

The objectives of radical feminists are not confined to the recruitment of converts through women's studies programs alone. Their aims are imperialistic. The feminist influence has spread to other departments and graduate schools. It is most visible to outsiders in the process of faculty recruitment, where preference is given to women and minorities. A young man I know went to the American Association of Law Schools convention in Washington, the traditional market for those desiring teaching jobs. He entered the hotel and passed a room marked "Women's Hospitality Room." Through the open door he saw young women having Danishes and coffee and chatting amicably with one another. Next he came to the "Minorities Hospitality Room," and observed the same activities. He walked on and discovered that there was no hospitality room he could enter. He and the other white males stood around the lobby until the interviewing began.

The same young man, possessed of splendid records at both Harvard College and Law School, and a clerk to a court of appeals judge and to Justice Anthony Kennedy, the sort of credentials law schools used to hunger for in their teaching applicants, applied for a position at the law school of the University of Texas. He was, however, in competition with a Mexican-American lesbian who had graduated well below the middle of her law school class. She got the job. A memorandum from a member of the appointments committee explained to the faculty that she should be hired because "She does appeal to three constituent groups."[33]

The point is not merely that white males are being subjected to sexual and racial discrimination in higher education, though that is certainly an outrage. The point is also that faculties are lowering their standards in hiring in order to be politically correct. That necessarily lowers the quality of education they offer their students and the standards of scholarly publication. A friend of mine, a law school professor, resigned from his school's appoint-

ments committee because the conversations he had with applicants likely to be hired were inferior in intellectual content to the
conversations he had with his students.

Radical feminist insistence upon seeing slights, harassment, and
male victimization of women everywhere has made campuses,
workplaces, and society less comfortable places. The eagerness of
radical feminists to see insult in every male action, coupled (if one
dare use that word) with the spinelessness of the supposedly
oppressive patriarchy, has led to so much discomfort and loss of
freedom. Some of women's complaints are merely funny, though
they do reveal a mindset: A young woman at the University of
Pennsylvania who wore a short skirt complained of a "mini-rape"
because a young man walked past her and said, "Nice legs."[34] At
the University of Maryland, some female students posted the
names of male students selected at random, young men about
whom they knew nothing, under the heading "Potential Rapists."
The message was that all men are potential rapists, though the
men actually named probably did not find much comfort in that.

Far more serious are the accusations of actual rape when
nothing of the sort occurred. A female student came to a male
student's quarters with her toothbrush, planning to stay the night.
The next morning she was seen having a peaceable breakfast with
the man. Later she charged him with rape and he was briefly held
in jail.[35] Accusations of date rape are flung freely by women who
consented and later changed their minds about what they did. Universities have capitulated by creating rape-prevention and sexual-
harassment workshops that offer virulently anti-male propaganda.
It is little wonder that young men are uncertain about themselves
and their relationship with women and, perhaps for self-protection,
perhaps because they have been brainwashed, tend usually to take
the women's side of issues.

Male faculty also feel the lash of feminist anger. The use of
"insensitive" language in the classroom often results in formal
complaints being filed, followed by a hearing notable for its lack of
the rudiments of due process, and then suspension or a requirement of submitting to sensitivity training. Required sensitivity
training is a humiliating experience, whether it is imposed by a
university or, as is increasingly frequent, by a corporation. (Corporations are heavily into diversity training, apparently in part

because federal regulators pressure them.) Nor is it usually possible for the professor or employee to retain his dignity by refusing to accept such coercion. That would bring dismissal, after which no other employment is likely to be available—other universities or businesses will be reluctant to hire someone found guilty of insensitivity to women. The feminists at the new organization will be alerted and will object to the man's employment. Who would want to hire the possibility, indeed the certainty, of more trouble with feminists?

Sensitivity training is often required even of people who have not displayed "insensitivity." Cornell's training session for resident advisers featured an X-rated homosexual movie. Pictures were taken of the advisers' reactions to detect homophobic squeamishness.[36] Thus, entering freshmen in colleges are increasingly subjected to sessions indoctrinating them in the correct attitudes not only to women but to homosexuals and members of minority groups. The object is thought control. As a reader of *Measure* (a publication of the University Center for Rational Alternatives, an organization dedicated to preserving the traditional virtues of scholarship and teaching in universities) said of compulsory training dictated by the Department of Education: "[It] is not enough for citizens to obey the law, they must be reeducated to love Big Brother."[37]

Often feminist complaints seem to reflect less a feeling of real outrage than a desire to provoke a confrontation and to intimidate. Radical feminists today, like the radical students of the Sixties, have discovered that they have the power to make the Establishment cringe and back down, and so their demands escalate. At Penn State University, a female English professor had to move her class into the arts building because of lack of space elsewhere. Hanging in the classroom were five museum reproductions: Goya's "The Naked Maja," a depiction of the crucifixion, a Madonna and child, the portrait of a youth, and a pastoral scene. Some male students snickered at the nude. Instead of ignoring them, telling them to grow up, or taking the picture down, the professor formally demanded that the administration remove it, thus forcing the school to take an official position. After lengthy negotiations which included considering the suggestion of a "diversity expert" to hang a painting of a nude male, the administration removed the picture. A spokeswoman for the Womyn's Concerns Committee said that "these older paintings served as a type of pornography—*Playboy* wasn't around back then." She added: "I don't think our society is capable of dealing with paintings such as these."[38] Society had dealt comfortably with Goya's masterpiece for well over a century, until a feminist chose to make a major issue of it.

Not the least of the feminists' sins is their mangling of the language. "Womyn" or "wimmin" for "women," just to avoid the hated letters M-E-N, is an atrocity. But it is not much better to go to a restaurant and be informed that your "waitperson" will be with you shortly. So ideologically crazed are some feminist academics that their seminars are now called "ovulars."

So alienating are the messages of the women's studies programs that Professor Sommers writes that she would like to see some of the more extreme institutions (e.g., Wellesley College, Mount Holyoke, Smith, Mills, and the University of Minnesota) put warning labels on the first page of their bulletins:

> We will help your daughter discover the extent to which she has been in complicity with the patriarchy. We will encourage her to reconstruct herself through dialogue with us. She may become enraged and chronically offended. She will very likely reject the religious and moral codes you raised her with. She may well distance herself from family and friends. She may change her appearance, and even her sexual orientation. She may end up hating you (her father) and pitying you (her mother). After she has completed her reeducation with us, you will certainly be out tens of thousands of dollars and very possibly be out one daughter as well.[39]

To that warning label Sommers might have added "You are also likely to have a badly educated daughter." The young women who are lured into women's studies should be spared what they obtain there: total immersion in a false world view coupled to a fourth-rate education. While other students are studying history, mathematics, science, languages, and similarly useful disciplines, those in women's studies programs are working on acquiring belligerent attitudes and misinformation. Instead of preparing students for the world, the programs impose severe handicaps upon them. Robert Nisbet offers the "affecting story" of a young woman who majored at her university in eco-feminism, and graduated with honors. She went to Washington, D.C., a city richly endowed with lobbies for ecology and feminism. Because of her dual degree, she assumed that a well-paying job would be waiting. "But even ecological and feminist lobbies require people who can read, write, count, and in general ratiocinate; she thus became one of the large number of genteel unemployables."[40]

When later in life the products of radical feminist education fail to achieve as they had hoped, they will undoubtedly blame the patriarchal system by which, they have been taught, they and all other women are oppressed. In compensation for providing poor educations, then, the women's studies programs offer their victims a ready-made, all-purpose alibi. They, and we, will be paying the price for years to come.

FEMINISM CONQUERS AMERICA'S ARMED FORCES

What has happened to education at all levels is paralleled by the ongoing feminization of the military. Because of the political strength of the feminist movement, women are assigned jobs close to combat and, in some cases, placed in combat roles. The result is certain to be additional lost lives—of men as well as women—and perhaps lost battles. Feminists advance two arguments for this disastrous policy. One is that putting women in combat is crucial to women's self-esteem and to men's respect for women. That has never been true in the past and it is impossible to see why it should be true now. The other, more effective argument in today's egalitarian culture is that combat roles are important to military advancement. With that observation feminists have framed the terms of the debate as one about fairness and the equality of women.

The question of whether equality in the military is worth the loss of additional lives and the decrease in our armed forces' fighting capability has virtually been ruled out of bounds as sexist. It has been entirely ruled out of bounds within the military. The military is to be used as a means for reforming society and not exclusively as the means of defending our country and our interests around the world.

The inevitable result is that training standards are lowered, and that fact is then ferociously denied. That has apparently already cost one woman her life. Navy Lieutenant Kara Hultgreen, one of the first female fighter pilots, was killed in October of 1994 on an approach landing to a carrier ship off the coast of San Diego. As she approached the landing deck, she over-corrected a mistake and plunged into the ocean. The episode triggered another debate concerning women's roles in the military. Congresswoman Pat Schroeder and columnist Ellen Goodman seized on reports that engine failure caused the Lieutenant's death. Goodman said: "So it was the engine after all. Not the pilot. Lieut. Kara Hultgreen did not die on the altar of political correctness or reverse discrimination."[41] But that is apparently precisely what did happen. Two formal investigations and a confidential Mishap Investigation Report cited "multiple instances of pilot error. The reports faulted Hultgreen's badly overshot landing approach, her excessive overcorrection and then her failure to follow the standard, designated procedures for recovering from a single-engine landing emergency," which resulted in her ejecting directly into the ocean.[42] The press, by and large, refused to investigate, and almost everything reported on the case was untrue. "[W]hile the Navy was saying publicly that Hultgreen was blameless, privately it had reached a different conclusion: Pilot error, not engine failure, was the principal cause of the crash. Political expedience, however, made it unwise to say so. And the real media story . . . was that so few reporters wanted to know."[43]

Lieutenant Hultgreen had failed the carrier landing phase of her training in April. Just after her failure, an admiral announced that he wanted to open combat positions to women, and it needed to be done quickly. Hultgreen took the training again, and passed. The Navy distributed a four-second video to the networks but had a twelve-second version that was passed around among present and former naval aviators, who were said to be appalled by what they saw.

Ironically, Hultgreen herself felt the pressures of militant feminism and gender quotas and wanted no part of it. On behalf of female naval aviators, she had earlier appealed to Rear Admiral Robert Hickey, saying, "Guys like you have to make sure there's only one standard. If people let me slide through on a lower standard, it's my life on the line. I could get killed."[44] Yet Hultgreen was permitted to continue although she had recorded seven crashes in combat conditions during training. That record would have grounded a male pilot.[45]

Unfortunately, those in the best position to testify on this subject, our career officers, would destroy their careers if they spoke objectively, so they are forced into silence or to repeating the feminist line. An official committee on Women's Issues headed by an admiral has recommended that "disagreement with the women-in-combat policy disqualifies officers from positions of leadership."[46]

The extent to which the armed forces have been intimidated by feminists and their allies in Congress is made clear by the case of Lt. Commander Kenneth Carkhuff. On July 26, 1994, Carkhuff's superior officer recommended him for early promotion ahead of his peers because he was an "extraordinary department head," a "superior officer in charge" with "unlimited potential . . . destined for command and beyond."

Six weeks later that same superior revised Carkhuff's fitness report to downgrade him in every category and to rate his "overall performance as unsatisfactory," so that he could not recommend him for promotion or even retention in the Navy. The intervening event that caused this drastic reevaluation was that Carkhuff, in a private conversation with his commanding officer, had said that his religious views made him doubtful about putting women in combat, though those views also required him to lead women into combat if ordered by his superiors. That remark led to the revised report, which criticized him for "His inability to fully employ and impartially judge the female members of his [helicopter] unit." The superior summed matters up quite succinctly: "A bright future has been lost and otherwise superb performance completely overshadowed by this glaring, irreconcilable conflict with Navy policy."[47] Even if you are willing to lead women in combat, your thought that that might not be suitable is sufficient to end your career. The Navy's Separation Board voted to discharge the Lieutenant Commander. The Navy threw away a man of great ability and gained peace with the feminists.

With such threats hanging over their heads, it is not surprising that career officers do not speak out about the performance of women in combat positions. It is not just the Navy that has been cowed. Though it is not discussed publicly, training in the other services has been made less arduous in order to accommodate women, and problems experienced in the field go unreported. David Horowitz offers specifics:[48]

¶ "Gender norming" is now the rule at all three service academies, so that women are measured against other women, rather than against men who outperform them. ¶ The official position at West Point is that there have been no negative effects from the admission of women. But a Heritage Foundation study by Robert Knight draws on the sworn courtroom testimony of a West Point official that women cannot perform nearly as well as men and that the men's training program has, for that reason, been downgraded. For example, men are no longer required to run carrying heavy weapons because women are unable to do that. ¶ William S. Lind, former defense adviser to Gary Hart, testified to the Presidential Commission on the Assignment of Women in the Armed Forces that the Army has not released detailed information on problems with female troops during the battle with the Iraqis. Pregnancies due to sex during the preceding phase, Desert Shield, was the primary reason the non-deployability rate of women was many times higher than that of men when the troops were called to battle in Desert Storm. ¶ Three "top gun" flight commanders had their careers destroyed because they were present at or performed in the Tom Cat Follies, which included a rhyme denigrating Pat Schroeder. President Bush and Vice President Quayle were also lampooned, but only parodying a fiercely feminist congresswoman was considered a grave offense.[49]

In physical fitness tests, very few women could do even one pull-up, so the Air Force Academy gave credit for the amount of time they could hang on the bar. Female cadets averaged almost four times as many visits to the medical clinic as male cadets. At West Point, the female cadets' injury rate in field training was fourteen times that of the men, and 61 percent of women failed the complete physical test, compared to 4.8 percent of men. During Army basic training, women broke down in tears, particularly on the rifle range.[50]

Since Desert Storm's pregnancy problems, it has been reported that Navy ships have had to be recalled from missions because of the pregnancy of female sailors. A male and a female sailor on the aircraft carrier *USS Dwight D. Eisenhower*, both married to others, videotaped themselves having sex in a remote part of the ship. There had been thirty-eight pregnancies since the crew went aboard the *Eisenhower*, fourteen of them after the ship was deployed. The Navy said there was no indication that any of the pregnancies resulted from sex on board the ship.[51] Those who wish to may believe that. Only someone who has never been with troops could not anticipate this result or fail to realize that it will be a major problem forever. The troops in question are very young, at an age when their hormones are, to put it mildly, fiercely insistent.

Effects on morale can be particularly adverse. The presence of women among male troops weakens combat readiness. All-male units in the field experience bonding that enhances unit cohesion and effectiveness. When women are introduced, men stop relating to each other and begin trying to attract the women. Nor can morale be improved when accusations of harassment are always a threat. Male officers leave the office door open or have a third person in the room when dealing with a female subordinate. An accusation of sexual harassment by the woman, even if unproven, would severely damage the man's service career, and both the man and the woman are acutely aware of that fact. They could hardly not be sensitive to the issue when, for example, Representative Pat Schroeder demanded and got sexual harassment training for all personnel in order to rid the Navy of bad attitudes.

The Israelis, Soviets, and Germans, when in desperate need of front-line troops, placed women in combat, but later barred them. Male troops forgot their tactical objectives in order to protect the women from harm or capture, knowing what the enemy would do to female prisoners of war. This made combat units less effective and exposed the men to even greater risks. In the Gulf War a female American pilot was captured, raped, and sodomized by Iraqi troops. She declared that this was just part of combat risk. But can anyone suppose that male pilots will not now divert their efforts to protecting female pilots whenever possible?

Our military seems quite aware of such dangers, but, because of the feminists, it would be politically dangerous to respond as the Israelis did by taking women out of harm's way. Instead, the American solution is to try to stifle the natural reactions of men. The Air Force, for example, established a mock prisoner of war camp to desensitize male recruits so they won't react like men when women prisoners scream under torture.[52] There is a very considerable anomaly here. The military is training men to be more sensitive to women in order to prevent sexual harassment and also training men to be insensitive to women being raped and sodomized or screaming under torture. It is impossible to believe that both efforts can succeed simultaneously.

It is clear that mindless feminist ideology is inflicting enormous damage on the readiness and fighting capability of the armed forces of the United States. Every other career is open to women. There is no reason why access to combat roles, for which they are not suited, has to be open as well. But political intimidation by radical feminists is so powerful that there seems little prospect that the continuing feminization of the U.S. military can be reversed. At least not until some engagements are lost, or won at unacceptably high costs, and women and the men who tried to protect them begin coming back in great numbers in body bags.

*　　*　　*

Perhaps the most vicious aspect of radical feminism is that it necessarily criticizes and demeans women who choose to work primarily as mothers and homemakers. They are made to feel guilty and told that their lives are essentially worthless. But feminists are not concerned with the human suffering they inflict. As Maggie Gallagher put it: "America today is a nation full of ironies. . . . [including a] female elite more fiercely committed to the good name of feminism than to the welfare of women."[53]

After watching human nature undo the culture that had been forced upon the young women of the Israeli kibbutz, the sociologist Melford Spiro reached very sensible conclusions. No social role should be denied anyone on the ground that it is inconsistent with the current system of sex-role differentiation. But to attempt to impose sex-role identity is an insult to basic human dignity. If the political or media influence of a group seeking to impose sex-role identity results in a measure of success, "the ensuing social and psychological dislocations for the larger society can be expected to be as serious as those attendant upon the reverse kind of staight-jacketing. . . . [A]ttempts to convince women that sexual equality . . . is worthwhile only in the 'identity' meaning of equality, and that 'feminine' careers—even if they achieve equality in its 'equiva-lence' meaning—are unseemly pursuits imposed on them by a sexist society, may (if successful) deprive them of important sources of human gratification."[54] If women are persuaded by this ideology but continue to feel powerful countervailing emotions, Spiro notes, that may cause "painful feelings of guilt and depres-sion. . . . That individuals and groups must be identical in order to be equal is surely one of the more pernicious dogmas of our time, and the fact that, ironically enough, it has become a liberal dogma does not make it any the less so."[55]

It should be a source of great pride to bear the next genera-tion and to train that generation's minds and morals. That is cer-tainly a greater accomplishment than churning out tracts raging at men and families. It is fine that women are taking up careers, but the price for that need not be the demoralization of women who do not choose that path.

Gallagher put the point succinctly: "Liberal feminism tri-umphed by telling a lie about nearly all women—and men. The work women do in families may not perhaps, seem great com-pared to oh, inventing a new morality, or discovering the cure to cancer. But it compares quite favorably, in value, meaning, and social productiveness with being a vice-president for public affairs of General Motors, say, or a partner in an advertising firm. And it is necessary that we start saying so."[56]

Saying so can be a problem. Radical feminism has a truly impressive capacity for moral intimidation. It is very difficult for men to counter its progress or point out its untruths and its mani-fold harms. To do so is to be exposed to heated accusations of being hostile to women and their rights, wanting to take away the gains women have made, and wishing to reduce them to subordi-nate positions. Most men, afraid of such allegations, choose cir-cumspection. That is why Kate O'Beirne, Washington editor of

National Review, said, "In the end, our girls are going to have to fight their girls." True, but after that, some males in the academic world, in the military, and in Congress are going to have to summon up the courage to begin to repair the damage feminism has done.

12

The Dilemmas
of Race

October 1995 was a sadly illuminating month.

Just as with the assassination of President Kennedy, everybody can remember where he was when he heard of the O. J. Simpson verdict. On October 3, I was looking out a window on Connecticut Avenue. Four or five black people stood on the sidewalk listening to the radio in a parked cab. A few minutes after one o'clock, the people on the sidewalk suddenly began shouting, leaping in the air, and pumping their fists. The driver honked his horn repeatedly and then got out of his cab to dance in the street. I knew at once that the verdict was in and what it was. Scenes like that happened all over America. Blacks of all levels of education and income were jubilant, even those who thought Simpson guilty.

Not quite three weeks later, on October 16, Louis Farrakhan, head of the Nation of Islam, convened his Million Man March in Washington. Despite Farrakhan's deserved reputation as a racist and anti-Semite, several hundred thousand men came. The event was billed as a day of atonement and reconciliation, but there was racist rhetoric from the platform and racist sentiment in the crowd. Six days later, during a visit to the United Nations, Fidel Castro went to a Harlem church in the evening and was greeted by enthusiastic chants of "Fidel, Fidel." Why? The black people in that church were hardly admirers of communism. It is difficult to avoid concluding that the Simpson verdict was cheered, Farrakhan's summons heeded, and Castro cheered because a great many black people wanted to express hostility to white people.

October jolted white Americans into a shocked and belated awareness that racial tranquillity is not in our immediate future, perhaps, or even probably, not in any foreseeable future. It has been over four decades since the Supreme Court's decision in *Brown* v. *Board of Education* ended governmental discrimination against blacks, over three decades since the 1964 Civil Rights Act outlawed private discrimination in employment and public accommodations, three decades since the Voting Rights Act of 1965 brought blacks to polling places as never before, and over two decades since the inception of affirmative action. Outside the welfare-ravaged inner cities, black economic and social progress has been dramatic.

Yet after all this, we learned that race relations had only grown worse. How could that be? The answers are complex, but, as black scholar Glenn Loury noted, the roots can be traced to the excesses of the 1960s: "We learned too well during the upheavals of that decade how to be America's pre-eminent victims."[1] He cites the series of killings of black children in Atlanta, which the activist Dick Gregory said was the work of a disease control center pursuing a cancer-fighting drug allegedly found in the tips of their sex organs. Jesse Jackson said: "It is open season on black people. . . . These murders can only be understood in the context of affirmative action and Ronald Reagan's conservative politics." There was great disappointment when the killer turned out to be black and was convicted before a black judge and a largely black jury.

In one way, there is no mystery to this. Americans have been intensely conscious of race throughout their history. Race has been central to our politics since Africans were brought to the colonies as slaves in the seventeenth century. Race was a difficult issue in the framing of the Constitution, which, in order to make union possible, awkwardly attempted to accommodate the fact of slavery, without ever using the word. Slavery caused the bloodiest war in our history. And race has been a subject of political and social agitation ever since. It is hardly a matter for surprise that the subject has not disappeared. Nor is it really surprising that blacks are not reconciled to their position in America. The underclass is, for the time being, largely black, and even blacks who have moved into the middle class often remain edgy. Memories of aggressive discrimination and oppression do not fade so quickly. Nor do suspicions that latent hostility is still present and may become overt once more.

But in another way, the intensely unsatisfactory state of race relations is a mystery. The opportunities for blacks to advance in the United States have never been greater. Despite the incessant talk about racism, by white liberals as well as by blacks, racism has never been at a lower ebb. Yet black anger seems at its zenith. Shelby Steele, a professor of English and black intellectual, offers a partial explanation that is remarkably similar to Midge Decter's explanation for the anger of the feminists. In both cases, the problem is the sudden and dramatic widening of choices about life, a new freedom and responsibility that frightens. For women the new choices are available largely because of technology, for blacks because of the success of the civil rights movement. Steele speaks of "race-holding" and defines a "holding" as any self-description that justifies to that person or camouflages his fears, weaknesses, and inadequacies. Race-holding allows a black to retreat into his racial identity as an excuse for not using his talents to the full out of fear that he really cannot compete. "With the decline in racism the margin of black choice has greatly expanded, which is probably why race-holding is so much more visible today than ever before. But anything that prevents us from exploiting our new freedom to the fullest is now as serious a barrier to us as racism once was."[2]

Steele thinks that the black students in his classes perform far below their abilities because they expect to do poorly and fail to recognize the margin of choice open to them. "I think they *choose* to believe in their inferiority, not to fulfill society's prophesy about them, but for the comforts and rationalizations their racial 'inferiority' affords them. They hold their race to evade individual responsibility. Their margin of choice scares them, as it does all people."[3]

Decter and Steele have identified a major part of the problem in each case. But neither of them would deny that there is more to the problems of male-female and black-white relations than the sudden expansion of choice. It is difficult for most whites to realize the intensity and depth of blacks' suspicion of whites. A *New York Times/CBS News* poll of black New Yorkers in 1990 found that 10 percent agreed that AIDS "was deliberately created in a laboratory in order to infect black people." Another 19 percent thought that it "might possibly be true." And 25 percent of blacks agreed that the government "deliberately makes sure that drugs are easily available in poor black neighborhoods," while another 35 percent said that was possibly true. Clarence Page, a black syndicated columnist for the *Chicago Tribune*, said, "There's a lot more talk about conspiracy than there used to be. You could call conspiracy theories about AIDS and drugs fringe ideas, but they seem to have a large following among the black intelligentsia. And it's present at the grass roots too. You find it at all levels." John Singleton, who made *Boyz 'N the Hood* said, "If AIDS was a natural disease, it would have been around 1,000 years ago. I think it was made in order to kill undesirables. That would include homosexuals, intravenous drug users and blacks."[4]

Paranoia is fed by the race hustlers, most visibly men like Farrakhan and Al Sharpton, but also by many others, including some university professors of black studies, who teach resentment and fear. These are persons whose careers would be diminished or ended by progress in racial reconciliation; it is in their interest to preserve and exacerbate racial antagonisms.

An additional factor which suggests we will never know racial peace is that the problem is not peculiarly American or black-white. It is more often the rule than the exception that different ethnic groups living in close proximity display hostility to one another. That is evident from Canada to the former Yugoslavia to Rwanda to Malaysia. There have been few, if any, completely peaceful multiethnic societies, and America is becoming ever more multiethnic. Still, matters are worse than they have to be.

Whites' responsibility for the present state of race relations goes beyond the obvious point that they oppressed blacks for centuries. Whites—and here I mean primarily modern liberals—deserve blame as well for the way they went about ending discrimination and seeking to eliminate discrimination's lingering ill effects. No one doubts the good intentions of modern liberals, at least on this topic, but there is every reason to doubt their intelligence and prudence. Radical egalitarianism leads them to believe that, absent discrimination, equality of results in every area of endeavor would be the natural outcome for different ethnic groups. Their cultural relativism insists that no culture is superior to any other in preparing individuals to succeed in a complex commercial society. The danger of tribalism is always present when ethnic groups share the same territory, but nothing could have been better calculated to intensify tribalism than the rhetoric and prescriptions liberals have advanced. For decades they have told blacks that their problems were caused entirely by racism. It should not be surprising that many blacks came to believe just that. It is human to want to blame your troubles on someone else and, in the case of American blacks, that message rang true because for centuries their troubles *were* caused by someone else. The unacknowledged difficulty was that if racism had utterly evaporated in 1964, most blacks were in no position to compete on equal terms. The years of segregation and discrimination had produced educational, attitudinal, and cultural disadvantages that would take years to overcome.

But liberal rhetoric continued on the line that discrimination was the only problem long after the dangers of that rhetoric had become apparent. The civil rights statutes and reforms were pushed on the implicit and sometimes explicit promise that all would immediately be well once discrimination was outlawed. It did not turn out that way, of course; it could not have, and black hopes were disappointed. For many blacks, indeed, the results of compassionate welfare policies made matters worse than they had been under segregation and discrimination. The predictable result was increased anger at whites, who must be responsible since whites themselves had said that racism was the only problem.

There were two other unhappy consequences. One was that some blacks developed a fatalistic attitude that hampered their progress. Why try if whites made it impossible to succeed? The second was the belief that nothing need be done but demand more laws, more subsidies, more affirmative action. Surely civil rights laws could have been advocated to deal with real discriminations without teaching such simplistic, false, and destructive lessons.

To make matters worse, white anger is rising, too, precisely because of the liberal effort to produce equality of results. Affirmative action, in the sense of preferential policies, is really a euphemism for quotas, and it is a perfect prescription for racial animosity. At the beginning of the civil rights movement's successes in the 1960s, what we now know as affirmative action was unthinkable. The 1964 Civil Rights Act explicitly forbade all forms of discrimination on the basis of race or sex. Even so, it would not have been enacted without the assurances of its backers, most prominently Hubert Humphrey, that there was no possibility of discrimination against white males. Today, that discrimination is everywhere, from schools and universities to employment, promotion, government benefits, and more.

When affirmative action was first mentioned, the policy was conceived as one of outreach. Governments and businesses would reach out to find qualified minority individuals, or individuals who could quickly become qualified, but who might not know of the opportunities available to them. The policy was enforced, however, by bureaucrats who believed that if significant numbers of minorities were not hired as a result of an outreach program, the employer was not trying. The Supreme Court made matters worse by ruling that any employer's test or practice that resulted in racial "imbalance" or had a "disparate impact" on minorities required extensive and often difficult justification. Hiring and promotion by the numbers began. This followed directly from the modern liberal notion that equality of results is natural. Instead of monitoring the good faith efforts made, the bureaucrats demanded results.[5] Goals and timetables were insisted upon. An employer who must reach a goal of a certain percentage of minority employees by a stated time is under a quota requirement. Affirmative action was transformed from an outreach program to a quota program, and the Supreme Court, in direct violation of the anti-discrimination provisions of the 1964 Civil Rights Act, approved.

The civil rights organizations changed direction. During the long judicial and legislative battles for anti-discrimination laws, they insisted over and over again that they wanted no special status for minorities. Now they sought special status and preferential treatment. The switch was surely partly due to the fact that blacks were not advancing as rapidly as these organizations had expected, so that something in addition to non-discrimination seemed required. But there were surely also individual and organizational imperatives. If individuals and organizations had been working full time for anti-discrimination laws for decades and decades and finally achieved those goals, what were they to do? Could the individuals concede that there was nothing more to do and seek other employment? Could the organizations admit that they had no further purpose and disband? Humans rarely act that way. Affirmative action, or preferences, provided a new purpose. The step was the easier to take because, being modern liberals, these folks found equality of results an even more congenial goal than equality of opportunity.

All of this was done mindlessly and without public debate. As happens all too frequently in the United States today, courts and bureaucrats made the important and sensitive decisions about public policy. The public was, at best, reduced to the status of onlookers. Nobody asked whether blacks should be the only group to benefit from affirmative action, how long the preferences would last, or what the effects would be on race relations. What happened in the United States is what has happened around the world where affirmative action has been tried. Thomas Sowell, a conservative black intellectual, made an international study of government-mandated preferences for government-designated groups and found common patterns:

    1. Preferential programs, even when explicitly and repeatedly defined as "temporary," have tended not only to persist but also to expand in scope, either embracing more groups or spreading to wider realms for the same groups, or both. Even preferential programs established with legally mandated cut-off dates, as in India and Pakistan, have continued far past those dates by subsequent extensions.

    2. Within the groups designated by government as recipients of preferential treatment, the benefits have usually gone disproportionately to those members already more fortunate.

    3. Group polarization has tended to increase in the wake of preferential programs, with non-preferred groups reacting adversely, in ways ranging from political backlash to mob violence and civil war.

4. Fraudulent claims of belonging to the designated beneficiary groups have been widespread and have taken many forms in various countries.[6]

The United States is no exception to the international experience. Preferential policies here were put forward as temporary measures, but Lyndon Johnson gave the game away when he announced that in "the next and more profound stage of civil rights" the object would be "not just equality as a right and a theory but equality as a fact and equality as a result."[7] We have been at affirmative action for over two decades now and, as could have been predicted, such equality of result as has been achieved is artificial. Proportional representation in various fields has been reached by diktat, by depriving people of freedom, which is what a policy of racial preference does.

We have expanded the area of tyranny by expanding the number of groups entitled to preferences. We now extend affirmative action to women, Hispanics, Asians, Aleuts, Pacific islanders, and American Indians. People who have suffered no discrimination whatever are entitled to preferences. As Terry Eastland points out, heavy immigration has brought large numbers of Hispanics and Asians who are at once entitled to preferences though they have suffered no wrong at the hands of this society.[8] A wealthy Spanish businessman who has just arrived in this country is entitled to preference in, say, getting a government contract, though a poor Frenchman would be entitled to no advantage whatever. Altogether, 60 percent or more of the population of the United States are entitled to preferential treatment. Only white males are not (unless they happen to be Hispanic) and only white males may be discriminated against.

It is inevitable that once the favoritism game begins, other groups will demand their share of its benefits. Those demands are difficult to resist precisely because there is no respectable rationale for preferential policies. Thus, there is no criterion that can be stated to explain why other groups are not entitled to favoritism. It is necessary, of course, that the group demanding advantages be able to articulate some way in which they have been unfairly treated, but that is not at all difficult. Simple lack of proportionate representation will do.

Here, as elsewhere, the scope of preferences keeps expanding. There are now 160 federal government preferences alone.[9] The number of state and municipal preferential programs is probably countless, and the private sector also practices affirmative action. Universities routinely practice discrimination in admitting students and hiring faculty. I know young lawyers looking for academic positions who suffer the very considerable handicap of being white males. One of them was told by a law school faculty member on the appointments committee that the school was hiring but had only one place for a white male. At another school, the interviewer looked over the young man's resumé and said, "This is very good. You have had two important clerkships, with Bork and then Scalia, and in the Solicitor General's Office you have argued cases in the Supreme Court. You have accomplished a great deal in a short time." He paused and then said thoughtfully, without a trace of irony, "Of course, it's not as good as being black."

Affirmative action is being pressed into areas where it will prove positively dangerous. "The application of the principles of affirmative action to medical education is significant, implying, as it does, that their proponents' ideological commitment makes them willing to risk the graduation of incompetent physicians."[10] The desire to graduate as many minority students as possible, who are often admitted with inadequate qualifications, creates a strong motivation for the administration to lower standards.

Either voluntarily or under pressure from the government, a large majority of major corporations engage in affirmative action. Some make managers' bonuses dependent on the preferential hiring of minorities and women. Paul Craig Roberts and Lawrence M. Stratton list seemingly endless programs of this sort.[11] Mortgage lending criteria must not have an adverse disparate impact on minorities; even small businesses are harassed to achieve proportional representation of women and minorities in their work forces; minority preferences govern the allocation of government contracts, broadcast licenses, and scientific research grants; disciplining of federal government workers must be racially proportional; the U.S. Merit Systems Protection Board measures merit in part by a civil servant's support for affirmative action; accreditation agencies take into account the proportion of minorities on the faculty and in the graduating classes of the schools they oversee.

Group polarization has increased. One has only to look into university dining halls to see the various races and ethnic groups clumped together with their own kind. Racial antagonisms on campuses are vastly worse than they were thirty years ago, and students agree that preferential admissions policies are the cause. Meanwhile, in employment as in academic admissions, people are changing the ethnic backgrounds they claim to ones more likely to bring benefits.

This has led to the systematic denigration of white, heterosexual males. Roberts and Stratton compare the rampant anti-Semitism among the educated classes even in pre-Hitler Germany to the assault in American universities on white males: "Like German anti-Semitism, the demonization of the white male is an *intellectual* movement."[12] And so it is. The most ardent advocates for affirmative action, and the most heated charges against white males are to be found in our universities. Nor is it hard to see why. In order to prefer certain groups it is necessary to harm others. Since the injustice of what is done is obvious, it is, unfortunately, human nature to justify it by imputing grave fault to the people harmed. For radical egalitarians who dislike the traditional culture of the West, moreover, it makes sense to attack those historically identified with that culture, white males. White females are exempt because it is politically astute to identify them as victims and so add to the coalition against white males, and because the powerful feminist movement is also hostile to Western culture. Besides, feminists make far more formidable adversaries than do white males. ·

Starting the policy of preferential treatment was a serious mistake. Continuing it would be a disaster. There is no respectable rationale for continuation. The most frequently heard argument is the claim that active discrimination against minorities and women continues in this country. For reasons to be discussed, it is extremely doubtful that such discrimination is at all common. Let us assume, however, that it is. The attempted justification fails, nonetheless. There are laws upon laws forbidding discrimination in employment and promotion, in housing, in voting, in access to places of public accommodation, in lending, and much more. We have the Civil Rights Acts of 1866, 1871, 1964, 1968, and 1991; we have the Voting Rights Acts of 1965, 1975, and 1982. There is agency upon agency devoted to finding and ending discrimination: the Civil Rights Division of the Department of Justice, the Equal Employment Opportunity Commission, the Office of Federal Contract Compliance Programs, the Department of Education's Civil Rights Office, civil rights sections in various government agencies, as well as state and municipal laws and enforcement agencies. There are thousands of such agencies, and more than 100,000 government lawyers, investigators, and agents who spend hundreds of millions of dollars enforcing the laws and regulations. If that were not enough, there are laws providing for private lawsuits and an army of private attorneys bringing discrimination claims. If discrimination is provable, we have far more than adequate means of dealing with it.

This means that affirmative action is generally applied to a pool of minorities who have suffered no discernible discrimination. Imagine a group of one hundred Hispanic men, ten of whom are to be admitted to Stanford under a policy of preference. In order to imagine that discrimination is being cured, it is necessary to suppose that, by a rare coincidence, preference is given to an individual who has actually suffered discrimination but cannot prove it, and may not even suspect it. If there are any victims of undetected discrimination in the pool of one hundred—suppose that there are ten—the likelihood is that none of them will receive preferential admission to Stanford or, at best, one or two will. Statistically, therefore, any person who has been the victim of unprovable discrimination will usually go without a remedy, while a person who has not been discriminated against will be given an undeserved benefit. It is difficult to see how a windfall for one cures an unsuspected injustice to the other. Affirmative action is simply irrelevant to discrimination.

This point is not met by shifting the accusation to one of institutional or structural racism and sexism. Not only does it raise the problem of the pool, just discussed, but structural charges are merely silly, a way of insisting that there must be discrimination although no one can see it. Structural racism or sexism would have to manifest itself in a series of individual acts of discrimination. That equally or better qualified blacks, Hispanics, or women were denied jobs or promotions in favor of white males would be provable and anti-discrimination laws and agencies would come into operation. Structural theories are simply an admission that actual discrimination cannot be shown, coupled with an unsupported assertion that it must nevertheless be pervasive. Only modern liberals and people with a vested interest in discovering racism would advance such an empty theory.

It is doubtful, in any event, that much discrimination occurs now that governments are no longer requiring it. Any fair-minded observer would have to admit that this country has undergone a drastic decline in racism. Discrimination is alleged much more often than it exists. When job discrimination complaints get a fair hearing, it usually turns out that the complainant was not hired because he or she had poor job qualifications.[13] Recently, to take another instance, there have been widely reported allegations of discrimination in mortgage lending, based on the observation that a higher percentage of blacks than whites are turned down. That kind of statistic, by itself, is meaningless, but most people, including government bureaucrats, take it as proving discrimination. The allegations were shown to be baseless by the fact that the default rates of the two races were the same. Had blacks been rejected who had financial qualifications equal to accepted white borrowers, so that blacks had to be more qualified to get loans, the default rates for whites would have been higher than those for blacks.

Mortgage lenders, not surprisingly, were more interested in economics than in race. What is true in that business is true generally. The prevalence of discrimination is to be doubted because it is economically irrational in any business where rivalry between firms exists. The employer who hires the best people, regardless of skin color or sex, will have a significant competitive advantage over any rival who discriminates. Hence discrimination is likely only where rivalry is muted or nonexistent.

As Thomas Sowell put it, "Prejudice is free but discrimination has costs."[14] That is the reason private businesses have resisted government-ordered discrimination. Even in South Africa, Sowell points out, private firms, run by folks presumably as racist as the government, persistently evaded the laws discriminating against blacks in employment. In the American South, bus companies publicly opposed and then tried to ignore municipal laws requiring separate seating of whites and blacks. The difference in attitudes was entirely due to the fact that governments bore none of the costs while businesses did. Discrimination against Jews was practiced far more often in regulated industries than in competitive ones, discrimination being costless where the firm was shielded from competition by regulators.[15] Businesses would, of course, discriminate when it paid, usually when their customers preferred not to associate with minorities. Hence the days of segregated lunch counters in the South. The phenomenon of private business resistance to discrimination when discrimination costs money is universal.

Sometimes preferential policies are justified as a form of reparations for a past history of discrimination. That would make sense, however, only if we ignore individuals and think of races as undifferentiated blocs whose members live forever. The individual beneficiaries and victims of past discrimination are now almost entirely unknowable. It is hardly sensible to prefer a person who has not suffered discrimination because a member of the same race or sex suffered it thirty years ago. Whatever happened in the past, in the present the policy does harm to guiltless individuals and benefits those who have suffered no harm. At some point, history must be accepted for what it is, history.

Though affirmative action has few if any legitimate benefits, it does have heavy adverse effects. To start with what many will think the least significant, it is obvious that jettisoning the achievement principle for reward according to skin color or genital arrangements has a serious economic cost. Peter Brimelow and Leslie Spencer estimated that affirmative action's direct and indirect costs in 1991 were about $115 billion; opportunity costs added another $236 billion; the lowering of the gross national product may have been about 4 percent.[16] Worse, it all may be wasted. The authors quote Charles Murray: "There's hardly a single outcome—black voting rights, access to public accommodation, employment, particularly in white collar jobs—that couldn't have been predicted on the basis of pre-1964 trend lines." "That's pretty devastating," the authors say. "It suggests that we have spent trillions of dollars to create an outcome that would have happened even if the government had done nothing."

If affirmative action had merely squandered trillions to accomplish little or nothing, that would be a considerable misfortune; but the truth is worse than that. This misbegotten policy has caused serious damage to blacks and Hispanics, to whites and those of Asian extraction, and to relations between those groups. Though these consequences are felt throughout our society, we may use the venue of higher education to illustrate the point.

Blacks and Hispanics do not currently perform as well on standardized tests or in school as do whites and Asian-Americans. If admissions were made on the basis of academic achievement, blacks and Hispanics would not be represented in the most prestigious and demanding universities in the same proportion that they bear to all university students. In their zeal to get minority numbers up, universities admit members of these groups with lower SATs and lower high school grades than they demand of whites and Asians. At many universities the practice is to compare black and Hispanic applicants only against others in the same ethnic group. The result is often startling differences in the academic qualifications of those groups and white and Asian students. Not only do some such admittees find themselves overmatched as they would not have at schools one rung down the prestige ladder, but the latter schools, deprived of minority students who would have done well there, must also admit lesser qualified minority students to get *their* numbers up. The result is a mismatching of universities and minority students at every level. This probably accounts for the higher drop-out rate for students who would have gotten good educations and graduated had the universities not done them so harmful a favor. Since everyone knows about affirmative action, those who do graduate are likely to be suspected by prospective employers and fellow employees of not really having the credentials their diplomas suggest.

Perhaps even worse than this, overmatching minority students may lead them to reject the standards for achievement that they will need to succeed after graduation. Sowell points out that the overmatched black or Hispanic student who does not keep up with his classmates has a choice. He can admit to himself that he is not qualified to compete at this level or, in an effort to retain his self-respect, he can attack as illegitimate the standards by which he is judged. It is hardly surprising that many choose the latter course. Most humans would. But a student who rejects the criteria by which our society judges achievement is himself handicapped, probably for life. The admissions office has done him no favor.

The problem is not simply that minority students are placed in universities where they have difficulty competing. The recipient of preferential admission has his self-doubt increased, which will in turn tend to encourage race-holding and underperformance. It is now fashionable to speak of seeking diversity, but the change in terms does not disguise the fact of preference. Whites seek innocence through absolution for their treatment of blacks in the past, while blacks seek power, which they can achieve by playing on white guilt. Shelby Steele writes,

> [D]iversity became a golden word. It grants whites an egalitarian fairness (innocence) and blacks an entitlement to proportionate representation (power).
>
> But the essential problem with this form of affirmative action is the way it leaps over the hard business of developing a formerly oppressed people to the point where they can achieve proportionate representation on their own (given equal opportunity) and goes straight for the proportionate representation. This may satisfy some whites of their innocence and some blacks of their power, but it does very little to truly uplift blacks.[17]

Of course, no minority (or majority either) will achieve proportionate representation in all fields of endeavor. Neither sex has done that, nor has any ethnic group. But Steele's point is entirely valid: preferential policies do not build the incentives for individual development that are necessary to uplift a formerly oppressed people, or anybody else for that matter.

The mistake the universities and society have made is to treat blacks and Hispanics by different standards from the rest of us. Christopher Lasch denounced the notion that "respect for cultural diversity forbids us to impose the standards of privileged groups on the victims of oppression." He calls this "clearly a recipe for universal incompetence (or at least for a disastrous split between the competent classes and the incompetent)."[18] A split between the competent classes and the incompetent would be disastrous for social stability. A more likely outcome is that if standards are lowered for minorities, they will also eventually be lowered for others. Since "privileged groups" and "victims of oppression" occupy the same classrooms and take the same tests, it will be impossible to demand different standards of the two. Just as the training of male cadets was scaled back to levels at which female cadets can perform, so educational standards will suffer in civilian universities if the standards of the privileged are not enforced on the formerly oppressed.

If preferential admission policies for blacks and Hispanics in colleges damages them, it certainly works a serious injustice on those who lose out because of preferences to others. A law professor referred to these results of affirmative action as "transitional inequities." That is a way of avoiding thinking about what you are doing. What the universities and employers are doing is inflicting permanent harm on people who have done nothing wrong. The inequities are not transitional or temporary for those who lose what they deserve on the merits because of their race or sex. If a white male does not get into Yale because of his race, he does not get into Yale forever, and chances are he forever does not get into Harvard, Stanford, etc. either. (Or, if he does, some other white male gets left out.) He may also not get the job he wants and that his talents and achievements qualify him for; he may well not get the promotion he has earned. Perhaps in ten or twenty years some other white male will be treated fairly, but that does not restore the life the first one who endured discrimination deserved to have. The damage to the individual is permanent, not transitional.

It may be thought that affirmative action is a way of buying social peace by enforcing proportional representation for all groups in all institutions. If so, it is obvious that the policy does not work. The results of affirmative action have been greater group antagonisms and self-segregation. The demand for equality of results is surely one cause of the increasing racial acrimony in our society. It is to be seen everywhere, from the new separation of the races on campuses to racial bloc voting on juries to workplace antagonisms. Nor is this just a problem between whites and blacks. Adjustments between races were difficult enough when that was only a question of those two races, but now we have large numbers of Asians and Hispanics, with many divisions within each group. By referring to non-whites generally as "persons of color," an attempt is made to range all non-whites against all whites. The tactic cannot work in an ethnic spoils system. The chancellor of a major university told me that blacks were calling him a racist. I asked why. He said, "Too many Asians." The prospects for racial and ethnic peace seem to be diminishing.

It is no wonder affirmative action creates racial hostilities. When a white male who has never discriminated against anyone loses out to a black male who has never been discriminated against, despite the former's superior qualifications, anger will flare up on both sides. The reason for the white's anger is obvious; the black will be angry because he knows that others know he has succeeded not on his own but because of his skin. The black is particularly likely to feel anger if he is placed by affirmative action in an environment in which he cannot compete equally. He may be college material but not ready for the college that takes him in. Perhaps, instead of being at Harvard, he should be at the University of Massachusetts.

It will be difficult to get rid of affirmative action. There is no reason to think that the infliction of inequities will come to an end at some unstated time in the future, at least not without acrimony and further racial anger. The rhetoric of victimhood will continue as long as there are benefits to be derived from it, which is to say as long as whites seek absolution. Judging by the universities' pusillanimity on this and similar issues for the past thirty years, unless authorities outside the universities intervene, affirmative action's inequities in the academic world will last forever, the period of transition will be eternity. Modern liberals have gotten us into a mistaken policy that we cannot continue and will have the greatest difficulty in ending.

Modern liberals in government agencies, universities, and elsewhere will do their utmost to preserve affirmative action. But there is a new mood in the public. There is a move to put the elimination of affirmative action in California to a vote in 1996, and the issue promises to become national. The initiative to be put to a vote in California states: "Neither the State of California nor any of its political subdivisions or agents shall use race, sex, color, ethnicity or national origin as a criterion for either discriminating against, or granting preferential treatment to, any individual or group in the operation of the State's system of public employment, public education or public contracting." This is an attempt to restore what Congress thought it was doing in the Civil Rights

Act of 1964. But the passage of the initiative would apply only to preferential policies put in place by the state or its subdivisions. Federal preferential policies override state law.

Interestingly enough, some liberals now think affirmative action has lasted too long. Joseph Califano, who pushed hard for affirmative action in both the Johnson and Carter administrations, wrote in 1989 that the policy was intended "only as a temporary expedient to speed blacks' entry into the social and economic mainstream" and that "its time is running out."[19] Susan Estrich, a law professor and campaign strategist for presidential candidate Mike Dukakis in 1988, said that "For all its good intentions, affirmative action was never meant to be permanent, and now is truly the time to move on to some other approach."[20] Ward Connerly, a black member of the Board of Regents of the University of California, said, "I tell you with every fiber of my being that what we're doing is inequitable to certain people. . . . To those who say, 'Affirmative action now, affirmative action as it is now'—that's what George Wallace said about segregation." The Board of Regents has ordered the California university system to stop preferences, but is said to be meeting covert resistance from educators and administrators.

On the other side of the issue, the head of the California branch of the National Organization for Women called the anti-affirmative action initiative "divisive scapegoating" and "one of the most significant attacks yet on our rights." A student at the University of California's law school, Boalt Hall, said of Proposition 187, which denies California benefits to illegal immigrants, and the civil rights initiatives that they were messages that "racism is O.K." and that "people of color are an O.K. target."[21] The fact that preferential treatment of those who are non-white and non-male is now their "right" merely confirms that many of its beneficiaries intend never to give up their privileged status. And the further charge that requiring non-discrimination for whites is "racism" shows how deeply anti-white racism has embedded itself in our culture.

One absurd consequence of minorities' admission to universities they are not fully qualified to enter is the self-esteem movement. The underlying idea is that achievement follows self-esteem rather than the other way round. A great deal of time is wasted at all levels of our educational system trying to build students' self-esteem, time that might better be spent teaching them skills and knowledge that would justify self-esteem. In higher education, self-esteem is promoted by programs dedicated to women and to ethnic groups. The results have been disastrous. The decline of, indeed disdain for, scholarly standards that is characteristic of the feminist movement and women's studies programs is also observable in ethnic studies programs. The most aggressive variety apparently is in African studies. The self-esteem of black students is, supposedly, raised by teaching them a false history of their race. Black students are, as Mary Lefkowitz puts it, taught myth as history.[22] The programs tend to be indoctrination rather than education. The presence of Afrocentrism on campus, like the presence of feminism, lowers scholarly standards generally. Professors outside the program refuse to object and refuse to demand evidence and logic when impossible claims are made.

A prominent Afrocentrist lectured at Wellesley, where Lefkowitz teaches, stating that Greek civilization was stolen from Egypt and that Egyptians were black. He claimed, among other things, that Aristotle stole his philosophy from the library at Alexandria. During the question period, Lefkowitz asked the lecturer why he made that claim when the library had been built after Aristotle's death. His only answer was that he resented the tone of the question. Several students accused Lefkowitz of racism. Her colleagues, who knew that the lecturer was making historical misrepresentations, remained silent.

When Lefkowitz went to the then dean of the college to point out that there was no evidence for some of what the Afrocentrists were teaching Wellesley students, the dean replied that each person has a different but equally valid view of history. When she made the point about Aristotle and the library at Alexandria at a faculty meeting, a colleague said, "I don't care who stole what from whom." Academics are afraid to challenge the misrepresentations of feminists and Afrocentrists. The likely penalty is to be called sexist and racist. Those terms have been flung about so indiscriminately that one would have thought they had lost their power to intimidate, but that is not the case. Worse than that, many professors and students feel that women and blacks, having been oppressed, have a right to their own histories, however false they may be.

The damage done by Afrocentric myths includes increased racial resentment. In order to make their claims—Socrates and Cleopatra were black, Greek philosophy was pilfered from the blacks of Egypt—even minimally plausible, it is necessary for the Afrocentrists to explain why the supposed debt of Greece, and hence of Western civilization, to the blacks of ancient Egypt is not widely known. The answer they offer is that whites not only stole their civilization from Egypt but have engaged in a massive cover-up ever since to maintain white supremacy. Blacks who believe that are naturally hostile to whites.

One reason Afrocentrists are not challenged is that race is becoming a subject it is almost impossible to discuss honestly in public. Professor Lefkowitz has been praised for her courage in call-ing the myths of Afrocentrism what they are. She has shown courage, given today's racial climate, although it should not require bravery to point out what amounts to scholarly fraud. But intimi-dation on matters of race is everywhere. A finalist for the presi-dency of Michigan State University was forced to withdraw his candidacy because four years earlier he had said: "As blacks begin to get into sports, their natural athletic abilities come through. They have actually done research on an average black athlete versus an average white athlete in basketball, where a black athlete can actu-ally outjump a white athlete on the average." An uproar resulted when those remarks became known at Michigan State. A black graduate student said, for example, "To try to justify racist views as science is preposterous. When other people in sports and entertain-ment have come up with those statements, they were axed imme-diately."[23] Everybody who has paid any attention knows that black athletes dominate most sports, not just basketball. That it is impossi-ble to say so without endangering your career is preposterous.

At the University of Pennsylvania, a professor trying to elicit discussion about the Thirteenth Amendment's prohibition of "involuntary servitude" referred to blacks as "ex-slaves" and said that as a Jew he was an ex-slave of Pharaoh. Several days later, when three black students complained, the professor apologized to them. Three months later, the Black Student League demanded his resignation, and the professor issued a public apology, to no avail. The university administration suspended him for two semesters and required him to attend sensitivity training sessions.[24]

In a faculty sensitivity session at the University of Cincinnati a woman was forced to stand up and be mocked as "a member of the privileged white elite" because she was blonde, blue-eyed, and well educated. The trainer implied that her three degrees from prestigious private schools were not really earned but were a genetic entitlement. When the trainer later ordered her to stand up again, presumably to be abused once more, she could only sit and sob. Not one of her one hundred colleagues who were present came to her defense.[25] This episode illustrates two things. Sensitivity sessions often turn into verbal assaults on representatives of a group deemed to dominate; here, whites. The more significant aspect of this episode, however, is that the woman did not respond with anger to an utterly unfair attack and that her faculty colleagues sat silent and allowed the attack to go on. We have become a submissive people, which is particularly true of whites where race is an issue.

Amity Schlaes, an editorial writer for the *Wall Street Journal*, wrote an article in the *Spectator* in January 1994, describing the white middle class' fear of blacks after Colin Ferguson murdered six whites on a Long Island commuter train, and after a jury in Brooklyn acquitted a young black despite powerful evidence that he had murdered a white. She wrote that whites were frightened because Ferguson's "manic hostility to whites is shared by many of the city's non madmen."[26] When copies of the article were circulated among Schlaes' colleagues at the *Journal*, she became an outcast. A number of her co-workers would get out of the elevator when she got on. People who had eaten with her in the staff cafeteria refused to sit at the same table. A delegation went to the office of the chairman of the company that owns the *Journal*. It did not matter that Schlaes had pointed out that minorities were the greatest victims of minority crimes or that nobody could show that a single element of her article was untrue or inaccurate. "Her crime," wrote the then editor of *The Spectator*, Dominic Lawson, "was far greater than being merely wrong. She had written the truth, regardless of the offence it might cause. And in modern America, or at least in its mainstream media, that is simply not done."[27] Paul Johnson makes the same point in "Gone is the time when Americans led the world in saying what they thought."[28]

Lawson goes on to account for the popularity of Rush Limbaugh and Jackie Mason by suggesting that they have "the role in modern America that underground satirists had in Russia during the late Soviet years. They were popular, and even loved, because they were the only people who could publicly demonstrate the absurdity of the official media dogma — the bogus brotherhood of man, promulgated in the USSR by *Pravda* and *Izvestia*, and in the USA by the likes of the *Washington Post* and the *New York Times*."[29] He came to realize why the American media are so neurotic, "why they are quite so slavish to the humourless ethos of political correctness. They realise that their own country is in fact riven by social divides along racial and religious lines. But no amount of silence on the matter will make the differences disappear."[30]†

It is ironic that racism and sexism have been discovered to be the deep, almost ineradicable, sicknesses of this culture at precisely the time when they have been successfully overcome. If they have not entirely disappeared, they are mere wisps of their former selves, except when it comes to white, heterosexual males. That discrimination is now so acceptable that it applies not only to matters like college admissions, hiring and promotion in government and in companies, but even to the design of the curriculum. The best known instance occurred at Stanford. The university had a very popular required course in Western culture. The idea was that students should have at least a nodding acquaintance with the minds and works that have shaped the West and that constitute our heritage. But radicals and minorities objected both because Western culture should not be celebrated, being racist, sexist, violent, imperialistic, and not at all like those wonderful Third World cultures, and because the authors that were assigned—Aristotle, Machiavelli, Rousseau, Locke, Shakespeare—were all white males. The culmination of the campaign consisted of a conga line snaking across campus, led by Jesse Jackson, the protesters chanting, "Hey, hey, ho, ho, Western culture's gotta go." And go it did. Universities routinely collapse when hit from that end of the cul-

---

†Some of what is happening is merely funny, or maybe it is pathetic. A few years ago some students at a major university gave a 1950s nostalgia party, using the music and dress of that decade. The next day the dean in charge of sensitivity delivered a reprimand, because the 1950s were not a good time for minorities.

tural and political spectrum. Stanford revised the course, eliminating some of the white male authors and replacing them with women and writers "of color," some of them bitterly hostile to Western civilization. This is a quota system for the curriculum. In capitulating, Stanford acquiesced in the claim that Western culture is at least highly suspect and that its great works are little more than justifications of white male dominance.

The problem is by no means confined to the universities. It is now rampant, for example, in the world of art. The *New York Times* carried an article asking "Is 'Quality' An Idea Whose Time Has Gone?" The story reports that the idea of quality has become a lightning rod for a stormy debate about Western values vs. non-Western values, men vs. women, and, of course, race. The division is also political, with those on the right generally embracing the word, those on the left generally deploring it. The word "quality" is denounced as racist, and those who reject the word in universities as well as in the art world, in the words of the article, "often exhibit an alarming readiness to set up a bogeyman called the heterosexual white male, make him the scapegoat for everything bad in human history, and try to discredit the word quality—and with it all of Western civilization—by identifying it with him alone."[31]

Getting ourselves out of this modern liberal swamp of discrimination will not be easy. The Supreme Court seems inclined to waffle on the issue.[†] Getting rid of affirmative action by democratic means may not be easy either. Though majorities of Americans of all races disapprove of this discrimination, the modern liberal elites will fight to retain it, and they have an impact on public policy out of proportion to their numbers.

Yet it is crucial that we do end this misbegotten policy. The objection to our current treatment of race is not only that it has made honest discussion virtually impossible, though it has. Nor is

---

[†]The Supreme Court ruled against a federal set aside program but only by a five-to-four vote, *Adarand Constructors, Inc.* v. *Pena*, 115 S. Ct. 2097 (1995), and some members of the majority are shaky on the question. Seven of the Justices, moreover, say that racial preferences may be used to remedy past discrimination, which merely means that the existence of past discrimination, perhaps only numerical imbalance, will be the new focus of litigation. We have already seen that past discrimination involving different people is no justification for present discrimination.

it simply that it is unfair to individuals, though it is. Nor that it will destroy incentives, though it will. Nor that it will make America less competitive precisely at the time when it needs to be more competitive. Nor even perhaps that it is intensifying racial hostility. The most basic objection is that it is destroying what America means, changing us from a society whose rewards may be achieved by individual merit to one whose rewards are handed out according to group identity.

13

The Decline of Intellect

I f, as Brigette Berger has quite plausibly asserted, "the fate of the modern university and the fate of Western civilization are inextricably intertwined,"[1] our prospects at the moment do not seem bright. Universities are central cultural institutions. Their preservation of the great works and traditions of Western civilization, including the traditions of rationality and skepticism, have been crucial to the growth of individual freedom, respect for the rule of law, and scientific progress.

Universities now threaten to abandon those ideals and to instruct the rest of society to abandon them as well. As the universities lose respect for intellect, that attitude spreads not only to lower schools but to the society at large. It is perhaps unclear whether the universities are instructing the culture at large in the joys of anti-intellectualism or whether the universities have been infected by a culture already lobotomized by television. Probably the influence runs both ways. The universities have an independent reason to abandon intellect: the barrier that rationality places in the way of politicization.

Whichever way the causation runs, the trend in question appears to be the result of an ever more insistent egalitarianism. America never has been enthusiastic about high intellect. "Again and again, but particularly in recent years," Richard Hofstadter wrote in 1962, "it has been noticed that intellect in America is resented as a kind of excellence, as a claim to distinction, as a challenge to egalitarianism, as a quality which almost certainly deprives a man or woman of the common touch."[2] He noted that anti-intellectualism "made its way into our politics because it became associated with our passion for equality. It has become formidable in our education partly because our educational beliefs are evangelically egalitarian."[3]

An egalitarian educational system is necessarily opposed to meritocracy and reward for achievement. It is inevitably opposed to procedures that might reveal differing levels of achievement. In the spring of 1953, as I left our apartment house for the last of a series of grueling law school exams, I met a young woman I knew to be in the school of education. I sympathized with her about how hard she must have been studying. She said she had studied not at all since there were no examinations. "How can they grade you, then?" "We are graded on class participation." That struck me as preposterous, but the full dimensions of the calamity such a philosophy portended did not then occur to me.

The problem was both that budding teachers of the young were allowed to avoid competition in the mastery of any subject matter and that educational faddishness—grading adults on class participation rather than knowledge—was apparent. The endless pursuit of fads is a way of avoiding conventional (bourgeois) methods and standards. A few years later, in a good private day school, my son was taught the "new math," in which, supposedly, he would learn the rationale behind arithmetic rather than engage in such foolishness as rote learning of the multiplication tables. Meanwhile, Japanese children were learning the multiplication tables by rote, and ended up far ahead of American children in mathematics.

Feminism, Afrocentrism, and the self-esteem movement, three other products of the egalitarian passion, divert resources from real education and miseducate. The United States spends more on education than do other Western industrialized nations, and gets less in return. This is not only harmful to individuals and to our competitiveness internationally, it is a likely source of considerable social unrest and antagonism. The failures of public education have had a devastating impact on poor black children. They are often not given even the most rudimentary education that might enable them to compete in the American economy. A growing uneducated black underclass, without prospects for a decent life, is creating social chaos and will create more.

The result of our egalitarian passion is that Americans, white as well as black, have allowed themselves to become progressively less competent. That fact is attested to in myriad ways: SAT scores keep declining; American students fall well behind the students of many other nations on international science and mathematics tests; even college students frequently lack basic historical and geographical knowledge. Our system of public education at the primary and secondary levels is not performing as well as it did half a century ago, and in places its performance is a disgrace. Universities must offer remedial courses to bring their entering freshmen up to the point they should have reached in mid-high school. Less and less of the four years of college can be spent on what we used to think of as college level studies. Intellectual rigor inevitably suffers as grades are inflated and graduate students are substituted for professors in teaching undergraduates.

Egalitarianism led Americans gradually to extend education to all youths, which was admirable, but egalitarianism also led to the notion that the education must be pretty much the same for all levels of ability. Those with higher levels of academic talent were no longer pressed to achieve as they once were. Not long ago a newspaper printed an examination that all high school graduates were once expected to be able to pass if they intended to go on to college. The test, if I recall correctly, was given between the turn of the century and World War I. I could not begin to answer most of the questions, nor could most of the educated people I discussed it with.

The difference between education today or education in the last sixty or seventy years and what it was before that is to be measured in light years. The future novelist Willa Cather's studies at the University of Nebraska in 1891 included three years of Greek, two years of Latin, Anglo-Saxon, Shakespeare and the Elizabethans, Robert Browning and the nineteenth century authors (Tennyson, Emerson, Hawthorne, and Ruskin), French literary classics, one year of German, history, philosophy, rhetoric, journalism, chemistry, and mathematics.

The self-indulgence of radical individualism has meant less homework and more television watching. Television, which is replacing reading as a leisure activity among the young, is a major contributor to vacuity. A professor of communications says that his students "tend to have an image-based standard of truth. If I ask, 'What evidence supports your view or contradicts it?' they look at me as if I came from another planet. It's very foreign to them to think in terms of truth, logic, consistency and evidence."[4] Though this is a problem across class lines, the situation becomes desperate for the poorly educated, who are less and less equipped to perform in a modern economy.

But lowered intellectual standards are by no means the whole tale of the degradation of primary and secondary education. We have seen that feminist and Afrocentric propaganda has made harmful inroads in the lower schools' curricula. But the sweep of modern liberal politicization is far wider. The most notable recent example is the National History Standards[5] funded by the National Endowment for the Humanities. The Standards were intended as guidance to teachers, curriculum planners, and textbook publishers. In keeping with the modern liberalism that dominates the education establishment, the Standards prescribed a multicultural curriculum that minimized the achievements of Europeans and their descendants in America in order to focus attention on Africans and Indians.

Although Africans were brought to America as slaves, it is difficult to see an important connection between American history and the direction to students in grades 5 to 6 to "Draw upon stories of Mansa Musa and his great pilgrimage to Mecca in order to analyze the great wealth of Mali, its trade in gold and salt, and the importance of its learning center in Timbuktu" or the direction to students in grades 7 to 8 to "Draw upon historical narratives of Muslim scholars such as Ibn Fadi Allah al-Omari and Ibn Battuta to analyze the achievements and grandeur of Mansa Musa's court, and the social customs and wealth of the kingdom of Mali."[6]

It is difficult to avoid the conclusion that this extensive detour into the achievements and grandeur of Mansa Musa has nothing to do with teaching American history and everything to do with promoting black self-esteem and demanding acknowledgment by white students of a marvelous African past. Whatever its place in a different course, the placement of this material in required American history courses is designed to make sure that students cannot avoid this propaganda.

Students in the seventh and eighth grades are asked how "Columbus's description of the peaceful and pleasant nature of the Carib Indians contrast[ed] with his treatment of them?"[7] One wonders whether students are to be informed that the Caribs' predations against their Indian neighbors forced the latter to migrate or that the Caribs were cannibals who tortured and ate their male captives. Never mind, since Columbus was a European, it is the Caribs on whom victim status is bestowed.

"Native American" and European views of land are contrasted, the latter believing in private property and the former believing that "land was not property, but entrusted by the Creator to all living creatures for their common benefit and shared use."[8] Were the students to be informed that private ownership results in greater preservation of land than does common use? Or that private ownership is a sign of advanced civilization, not suitable to primitive and often nomadic Indian tribes? On and on it goes. William Penn's friendly relations with some tribes is contrasted with wars between settlers and Indians in Virginia and Massachusetts. The comparison is misleading. Penn's friendly relations with the Indians was not a model to be emulated, as the Standards seem to suggest. Indians ravaged the settlements of western Pennsylvania. The settlers begged Philadelphia for help, but the Quakers there preferred to ask themselves what they had done to justify the savagery to the west. Where had they gone wrong?[9]

Lynne Cheney, as chairman of the National Endowment for the Humanities, authorized a grant that went to the development of the Standards, an act she has come to regret. She points out that the Standards do not mention the Constitution even once. Students are told to conduct a trial of John D. Rockefeller for his "unethical and amoral business practices . . . in direct violation of the common welfare." No matter that much recent scholarship has shown that the legends about the "robber barons" are without foundation and that Rockefeller, in addition to being a philanthropist on a gigantic scale, developed the oil industry to the benefit of American consumers. Students are instructed to consider the achievements of Aztec civilization but not the practice of human sacrifice. McCarthy and McCarthyism get nineteen mentions, the Ku Klux Klan seventeen. Harriet Tubman, a black who helped rescue slaves through the Underground Railroad, is mentioned six times. By contrast, Henry Clay and Ulysses S. Grant are each mentioned once. There is no mention at all of Daniel Webster, Robert E. Lee, Alexander Graham Bell, Thomas Edison, Albert Einstein, Jonas Salk, or the Wright brothers. George Washington appears fleetingly but is not identified as our first president. The foundings of the Sierra Club and the National Organization for Women are considered noteworthy, but the first gathering of the U.S. Congress is not.[10]

The National Standards were politically correct. The contributions of the West were trivialized or ignored while those of Africans and Indians were magnified; males who had played important roles in our history were dropped out; organizations and events that reflected poorly upon us were stressed. So outrageous were the messages the Standards would have foisted upon the young that Congress rebelled. The Senate condemned them by a vote of 99 to 1, and the lone dissenter thought the condemnation inadequate.

A new version of the history Standards, much less political and biased against America, appeared in April 1995. But bias is still prominent. Students are to learn about the religious beliefs of American Indians and Africans but are to be given nothing about European religion (i.e., Christianity). Students are to analyze modern feminism, described as "compelling in its analysis of women's problems and the solutions offered," and fifth and sixth graders must be able to explain why the National Organization for Women (NOW) was formed. Fifth graders receive a thorough indoctrination in Watergate and are informed that Ronald Reagan was called "Herbert Hoover with a smile."[11]

The new standards are widely praised in the universities, though why words like "non-ideological" and "non-partisan" should be used is something of a mystery. Perhaps the warm reception is given because another battle is too painful to contemplate. More likely, Standards that ignore Christianity, advocate feminism, and lean to the left politically seem balanced to the modern liberals of the universities.

Matters do not improve at the university level. Anyone who

reads newspapers and magazines is surely aware of the politically correct terror that has overtaken many of our institutions of higher learning, and is probably aware of the preposterous courses being offered in matters such as comic books and of the inflation of grades. But what the press reports is usually anecdotal. The National Association of Scholars (NAS), by contrast, has conducted a systematic study of what has happened to university educations over a period of almost eighty years in fifty highly selective institutions.[12] The NAS studied the catalogues of these universities for the academic years beginning in 1914, 1939, 1964, and 1993. The findings are devastating. They bear out in full columnist Robert J. Samuelson's conclusion: "You should treat skeptically the loud cries now coming from colleges and universities that the last bastion of excellence in American education is being gutted by state budget cuts and mounting costs. Whatever else it is, higher education is not a bastion of excellence. It is shot through with waste, lax academic standards and mediocre teaching and scholarship."[13]

What has gone wrong appears to flow from a poisonous combination of radical egalitarianism and radical individualism. Egalitarianism means that faculties have lost the self-confidence to tell students what it is they ought to learn. Radical individualism causes students to resist dictation by college authorities and faculty, to prefer following their own interests to learning what the institution wants taught. These two forces press higher education in the same direction. Hence the startling decline in required courses. But, as the NAS points out, the existence, number, and nature of required courses indicates an institution's educational priorities, what it thinks an educated person should know. To the degree that higher educational institutions have such priorities and tend to agree with one another, they help maintain a common culture.

Yet the number of required courses has undergone a rapid decline in recent years. The NAS report deals with this in a chapter entitled "The Dissolution of Structure," which shows that the dropping or easing of requirements—begun as a slow evolution by 1939—had become a rush by 1993. General education programs were 55 percent of requirements in 1914 and only 33 percent in 1993. That does not tell the full story because in 1914 no exemptions from general education requirements were allowed in 98 percent of the courses, but by 1993 that had dropped to 29 percent. The loss of general education requirements is an educational disaster, producing students who have information about narrow corners of subjects but no conception of the larger context that alone can give the niches meaning. In college, my son was not offered a survey course in history and wound up studying such niches of history as the Weimar Republic. The college had given up on the idea that there was a central body of historical knowledge all educated persons should have. That is true across the board, not just in history. It will be a few years yet before America discovers what the decline of general knowledge means for our well-being.

The other two chapters of the report make equally dismal reading. "The Evaporation of Content" reveals, for example, that from 1914 to 1939, the percentage of institutions with literature requirements fell from 57 percent to 38 percent, where it held steady into the Sixties. By 1993, only 14 percent of institutions had such requirements. The same pattern held true in philosophy, religion, social science, natural science, and mathematics. Though distribution requirements increased, so many courses are often included in each curriculum category that the purpose once served by required general courses is not served.

"The Decline of Rigor," the third and last chapter, states that the data from the catalogues "paint a discouraging portrait of diminishing rigor at the most prestigious colleges and universities in our land. Thus, by 1993 students graduating from these elite schools not only had fewer assignments to complete but were asked to do considerably less in completing them." The NAS stated that the degree of rigor in a curriculum is important to more than how much the student learns. "It also has implications for character formation. The ability to work hard, to persevere in exacting tasks, and to master detail are all critical in determining individual achievement. By the same token, the degree to which these qualities are found among a society's leadership has a direct influence on that society's overall strength and vitality."[14]

The evidence showed a decline in freshman preparation. Between 1964 and 1993, combined verbal and mathematics SAT scores declined 7.3 percent, and this was concentrated especially within the highest percentiles of test takers, the group from which the elite schools draw their students. The catalogues also revealed severe drops in admission requirements. This in turn led to the need for remedial courses in a variety of subjects. These were attempts to bring students up to the level at which they could do college work. Colleges were teaching what high schools should have taught. In 1939 and 1964, no college offered credit for completing what was essentially a high school course, and students who completed the remedial course were invariably required to take and complete the standard college course on the subject. The situation with respect to writing or composition courses is illustrative. By 1993, thirty-one out of thirty-five schools with remedial courses offered college credit for them, and in only four of the twenty-six cases where a regular writing requirement existed was the subsequent completion of that course required. One can only conclude that students were permitted to go forward without college level writing skills or, perhaps more likely, that the standard offering had been diluted so that it hardly differed from the remedial course.

What seems conclusive evidence of the decline of rigor is that the average number of days classes were in session during the academic year dropped precipitously over the period examined. The average was 204 days in 1914, 195 in 1939, 191 in 1964, and then a dramatic drop to 156 classroom days in 1993. The length of the standard class period, which was 59.8 minutes in 1914, had declined by 6.1 minutes by 1993. Equally telling is the trend of the days of the week in which classes are in session. In 1914, 98 percent of the institutions studied scheduled Saturday classes. This percentage kept declining until in 1993 only 6 percent had Saturday classes. The NAS refers to the "widespread impression within academe" that "even Friday classes are becoming a rarity."

The willingness of students to attend Saturday classes is as good an indicator as any of the seriousness with which they take their studies. When I first went to Yale law school to teach in 1962, Saturday morning classes were standard. I scheduled all my classes for Thursday, Friday, and Saturday, and thus had the three days of the first half of the week free for writing. The students did not mind the arrangement, some of them brought their weekend dates to class. When I returned to the law school from government in 1977, I learned that students would not take courses with Saturday classes and most would not attend Friday afternoon classes. The object was to get out of New Haven for the weekend as rapidly as possible. The change signified a loss of seriousness about education and intellectual work. The faculty accepted the new attitude, as indeed they had to unless they banded together to insist upon offering Saturday classes. The faculty, in this and other matters, did not care enough to act.

Not long ago I was asked to tape a discussion of the judiciary to be used in conjunction with a college textbook on American government. I asked why a tape was needed for college students and was told, "They don't read. They don't even read for pleasure. If they are given a reading assignment, they feel agony—which is why the textbooks are becoming shorter and dumber." As somebody said, this is a generation that watches and rewinds. "There is a name for what happens when people pursue a pleasure so relentlessly that the more they ingest in the pursuit of happiness, the more they need, and the less happy, in general, they end up. . . . The word is addiction. Entertainment is the national dope."[15]

In chart after chart in the NAS report, one sees a number (of required courses, class days, etc.) in 1914, then a gradual falling off in 1939 and 1964, followed by a precipitous decline to 1993. This confirms a pattern repeatedly suggested in this book: trends slowly moving through an area of life, in this case higher education, until the Sixties when those trends accelerated rapidly. This suggests, as noted earlier, that we would in any event have eventually arrived where the Sixties took us but perhaps two or three decades later. Which in turn suggests that we are merely seeing the playing out of qualities—individualism and egalitarianism—inherent in Western civilization and to some degree unique to that civilization.

Decreasing competence is only the beginning of the story. Intellect loses its virtue when it ceases to seek truth and turns to the pursuit of political ends. Not all of this is seriously intended. We have reached the point described by Ortega y Gasset in which many of our intellectuals have abandoned the traditional standards of scholarship and have begun to kick up their heels and stand on their heads to pass the time. Even during the student rebellions of the Sixties and early Seventies it was evident that many of the rebels were playing at being revolutionaries, having fun watching the faculties and administrations cower. On today's faculties they continue to ridicule bourgeois standards, and their effects are pernicious.

But there are more serious types, teachers who see themselves as political activists whose campaign headquarters just happen to be the classroom. Professors openly describe themselves as advocates for radical change in the society. They teach courses to make converts to an ideology, always a liberal to left ideology. One might suppose that this proselytizing would be done covertly, as the milder forms of liberal propaganda used to be spread before the Sixties radicals became tenured faculty, but that is not the case. Radical faculty openly boast of their purposes and offer two justifications. The first suggests that standards may be subverted or abandoned if the need is great enough. That is the case today because this society is corrupt and oppressive and urgently needs drastic reform or restructuring. The second justification argues that standards are actually not being altered or abandoned: all teaching is inevitably political—if a professor tries to teach a subject objectively, he is a knave or a fool, since he is, knowingly or unknowingly, reinforcing a corrupt status quo.

The first argument we may simply brush aside. America today is the least oppressive and corrupt society, in the sense the radicals mean, in the history of the world. Whole shelves of books have been written to prove that what looks like openness and tolerance is actually a subtle form of repression. But these books are by fools and knaves, the sort of people who were assuring us that one communist government after another was a workers' paradise while the actual workers were doing their utmost to escape those paradises and, often enough, losing their lives in the attempt.

The second justification for political teaching and scholarship is true, up to a point. If a professor of traditional views protests that he never used his classroom authority for political ends, the response is that of course he did, he was just not sufficiently self-aware to realize the political nature of all teaching, thought, and scholarship. Indeed, the effort to abide by traditional standards of scholarship, and teaching itself, rest upon a political (or moral) judgment. As of course they do: the judgment is that men will be freer and happier if truth is sought, and the results of the search confirmed or rejected, without regard to the political implications of the outcome. The ultimate premise of the enterprise is political and moral, but it is a politics and a morality that command that the inquiry set in motion be nonpolitical and neutral.

The politically motivated scholar and teacher is engaged in a dishonest act: pretending that his conclusions are reached impartially when they are not. This is particularly pernicious when the modern liberal scholar speaks to the public as an expert but is really concealing a political agenda behind his credentials. During Edward Levi's tenure as Attorney General of the United States, a highly charged dispute about his duties under a statute arose between the Department of Justice and a congressional committee. Liberals were on the side of the committee, and soon professors of law were being recruited to sign a statement that there was no legal validity to Levi's position. One such canvasser approached a friend of mine for his signature. My friend declined on the ground that he knew nothing about that area of the law and could not judge whether the committee or the Attorney General was right. The law professor doing the canvassing said: "You don't understand. This isn't a legal issue; it's political." Yet the petition was to be presented to the press and the public as the expert opinion of law professors on a question of law. Again and again, one sees university faculty speaking to issues and demanding respect for their opinions because of their special competence and expertise when what is offered is no more than a camouflaged political statement. This is so common that it is taken for granted in the academic world. If you see a letter or a petition with many signatories and purporting to state an expert opinion, you can be almost certain that a majority of those signing have never read the relevant materials and their opinions are politics masquerading as professional expertise.

It is obviously easier to politicize fields like law or history or literature, but not even the natural sciences are wholly immune. A few years back the *New York Times* reported that paleontologists who doubted the theory that dinosaurs' extinction was caused by the impact on the earth of an enormous meteor were called "militarists" by their colleagues and felt their careers threatened. The reason was that the theory was used as support for the notion that nuclear war would throw up enormous quantities of dust that would block sunlight and cause a "nuclear winter," writing finis to the human race. The dinosaur extinction theory was too valuable to one side of a political argument about nuclear weapons to be decided on its scientific merits.

This is but a small example of the tyranny of political correctness that has spread across American campuses. A few years back there was a burst of denunciation from all segments of the political spectrum when the phenomenon became known. A friend of mine laughed and said, "It's a rout. They are discredited completely." Unfortunately, it was not a rout. The janissaries of the Left are infinitely adaptable in their tactics but they do not abandon their strategic objective. They denied there was such an animal as political correctness, they claimed it was a term invented by extreme right-wingers to discredit liberals. (Conservatives are always referred to as extreme and right-wing to distinguish them from radicals of the Left who, we are to understand, spend their time in the middle of the road.) Meanwhile, however, the tyranny of political correctness goes on. As the sociologist Paul Hollander describes the situation:

> PC is, above all, a climate of opinion, a complex of social and institutional pressures and threats, beliefs and taboos which have come to dominate the campuses and academic public discourse over the past quarter century. . . .
>
> There are at least five areas to which PC applies and where it succeeded in imposing a fair amount of conformity. They are: 1) race-minority relations; 2) sexual and gender relations; 3) homosexuality; 4) American society as a whole; 5) Western culture and values. In regard to each, PC prescribes publicly acceptable opinions and attitudes which are often conveyed on the campuses by required courses, freshman orientation, sensitivity training, memoranda by administrators, speech codes, harassment codes, official and student publications and other means.
>
> Deviation from the norms of PC may result in public abuse, ostracism, formal or informal sanctions, administrative reproach, delayed promotion, difficulty of finding a job, being sentenced to sensitivity training, etc.[16]

It is impossible to imagine that academic inquiry flourishes where thought police abound. Indeed, the intellectual apparatus of the Sixties radicals now dominating the universities is built for intellectual repression and not for inquiry. "The 'sixties' culture had tried to reinterpret history in terms of race, class, and gender."[17] These categories played little part in recent history, including such momentous developments as the collapse of communism in the Soviet Union and its satellites. The important factors there were ones the New Left had ignored or derided—nationalism, religion, and the struggle for freedom and democracy through a free-market economy. Their analysis failed when applied to the United States as well. "The [race-class-gender] model, however, was flawed because it did not make adequate allowance for those multiple loyalties that transcended those of mere race and ethnicity." Race, class, and gender are not adequate tools of analysis; they are expressions of resentment, claims of oppression. They are thus better suited to attack than to analysis.

Intellect is in decline in other ways, however. One is the refusal of many Americans to apply reasoning to their beliefs.[18] Another is the rejection of the very idea of rationality. As to the first, we have become so accustomed to the astrology column in the daily paper that we no longer reflect on just how preposterous it is that people in a highly scientific and rational culture should pay any attention at all to astrology, a subject that should have died with pre-scientific ages. Yet a psychiatrist told me he estimated that about 25 percent of his colleagues believed in astrology. Important people, like a First Lady of the United States, arrange their affairs according to astrologers' advice. There are, in fact, ten times as many astrologers as astronomers in this country.

I remember laughing out loud when on the cab ride from LaGuardia airport to Manhattan I saw a billboard offering psychic counseling over a 900 telephone number. Who could be foolish enough to pay to listen to a psychic? Lots of people, apparently. Now the psychics advertise on television. Television, in apparently respectable programs, hosted by men with deep authoritative voices, informs us of the mysteries of the Bermuda Triangle, the mystic powers of Egyptian pyramids, the landings of extraterrestrial spacemen among primitive peoples millennia ago, the lost continent of Atlantis, the enigma of crop circles, sightings of Big Foot and the Loch Ness Monster.[†]

That all of this is nonsense is never allowed to intrude upon the flow of misinformation. It is perhaps no wonder, then, that Americans believe so much that simply is not so. That might not be a problem, except that many of them arrange their personal lives in accordance with these myths and probably form their opinions of public policies on the same basis.

Quite another form of irrationality afflicts portions of our intelligentsia: the astounding claim that rationality itself is neither possible nor legitimate. We have seen that some radical feminists make this claim, as do some racial essentialists; in both cases they claim that what counts as rationality is socially constructed, that there are different ways of knowing, which means that reality has no stable content, not even in principle. The denial that rationality, now routinely derided as "logocentrism," is legitimate or perhaps even possible is closely related to the politicization of intellectual fields.

In the universities, as John R. Searle notes, there are challenges "not just to the content of the curriculum but to the very conceptions of rationality, truth, objectivity, and reality that have been taken for granted in higher education, as they have been taken for granted in our civilization at large." These qualities are rejected "*even as ideals*."[20] This did not occur because a large number of people recently had the insight that these ideals were false or impossible of achievement. This rejection occurred, rather, because the more advanced modern liberals saw that their political and cultural agendas were vulnerable to rational thought. That was the reason the European fascists rejected rationality as a prop to the

---

[†]The phenomenon may be common in the West and on the increase. The French have experienced increased demand for clairvoyants, numerologists, those who seek underground water with dowsing rods, heal the sick by telephone, read stones and runes. Irrationality is so widespread and accepted that the practitioners of such arts gather annually at the Paris Fair for Parapsychology. A disheartening sign of the change in Western culture is that men, who rarely patronized clairvoyants a few years back, now come openly, and, according to one adept, "What's more, the men cry. They didn't 10 years ago."[19] The increasing manifestation of superstition in the West is bad enough. The fact that men, who did not cry ten years ago, now do so indicates that something has gone high and soft in the culture.

old, corrupt order—just as our American fascists, the New Left, decried objectivity for that reason. Those issuing such challenges today are the emotional—one hesitates to say intellectual—heirs of the New Left, and in many cases are not the heirs but the same people.

This is anti-intellectualism carried as far as it can possibly go. Hofstadter assumed, as was conventional among academics of his time, that anti-intellectualism was a right-wing phenomenon. If that was ever true, it is certainly not the case today. In an excellent book, *Higher Superstition*,[21] Paul R. Gross and Norman Levitt profess a certain puzzlement that the attacks on science and indeed on rationality should now come not just from within the universities but from the academic left. "What defines [that left], as much as anything else, is a deep concern with cultural issues, and, in particular, a commitment to the idea that fundamental political change is urgently needed and can be achieved only through revolutionary processes rooted in the wholesale revision of cultural categories."[22] The academic left does not offer a consistent body of doctrine but rather a variety of doctrines, many of them in conflict with one another. "What enables them to coexist congenially, in spite of gross logical inconsistencies, is a shared sense of injury, resentment, and indignation against modern science."[23]

That sense of injury, resentment, and indignation attaches to much else besides science. The attack on the natural sciences is but part of a larger rejection of the culture of the West, one more continuation of the Sixties: "[M]any of the academics who are most actively hostile toward standard science are affiliated, formally or informally, with areas of study that first arose during the sixties—women's studies, ethnic studies, environmental studies, and so forth."[24] These studies are, almost by definition, anti-intellectual. With respect to science as with respect to the other objects of their hostility, the Left, and not least its academic branch, is ill-informed and illogical.

Gross and Levitt argue that scientific skepticism, its insistence on internal logical consistency and empirical verification, has been an invaluable weapon against intellectual authoritarianisms that sustained social systems based on exploitation, domination, and absolutism. Thus, the scientific enterprise was egalitarian and seen as a leading feature of the progress of liberalism. They then remark that our era is singular in that this understanding has "come under strident and increasingly scornful attack, not from reactionaries and traditionalists, who have always feared science, but from its natural heirs—the community of thinkers, theoreticians, and activists who challenge both the material injustices of the existing social system and the underlying assumptions and prejudices that perpetuate them."[25]

It is necessary here to protest a bit. It is not at all clear that the "natural heirs" of the scientific enterprise would perceive material injustices or false assumptions that perpetuate injustices in the existing social system. This sounds like a call for the massive restructuring of society without making the point explicit. A minor annoyance of the book is that the authors repeatedly strain so hard to distance themselves from anything that might sound conservative that they are in danger of throwing their backs out. It is typical that in a footnote, they offhandedly deplore multinational corporations. The authors assume an equivalence in bad faith between the "academic left" and the "academic right." What academic right? There is no academic right. The academic world is not symmetrical. The Left is fundamentally hostile to American culture and the economy. It would like to overthrow basic institutions and remake the world. This Left has been that way since the Sixties. There is no comparable group on "the right." There are a few academic conservatives, but they do not propose any attack upon our culture, polity, and economy with the object of drastic restructuring. Today's academic conservatives attempt to preserve what is left of a culture the Sixties virtually destroyed or, at their most ambitious, to reconstitute such parts of that culture that seem valuable. They hardly deserve to be equated with the dishonest and destructive academic Left.

The explanation for the Left's new hostility to science—or, more broadly, to rationality—may not be as mysterious as the authors think. The scientific temper may have been an invaluable ally to egalitarians when there were powerful intellectual authoritarianisms (or hierarchies) to be battled, but of what use is that temper to egalitarians when the authoritarianisms have been routed? It is even somewhat difficult to think of authoritarianisms that needed opposition in recent memory. There is, of course, an increasingly authoritarian federal government, but the scientific temper has been no threat to the incursions of government, nor would egalitarians wish government power to be opposed. They need government's coercive power to impose their (so far) mini-tyrannies. The only other institution to presume to speak authoritatively in this century in America has been religion. And science, or a dogmatic and inflated version of the scientific outlook, has certainly diminished the authority of religion. So scientific skepticism and rationality, having finished their work (so far as egalitarians are concerned), are now superfluous or, worse, dangerous.

They are dangerous to the Left because radical individualism and radical egalitarianism are pernicious points of view that cannot withstand empirical investigation and rational analysis. Most women's studies, racial and ethnic studies, and gay and lesbian studies are intellectual hoaxes, programs of propaganda and mutual support. It is hardly surprising that denials of the possibility of rationality should come from groups whose excuse for existence is threatened by rational inquiry. The knowledge that science produces, moreover, often results in a picture of the world that is anathema to the more rabid egalitarians, for that knowledge may demonstrate that there is a hard, concrete reality blocking the egalitarians' path forward. Radical feminism is put in peril by scientific proof that some sex-role differences are inherent and cannot be dismissed as mere social constructs. To multiculturalists, empirical investigation is dangerous because it will demonstrate that not all cultures are equal in their capacity to equip their members for success in the modern world. Contrary to the claims of the multiculturalists, there are not different ways of knowing. There is one way and, though it is accessible to people of all cultures, it had its origins, or at least was brought to its fullest development, in Europe.

For egalitarians, there is always lurking the nightmare that there may be genetic differences between ethnic groups that result in different average levels of performance in different activities. Only that fear can explain the explosive rage with which some commentators received *The Bell Curve* by the late Richard Herrnstein and Charles Murray, which, as a small part of a much larger thesis, concluded that there are heritable differences in cognitive ability among the races.[26] Some comments expressed respectful and thoughtful disagreement, some asked for careful reexamination of the data and arguments, but some did little more than shout "Nazi." Herrnstein and Murray are not racists but serious scholars. They may be right or they may not, but the episode indicates the degree to which the ideology of egalitarianism censors expression and thought in sensitive areas.

Then, too, science may be offensive to egalitarians because it is a difficult enterprise, reserved in its most important spheres for people of high intelligence who have put in years of arduous study and work. Scientific knowledge is increasingly arcane, beyond the understanding of most of us. This exposes scientists to envy and hence to the inevitable charge of elitism. Radical egalitarians enjoy nothing more than lowering or destroying the prestige of an elite class. This suggests that the scientific temper's role in destroying the intellectual authoritarianisms of the past—religious and political—was not valued entirely, or perhaps even primarily, for the good supposedly done humanity but rather for the simple reason that elite classes were being brought down. Now it is the scientists' turn.

This development can be seen in any number of academic, previously intellectual, fields. Sometimes called post-modernism or post-structuralism, this denial of truth is, as Gertrude Himmelfarb says, "best known as a school of literary theory. But it is becoming increasingly prominent in such other disciplines as history, philosophy, anthropology, law, and theology. . . ."[27] It is also becoming increasingly difficult to call some of those subjects "disciplines." In every case—the attack on reason, on the concept of truth, and on the idea that there is an objective reality to which we must attempt to make our words and theories correspond—the impetus behind such assaults comes from the political left. Himmelfarb demonstrates that fact about history, Searle about curricular reform, Gross and Levitt about science, David Lehman about literary studies,[28] and I have attempted to do so about academic constitutional theory.[29] Nonsense these attacks may be, but, as the history of our century teaches, there is no guarantee that nonsense will not prevail, with dire results. In law, philosophy, literary studies, and history, among other subjects, we are raising generations of students who are taught by the "cutting edge" professors that traditional respect for logic, evidence, intellectual honesty, and the other requirements of discipline are not merely passe but totalitarian and repressive, sustaining existing social, political, and economic arrangements to the benefit of white, heterosexual males. To change society in radical directions, it is said, it is necessary to be rid of the old apparatus.

The nonsensical denial of objective truth reached its apogee with physicist Alan Sokal's hilarious unmasking of the social constructionists' approach to science. He wrote an article entitled "Transgressing the Boundaries: Toward a Transformative Hermeneutics of Quantum Gravity," which was accepted and published by the magazine *Social Text* in a special issue about "Science Wars." Sokal took care to appeal to the editors' ideological preconceptions, asserting that

> deep conceptual shifts within twentieth century science have undermined [the] Cartesian-Newtonian metaphysics . . . ; revisionist studies in the history and philosophy of science have cast further doubt on its credibility . . . ; and, most recently, feminist and poststructuralist critiques have demystified the substantive content of mainstream Western scientific practice, revealing the ideology of domination concealed behind the facade of "objectivity". . . . It has thus become increasingly apparent that physical "reality," no less than social "reality," is at bottom a social and linguistic construct. . . .[30]

When he revealed his coup, Sokal said "Anyone who believes that the laws of physics are mere social conventions is invited to try transgressing those conventions from the windows of my apartment. (I live on the twenty-first floor.)"[31] He said that any competent undergraduate physics or math major should have spotted the article as a spoof that had no logical sequence of thought, but relied upon strained analogies and bold assertions.[32]

The arrogant relativism that Sokal exposed as intellectual nonsense is a peculiar semi-nihilism. While it professes to be rid of logic and principles, it also has a fierce left-wing political and cultural agenda, which it could not have without accepting some principles. Thus, this component of the academic left preaches nihilism only to attack their opponents' certitudes. Their own left-wing certitudes may not be attacked, precisely because the attack must rest on rationality, the possibility of which they have denied.

Concerned about the breadth of the attacks on rationality, some 200 scientists, doctors, philosophers, educators, and thinkers met at the New York Academy of Sciences. "Defenders of scientific methodology were urged to counterattack against faith healing, astrology, religious fundamentalism and paranormal charlatanism. But beyond these threats to rational behavior, participants at the meeting aimed their barbs at 'post-modernist' critics of science who contend that truth in science depends on one's point of view, not on any absolute content."[33]

The conferees deplored the distortion of scientific ideas, such as the physics of relativity and quantum mechanics (pillars of twentieth-century thought), into arguments that nothing in science is certain and that mystery and magic have an equal claim to belief. At risk was not only science but every subject dependent on disciplined, rational thought. Dr. Paul Kurtz, a professor of philosophy at the State University of New York at Buffalo, argued that post-modernists of both the political left and right denied that scientific knowledge was possible. This causes an "erosion of the cognitive process which may undermine democracy."[34]

The conferees were quite right to be concerned about the decline in rationality, but the connection between the cognitive process and democracy is not a simple one. No one who observes the state of democratic public discourse can believe that it relies heavily on either the cognitive process or rationality. Our quadrennial presidential debates are not the displays of reasoning and sustained argument that the Lincoln-Douglas debates were. If, contrary to the evidence, the candidates were up to such a discourse, the electorate would not want it. If there were a demand for politicians who engage in rational exploration of the issues, we would have such politicians. Instead, we have proposals that are demonstrably irrational—the balanced budget to the Constitution (with no discussion of how it could possibly be enforced), reviving the Tenth Amendment to confine the federal government to the enumerated powers (an idea Americans would not tolerate if anybody explained that it meant, among other things, the end of Social Security and Medicare), and raising the minimum wage.

The balanced budget amendment came within a single vote in the Senate of being proposed for ratification by the states. A rise in the minimum wage is approved by a large majority of Americans, yet its pernicious effects are plain and indisputable. A simple and fundamental principle of economics is that if the price of anything is raised, less of it will be purchased. Any minimum wage that raises wages above the market price will inevitably mean that fewer workers are hired or retained in their jobs. If anybody could show that this was not so, he would achieve immortality in history by destroying a centuries-old foundational principle of economics. Yet the policy rolls on, propelled not by any cognitive process but by irrational demagoguery. The case for democracy is not that it produces policy by deep thought, but that it is the safest form of government for its citizens.

The professor is right to the extent that an increase in irrationality will lead to even worse democratic results. Erosion of the cognitive process will also produce a society that is less competent in fields from economic activity to scholarship. A less competent society is a less affluent one and a less happy one. These are reasons enough to resist the decline of intellect in all of its manifestations.

14

The Trouble in Religion

S ome of the most acute observers have thought that religion
is essential to the health of American culture and, perhaps, to
the survival of our democratic institutions. Most of these
commentators viewed religion as the basis of morality, which is
fundamental to all else. It is significant, then, that religion was seen
as secure and central to American life in the nineteenth century
but has appeared increasingly problematic and peripheral in the
twentieth.

Alexis de Tocqueville thought it important that America's
women were supremely religious because women are the protec-
tors of morals. Christianity reigns without obstacle, by universal
consent, he said, and the consequence is that every principle of the
moral world is fixed and determinate. While the law permits
Americans to do as they please, religion prevents them from contemplating, and forbids them to commit, what is rash or unjust.
Americans hold religion to be indispensable to the maintenance of
republican institutions. Despotism may govern without faith, but
liberty cannot. These observations, contained in the first volume of
Democracy In America,[1] were written in 1834. They could hardly
have expressed greater confidence about religion's beneficial role
in our national life.

In volume two, published in 1840, Tocqueville's remarks about religion's prospects were less optimistic. Perhaps further reflection had suggested the presence of a worm in the American apple. He noted that Christianity had felt, to some degree, the influence that social and political conditions exercise on religious opinions. He saw the struggle of religion with that spirit of individual independence which is her most dangerous opponent. In discussing the progress of Roman Catholicism in the United States, Tocqueville said: "One of the most ordinary weaknesses of the human intellect is to seek to reconcile contrary principles and to purchase peace at the expense of logic. There have ever been and will ever be men who, after having submitted some portion of their religious belief to the principle of authority, will seek to exempt several other parts of their faith from it and to keep their minds floating at random between liberty and obedience." Finally, he remarked that democratic nations incline to pantheism.[2]

That was a remarkable performance. In a few pages Tocqueville not only recognized that the zeitgeist was capable of changing the substance of religion but anticipated the ravages that radical individualism would inflict upon religion. Thus, he also foresaw the emergence of "cafeteria Catholics," who obey only those teachings of the Church they find congenial, and the coming of pantheistic New Age religions. Those observations may certainly be read as predictions of trouble in religion in America, and, given the centrality Tocqueville accorded religion, as predictions of trouble in morals, culture, and self-government. If so, the predictions have been lavishly borne out.

Whether the link between religion and morality can be demonstrated conclusively, as I have come to believe it can, it is true that the coming of trouble in our culture coincided with a decline in the influence of religion. "In the mid-nineteenth century England and America reacted to the consequences of industrialization, urbanization, immigration, and affluence by asserting an ethos of self-control," James Q. Wilson writes, "whereas in the late twentieth century they reacted to many of the same forces by asserting an ethos of self-expression."[3] Religion and the voluntary associations inspired by religious life were the source of the ethos of self-control working through the processes of habituation in the family, the schools, the neighborhood, and the workplace. The secular ethos of self-expression led to excesses, according to Wilson, because of the unwillingness of certain elites to support those processes of habituation. He does not draw a conclusion about the importance of religion, but his observations do more than merely suggest that importance.

The late Christopher Lasch, who was by no means a conservative, asked "what accounts for [our society's] wholesale defection from the standards of personal conduct—civility, industry, self-restraint—that were once considered indispensable to democracy?" He answered that a major reason is the "gradual decay of religion." Our liberal elites, whose "attitude to religion," Lasch said, "ranges from indifference to active hostility," have succeeded in removing religion from public recognition and debate.[4]

There is a very considerable additional danger in removing religion from public recognition and debate, as Richard John Neuhaus persuasively argued in *The Naked Public Square*.[5] There is in many people a need for a belief in the transcendent to give meaning to their lives. By removing religion from the public space, we marginalize it, we deny its importance to society and relegate it to the private sphere. But if men need a transcendence that can be brought to bear on public affairs, and if religion is denied that role, other forms of transcendence, some of them quite ugly and threatening, may move in to occupy the empty space. In part, that has already happened. Many of the causes of the day—from environmentalism to animal rights—are pressed with an enthusiasm, a zealotry, that can only be called religious, and sometimes violence has resulted. There is also a splintering of morality when religion no longer provides a common set of moral assumptions.

It is by no means universally conceded that morality flows from religion. A denial that religion is essential to morality comes from a surprising source. C. S. Lewis, a devout Anglican, wrote: "Men say, 'How are we to act, what are we to teach our children, now that we are no longer Christians?' You see, gentlemen, how I would answer that question. You are deceived in thinking that the morality of your father was based on Christianity. On the contrary, Christianity presupposed it. That morality stands exactly where it did; its basis has not been withdrawn for, in a sense, it never had a basis. The ultimate ethical injunctions have always been premises, never conclusions. . . . Unless the ethical is assumed from the outset, no argument will bring you to it."[6]

Lewis seems to make morality the basis for religion rather than the other way round. But morals or ethics, as he says, cannot be reached by reason, so the question becomes where does morality come from. What can cause humans to assume the ethical from the outset? If morality can be created and maintained independently of religion, if it is prior to religion, then the decline of religion need not be a matter of overwhelming social concern; religion becomes a matter of individual salvation after death, of overwhelming importance to the individual but of little social concern. Yet it is observable that religion and morality have declined together.

James Q. Wilson argues in *The Moral Sense* that people have a natural moral sense that is in part biological and in part derives from family life and natural human sociability. He does not deny religion a role but does not discuss it. In *On Character*, however, he refers to "processes of habituation that even in the absence of religious commitment lead to temperance, fidelity, moderation, and the acceptance of personal responsibility."[7] The question is, of course, whether secular habituation can sustain itself over generations. I was inclined at one time to think that it could, that each generation would teach its children virtues that they in turn would pass to their offspring. We all know persons without religious belief who nevertheless display all the virtues we associate with religious teaching. That might seem to suggest that religion is unnecessary to morality, but the counter argument is that such people are living on the moral capital of prior religious generations. Since secular habituation is grounded only in tradition, that moral capital will be used up eventually, having nothing to replenish it, and we will see a culture such as the one we are entering.

This is not to dismiss Wilson's persuasive showing that humans have a natural moral sense, but the evidence so far suggests rather strongly that the natural moral sense is not of itself adequate to provide the level of morality necessary to save a culture. Wilson himself suggests that conclusion: "Having thought about the matter for many years, I can find no complete explanation for the worldwide increase in crime rates that does not assign an important role to a profound cultural shift in the strength of either social constraints or internal conscience or both, and I can find no complete explanation of that cultural shift that does not implicate to some important degree our convictions about the sources and importance of moral sentiments."[8] The natural sources of moral sentiments that he discusses are, presumably, what they always have been. Thus, something additional must be found that accounts not only for rising crime rates but for the more general cultural degeneration that is the subject of this book. I find it difficult to imagine what that something else might be, for America, other than the ebbing of religious faith.

There are, of course, countries with high ethical standards—low rates of divorce and illegitimacy, for example—that are not only not Christian but are not religious in any Western sense. Japan appears to be such a country. Japan, however, is also not a Western culture. Its religion, Shinto, features ancestor worship, which is a way of revering traditional virtues and thus enforcing morality. The homogeneity of the Japanese population also makes it possible, for the time being at least, to maintain morality through tradition.

Irving Kristol points out also that relatively small societies may be able to maintain morality by tradition, but once a society becomes large and complex, particularly if its population is heterogeneous, tradition cannot be adequate to the maintenance of morality and a healthy culture. It is also now obvious that reason alone cannot provide a morality. Moral reasoning, like all reasoning, requires a place to start; it requires major premises. Philosophy cannot provide major premises, though for a long time, since the Enlightenment perhaps, it was thought that reason could and ultimately would do so. The realization that it cannot has begun to sink in and has produced most unhappy results. "Secular rationalism," as Kristol put it, "has been unable to produce a compelling, self-justifying moral code. Philosophy can analyze moral codes in interesting ways, but it cannot create them. And with this failure, the whole enterprise of secular humanism—the idea that man can define his humanity and shape the human future by reason and will alone—begins to lose its legitimacy. Over the past 30 years, all the major philosophical as well as cultural trends began to repudiate secular rationalism in favor of an intellectual and moral relativism and/or nihilism."[9]

The only other possibility is that men may learn from experience what behavior produces a satisfactory or good life. Reflection on experience can provide the major premises and the minor premises from which conclusions about morality follow. If one is to have a satisfactory life, it is better not to covet your neighbor's wife. Not only are you less likely to be shot or sued, but if others follow the same rule, you can, with considerable confidence, take serious interest in raising your wife's children. It is probably possible, in short, to reconstruct most of the Ten Commandments in this way. But to suppose that an entire society may be made moral in this fashion is merely laughable. We are not a community of over 250 million reflective men and women able to work out the conditions of contentedness and willing to sacrifice near-term pleasure for long-term benefits.

It thus appears, at least for society as a whole, that the major and perhaps only alternative to "intellectual and moral relativism and/or nihilism" is religious faith. That conclusion will make many Americans nervous or hostile. While most people claim to be religious, most are also not comfortable with those whose faith is strong enough to affect their public behavior. That can be seen in the reaction of many Americans to the appearance in the public square of religious conservatives. A letter to the editor, for example, proclaims, "The 'ardor' shown by many people of the religious right is often intolerance masquerading as principle. In seeking to impose its ideas about school prayer, abortion and a host of other issues on society at large, the religious right is pursuing a program of bigotry and demagoguery that is antithetical to the U.S.'s pluralistic heritage."[10]

The fear of religion in the public arena is all too typical of Americans, and particularly the intellectual class, today. Religious conservatives cannot "impose" their ideas on society except by the usual democratic methods of trying to build majorities and passing legislation. In that they are no different from any other group of people with ideas of what morality requires. All legislation "imposes" a morality of one sort or another, and, therefore, on the reasoning offered, all law would seem to be antithetical to pluralism. The references to "bigotry" and "demagoguery" seem to mean little more than that the author would like to impose a very different set of values.

Today's religious conservatives take Christianity and Judaism seriously, but that does not place them outside a very long moral tradition. C. S. Lewis: "The number of actions about whose ethical quality a Stoic, an Aristotelian, a Thomist, a Kantian, and a Utilitarian would agree is, after all very large."[11] And again: "A Christian who understands his own religion laughs when unbelievers expect to trouble him by the assertion that Jesus uttered no command which had not been anticipated by the Rabbis—few, indeed, which cannot be paralleled in classical, ancient Egyptian, Ninevite, Babylonian, or Chinese texts. We have long recognized that truth with rejoicing. Our faith is not pinned on a crank."[12]

Only religion can accomplish for a modern society what tradition, reason, and empirical observation cannot. Christianity and Judaism provide the major premises of moral reasoning by revelation and by the stories in the Bible. There is no need to attempt the impossible task of reasoning your way to first principles. Those principles are accepted as given by God.

For most people, only revealed religion can supply the premises from which the prescriptions of morality can be deduced. Religion tells us what the end of man should be and that information supplies the premises for moral reasoning and hence a basis for moral conduct. Philosophers cannot agree on the proper end of man and hence cannot supply the necessary premises. Religion is by its nature authoritative and final as to first principles. It must be so or it would be valueless. Those principles are given on a stone tablet, either literally or figuratively, and, so long as you believe the religion, there is simply no possibility of arguing with what is on the tablet.

Ortega y Gassett put the importance of authoritative religion very well:

Decalogues retain from the time they were written on stone or bronze their character of heaviness. . . . Lower ranks the world over are tired of being ordered and commanded, and with holiday air take advantage of a period freed from burdensome imperatives. But the holiday does not last long. Without commandments, obliging us to live after a certain fashion, our existence is that of the "unemployed." This is the terrible spiritual situation in which the best youth of the world finds itself today.

By dint of feeling itself free, exempt from restrictions, it feels itself empty. . . . Before long there will be heard throughout the planet a formidable cry, rising like the howling of innumerable dogs to the stars, asking for someone or something to take command, to impose an occupation, a duty.[13]

Hence, among other things, the "politics of meaning."

Religion supplies the major premises from which moral reasoning begins, but after that trouble may begin. The difficulty is not with the major premises religion provides but with the minor premises that must be provided by secular reasoning and secular disciplines. These are essential to discern what the major premises require for their fulfillment in a variety of worldly circumstances. The reasoning and discernment must be done by both clergy and laity. One reason for humility is that often the persons concerned will lack the essential knowledge and will leap to a conclusion that retards rather than advances the religious value in question. The Roman Catholic Church, for example, long ignored or misunderstood economics, with the result that it advanced such intellectual bloomers as the just wage doctrine, which, if it had been effective, would have inflicted the same harm—unemployment—as the minimum wage. But religious belief coupled with sound secular reasoning is of enormous benefit to a society.

In that case, it may be asked, why is America's culture not thriving rather than degenerating? How could Lasch speak of the "gradual decay of religion"? We are, after all, regularly assured that Americans are the most religious people among the industrial democracies; 90 percent of Americans say they believe in God, over half report they pray at least once a day, and more than 40 percent claim to have gone to church in any given week. Surely that demonstrates the continuation of the vibrant religious belief Tocqueville saw, and surely it refutes Lasch.

The truth is that, despite the statistics on churchgoing, etc., the United States is a very secular nation that, for the most part, does not take religion seriously. Not only may the statistics overstate the religious reality—people may be telling pollsters what they think makes a good impression—but statistics say nothing of the quality or depth of American religious belief. It is increasingly clear that very few people who claim a religion could truthfully say that it informs their attitudes and significantly affects their behavior.[14]

The practices and beliefs of the Catholic laity offer a good test case because the Catholic Church's teachings on contraception, abortion, divorce and remarriage, and the infallibility of the pope on matters of faith and morals, are unusually clear. Yet it is also clear that many of the laity display the Tocqueville syndrome and "keep their minds floating at random between liberty and obedience." A 1985 *New York Times/CBS News* poll shows that 68 percent of Catholics favored the use of artificial birth control, and 73 percent thought Catholics should be allowed to divorce and remarry, and 79 percent believed you can disagree with the pope on these issues and still be a good Catholic. Catholics even have higher abortion rates than do Protestants and Jews.[15] I have no figures on comparative divorce rates, but anyone with a large Catholic acquaintance has seen a large number of divorces. The Church has accommodated itself to this reality, the zeitgeist, by granting annulments, even of long-standing marriages that have produced children. In short, Catholics' obedience to their doctrines would seem to run at the same level as Protestants' to theirs.

Conformity to the spirit of the times appears to characterize the clergy as well as the laity. In 1968 Pope Paul VI issued an encyclical on birth control that, to state the matter gently, was thoroughly counter to the zeitgeist and highly unpopular. The American bishops decided to give the position only verbal support and, according to James Hitchcock, a Catholic writer, thereby "made the fundamental strategic mistake which has been the undoing of liberal Protestantism. For over a century liberal Protestantism has steadily surrendered Christian positions deemed incredible by a particular historic age, the better to protect the core of the faith. But in each generation, more such surrenders are demanded, until there is finally nothing left, and surrender itself becomes the chief expectation which liberals must meet."[16] The result, he says, has been the "steady erosion of every distinctively Catholic moral position." That much seems clear, as the figures above about the disagreement of the laity with Church doctrine demonstrate.

What Frederick Lewis Allen noted of the 1920s was true for a long time previously and remains true today: religion is declining because those identified with it do not actually believe in it.[17] It seems impossible to say that a person believes in a religion when he rejects what the religion proclaims. It is difficult to say that a religion even exists if it keeps giving up its tenets to appease its members and critics. If belief, in some sense, can be said to be present, it is a weak and watery belief that is no match for parishioners' personal, secular concerns.

The first question, then, is why belief evaporated, why the West has become so rapidly secularized. A number of factors might be cited, but underlying them and giving them force I would put the advance of egalitarianism and individualism together with the progress of technology that made lives easier. Those of us used to the soft, therapeutic religions of the present day forget how rigorous religion used to be, Protestant as well as Catholic. As life became easier and diversions more plentiful, men are less willing to accept the authority of their clergy and less willing to worship a demanding God, a God who dictates how one should live and puts a great many bodily and psychological pleasures off limits.

It was tempting for men who wanted freedom from religious prohibitions to accept the idea that science was steadily disproving religion's claims. The three most influential thinkers of the modern era, men who advanced their theories as science, either were bitterly hostile to religion or espoused theories that could be read to undercut faith. Sigmund Freud assailed religion "in all its forms as an illusion and therefore recast it as a form of neurosis."[18] Karl Marx viewed religion as superstition that opposed the progress of the working class. Charles Darwin offered the theory of evolution that was taken by many to disprove the theory of a Creator. Many people were particularly attracted to what they took to be the message of the new science of psychology: sex is the driving force of life and inhibitions are not only passé but dangerous.

The lures of hedonism aside, the intellectual prestige of science was high because of its increasing ability to predict and explain much that had previously been mysterious, and also continually to improve the material conditions of life. Science is assumed to be hostile to supernatural theories. Most people would say that religious belief requires an act of faith while a belief that science can compass all reality does not. A belief that science will ultimately explain everything, however, also requires a leap of faith. Faith in science requires the unproven assumption that all reality is material, that there is nothing beyond or outside the material universe.[19] Perhaps that is right, though it seems counterintuitive, but it cannot be proven and therefore rests on an untested and untestable assumption. That being the case, there is no logical reason why science should be hostile to or displace religion. There are, in fact, arguments that materialism as a philosophy is now dead,[20] but I need go no further than to assert that the belief that science has demonstrated the falsity or improbability of religious beliefs is itself false.

Refuting the supposed opposition between religion and science, however, will have no noticeable effect in reinvigorating religion. We have gotten used to its effective absence. Many people go through life with no particular beliefs, and appear untroubled by it. Others have substituted some political movement as their religion—environmentalism, animal rights, feminism, incremental socialism. The churches themselves have turned left. This has been blamed on the Sixties: "The New Left also affected religious life in the West. The Protestant mainline churches turned to the left; the World Council of Churches identified itself with the Third World as against the West. . . . Liberation theology affected young Catholic priests and nuns who became soldiers in the antiwar, anticapitalist, and anti-American empire movements of the late 1960s and 1970s. While they condemned 'cutthroat capitalism,' they seldom criticized 'cutthroat socialism.'"[21] All quite true; the Sixties jump-started the leftist politicization of the churches, but the process was under way before that.

Clergy and church bureaucrats are members of the intellectual class and look to that class for approval, an approval they cannot win through their merits as religionists, but only through their political attitudes and political usefulness. Too often it is clear that the president of Notre Dame would much prefer the approval of the presidents of Harvard and Yale to that of the pope. On domestic issues other than abortion, the Catholic bishops often look like the Democratic Party in robes. They claim to be for welfare reform, for example, but they oppose the Republican bill for the same reasons the Democrats do. On issue after issue, they line up with the Democrats and against the Republicans.

The mainline Protestant churches are further to the left. The

National Council of Churches of Christ in the United States of America (NCC), which represents most mainline Protestant denominations, has consistently taken liberal left positions on domestic issues and has been strongly critical of the foreign policy of the United States while much more favorable to the foreign policies of the Soviet Union and other Communist regimes. The NCC

> has taken the ideas of the liberal-left, clothed them in theological garments, and accorded them the status of quasi-dogma. Political "liberation" seems more important than spiritual salvation; sin, now only rarely personal, is often identified with "unjust structures"—capitalism or anything "reactionary"; an earthly kingdom of "justice for the oppressed" displaces or even claims to be the Kingdom of God; and corporations, the military, and the United States are labeled "demonic powers." Revolutionary movements, on the other hand, are "new thrusts for human dignity and freedom"; revolutionary leaders, the new messiah figures, are "co-workers with God."[22]

The World Council of Churches is, if anything, worse. During the Cold War, the WCC regularly took positions that were pro-communist and anti-United States. The Sixth Assembly of the WCC met in Vancouver in 1983 and adopted resolutions on the war in Afghanistan and the conflicts in Central America, especially the fighting in Nicaragua where the Sandinista regime was instituting a violent communist dictatorship. As Ernest W. Lefever, a political commentator, noted, the WCC's position on Afghanistan carefully did not blame the Soviet Union for invading, but did call for "'an end to the supply of arms to the opposition groups from the outside,' meaning that military supplies to the freedom fighters, primarily from the United States, should cease." The Russian Orthodox Church, a member of the Council and a tool of the Soviet government, called this "balanced and realistic." Lefever wrote that the "Central American resolution repeatedly portrayed the United States as the only external aggressive, militaristic, and repressive force in the region"; "Respected scholars on Central American affairs could discern no difference in the WCC resolution and the views espoused by Moscow and Havana." Capitalism was defined as a system of "economic domination and unjust social structures" that suppresses the "socio-economic rights of people, such as the basic needs of families, communities, and the rights of workers."[23]

The members of the American denominations represented by the NCC and the WCC are far more conservative than the controlling bureaucracies of those organizations. But many of the member church bureaucracies are themselves to the left of the parishioners. There was something of an uproar when a Presbyterian official and other NCC leaders visited the White House, "laid hands" on President Clinton, and prayed for him to be "strong for the task" of resisting the Republican Congress.[24] A unit of the Episcopal Church, Women in Mission and Ministry, co-sponsored a National Feminist Exposition, characterized by the Institute on Religion and Democracy, a Washington think tank, as a "left-wing, partisan political extravaganza" showcasing a "pantheon of radical feminist leaders." The major agenda item was to "galvanize opposition to the Republican Congress during the 1996 elections."[25]

The United Methodist Church was particularly busy. At its 1995 fall meeting, the UM Board of Church and Society asked President Clinton to release fourteen Puerto Rican "political prisoners." The "political" acts that got them into prison included a hundred bombings in five cities during the late 1970s and early 1980s, which killed five people, caused eighty injuries and produced more than $3.5 million in damage. The Board's resolution compared the terrorists to American patriots during the Revolutionary War as well as to the apostles Peter and Paul. The terrorists wanted Puerto Rican independence, which their fellow Puerto Ricans regularly reject at the polls. The UM Board nevertheless said that the terrorists had "taken up arms against the colonizer," the United States, and regretted that their "resistance" had been "criminalized."[26]

At another fall meeting, the United Methodist Board of Global Ministries defended affirmative action against what it perceived as an increasingly racist America. One Board member said, "We live in terrifying times," and identified radio talk shows as a "hotbed" of the thinking she feared. Another referred to the "climate of hate and violence" and said, "White, male supremacists now wear suits. They talk states rights and anti-taxes." Yet another argued that the United States and China are equivalent in their human rights problems and claimed that "domestic battering" is the "number one cause of death for women in the U.S."[27] These people live in a leftist dream world so powerful that they can repeat lies like that without shame, perhaps without even realizing that what they are saying has no relation to reality.

Leftishness usually means hostility to the United States and that is abundantly present in the old mainline Protestant churches. This was in evidence before and during the Gulf War:

> Most oldline voices seemed to experience no doubt about the moral correctness of rejecting the use of force. Amidst ambiguities and uncertainties, the worst case was almost always assumed regarding the result of further war and the United States' role in it. What some religious leaders affirmed as necessary about the American leadership in the crisis was heavily qualified with accusations of hypocrisy on the part of political leaders, while the worst fears of church leaders regarding American involvement in the Gulf were expressed in terms of a militaristic, imperial conspiracy. On the other hand, the best case was always assumed for multilateral diplomacy and negotiation to bring a just peace. . . . The more power in the hands of the Secretary General of the U.N., and out of the hands of President Bush, the better.[28]

It was not just the Gulf War that evoked such sentiments. During 1985–1988, the leadership of the Presbyterian Church (USA) was seeking support for its document "Presbyterians and Peacemaking: Are We Now Called to Resistance?" which "condemned the United States for its 'idolatrous' possession of nuclear weapons, and suggested that Presbyterians 'resist' the idolatry by acts of civil disobedience such as refusing to pay taxes."[29]

It is hardly surprising that such churches have lost substantial membership. The situation of the mainline Protestant denominations was described by the Roper Center for Public Opinion Research:

> As recently as the 1950s, their memberships' rates of growth equalled or surpassed that of the US population as a whole. But their growth slowed in the early 1960s, and by the latter part of the decade they were losing ground in overall membership. This decline has continued right to the present. By 1990, the old

mainline Protestant churches had lost at least one-fifth and per-haps as much as one-third of the membership total they claimed just a quarter-century earlier. The extent and persistence of this drop-off in membership has no parallel in US religious experi-ence. The proportion of Americans affiliated with mainline Protestant denominations is now at its twentieth-century low. And, in considering these data, it's important to keep in mind that church membership overall has been rising over this span.[30]

The mainline Protestant churches have melded too much with the secular culture so that their members see less reason to attend.[31] It would be more accurate to say that these churches have melded with the far left wing of the secular culture. The decline in membership would be even more dramatic if parishioners were aware of just how extreme many of the church bureaucracies have become.

The problem is not merely that much of the hierarchy has gone politically left. There is also the problem Tocqueville identified: the influence of the surrounding culture on the churches, in this case, the elite culture. The most striking manifestation of that is, of course, the ordination of practicing gays and lesbians as denomina-tional ministers. That is a flat rejection of biblical principles for a secular, egalitarian, and therefore permissive, outlook. It is uncertain that the mainline churches could prevent this even if they wanted to; discipline has broken down within the church hierarchies. Thus, Episcopal Bishop John Spong of Newark, New Jersey, reportedly said that he will continue to ordain homosexuals even if his church instructs him not to do so.[32] In other ways, too, the mainline Protes-tant churches have conformed their standards to those of the secular culture, on the theory, which has proved mistaken again and again, that to remain "relevant" and keep its members, a church must change with the times. The Roman Catholic Church has made the same mistake, but to a somewhat lesser degree.

The obtrusive fact is that the churches that make the highest demands on their members, that focus on salvation, community, and morality, that stand against the direction of the secular culture, are the churches that have gained in membership. Evangelical denomi-nations are examples of this. The same phenomenon is observable within denominations. The Catholic Church suffers from a shortage of priests and men seeking to become priests, but there is no shortage of vocations in the orthodox dioceses.

If the factors just discussed were not enough cause for concern, there are yet stronger forces seeking to remake religion and to marginalize it. The strongest force seeking to destroy traditional religions is feminism. Radical feminists have very little use for religion or churches as they are, but they do not leave the churches whose doctrines and liturgies they find objectionable. They work within to change the churches so that the final product will bear little resemblance to Christianity. The feminists call for "reimagining" the Christian religion, which means rejecting all traditional doctrine. One form of reimagining is to reject the gospels because they were written by men and replace them with a history that pleases feminists. Feminists see no problem with that, according to Catholic theologian Joyce Little, because they believe that written history is merely the record of the victors, and that includes the Bible. "Everything is a form of propaganda pushing somebody's ideology. Nothing is to be trusted at face value. This is what the feminists mean by their 'hermeneutics of suspicion'. And on this foundation of suspicion the feminists have constructed their ideological alternative to Christian faith."[33] The implications of this approach for honest investigation are obvious: anything goes. "The purpose of scholarship has become, not the discovery of truth, but the nurture of feminist consciousness," wrote theologian William Oddie, then an Anglican, in the process of analyzing the views of a feminist theologian teaching at Notre Dame.[34] Thus, biblical history is rewritten, without evidence to support the rewriting, so that it better fits the feminist view of what women must have done, what ought to have happened.

Feminist gatherings within traditional denominations celebrate and pray to pagan goddesses. Witchcraft is undergoing an enormous revival in feminist circles as the antagonist of Christian faith. The damage done to traditional religion that is most obvious to the people in the pews is the feminist drive to make the language of the scriptures and the liturgy "inclusive." As in all of feminism's endeavors, the charge is that the traditional—in this case the English language and the original language of the Bible—are unjust and offensive because they make women feel left out.

The complaint is both silly and one more instance of feminists' ability to find offense everywhere and whine about it. But in churches as in universities and the military, the opposition collapses at once when belligerent women claim to be offended. One of the results of the inclusive language drive has been ludicrous alterations in religious texts. "Masculine words are no longer used in reference to God; instead of the use of pronouns, the word 'God' is repeated over and over ('God sent God's Son to redeem God's people'); the word 'Father' is eliminated because it is patriarchal; the names for the persons of the Holy Trinity are changed to Creator, Redeemer, and Sanctifier."[35] There are also, of course, efforts to avoid referring to "man," although, in English, generic references to "man" have always been understood to mean all humans.

Paul Mankowski, a brilliant young Jesuit, points out that changing the wording to the supposedly more inclusive

> "men and women" won't quite do, for it excludes children and hermaphrodites, who are themselves entirely human, in need of redemption, and addressees of the Word. Even "men, women, children, and those of indeterminate gender" is inadequate, because someone, sometimes, might well hear "children" and infer that it excludes infants. Notice: this proliferation is stark nonsense, but the only objection that can be tendered by the champions of inclusive language—namely, that the unmarked locution includes the various marked forms—is one that precisely invalidates their own claim. They can't have it both ways; the dilemma is fatal.[36]

The dilemma is logically fatal, but logic is not what the feminist assault on scripture and liturgy is about. What it is about is sweeping change in the Roman Catholic Church—the ordination of women as priests, and acceptance of gay and lesbian sexual practices, for example. But the motivation may go deeper than that, as one suspects upon learning that the feminists within the church engage in neo-pagan ritual magic and the worship of pagan goddesses. Donna Steichen concludes: "[The feminists'] ultimate rebellion, against God the Father and his Son, the male Savior Jesus Christ, has been disguised for public consumption as a campaign for 'inclusive' liturgical language. On its face, it is a child's complaint against grammatical convention, to be addressed in an introductory course on the structure of English language. But in private, and in their own publications, feminist theologians reveal, behind that mask, naked denial of the objectively existent, transcendent Father God."[37] The inclusive language campaign serves that objective by altering what has come down to Catholic and Protestant churches so that we will accept that there is no permanent truth in religion, but only the need to respond to whatever resentments and sensitivities prevail today.

If religion is being altered internally by the forces of feminism and left-wing ideology, it is simultaneously being marginalized in our public life by the hostility of the intellectual class. The two most significant manifestations of that hostility are the federal judiciary's wholly unwarranted expansion of the First Amendment's prohibition of the establishment of religion and the national press's ignoring of religion as a topic of any importance.

The First Amendment begins quite simply: "Congress shall make no law respecting an establishment of religion. . . ." At the time, an establishment of religion was understood to be the preference by government of one or more religions over others. Sometimes this is referred to, inaccurately, as mandating the separation of church and state. The difficulty is that within the last several decades, the Supreme Court, at the urging of organizations such as the ACLU, has read the clause as though it commanded the separation of religion and society. It is one thing to say that government may not sponsor or support particular churches; it is quite another to say that wherever government appears, however passively, as in the ownership of parks, the symbols of religion must be banished.

That was not the historical meaning of the First Amendment.[38] The first Congress, which proposed the First Amendment for ratification by the states, also appointed chaplains for the House, Senate, and the armed forces. The early Congresses regularly petitioned the president to issue Thanksgiving Day proclamations addressed to God. The framers and ratifiers could not conceivably have anticipated that the Supreme Court, sitting in a courtroom with a painting of Moses and the Ten Commandments, would hold it an unconstitutional establishment of religion for a high school to have a copy of the Ten Commandments on a wall. Nor

could they have supposed that when a public school system provided remedial education to educationally deprived children, those
children from religious schools would have to leave the premises
and receive the instruction in trailers.

Lower courts have joined in, detecting the horrid "establishment of religion" in the most innocuous practices. One judge held
it unconstitutional for a high school football team to pray before a
game that nobody be injured. A federal court of appeals held that
a Baltimore ordinance forbidding the sale of non-kosher foods as
kosher violated the establishment clause. Apparently Baltimore is
free to ban every form of fraud except fraud that causes an obser-
vant Jew to eat pork. Another federal court decided that a school
principal was required by the First Amendment to prevent a
teacher from reading the Bible silently for his own purposes during a silent reading period. The great danger was that students,
who were not shown to know what the teacher was reading,
might, if they found out, be influenced by his choice of reading
material. He would be perfectly free, of course, to read the Communist Manifesto and even show it to his students. The speech
clause of the First Amendment protects that. The list of these anti-
religion decisions is almost endless.

There can be no doubt that the systematic hostility of the
courts to religion has lowered the prestige of religion in the public
mind. Indeed, the message that any contact between religion and
government, even a non-sectarian prayer at a school commencement, violates the document upon which our nation is formed
can only send a message that religion is dangerous, perhaps sinister.
Justice Potter Stewart put the matter well in a dissent:

> [A] compulsory state educational system so structures a child's life
> that if religious exercises are held to be an impermissible activity
> in schools, religion is placed at an artificial and state-created dis-
> advantage. Viewed in this light, permission of such exercises for
> those who want them is necessary if the schools are truly to be
> neutral in the matter of religion. And a refusal to permit religious
> exercises thus is seen, not as the realization of state neutrality, but
> rather as the establishment of a religion of secularism, or at the
> least, as government support of the beliefs of those who think
> that religious exercises should be conducted only in private.[39]

The other marginalizing factor to be mentioned is the hostility or indifference of the national media to religion. Despite the fact that religion is a major feature of American life, it is the subject of only 1 percent of news stories on the four major networks and the national print press, and those are typically hostile. Journalist Fred Barnes, for example, reports a dinner with then Governor Mario Cuomo and a dozen journalists during which Cuomo said he sent his children to Catholic schools because "The public schools inculcate a disbelief in God." Barnes wrote, "From the reaction of my colleagues, one might have thought Cuomo had advocated mandatory snake-handling as a test of faith for the state's students." They peppered the Governor with dozens of hostile questions. There is, Barnes says, a "peculiar bias in mainstream American journalism against traditional religions. . . . [W]henever religion comes in contact with politics or public policy, as it increasingly does, the news media reacts in three distinct ways, all negative. Reporters treat religion as beneath mention, as personally distasteful, or as a clear and present threat to the American way of life."[40]

It was apparently the third sentiment that led the *Los Angeles Times* to pull Johnny Hart's cartoon strip "B.C." when at Easter it depicted his caveman character writing a poem that ended "Never to mourn the Prince who was downed,/For He is not lost! It is you who are found." A spokesman for the *Times* said the strips were "insensitive and exclusionary."[41] According to that standard, no one should be allowed to mention any religion in public. Hart's problems with the censorship of religion are merely symptomatic of the press's general hostility.[42] When Justice Scalia made a speech at a prayer breakfast sponsored by a religious society stating his faith and anticipating the "scorn of the sophisticated world," he got just that from journalists who had trouble stating why it was wrong for a Justice to mention his religion in public but were sure there was something sinister about it. So weakened and out of fashion is Christianity that a travel writer can, apparently without reproof, flippantly remark of the Church's battle with thirteenth-century heretics that "Even the enemies of the Cathars agreed that they behaved like good Christians, which is no doubt why the church resorted to such dramatic measures to exterminate them."[43] As the courts keep pushing religion out of sight, the press either ignores it or treats it as some sort of emotional affliction. It is hardly any wonder that religion slowly loses its grip on the popular mind.

Radical egalitarianism and individualism have altered much in American life. The question of just how irresistible they are, the test case of whether any institution can maintain its integrity in the face of the deforming pressures of a modern liberal culture is, of course, the Roman Catholic Church. What is to be seen is whether the Church can maintain its doctrines and its institutional structure in the face of pressure both from without and from within.

The Roman Catholic Church is the test case because, as Hitchcock put it, "few religions in the history of the world have placed more emphasis on doctrinal purity, liturgical correctness, and moral authenticity than has the Catholic Church. . . . If at almost all times in the history of the Church, a concern for orthodoxy has been paramount, the contemporary Church has an eerie feel about it precisely because of the absence of that concern."[44] If, despite a powerful and orthodox pope who has appointed many orthodox American bishops, orthodoxy is no longer a major concern in the American Church, that is surely a sign that the Church is giving way to the culture. The Church's opposition to abortion, homosexual conduct, and the ordination of women is under attack and appears to be a minority position among the Catholic laity, perhaps even among the American bishops. If the Church gives way on any of those issues, the culture will have effectively destroyed it.

The other reason the Church arouses hostility is that its structure is hierarchical and authoritative, in addition to the fact that its priesthood is male. It has clear lines of authority on matters of faith and morals, culminating in the authority of the pope. These are matters that create no small outrage in the egalitarians of our time, and one sees even within the Church demands that it be democratized, that it accept beliefs and behavior it has always condemned, and that it accept radical alterations of its ancient structure. Columnists pronounce the Church out of touch with the people in the pews and find that reason for the church to change.

That is not reason for the Church to change. The Protestant mainline denominations are out of touch with the people in the pews because the churches' leadership changed, moving well to the left of their membership. That is a different situation than a church that is trying to remain unchanged while the culture changes its members.

If a church changes doctrine and structure to follow its members' views, it is difficult to see the value of that church and its religion. Religions must claim to be true and, in their essentials, to uphold principles that are universal and eternal. No church that panders to the zeitgeist deserves respect, and very shortly it will not get respect, except from those who find it politically useful, and that is less respect than disguised contempt.

It is not helpful that the ideas of salvation and damnation, of sin and virtue, which once played major roles in Christian belief, are now almost never heard of in the mainline churches. The sermons and homilies are now almost exclusively about love, kindness, and eternal life. That may be regarded, particularly by the sentimental, as an improvement in humaneness, indeed in civility, but it also means an alteration in the teaching of Christianity that makes the religion less powerful as a moral force. The carrot alone has never been a wholly adequate incentive to desired behavior.

The current resurgence of religion is taking place both within and without the traditional churches. The evangelical movement within these churches is strong and growing and may ultimately reinvigorate them. A religious revival outside any traditional church may be seen in the phenomenon of the men's movement Promise Keepers. The idea of University of Colorado football coach Bill McCartney, the movement started in 1990 with a meeting of 72 men. By 1995, more than 720,000 men had packed thirteen sites around the country to hear the Keepers' growing list of top speakers, to pray, and to enjoy fellowship. Promise Keepers has a staff of 300 and a budget of more than $60 million.[45] At the highly emotional meetings, the men vow to be faithful in marriage, to be good family men, and to seek denominational and racial unity. They work with their local churches. Some anxiety has been expressed that Keepers is a theological and doctrinal hodgepodge, but that is not terribly relevant to the question of whether the movement can help restore the moral tone of society. Perhaps Keepers' highly emotional commitment can do more to alter personal behavior and elevate cultural standards than the traditional churches have been capable of doing, or willing to try to do, in recent years. At a different level, Pope John Paul during his eighteen-year pontificate has been laying the intellectual foundations for a revitalization of the Church and Catholic life. Whether his vision will influence the entire Church remains to be seen.

Much of the outlook of American churches today can be capsulated in the phrase "liberty, equality, fraternity," which James Fitzjames Stephen over a century ago called the Religion of Humanity: "It is one of the commonest beliefs of the day that the human race collectively has before it splendid destinies of various kinds, and that the road to them is to be found in the removal of all restraints on human conduct, in the recognition of a substantial equality between all human creatures, and in fraternity or general love."[46] He added, "I do not believe it." Neither does anyone with eyes to see and even a trace of common sense. The Religion of Humanity is not Christianity or Judaism but tends to oust those religions or soften them to irrelevance.

The major obstacle to a religious renewal is the intellectual classes, who are highly influential and tend to view religion as primitive superstition. They believe that science has left atheism as the only respectable intellectual stance. Freud, Marx, and Darwin, according to the conventional account, routed the believers. Freud and Marx are no longer taken as irrefutable by intellectuals, and now it appears to be Darwin's turn to undergo a devaluation.

The fossil record is proving a major embarrassment to evolutionary theory. Though there is ample evidence of evolution and adaptation to environment within species, there is not evidence of the gradual change that is supposed to slowly change one species into another. A compelling argument for why such evidence is missing is provided by the microbiologist Michael Behe. He has shown that Darwinism cannot explain life as we know it.[47] Scientists at the time of Darwin had no conception of the enormous complexity of bodies and their organs. Behe points out that for evolution to be the explanation of features such as the coagulation of blood and the human eye, too many unrelated mutations would have to occur simultaneously. This may be read as the modern, scientific version of the argument from design to the existence of a designer.

The argument from design is now bolstered by the findings of physics concerning the Big Bang. We now know that there were a great many "coincidences" at the outset of the universe that were essential if life was to exist. Surveying this developing literature, Patrick Glynn lists values such as Planck's constant, the gravitational constant, the relative masses of subatomic particles, the precise rate of expansion of the universe in the tiny fractions of a second after the Big Bang, the precise strength of the nuclear weak force, the nuclear strong force, and electromagnetism. "[S]cientists now understand that minuscule alterations (often as little as one part per million) in those values and relationships, or in scores of others, would have caused catastrophic derailments in the series of events following the universe's beginning. . . . [E]ven the slightest tinkering with a single one of these values, most scientists now agree, would have foreclosed the possibility of life."[48]

Religion will no longer have to fight scientific atheism with unsupported faith. The presumption has shifted, and naturalistic atheism and secular humanism are on the defensive. Evidence of a designer is not, of course, evidence of the God of Christianity and Judaism. But the evidence, by undermining the scientific support for atheism, makes belief in that God much easier. And that belief is probably essential to a civilized future.

The nature of a world without such religion, as Paul Johnson argued, is likely to be very unpleasant:

> Certainly, mankind without Christianity conjures up a dismal prospect. The record of mankind *with* Christianity is daunting enough. . . . The dynamism it has unleashed has brought massacre and torture, intolerance and destructive pride on a huge scale, for there is a cruel and pitiless nature in man which is sometimes impervious to Christian restraints and encouragements. But without these restraints, bereft of these encouragements, how much more horrific the history of these last 2,000 years must have been! . . . In the last generation, with public Christianity in headlong retreat, we have caught our first, distant view of a de-Christianized world, and it is not encouraging.[49]

15

The Wistful Hope for Fraternity

Where modern liberalism's radical versions of liberty and equality hold sway, there can be no fraternity. From the French Revolution to the Sixties rebellions, radicals who worship liberty and equality also invariably yearn for fraternity, community, brotherhood. They will never achieve it, because the dynamic of radicalism in general and modern liberalism in particular is to shatter society. Talk of fraternity refers only to the rebels; everybody else is despised and to be coerced.

A bourgeois or non-radical society, one that is not politicized in all its departments, can achieve a degree of unity through a common culture. America once had such a culture. Periods of heavy immigration of a wide variety of races and ethnic groups produced evolution in that culture without destroying its essential nature. Assimilating large numbers of persons from very different cultures is difficult but doable, as our experience proves. What may make the task impossible is that the powerful agents of modern liberalism—primarily the universities, high schools, primary schools—are working not only to fracture our culture but to suppress its historic sources of strength. This fracturing does not result from immigration but from ideology. It is difficult to overstate the importance of the cultural unity that is being deliberately destroyed.

From the beginning of our nation, men regarded it as important that America had a single culture. In Federalist No. 2, Publius (John Jay) wrote:

> Providence has been pleased to give this one connected country, to one united people, a people descended from the same ancestors, speaking the same language, professing the same religion, attached to the same principles of government, very similar in their manners and customs. . . .
>
> This country and this people seem to have been made for each other, and it appears as if it was the design of Providence, that an inheritance so proper and convenient for a band of brethren, united to each other by the strongest ties, should never be split into a number of unsocial, jealous and alien sovereignties.

Publius described a land populated by people descended from Englishmen, speaking English, professing Protestantism, attached to principles of self-government, and so, not surprisingly, very similar in their manners and customs. In fact, it would be untrue to say that the culture at America's foundation was European or, as we now say, Eurocentric. It was nowhere near as inclusive as that. It was Protestant English. There were other nationalities, of course, but by far the dominant culture was as Publius stated it. He might have added that our prospects for nationhood under a common culture were enhanced by Americans' common political experiences of living as colonies of England, of the Revolutionary War, and of living together, albeit rather loosely joined, under the Articles of Confederation.

Change came with the initial heavy waves of immigration of other Europeans with different ancestors, different languages, and different religions. Germans came in massive numbers, then Irish, Italians, Slavs, and European and Eastern European Jews, among others. The culture was enriched but did not alter fundamentally. It gradually changed from Anglocentric to Eurocentric, with a new and distinctively American accent. Those who came later were certainly not primarily English Protestants, but they assimilated because they wanted to become Americans and believed that meant adopting the language and many of the attitudes they found here. There were resentments between groups, of course, ethnic politics, social and religious discrimination, and sizeable pockets of bigotry. But there was certainly no concerted rejection of the dominant culture.

The United States now faces the question of how far a culture can stretch to accommodate more and more ethnic groups and religions and still remain recognizable as a culture rather than an agglomeration of cultures. Which leads to the further question: Can a national identity, something resembling a national community, be maintained when cultural unity is destroyed? We are, after all, no longer one united people, descended from the same ancestors, speaking the same language, professing the same religion, attached to the same principles of government, and very similar in our manners and customs. We are no longer a people joined by common political experiences and memories. And with every year that passes, we are less like that.

So far as I know, no multiethnic society has ever been peaceful except when constrained by external force. Ethnicity appears to be so powerful that it can overcome rationality. Canada, for example, one of the five richest countries in the world, is torn and may well be destroyed by what, to the outsider, look like utterly senseless ethnic animosities. Since the United States has more ethnic groups than any other nation, it will pass as a miracle if we maintain a high degree of unity and peace.

Had we been at the Founding a people as diverse and culturally disunited as we are today, there would have been no Founding. A Constitution and Bill of Rights would not have been proposed, and, if proposed, would have provoked political warfare that would have torn the country too deeply for any hope of unity. It was only the momentum of the original cultural unity that carried us forward with a single dominant culture for so long.

It was still possible to think of the United States as more or less culturally unified into the 1950s. But now we are reversing direction and becoming a chaos of cultures that cannot, or more accurately will not, be unified. What we are discussing are cultural disintegrations in addition to those caused by a number of other groups with feverishly adversarial stances. Radical feminists, race demagogues, homosexual activists, animal rights fanatics, and yet others, play major roles in fracturing the culture. But the phenomenon known as multiculturalism adds a new and powerful dissolvent. It addresses not a single group, as does feminism, for example, but all groups—other than white, heterosexual males. Each is urged to become or remain a separate tribe.

Some of this was to be expected. No immigrant racial or ethnic group assimilated immediately; typically, newly arrived groups bunched together for a generation or two. Though they assimilated more rapidly than most, German immigrants clustered in Milwaukee and on farms in eastern Pennsylvania. Irish and Italians stayed together in their own urban neighborhoods, as did Jews in areas like the Lower East Side of Manhattan. Chinatowns grew up in a number of American cities. The children and grandchildren of these groups moved out, intermarried, and, though preserving aspects of their original culture, by and large melded into the larger culture.

The arrival of groups of non-European backgrounds would make the task of assimilation much harder in any event, but what bids fair to make it impossible is the recent phenomenon of groups who do not wish to assimilate but to live in America as indigestible lumps in our society. While most immigrants still wish to become Americans, some of them do not learn English and do not apply for American citizenship when they become eligible. These groups are told by ethnic activists and academic leftists that they should not move into the older American culture but should remain separate, preserving their distinctive cultures, no matter how ill-suited to success in this society those cultures are. Hispanics, who will outnumber blacks in the United States by the end of the century, often do not regard this country as their own. During the heated demonstrations against California's law denying various social services to illegal immigrants, a number of the demonstrators waved Mexican flags, apparently, regardless of citizenship, regarding themselves as Mexicans who were here for economic benefits only.

Muslim immigration adds a group whose religion and culture causes some of them to reject much of what we regard as essential features of American culture and government. This "ominous development," as the British political philosopher John Gray calls it, is well under way in Britain, "where a minority of fundamentalist Muslims that is estranged from whatever remains of a common culture, and which rejects the tacit norms of toleration that allow a civil society to reproduce itself peacefully, has effectively curbed freedom of expression about Islam in Britain today."[1] Some conservative Muslims in the United States fight assimilation, while the fundamentalists speak of living here "in the depths of corruption and ruin and moral deprivation." They assert that "Islamic civilization is based upon principles fundamentally opposed to those of Western civilization."[2] This is, of course, not true of all Muslim immigrants or even most of them, but that it is true of some may well pose a problem. The British experience may not be a guide, since the British, unlike the Americans, have no tradition of welcoming newcomers. It is important, nevertheless, that we do all we can to counter the separationist tendencies of some Muslims, even if there is some truth in their statement that we live in a state of moral deprivation.

Americans of Asian extraction had seemed to be immune to this rejectionist impulse. They had, after all, produced startling rates of achievement in academic endeavors, science, and business. Yet, perhaps feeling that ethnic grievance is necessary to one's self-respect, Asian-American university students are beginning to act like an ethnic pressure group, demanding the paraphernalia—separate dormitories, courses, etc.—of campus tribalism.

Ethnic separatism and hostility to other ethnic groups may be inbred in mankind, requiring no explanation peculiar to any particular society. Thus, it is possible to question historian Arthur Schlesinger's proposition that "The rising cult of ethnicity was a symptom of decreasing confidence in the American future."[3] If the cult of ethnicity is a universal phenomenon—running from Bosnia to Sri Lanka to Liberia to Indonesia, and a dozen or so other places—surely the cause is more general than decreasing confidence in the American future. It seems far more likely that the causal arrow runs the other way: decreasing confidence in the American future is a symptom of the rising cult of ethnicity.

The natural centrifugal tendencies of ethnicity were once counteracted by a public school system that stressed indoctrinating immigrants to be Americans. The schools were agents of cultural unification. They taught patriotism and standards derived from European cultures. Part of our national lore, and glory, is the fact that youngsters speaking not a word of English were placed in public schools where only English was used and very shortly were proficient in the language. That was crucial to the formation of an American identity. Now, however, the educational system has become the weapon of choice for modern liberals in their project of dismantling American culture. Our egalitarians view every culture (other than European) as equal. They resent and resist attempts to Americanize immigrants, and the crucial battleground is language.

That is the reason for bilingual education. Initially, some well-meaning souls saw bilingual education as a way of easing the immigrant child's entry into American culture. The child would take courses in English but learn many subjects in his native tongue, usually Spanish. Within two or three years, the argument ran, the child would be able to take all of his courses in English. It is now clear, however, that the program is designed not to facilitate but to delay entry into American culture, and, to the degree possible, make certain that assimilation is never complete.

So many languages are spoken by immigrants that it is impossible to provide bilingual education for all. That is why bilingual education is so often in Spanish, the language most immigrants speak. But that fact gives away the real reason for the programs. Vietnamese and Polish children were put into English-speaking classes and were competent into English long before the Hispanics in bilingual schools.[4] That leaves the partisans of bilingualism only the choice of saying that Hispanic children are not as capable as others or admitting that they, the educators, are driven by hostility to American culture, and the rewards to be had by teachers' unions and educational bureaucrats. The rewards would not be there, however, if ideology had not created the situation.

Often, the bilingualists do not care whether immigrant children learn English. The key to success for the students is "self-esteem. . . . Children do badly in school because of their feelings of 'shame' at belonging to a minority group rather than the 'dominant group.' For the children to do better, teachers must 'consciously challenge the power structure both in their classrooms and schools and in the society at large.'"[5] As Richard Bernstein writes, "Bilingual education . . . is an act of rebellion against white, Anglo cultural domination." And the "animus against assimilation, is not an implicit part of the emerging educational philosophy. It is explicit, open, out there, a standard belief. 'The psychological cost of assimilation has been and continues to be high for many U.S. citizens,' declares the National Council of Social Studies (NCSS), in Washington, D.C., in its 1992 'Curriculum Guidelines for Multicultural Education.' 'It too often demands self-denial, self-hatred, and rejection of family and ethnic ties.'"[6] This pathetic whine is not insignificant since the NCSS is the country's largest organization devoted to social studies education.

Public dissatisfaction with the linguistic fracturing of society has led to calls for an English-only amendment to the Constitution. The frustration is understandable, but there is no need to amend the Constitution to achieve an English-speaking nation. All that need be done is the abolition of bilingual education and the repeal of the Voting Rights Act's requirement of different language ballots. Children from other countries will learn English in public schools as they used to do. Their parents will accept the change once they begin to see its results. Immigrant parents want their children to learn English and become Americans. The opposition to that, manifested in bilingual education, comes from American elites who form an adversarial culture, alienated from the culture of the West and wishing to weaken it.

In 1989, the Commissioner's Task Force on Minorities in New York concluded: "African Americans, Asian Americans, Puerto Ricans/Latinos, and Native Americans have all been the victims of an intellectual and educational oppression that has characterized the culture and institutions of the United States and the European American world for centuries." All young people were being "miseducated" because of a "systematic bias toward European culture and its derivatives." Bernstein asks, rhetorically, "Could the multicultural animus against 'European culture and its derivatives' emerge more clearly than that? Here we have a direct statement that the Western culture is harmful to nonwhite children."[7]

Despite the evidence and the frankness of its advocates, most people, including very astute people, tend to accept the beneficent view of multiculturalism put forth by its less candid partisans. Thus, one can find diametrically opposed views of the phenomenon, one put forward, for example, by Richard Bernstein and another articulated by Conor Cruise O'Brien. Bernstein writes, "Multiculturalism is a movement of the left, emerging from the counterculture of the 1960s. . . . It is a code word for a political ambition, a yearning for more power, combined with a genuine, earnest, zealous, self-righteous craving for social improvement. . . ." He says we are "likely to end up in a simmering sort of mutual dislike on the level of everyday unpleasantness. . . ."[8]

O'Brien, on the other hand, thinks that multiculturalism and diversity are "actually both a mask for, and perhaps an unconscious mode for achieving, a unity which would be broader-based and to that extent stronger. . . . The real agenda is the enlargement of the American national elite to include groups of persons who have traditionally been excluded from the same, mainly for reasons associated with race and gender. What is in view is the enlargement and diversification of the composition of the future governing class of the United States of America."

I am afraid it is clear that Bernstein has it right and O'Brien has it wrong. Multiculturalism is advertised by its less candid practitioners as opening students to the perspectives and accomplishments of groups that have been largely ignored and undervalued in conventional curriculums. The goal, it is said, is to enrich the student's understanding of the world and to teach him respect for and tolerance of others who are different. It substitutes an ethic of inclusion for the older ethic of exclusion. This is the movement's self-portrait, and O'Brien seems to have accepted it at face value. If there were truth in that advertising, if that were what the goal really is, no one could legitimately object to what is taking place in the American educational system. Unfortunately, there appears to be very little truth in the pretensions of the multiculturalists.

Bernstein took a two-year leave of absence from the *New York Times* to gather the facts of the multicultural ideology and its opponents. His is not an impressionistic book or one based on an ideological predisposition; it is a report of empirical findings. He points, for example, to the remarkable change in attitude towards Christopher Columbus between 1892 and 1992. Though not a single new fact about Columbus's life and exploits had been uncovered, the country's mood swung from one of uncritical adulation to one of loathing and condemnation, at least among the members of the "intellectual" class. The change was accomplished by the aggressive ideology of multiculturalism. The Columbus turnaround is merely a specific instance of more general alterations in our moral landscape.

What it signifies, and what becomes increasingly obvious, is that multiculturalism is a philosophy of antagonism to America and the West. The hostility of the multiculturalists to this nation and its achievements can hardly be overstated. Lynne Cheney, the former head of the National Endowment for the Humanities, quotes a professor who is pleased that multiculturalism has the "potential for ideologically disuniting the nation" by stressing America's faults so that students will not think this country deserves their special support.[9]

That multiculturalism is essentially an attack on America, the European-American culture, and the white race, with special emphasis on white males, may be seen from the curriculum it favors. A curriculum designed to foster understanding of other cultures would study those cultures. Multiculturalism does not. Courses are not offered on the cultures of China or India or Brazil or Nigeria, nor does the curriculum require the study of languages without which foreign cultures cannot be fully understood. Instead the focus is on groups that, allegedly, have been subjected to oppression by American and Western civilization—homosexuals, American Indians, blacks, Hispanics, women, and so on. The message is not that all cultures are to be respected but that European culture, which created the dominance of white males, is uniquely evil. Multiculturalism follows the agenda of modern liberalism, and it comes straight from the Sixties counterculture. But now, in American education, it is the dominant culture.

Bernstein catalogues the basic changes multiculturalism has made in the nature of public discourse.

> First is the elimination from acceptable discourse of any claim of superiority or even special status for Europe, or any definition of the United States as derived primarily from European civilization.
>
> Second is the attack on the very notion of the individual and the concomitant paramount status accorded group identification. . . .
>
> Third is the triumph of the politics of difference over the politics of equality, that great and still-visionary goal of the civil rights movement. Multiculturalism here is the indictment of one group and the exculpation of all the others. . . .
>
> This obsession with the themes of cultural domination and

oppression [by whites] justifies one of the most important departures from the principal and essential goal of the civil rights movement, equality of opportunity. Multiculturalism insists on equality of results.[10]

Hence it is that multiculturalists have turned Martin Luther King, Jr.'s dream into a nightmare. He asked that his children "not be judged by the color of their skin but by the content of their character," which, as Bernstein says, is the "essential ideal of liberalism." But multiculturalists say, "Judge me by the color of my skin for therein lies my identity and my place in the world."[11]

Multiculturalism requires the quotas or affirmative action that create group dislike of other groups and self-segregation. There is no other way to ensure that each valued ethnic group is represented in the student body and on the faculty. Of late, educators have begun to speak of diversity instead of multiculturalism, but it is the same thing. University presidents and faculties, secondary and primary school principals and teachers, all chant the diversity mantra. So powerful has this harmful notion become that it not only dictates who is admitted to a school but sometimes determines who may leave.

Students of Asian ancestry, for example, have tried to transfer to public schools whose curriculum was better suited to their ambitions but been denied the transfer on the grounds that their departure would lessen diversity. One father complained that his adopted Korean daughter could contribute no non-western perspective to the school she sought to leave because she had been brought to this country at the age of five months. No matter; she was of the requisite racial group. When the controversy was reported in the newspapers, she was allowed to transfer. But the episode demonstrates that the multiculturalists are sometimes willing to force a person into a cultural identity that person does not have on the grounds of ancestry alone.

The quality of education must necessarily decline as students turn from substantive subjects to ideologically driven resentments, in the case of non-whites, or guilt, in the case of whites. Although white students are often required to study America's "oppressed" subcultures and their allegedly superior qualities, it is regarded as racist to require that non-whites study Western culture. That was the meaning of the radicals' attack on Stanford's Western Culture program in which students were required to sample the writings of men who had helped shape Western culture—Shakespeare, Dante, Locke, etc. A black student who objected to the program said its message was "Nigger, go home."[12] That exclusionary interpretation is precisely the opposite of the real message of the program, which was "Let us study what we have in common as inheritors of a tradition." The black student's objection follows from the perverse teaching of multiculturalism that those who have been "traditionally excluded" must now reject inclusion.

This has the odd effect of damaging all groups. The insistence on separate ethnic identities means that persons in each group can study their own culture, often in highly flattering and historically inaccurate form. Multiculturalism then means not the study of others but of oneself. The student who immerses himself in multicultural studies, who lives in a dormitory where admission is defined by ethnicity, who socializes only with members of his ethnic group, does not acquire the knowledge and discipline that he might have and does not learn how to deal comfortably with those of other ethnicities. One of the ways in which cultures improve is by borrowing from other cultures. Europe borrowed important aspects of mathematics, for example, from the Arab world. But the essence of multiculturalism is the isolation of groups so that they do not borrow from one another. The result is the relative cultural impoverishment of all groups.

In education at all levels, the substance of the curriculum changes to accommodate multiculturalist pressures. We have already seen this in feminist and Afrocentric studies, but it is everywhere. In New York state it is official educational doctrine that the United States Constitution was heavily influenced by the political arrangements of the Iroquois Confederacy. The official promulgation of this idea was not due to any research that disclosed its truth. Nor has any other state adopted this nonsensical idea. New York adopted it because the Iroquois mounted an intensive lobbying campaign directed at the State Department of Education. Far from this being a beneficial borrowing from another culture, it was a detrimental forcing of a false notion by one culture on another. John Leo notes that the decision "shows that some school authorities, eager to avoid minority group pressure and rage, are now willing to treat the curriculum as a prize in an ethnic spoils system."[13] That it is ideologcally driven by guilt and not an attempt to pacify a large bloc of voters is clear from the fact that there are only a little more than 38,000 Indians in New York state, most of whom probably have no interest in the myth of the Iroquois and the Constitution.

This sort of thing is happening across the country as various ethnic groups and feminists demand that history be rewritten according to their party lines. This not only debases history but pits the various groups against one another as they struggle for space in the textbooks. New York's "interest in history is not as an intellectual discipline," Schlesinger writes, "but rather as social and psychological therapy whose primary purpose is to raise the self-esteem of children from minority groups."[14]

Those who have traditionally been excluded because of race or gender are not helped by multiculturalists who teach them that European culture and standards are the cause of their difficulties and may be jettisoned, that history has no content aside from its ideological usefulness, that there are different ways of knowing, that linear thinking is a white male stratagem to oppress those who are not white or male, that standard English is no better than a variety of dialects such as "black English." To the extent the traditionally excluded believe any of this, they are additionally handicapped in life, and further excluded. To the extent they are taught that self-esteem comes before achievement and leads to achievement, they are lied to and held back.

In confidence games, there is a strategy called "cooling out the mark." One of the con men, not known to be such by the victim, stays behind to sympathize, to point out that being taken wasn't his fault, and generally to console and calm him so that he will be less likely to go to the police or pursue those who cheated him. Intentionally or not, multiculturalism is like that. It consoles low achievers by telling them that achievement has been falsely defined by white male, Eurocentric standards so that there is really no need to try to meet those standards. The result will be more failure, but the cooled-out minority student will have the consolation of knowing it was not his fault. There could be no strategy better suited to prevent what O'Brien thinks is the purpose of multiculturalism: "the enlargement and diversification of the composition of the future governing class of the United States of America." If there were a conspiracy by white males to consolidate their hegemony, they would find multiculturalism one of their best methods of oppression.

The adverse consequences of the multiculturalist relativism do not end there. If members of one ethnic group succeed more often in particular lines of work than members of other cultures, then, according to the multiculturalist philosophy, the reason must be discrimination; it could not be that some cultures are superior to others in preparing people for success in the modern world. If overt discrimination cannot be found, as is often the case because it does not exist, then discrimination must be built into our institutions and standards. These are said to be Eurocentric, as indeed they are. They are also said to be designed to buttress the hegemony of white, heterosexual males. Multiculturalism, therefore, necessarily requires affirmative action. If the standards are rigged against some groups, the solution is to use group membership as the basis for advancement. Thus, the multiculturalists have arranged matters so that our diversity does not enrich but festers.

Multiculturalism, or diversity, also requires "sensitivity." We cannot, after all, value another person's culture and outlook equally with our own unless we are sensitive to that which might offend him. Sensitivity, in turn, requires small tyrannies and personal humiliations, or worse. Worse is the destruction of careers and reputations. The only people ordered to take sensitivity training, so far as I am aware, are whites.

If anyone accused of insensitivity objects that he does not have racist or sexist attitudes, the sensitivity guru, sometimes genially, sometimes accusingly, is likely to respond that everyone, himself included, is a racist and a sexist. There is no way to argue with that. If someone insists that you have attitudes that you yourself are not aware of, it will be impossible for you to prove a negative. You might as well tell a psychoanalyst that you are sure you have no Oedipus complex. He knows better. "By its very nature," Bernstein writes, sensitivity training "thrusts the concepts of 'racism' and 'sexism' and the various other isms to the forefront, turning them from ugly aberrations into the central elements of American life and implicitly branding anyone who does not share that assumption to be guilty of the very isms that he feels do not lie in his heart."[15] It is as if a prisoner pleading not guilty to a charge of armed robbery merely by denying his guilt became eligible for five to ten years in the penitentiary.

Only some groups have the right to demand sensitivity of others. Hispanics, Asians, blacks, American Indians, Aleuts, Pacific Islanders, homosexuals, and women have that right; heterosexual white males alone do not. So strong is the claim of such groups to sensitivity that it excuses them in the commission of what would otherwise be crimes. There was the notorious instance at the University of Pennsylvania when black and Hispanic students stole every copy of the student newspaper because a conservative columnist had criticized affirmative action. Penn's president, Sheldon Hackney, whom President Clinton soon appointed to head the National Endowment for the Humanities, did not discipline the students but reprimanded campus police who had tried to stop the theft. One can imagine what would have happened had the students been whites stealing a black student newspaper. They would have been expelled or suspended and police would have been fired if they did *not* try to stop the theft.

More recently, at DePaul University in Chicago, the school newspaper ran a front-page story about a dance party sponsored by a black student publication that was broken up by police responding to a disturbance complaint. The article quoted a police report that identified some of the disruptive partyers as black males. Black students claimed insensitivity and demanded a front-page apology; when they got none, a group of them destroyed all the copies of the paper they could find. A supporter said, "If you're going to have freedom of speech then it should be correct freedom of speech."

DePaul's president reprimanded those who mismanaged the party but also said that university departments were to respond with "sensitivity and diversity programs for staff," a "university-wide diversity awareness program," and enhancement of "multicultural staffing initiatives." Not satisfied, a month later twenty to thirty black students seized the offices of the student newspaper, demanding the resignation of the article's author and the paper's faculty adviser, that the paper's staff attend sensitivity sessions, and that at least one issue a year and one page each week be devoted to minority issues. The president told the paper it could not publish until it met some of these demands. He agreed, among other things, to give the occupiers amnesty, provide tutoring to make up for the classes they missed during their ten-day occupation, increase the number of minorities on the faculty, establish a Diversity Council, and recruit and retain more minority students. The protest leader proclaimed an "almost complete victory" that gave them more than they expected.[16]

Minority students should, of course, be held accountable for their actions in precisely the same way and to the same degree as white students. That said, it must also be said that minority students are only partially to blame for their behavior on campuses. The faculties and administrations who encourage that behavior in immature students are to blame. It is easy to see why the message of multiculturalism appeals to the minority student. If he comes from an ethnic or racial enclave, the university will be his first intense experience of pluralism. Even if he comes from a middle-class home in an integrated environment, entry into a university will be, as it is for most students, a somewhat disorienting experience. As Peter Berger points out, the opening of choices about values and vocations produces a process of individuation, which may then produce a backlash of de-individuation.[17]

A youngster faced with a bewildering variety of choices and no longer embedded in the certainties of the culture and family from which he came becomes more individualistic but is also more inclined to feel lost and unhappy without those certainties. The multiculturalists on the faculty, in the administration, and in the student body come to the rescue by offering the lonesome and unhappy student the companionship and comfort of his ethnic group. All that is asked in return is that his primary loyalty be to that group. Group identity is the road to de-individuation. Henceforth, the student is not an individual but only a representative. The individual cannot easily reject an ethnic identity for an American identity, not only because of the anger of his or her group which will say the person is "acting white," but because so many rewards, including friendship, depend upon insisting upon one's ethnic identity.

So powerful has the fantasy world of multiculturalism become that many of us have accepted the myth that only a minority person can understand the thoughts and emotions of a person of the same minority. That is a denial of the universality of human qualities. If that were true, a common culture and a peaceful society would be impossible. The multiculturalists, albeit inadvertently, make the case for a highly restrictive immigration policy, one that admits only people of European descent.

A white academic feminist is even prepared to concede that she cannot adequately interpret black literature because it is set within a history of racial oppression. The white scholar's perspective is said to be utterly foreign to the culture from which the black literature issued.[18] It would seem to follow that black scholars cannot adequately interpret literature issuing from white culture and should not be allowed to teach it. Why should one of the oppressed be better able to interpret the literature of the oppressor race than the other way around? There is no reason, merely the fact that multiculturalism always sees the victim as uniquely insightful and comprehending.

Multiculturalism is a lie, or rather a series of lies: the lie that European-American culture is uniquely oppressive; the lie that culture has been formed to preserve the dominance of heterosexual white males; and the lie that other cultures are equal to the culture of the West. What needs to be said is that no other culture in the history of the world has offered the individual as much freedom, as much opportunity to advance; no other culture has permitted homosexuals, non-whites, and women to play ever-increasing roles in the economy, in politics, in scholarship, in government. What needs to be said is that American culture is Eurocentric, and it must remain Eurocentric or collapse into meaninglessness. Standards of European and American origin are the only possible standards that can hold our society together and keep us a competent nation. If the legitimacy of Eurocentric standards is denied, there is nothing else. There are no standards from any other quarter of the globe that we can agree upon. Islam cannot provide standards for us, nor can Africa or the Far East. Yet a single set of standards is essential to a sense of what authority is legitimate, what ideals must be maintained. The alternative to Eurocentrism, then, is fragmentation and chaos.

The attack on Eurocentrism is ignorant and perverse in an additional way. Europe made the modern world. Europe and America made the world that people from around the globe desperately desire to enter. It is insane to say that they should enter this world in order to reject the culture that made it. European-American culture is the best the world has to offer, if one judges by where the people of the world want to immigrate. It is not hard to see what makes this culture superior. Europe was the originator of individualism, representative democracy, free-market capitalism, the rule of law, theoretical and experimental science, applied science or advanced technology, and so on through a list of achievements that have made the life of mankind much more free and prosperous. The static societies of Asia and Africa finally achieved dynamism, or varying degrees of it, only under the influence of European culture.

Today's revolt against European standards is probably merely a continuation of the revolt against bourgeois rationalism that has marked this century. Ortega y Gassett characterized the phenomenon:

> Europe had created a system of standards whose efficiency and productiveness the centuries have proved.... Now, the mass-peoples have decided to consider as bankrupt that system of standards which European civilisation implies, but as they are incapable of creating others, they do not know what to do, and to pass the time they kick up their heels and stand on their heads.[19]

Standing on your head is not a bad description of multiculturalism. Unfortunately, it involves standing a civilization on its head. Fascism and Naziism were both romantic, anti-bourgeois movements. Communism, while pretending to scientific certainty, was clearly a religious movement impervious to rational argument. Perhaps hostility to rational, bourgeois culture reflects an irrationality in humans, a desire to escape rationality and firm standards. Sixties radicalism was acutely anti-bourgeois and romantic. Its family resemblance to fascism has already been noted. At a weaker, less fanatical level, the hostility to rationality is evidenced by American fascination with such farcical subjects as psychics, astrology, channeling, UFOs, and so on. Multiculturalism, as well as all of modern liberalism, belongs to this family of anti-rationalistic enterprises.

Is there hope that multiculturalism will fade as other passions have? The best guess is that it will not. We have started down the road that other societies have taken, societies that are now riven with ethnic violence, and ethnic violence seems to cease only when a stronger force imposes peace. The center of the agitation in America is the educational system, and particularly the universities. Will they abandon the multiculturalist enterprise? Some think so. Arthur Schlesinger, Jr., is one of the optimists: "The situation in our universities, I am confident, will soon right itself once the great silent majority of professors cry 'enough' and challenge what they know to be voguish nonsense."[20] Well, they have had thirty years to cry "enough" to voguish and pernicious nonsense and haven't done so yet. This silent majority seems to be like the previous ones we have heard about, permanently silent. That is what Morson's Law would predict.

We are, then, entering a period of tribal hostilities. Some of what we may expect includes a rise in interethnic violence, a slowing of economic productivity, a vulgarization of scholarship (which is already well under way), and increasing government intrusion into our lives in the name of producing greater equality and ethnic peace, which will, predictably, produce still greater polarization and fractiousness. Since multiculturalism is a movement of the left and a yearning for more power, which is necessarily government power, its spread and entrenchment also bodes ill for the institutions of capitalism.

As Ortega y Gasset said, "Civilisation is before all, the will to live in common. . . . Barbarism is the tendency to disassociation. Accordingly, all barbarous epochs have been times of human scattering, of the pullulation of tiny groups, separate from and hostile to one another."[21] Multiculturalism is barbarism, and it is bringing us to a barbarous epoch.

PART III

Part III

16

Can Democratic Government Survive?

Sir Henry Maine made the point that, looking back, we are amazed at the blindness of the privileged classes in France to the approach of the Revolution that was to overwhelm them.[1] Yet Maine finds "the blindness of the French nobility and clergy eminently pardonable. The Monarchy . . . appeared to have roots deeper in the past than any existing European institution."[2] In his own place and time, men looked upon popular government and the democratic principle as destined to last forever. Maine asked whether the confidence of the French upper classes just before the Revolution "conveys a caution to other generations than theirs."[3] In the following century, of course, nations that had adopted the democratic principle, in whole or in part, rejected it for totalitarian systems.

Yet we seem at least as sanguine about the prospects for democratic government as were Maine's contemporaries.[4] The democratic principle is in rhetorical ascendancy everywhere, and yet it is worth asking whether in actuality, as a matter of practice rather than declamation, it is not in retreat, particularly in what had been its strongest bastion, the United States. Unlike the sudden cataclysm that overtook the French monarchy, ours appears to be a slow crisis, a hollowing out of democracy from within, that gives ample warning of the unhappy condition towards which matters tend.

Modern liberalism is fundamentally at odds with democratic government because it demands results that ordinary people would not freely choose. Liberals must govern, therefore, through institutions that are largely insulated from the popular will. The most important institutions for liberals' purposes are the judiciary and the bureaucracies. The judiciary and the bureaucracies are staffed with intellectuals, as that term is used in this book, and thus tend to share the views and accept the agendas of modern liberalism.

In his First Inaugural Address, Abraham Lincoln asserted: "The candid citizen must confess that if the policy of the Government upon vital questions affecting the whole people is to be irrevocably fixed by decisions of the Supreme Court . . . the people will have ceased to be their own rulers, having to that extent practically resigned their Government into the hands of that eminent tribunal." Lincoln was thinking of *Dred Scott*, the infamous decision that created a constitutional right, good against the federal government, to own slaves. Today, however, his observation is even more pertinent, as we have resigned into the hands of the federal judiciary ever more vital questions affecting the whole people. We have in very significant measure ceased to be our own rulers.

Chapter Six discussed the manifold ways in which the Supreme Court, without authorization from any law, has changed our politics and our culture. That process continues as the lower federal courts and state courts are following the Supreme Court's example. The courts, without authorization from law, are taking out of the hands of the American people the most basic moral and cultural decisions.

There seems no possibility of retrieving democratic government from the grasp of the Supreme Court, which now governs us in the name of the Constitution in ways not remotely contemplated by the framers and ratifiers of that Constitution. Lino Graglia, a professor of law at the University of Texas, concludes:

> The hope that this situation can be changed by shifts in person-
> nel on the Court has been shown to be futile. Eleven consecu-
> tive appointments to the Court by Republican presidents
> pledged to change the Court's direction have not resulted in the

overruling of a single major ACLU victory or even halting the
flow of ACLU victories. . . . The Court will continue to serve as
the mirror, mouthpiece, and enacting arm of a cultural elite that
is radically alienated from and to the left of the ordinary
citizen. . . . Judicial activism presents the . . . currently crucial
question whether and how we can return to the federalist system of representative self-government that the Constitution
contemplates, a return which is necessary if we are to reverse
the socially destructive policies that judicial activism has
imposed.[5]

Graglia is quite right about what the Court has become, but
he does not suggest how we can return to the system of representative self-government that the Constitution contemplates and that
the courts, most especially the Supreme Court, are gradually but
inexorably destroying. As we saw in chapter 6, the only practical
way of reining in the Supreme Court is a constitutional amendment making its rulings subject to democratic review. As matters
now stand, the Court's assumption of complete governing power
is intolerable, and yet, absent a constitutional amendment, we have
no way of refusing to tolerate it.

The question is not only one of the illegitimacy of the Court's
performance in usurping powers that belong to the people and
their elected representatives. The judiciary is slowly disintegrating
the basis for our social unity. Our cultural elites, the modern liberals, have contempt for democracy because it produces results and
elects politicians they disapprove of. The courts have long since
run out of ways to derive modern liberal results from even distor-
tions of the original understanding of the Constitution. They, and
the academic commentators who sustain them and urge them on,
have, therefore, resorted to increasingly abstract and meaningless
moralistic arguments and to lifeless legalisms.

We too often forget that the liberties guaranteed by our Constitution were not based on legalisms or moral theorizing but
upon the historical experience of being governed by the British
Crown. Our Constitution, and most particularly our Bill of
Rights, were designed to prevent the federal government from
becoming as oppressive as British rule was perceived to be. But as
the historical meaning of the Constitution fades from memory, or

is regarded as irrelevant, its guarantees begin to change. We have a student who can say, with no sense of incongruity, that speech should not be free unless it is also correct. Far worse, constitutional adjudication has become the battleground of warring minorities who seek to capture the Supreme Court, and who have, on significant occasions, including the present, done so.

As it departs from the constitutional text and history that give our rights life, rootedness, and meaning, and substitutes abstractions reflecting modern liberalism's agenda, the Supreme Court brings itself and the entire concept of the rule of law into disrepute. It expends a dwindling moral capital and weakens both political authority and the possibility of a common culture. The increasing legalization of our culture is a sign of the fracturing of that culture, the continuing disappearance of the vestiges of unity. John Gray, after discussing the fragmentation of British culture, noted:

> We may see the same somber development occurring on a vast scale in the United States, which appears to be sliding inexorably away from being a civil society whose institutions express a common cultural inheritance to being an enfeebled polity whose institutions are captured by a host of warring minorities, having in common only the dwindling capital of an unquestioned legalism to sustain them. . . . The idea that political authority could ever be solely or mainly formal or abstract arose in times when a common cultural identity could be taken for granted. For . . . the framers of the Declaration of Independence, that common cultural identity was that of European Christendom. In so far as this cultural identity is depleted or fragmented, political authority will be attenuated.[6]

A variety of forces are destroying America's political and cultural unity, and judicial activism must surely be ranked among them. As the courts recklessly squander our common cultural inheritance in the names of radical individualism and radical egalitarianism, they necessarily offer themselves and their authority over law as the only institution capable of holding our turbulent society together. But that task will prove beyond the capabilities of the courts. It takes more than legalisms, abstractions, and judicial diktats to hold a community together. Indeed, by its emphasis on individual and group rights—rights it has invented—against those of the larger community, the Court denigrates the idea that there is value in community, the idea that the collectivity should exert a centripetal force. What the Court is doing is forcing the libertarian-egalitarian philosophy of our cultural elites upon the rest of us.

The parochial morality of an arrogant intellectual class cannot sustain a democratic consensus about the legitimacy of law. As one abstract theory after another collapses in intellectual shambles, we head towards constitutional nihilism. No one knows what will happen if Americans see the judiciary for what it is, an organ of power without legitimacy either in democratic theory or in the Constitution. Perhaps we will simply accept the fact that the courts are our governing bodies. Perhaps, though it is highly unlikely, we will amend the Constitution to reassert ultimate democratic control. There does not seem to be a third choice except civil disobedience by legislatures and executives. The most likely outcome seems, at the moment, to be passive acceptance of the ukases of the Court.

The other institution that may seem to hold the prospect of unifying a multiethnic and increasingly contentious society is the federal government, by which I mean the federal bureaucracies, for it is the bureaucracies that directly and pervasively impinge on the lives of people. Bureaucracies tend to be levelling institutions. A strong egalitarian philosophy implies extensive regulation of individuals by law (because equality of condition does not come about naturally) and a depreciation of the value of democratic processes. Egalitarianism is reinforced by the need of bureaucracies for uniform rules required for ease of administration.

If equality is the ultimate and most profound political good, there is really very little to vote about. Only a society with a profusion of competing values, all regarded as legitimate, needs to vote. In such a society, there being no way of saying that one outcome is *a priori* better than another, it is the legitimacy of the process that validates the result; not, as in a thoroughly egalitarian society, the morality of the result that validates the process. There is thus a built-in tension between the ideal of equality of condition and the ideal of democracy. That tension is not merely philosophical, which is how it has just been stated, but exists as well at the level of practical governance.

A modern society whose predominant value is equality necessarily displays three related symptoms: a strong sense of guilt; a consequent feeling of personal insecurity; and, as a direct result of the first two, the spread of an oppressive and excessive legalism throughout the social body.

A society whose morality is egalitarian but whose structure is inevitably hierarchical, a society that feels there are unjustifiable inequalities throughout its social, political, and economic order, is a society that feels guilty. It may seem odd that people who understand that a complex, vital society is necessarily hierarchical can simultaneously feel that the existence of hierarchies is somehow immoral. Yet it is plain that many of us do feel that way. Bad social conscience is taught to the young as dogma. Randall Jarrell wrote of a fictional but not untypical New England college that could have carved on an administration building: *Ye shall know the truth, and the truth shall make you feel guilty.*[7] In certain academic circles, with which I was once familiar, a sense of guilt became as essential to good standing as proper manners used to be.

It is also true that at a time when we have achieved greater personal security for the individual than ever before in recorded history, we have become increasingly anxious. Every newspaper, every television talk show, has been loud in lamentation of today's job insecurity. It is a myth. The truth, as James K. Glassman reminds us, is far different. "Unemployment has dropped from 7.7 percent to 5.5 percent since 1992, workers keep their jobs as long as they ever did, and many companies (including AT&T) are surprisingly generous with the employees they lay off."[8] Overall job stability has changed little. In fact, length of job tenure has been increasing. Glassman attributes the uproar to the baby boom generation turning 50. That is the generation that is most likely to feel guilt not only about economic and social hierarchies but about having arrived themselves pretty far up in those hierarchies. Those sentiments magnify the sense of being at risk that that generation displays. The demand that all should be insulated from risk is an egalitarian response to the prospect of varying individual fortunes.

Security has become a religion. We demand it not only from government but from schools and employers, we demand it not only from major catastrophe but from minor inconvenience; not only, to take health plans as an example, from the financial disaster of major surgery and prolonged hospitalization but from having to pay for a medical checkup—and we demand it as of right. So it is in all our relationships. We have even thrown constitutional protection around the imposition of minor disciplinary measures by school authorities. David Riesman's picture of university students some forty years ago seems a passingly accurate description of our society now.

Riesman had his students read about the cultures of the Pueblo and Kwakiutl Indians, and asked which most closely resembled the culture of the United States. The Pueblo were described as a peaceable, cooperative, relatively unemotional society, in which no one wishes to be thought a great man and everyone wishes to be thought a good fellow. Kwakiutl society, on the other hand, was pictured as intensely rivalrous, marked by conspicuous consumption, competition for status, and power drives. The great majority of the students questioned saw American society as essentially Kwakiutl. Riesman points out that this self-image is wide of the mark, that Americans tend to be a mild and cooperative people and bear a good many resemblances to the characteristics ascribed to the Pueblo.[9]

Only modern liberalism, which was on the way when Riesman's students responded, could persuade anyone that our relatively safe and cooperative society is actually egomaniacal and ruthless. The students made their assessment before the violence of the underclass had exploded. People who regard mainstream American culture as comparable to Kwakiutl are obviously highly insecure. It is perhaps for that reason that they continually seek additional protection and security, and seek much of it through government.

A society whose members feel insecure and guilty seeks the antidotes of security and expiation by trying to legislate equality. Our legislatures, our bureaucracies, and our courts are attempting to guarantee every right, major or minor or merely symbolic, people think they ought ideally to possess. There is no reason to suppose that we will achieve equality of condition. We will not. In saying that we are necessarily a hierarchical society, I mean simply to state the obvious: any big, complex society must depend upon differential rewards of some kind to operate effectively. There is, as has been remarked, a "natural tyranny of the bell-shaped curve" in the distribution of the world's goods. Because of the inefficiency it imposes, the effort to achieve equality may, as in communist countries, result in everybody having less, but what there is will still be distributed unequally.

But the enormous profusion of egalitarian regulations is incompatible with democratic processes in still another way. Democratic government is limited government for the simple reason that there are economies of scale in governmental institutions, as in all others. Since we can hardly have a dozen congresses and presidents simultaneously at work, the only available alternative is government by semi-independent and increasingly independent bureaucracies.

As government spreads, bureaucracies get beyond the power of the elected representatives to control. Government is too big, too complicated, there are too many decisions continually to be made. The staffs of both the President and Congress have been so enlarged in the effort to cope with the workload that both institutions have become bureaucratized. The result is a serious institutional overload for all branches of government.

Democratic processes become increasingly irrelevant. They simply are not the processes by which we are ruled or can be ruled. And there is increasing acceptance of this condition, in part because egalitarians do not care greatly about process. That is why they prefer an activist Supreme Court as a means of displacing democratic choice by moral principle. That was the reason for the Equal Rights Amendment, which provided that it should be primarily the function of the judiciary to define and enforce equality between the sexes. The amendment, we were assured, did not mean that no distinctions whatever may be made between men and women, that women must, for instance, be conscripted for combat duty or that unisex bathrooms are required. Yet it was proposed that the Supreme Court rather than Congress or the state legislatures make the necessary detailed and sensitive political choices to write a gender code for the nation. In that sense, the amendment represented less a revolution in sexual equality than a revolution in our attitudes about constitutional methods of government. The intellectual class, it hardly needs saying, was in favor of the ERA. Had it not been for instense political activity by people like Phyllis Schlafly, the ERA would have been adopted.

This episode is characteristic. When a controversial proposition is put to the nation for an up or down vote, an effective political leader like Schlafly can rally the electorate and their representatives to stop a departure from democratic governance. But the issue is rarely put that way. There was nothing Schlafly or anyone else could do to stop the judicial enactment of the ERA or the judicial approval of homosexual marriages. Still less is it possible to mount effective opposition across the board to myriad bureaucratic usurpations of democratic control. With scores of agencies and the executive departments all churning out regulations, it is apparent that the bureaucracies make most of the law by which we are governed. Regulations issued in 1994 took up nearly 65,000 pages in the Federal Register; in 1995, the number was 67,518.

It is true that Congress can alter the decisions made by bureaucracies, but that is by no means an adequate answer. So much law is made non-democratically, by bureaucracies, that no legislature can focus on more than a small fraction of the choices made. Moreover, the bureaucracies develop rather small but intense constituencies, which often have more political influence than an electorate aggrieved by the total amount of regulation but rarely unified in opposition to any one regulation.

The prospect, then, is the increasing irrelevance of democratic government. What replaces it is bureaucratic and judicial government, which may be benign and well intentioned, and may respond somewhat to popular desires, though by no means always, but cannot by definition be democratic. Matters are not helped by the fact that the leadership of one of our political parties is not fully committed to the traditional American system of government. "[T]here seems to be a rising undercurrent of discontent with the American system among elite Democratic supporters. System alienation becomes a significant factor after the 1968 election and remains so. One suspects that a study today would find it playing an even more significant role."[10]

Tocqueville, it will be remembered, warned of a soft form of despotism that would suffuse society with small complicated rules that would soften and guide the will of man to acceptance of a "servitude of the regular, quiet, and gentle kind." That, he saw, was not at all incompatible with the sovereignty of the people; it is just that sovereignty, the ability to elect representatives from time to time, becomes less and less important.[11]

The effect of such servitude upon the character of the people, Tocqueville saw, could be disastrous.[12] It does not seem far-fetched to think there may be a connection between the rise of egalitarian bureaucracies, the proliferation of "small complicated rules," our sense of guilt, the paramountcy of security among our domestic gods, and the symptoms of enervation and loss of self-confidence that seem to afflict all Western democracies, in domestic matters as well as international. That there is a decline in self-confidence seems plain. It takes confidence in your values to punish for crime, and yet punishment rates in the United States and all of the Western world have declined even as crime rates soared. It takes assurance to enforce community standards of behavior, but, though most of us do not like the fact, pornography has become a national plague.

If there is a connection, as seems highly likely, then something very ominous and perhaps irreversible is happening to us as a people and as a community. It is disturbing in many respects but in none more so than in relation to the prospects for democratic government. A people without energy and self-confidence runs a greater risk of tyranny, albeit of the soft variety.

Tocqueville thought he saw a protection against this but it is now proving illusory. Aristocratic countries, he said, abound in powerful individuals who cannot be easily oppressed and "such persons restrain a government within general habits of moderation and reserve." Democracies contain no such persons, but their role, Tocqueville thought, may be played by great private corporations and associations, each of which "is a powerful and enlightened member of the community, which cannot be disposed of at pleasure or oppressed without remonstrance, and which, by defending its own rights against the encroachments of the government, saves the common liberties of the country."

He did not foresee that in an age of egalitarian passion these great institutions might play the role of aristocrats not by succeeding to their power but by sharing their fate. Egalitarians necessarily dislike any center of power other than government. The great private institutions that were supposed to intermediate between the individual and the power of the state are becoming instead the conduits by which government regulation controls the individual. In the process the strength of these institutions is sapped. They do not remonstrate with government so much as seek a truce with it, a truce that never holds for long.

The great business corporations have long since ceased to seek much more than an accommodation. Now other institutions are being drawn into the web of regulation. Private universities have become unhappily aware of the regulation they accepted when they started taking federal money. The question arises whether any private university or any other institution can live apart from the federal government. Government has devised, as Robert Nisbet points out, new, softer, and less resistible modes of coercion.[13] Its motives are sometimes benign, and, indeed, the institutions ask for subsidies or contracts to which conditions will be attached.

The world proves more resistant to public policy than regulators expect. People can be regulated but the expected results often do not appear. The regulator's response is to demand more complete control of people and of the social process. Martin Mayer states the progression of regulation in the field of racial equality: "nondiscrimination became equal opportunity became affirmative action became goals became quotas became 'equality of outcomes.'"[14] Non-discrimination, as an ideal, was an objection to government interference in free social processes, but the results were not the expected millennium, and hence the movement, by stages, to equality of outcomes, which, as an ideal, is government objection to free social processes. The same progression may be traced in a variety of fields of regulation.

The gradual displacement of democratic government by bureaucratic government does not necessarily suggest that the relatively mild and well-intentioned, though insistent, reign of the bureaucracies will be stable. If it is true that bureaucratic egalitarianism suffocates the spirit, and weakens the morale and self-confidence of the community while it saps the strength of intermediate institutions, then it leaves society as an aggregation of individual particles ranged against the state. That kind of society— anxious, insecure, irritated, bored, the people an undifferentiated mass—may perhaps more easily be swept by mass movements joined to populist rhetoric and transcendental principles. Such movements create excitement and a sense of purpose; they promise the restoration of the lost but longed-for sense of community. In a word, a society so reduced is more vulnerable to one or another form of authoritarianism.

The intellectual class contributes heavily to social guilt, insecurity, and egalitarian policies. It is impossible in short compass to give an adequate impression of the amount of intellectual energy, in both teaching and writing, that is devoted to attempts to prove free economic and social processes so defective that legal intervention is required. Much of the literature is itself so deficient, so palpably illogical and at variance with observable fact, that one must conclude it is the rationalization of prejudice rather than the explanation of positions arrived at by a process of intellection. The weight of this intellectual product upon legislative opinion in the middle and upper middle classes is enormous. The effect of it upon the disseminators of popular information and upon policy-makers in government is profound. That is why the alliance or, perhaps more accurately, the congruence of intellectual opinion with populist politics has such a profound impact upon the direction of our society.

Perversely enough, the spread of secondary and higher education, along with the extension of the suffrage, has reinforced these trends. The complexity of institutions and relationships in our society was never well understood, and the freedom and power of those institutions and relationships rested in no small measure on an unreasoned, awed acceptance of them. The spread of education, particularly university education, has served to decrease that awe without increasing, in the same proportions, the reality of understanding. We are left unhappily in between. Respect founded in ignorance is lost but is not fully replaced with respect founded in sophistication.

Democratic government requires something that democratic government has badly damaged in the past half century and continues to damage today—civil society. By that is meant the institutions that serve public (as well as private) purposes but are not government—neighborhoods, families, churches, and voluntary associations, to name the ones discussed by Peter L. Berger and Richard John Neuhaus in their influential pamphlet *To Empower People*.[15] What we are talking about are institutions that shape and maintain values; the bridge club is not on the list. These are also institutions that assist people who need assistance, giving charity or advice or consolation or companionship.

One of the most important aspects of these institutions—Berger and Neuhaus call them "mediating structures"; Nisbet calls them "intermediate associations"—is that they stand as buffers between the individual and the state. They do that, in part, by performing functions for individuals that the state would otherwise perform. The difficulty is that, ever since the New Deal, the state has increasingly ousted the institutions of civil society and taken over their functions or controlled them.

It is proposed to attempt to restore these intermediate institutions, but it may be quite difficult to do so. In the first place, if government attempts the restoration, the result is likely to be more bureaucratic interference and hence damage to civil society. In the second place, churches are among the most important of the intermediate institutions and should lead in the restoration of other institutions and in value maintenance. The difficulty is that if government were to try to cooperate with or assist churches in their efforts, the courts, which have made a mess of the religion clauses of the Constitution, might well intervene to stop the effort.

In the end, however, all of these threats to the survival of democratic government derive from modern liberalism, which has now turned classical liberalism upside down with respect to both liberty and equality. "Traditional liberalism called for economic freedom within a framework of emotional and expressive restraint. The new liberalism discards expressive restraints but adds economic controls."[16] Rothman adds that the failure of Soviet-style economies has had little impact on this ideology. Nor have the obvious failures of American cultural libertinism and coerced equality had any impact on modern liberalism.

Modern liberalism, moreover, changes the nature of legislative opinion in the public at large. Decades of government delivery of favors have induced the belief that we are entitled to big government that coddles us. Thus it happens that the same persons who object to the cost of government and the ubiquity of bureaucratic regulation also frequently insist that government deal with still more problems. Much of the public demands of government the very programs whose implementation irritates them. We may, therefore, be creating conditions in which public policy is bound to be perceived as consistently failing. Institutions are thought to be incompetent because they have been assigned tasks in which competence is not possible. The failure to understand that our demands are the source of our dissatisfactions thus generates a public mood that is not favorable to the survival of democratic government.

Modern liberals will continue to try to govern through the judiciary and the bureaucracies. To the degree they have already succeeded, democratic government has not survived. As the behavior of modern liberal politicians, the courts, and the bureaucrats demonstrates, they have no intention of relinquishing any of their power to the popular will.

17

Can America Avoid Gomorrah?

There is ample room for pessimism, but there may be room for hope as well. Analysis demonstrates that we continue slouching towards Gomorrah. We are well along the road to the moral chaos that is the end of radical individualism and the tyranny that is the goal of radical egalitarianism. Modern liberalism has corrupted our culture across the board.

The imperative question is whether there is any possibility of avoiding the condition of Gomorrah. What can halt or reverse the march of modern liberalism? What can keep us from reaching a servile condition punctuated by spasms of violence and eroticism?

The answer, if there is to be an answer, lies in the thought expressed by the French novelist Romain Rolland. He spoke of the pessimism of the intellect, but the optimism of the will. Our trends may not move inexorably to their logical conclusion in squalor. What mistaken, and sometimes ill-intentioned, people have done can perhaps be undone. Americans, having seen what modern liberalism has wrought, seem more likely than they were in the Sixties and early Seventies to mount an effective resistance and restore much of what has been lost. The issue is our will.

The outlook may seem unpromising when one considers that individualism was the distinctive mark of Western civilization from the beginning. It enabled the West to surpass other civilizations in freedom and wealth. But individualism is valuable only when it is balanced by opposing forces. Now those forces—religion and morality, primarily—have been so weakened that individualism is breaking loose and becoming radical and destructive. Egalitarianism is more difficult to trace. It appears to be the product of envy. While envy is known to all cultures, it has often been held in check by repressive caste systems or social pressures that confine people to particular ranks in society. Individualism releases us from those bonds so that we can make our envy effective.

We are, furthermore, encumbered, perhaps permanently but certainly for the foreseeable future, with culturally powerful intellectual and artistic classes, who are well to the left of center and who press the culture always in that direction. They attack the existing order and their hostility cannot be placated even by the changes they demand. Appeasement leads only to further attacks. The problem, of course, is not merely the inclination of the intellectual classes, nor even the attitude of courts that increasingly accept nihilism as a constitutional value. Much of the general public must be brought back to the virtues we practiced not long ago. Many Americans, after all, have grown up and lived in a powerfully corrupting culture for thirty years.

We must, then, take seriously the possibility that perhaps nothing will be done to reverse the direction of our culture, that the degeneracy we see about us will only become worse. The impetus is now with modern liberalism. Writing well before the Sixties revealed the full power and the pathologies of today's liberalism, Friedrich Hayek said that the decisive objection to any true conservatism is that "by its very nature it cannot offer an alternative to the direction in which we are moving. . . . It has, for this reason, invariably been the fate of conservatism to be dragged along a path not of its own choosing. The tug of war between conservatives and progressives can only affect the speed, not the direction, of contemporary developments."[1] The task of conservatism, so understood, is merely to hold on as long as possible to the institutions and beliefs that liberalism attacks. In the contest between the two, just as in the contest between waves and rocks, there is no doubt which will ultimately prevail. In the 1960s, under the moral assault of modern liberalism, what we had thought to be rocks turned out to be papier-mâché.

The passive conservatism that Hayek described is characteristic of those Republicans the press loves to describe as "moderates." As former Senator Malcolm Wallop put it: "If the Democrats were to suggest burning down every building on Capitol Hill, the Republican moderates would say, 'That's too radical. Let's do it one building at a time and stretch it out over three years.'" There is, however, a more aggressive conservatism, or traditionalism, and it is there that our salvation must be found, if it is to be found at all.

In our time, the opposing forces are ill-named. Conservatism does not merely conserve and liberalism has become illiberal. But the labels are so firmly attached that there is no point in trying to create new ones. We may examine the possibility that liberalism will decline of itself, a victim of its own incoherence, or whether it must be actively attacked and defeated by conservatism.

There are optimistic suggestions that modern liberalism may die a natural death. Professor Paul Hollander, for example, suggests that political correctness, almost a synonym for modern liberalism, is fading as the Sixties generation ages and begins to pass on to its reward.[2] He notes that there are almost no prominent radicals under the age of fifty. There may, however, be an explanation of that fact that is not so cheerful. Radicals whose names we know today achieved celebrity status in the late Sixties and early Seventies by being conspicuously, and usually outrageously, opposed to traditional American values and institutions. Younger radicals today are less likely to achieve celebrity because they run the institutions they formerly tried to burn down. It may not be that radicalism is dying with the Sixties generation but that the Sixties generation has so completely triumphed that there are no longer occasions for acts of defiance or destruction that confer celebrity.

There is also the optimistic view that modern liberalism will fail of itself because it is incoherent as well as intellectually and morally bankrupt. But history teaches that neither intellectual nor moral insolvency necessarily leads to failure. Bankrupt enterprises can survive and do extensive damage for long periods of time, as both the Soviet Union and its spiritual predecessor, the Mongol Empire, demonstrated. The inmates of universities and think tanks are fond of reassuring one another that ideas not only have consequences but are ultimately decisive. That is true but not necessarily consoling. There is no guarantee that the best or most benign ideas will win out.

Justice Oliver Wendell Holmes, Jr., spoke of the "marketplace of ideas." As is often the case, an arresting metaphor has paralyzed thought. The winner in that marketplace is not always, or perhaps even usually, the superior product. The economic marketplace penalizes bad decisions. The intellectual and cultural "marketplace"—in which the ideas of politics, the humanities, and most of the social sciences, and popular entertainment are offered—imposes few or no penalties for being wrong, even egregiously wrong. In fact, patently foolish ideas are likely to be regarded as daring. At Yale there was always a sizable minority on the law faculty ready to hire candidates who rejected all the conventional learning in their fields but had nothing to put in their place. It was said of such intellectual adolescents that they had "gone to the frontier." If only they had. The left-wing intellectual—take John Kenneth Galbraith as the prototype—can go on selling defunct ideas for decades. The forces that put the Edsel out of business do not apply to Harvard professors.

These somber reflections may seem to suggest that the best strategy for those of us who detest modern liberalism and all its works may be simply to seek sanctuary, to attempt to create small islands of decency and civility in the midst of a subpagan culture. Gated communities and the home-schooling movement are the beginning of such responses—one an attempt to find safety, the other an effort to keep children out of the corrupting embrace of public school systems run by modern liberals. The creation of enclaves to preserve the virtues that the West has so assiduously cultivated, until now, is not a solution to be despised. Thomas Cahill describes how Irish monasteries, on the fringe of civilization, kept alive religion and classical learning during Europe's Dark Ages:

> [A]t the beginning of the fifth century, no one could foresee the coming collapse. But to reasonable men in the second half of the century, surveying the situation of their time, the end was no longer in doubt: their world was finished. One could do nothing but, like Ausonius [a Roman administrator and poet],

retire to one's villa, write poetry, and await the inevitable. It never occurred to them that the building blocks of their world would be saved by outlandish oddities from a land so marginal that the Romans had not bothered to conquer it. . . . As Kenneth Clark said, "Looking back from the great civilizations of twelfth-century France or seventeenth-century Rome, it is hard to believe that for quite a long time—almost a hundred years— western Christianity survived by clinging to places like Skellig Michael, a pinnacle of rock eighteen miles from the Irish coast, rising seven hundred feet out of the sea."[3]

The shrine of Skellig Michael (named after St. Michael, and actually seven miles off the coast) consisted of six stone beehive cells and a small oratory.[4] The pinnacle's sheer rock sides and the fierce Atlantic gales made it an uncomfortable and dangerous place for the monks. When the Continent was once more ready for civilization, the Irish reintroduced Christianity and the religious and secular classics their monks had copied.

For some, it may be possible to view the coming of a new Dark Ages with equanimity. During the worst of the Clarence Thomas hearings, the nominee for Associate Justice of the Supreme Court was subjected to scurrilous and vulgar sexual allegations that were telecast internationally. The shock of seeing how far our governing processes had descended was so great that I went to a friend's office and said, "Television is showing the end of Western civilization in living color." He replied, "Of course it's coming to an end. But don't worry. It takes a long time, and in the meantime it's possible to live well." That is the Ausonian philosophy.

It is not necessarily true, however, that the collapse will proceed in slow motion. Cultural calamities can happen quickly. The Sixties, for example, were upon us before we knew it. Nor is the prospect of sheltered enclaves entirely consoling. It is possible that we will not be allowed to create islands of freedom and decency. Christianity and learning survived on Skellig Michael and in other monasteries only because the barbarian hordes did not think Ireland worth conquering. Had they done so, Western civilization, if it still deserved that name, would be very different and much poorer in spirit and intellect than it became. In contrast, modern liberals, today's barbarians, would impose their entertainments, their laws, their regulations, and their court decrees into whatever sanctuaries we may create. One must never underestimate what Richard John Neuhaus called "the profound bigotry and anti-intellectualism and intolerance and illiberality of liberalism."[5] It is an open question, therefore, whether an Ausonian strategy will prove feasible in our time.

What may be feasible is a moral regeneration and an intellectual understanding capable of defeating modern liberalism. In a discussion of that possibility with friends, we came up with four events that could produce a moral and spiritual regeneration: a religious revival; the revival of public discourse about morality; a cataclysmic war; or a deep economic depression. Though there was increased social discipline during the Second World War and, perhaps even more, during the Great Depression, we may safely drop the last two items on that list as, to say the least, social policies lacking broad public support.

Perhaps the most promising development in our time is the rise of an energetic, optimistic, and politically sophisticated religious conservatism. It may prove more powerful than merely political or economic conservatism because religious conservatism's objectives are cultural and moral as well. Thus, though these conservatives can help elect candidates to national and statewide offices, as they have repeatedly demonstrated, their more important influence may lie elsewhere. Because it is a grass roots movement, the new religious conservatism can alter the culture both by electing local officials and school boards (which have greater effects on culture than do national politicians), and by setting a moral tone in opposition to today's liberal relativism.

We may be witnessing a religious revival, another awakening. Not only are the evangelicals stronger than ever in their various denominations but other organizations are likely to bring fresh spiritual forces to our culture and, ultimately, to our politics. The Christian Coalition, the Catholic Campaign for America, and the resurgence of interest among the young in Orthodox Judaism are all signs that religion is gaining strength. If so, religious precepts will eventually influence political action.

Promise Keepers, like earlier religious awakenings that benefited America, adds an emotional fervor to churches that too often lacked it. It may be a crucial question for the culture whether the Roman Church can be restored to its former strength and orthodoxy. Because it is America's largest denomination, and the only one with strong central authority, the Catholic Church can be a major opponent of the nihilism of modern liberal culture. Pope John Paul II has been attempting to lead an intellectual and spiritual reinvigoration, but there is resistance within the Church. Modern liberal culture has made inroads with some of the hierarchy as well as the laity. It remains to be seen whether intellectual orthodoxy can stand firm against the currents of radical individualism and radical egalitarianism. For the moment, the outcome is in doubt.

Liberals of the modern variety are hostile to religious conservatism in any denomination. They realize, quite correctly, that it is a threat to their agenda. For that reason, they regularly refer to the "religious right," using the term as a pejorative to suggest that anything conservative is extreme. No conservative, religious or secular, ought to accept the phrase. There is no symmetry of "left" and "right" in religion, in our culture, or in our politics. The Left, as has been apparent throughout our history, and never more so than in the Sixties, is alienated and hostile to American institutions and traditions. They will destroy those institutions and traditions if they can. There is no group of comparable size and influence to balance the extremists of modern liberalism, no "right" that has a similarly destructive program in mind.

Modern liberals try to frighten Americans by saying that religious conservatives "want to impose their morality on others." That is palpable foolishness. All participants in politics want to "impose" on others as much of their morality as possible, and no group is more insistent on that than liberals. Religious conservatives are not authoritarian. To the degree they have their way, it will be through democratic processes. The culture would then resemble the better aspects of the 1950s; and that would be cause for rejoicing.

Religion is, of course, not the only source of morality. The English philosopher Roger Scruton argues that "It would be a great mistake to suppose that religious belief is the only antidote to this [liberal] ideology."[6] That is certainly true. Whether, as Scruton proposes, "piety," divorced from religion but anchored in an unconscious awareness that customs and traditions embody great wisdom, is sufficient to restore virtue to a degenerate culture is more dubious. Piety in this sense is an aristocratic notion that depends on an unquestioning acceptance of tradition. Once that is lost, however, it would seem impossible to regain. People can hardly be argued into accepting a view unconsciously.

There is, of course, a secular language of morality, but it is self-conscious rather than unaware. While hoping for a religious reawakening, we had best also speak the language of secular morality to a society that has become largely secular. The language of secular morality is spoken increasingly by conservative commentators in the press and on talk radio. That language takes the form of ridiculing the idiocies of modern liberalism and extolling traditional values. Talk radio, in particular, provides a way to reach the public by bypassing the print press and television, which remain overwhelmingly liberal. The effectiveness of talk radio may be gauged by the hysteria it generates in the liberal press and among liberal politicians.

We need not decide here whether secular morality is merely the dwindling moral capital of religious belief that has faded. C. S. Lewis made the argument that ethics or morality precedes religion. But in that case there would be little social value to religion; secular ethics would be sufficient to maintain a society's virtue. The evidence is running rather strongly against that point of view. Perhaps a society—at least a Western society in which Christianity had been dominant—cannot retain its virtue when religion has lapsed.

One indication that morality, secular or religious, still retains strength is that our politics are becoming increasingly, if erratically and inconsistently, conservative. Our two political parties are increasingly polarized on cultural issues and the Republican electoral victory of 1994 surely reflected dissatisfaction with the degenerate culture liberals have made. Bill Clinton's subsequent adoption of Republican rhetoric and policies as his own, however insincere, is another sign that a conservative cultural as well as political revival is probably underway. It is quite possible, however, that the party of cultural conservatism will be defeated by the public appetite for the welfare state. The electorate balks at conservative programs that would deprive them of the slightest amount of the entitlements and benefits they now enjoy. Campaigns and elections are crucial, nevertheless, precisely because our parties have, by and large, lined up on opposite sides of the cultural divide. Elections are important not only because of the policies adopted and laws enacted but as symbolic victories for one set of values or the other.

But it is well to remember the limits of politics. The political nation is not the same as the cultural nation; the two have different leaders and very different views of the world. Even when conservative political leaders have the votes, liberal cultural leaders operate and exercise influence where votes do not count. However many political victories conservatives may produce, they cannot attack modern liberalism in its fortresses. If conservatives come to control the White House and both Houses of Congress, there will be very little change in Hollywood, the network evening news, universities, church bureaucracies, the *New York Times*, or the *Washington Post*. Institutions that are overwhelmingly left–liberal (89 percent of journalists voted for Bill Clinton in 1992) will continue to misinform the public and distort public discourse. The obscenities of popular entertainment will often be protected by the courts. The tyrannies of political correctness and multiculturalism will not be ejected from the universities by any number of conservative victories at the polls. Modern liberals captured the government and its bureaucracies because they captured the culture. Conservative political victories will always be tenuous and fragile unless conservatives recapture the culture.

The election of Ronald Reagan and the defeat of a clutch of very liberal Democratic senators in 1980 seemed to many of us a decisive turn for the better in our culture. The "Reagan Revolution" was to be a sharp break with liberal trends. Liberals thought otherwise. If their response to the 1980 elections is any guide, in reaction to future conservative victories at the polls, modern liberals will only become more intolerant, untruthful, venomous, and abusive. The cultural phase of the revolution petered out; Reagan lost the Senate in 1986 and was followed by Bush and Clinton. Today, more is wrong with our culture than was the case in 1980. If the conservative political revival persists and gathers strength, we may see a long period of an antagonistic standoff between the political nation and its culture, on the one hand, and the culture of the elites, on the other.

Victory over modern liberalism will require a robust self-confidence about the worth of traditional values that the relativism of modern liberalism has already seriously damaged. When the barbarians struck in the Sixties, America did not show confidence in its own worth and values. We were taken by surprise, but we have had time to recover and form a new center that just may hold. Now that we have seen the emptiness of the liberal criticism of America, now that we have seen the catastrophes that the ideas of modern liberalism have produced and are producing, perhaps we will shed our guilt and forthrightly speak and act on the understanding that the evolution of traditional values will produce a far better society than the nihilism of the Left.

This is at bottom a moral and spiritual struggle. Speaking of the high rates of divorce, illegitimacy, and drug abuse, and of the lewdness, cruelty, and senseless violence with which we have become familiar, James Q. Wilson says there are many causes and one must resist the temptation to blame them all on moral failure. But he then places a large part of the blame precisely on moral failure:

> These unpleasant actions are chiefly the behavior of young people who in all cultures in every epoch test the limits of acceptable behavior. Testing limits is a way of asserting selfhood. Maintaining limits is a way of asserting community. If the limits are asserted weakly, uncertainly, or apologetically, their effects must surely be weaker than if they are asserted boldly, confidently, and persuasively. How vigorously and persuasively we—mostly but not entirely older people—assert those limits will surely depend to some important degree on how confidently we believe in the sentiments that underlie them. Some of us have lost that confidence. The avant-garde in music, art, and literature mocks that confidence.[7]

In a word, everything ultimately depends on the temper of the American people. That temper is uncertain. There may be reason to think that a major portion of the American public has changed its values over the past thirty years, and that much of the public is no longer concerned with issues of personal morality and responsibility. The evidence frequently offered is the President of the

United States. William Jefferson Clinton is the very model of the modern liberal. He epitomizes the leading edge of the trends this book has discussed. The London *Spectator*, shortly after the 1992 presidential election, saw the election result as representing a moral and cultural sea change in the United States:

> The election of Governor Bill Clinton is nothing less than a cultural revolution.... [Americans] have chosen a youngish man, with little experience beyond the parochial politics of Arkansas, dogged by accusations of indiscriminate marital infidelity, and with no record of military service (to put it politely) to embody the aspirations and values of the nation.... [T]his suggests that the America of the Baby Boomers is a radically different place from the America of their parents....
>
> It is hard to avoid the conclusion that a large part of the American people have turned their backs on that old-fashioned quality: Virtue—private and public Virtue.[8]

Because it did not allow for the unpalatability of the alternatives American voters had—the feckless George Bush and the unstable Ross Perot—the *Spectator* may have been somewhat too hard on us. Still, thirty years ago, Clinton's behavior would have been absolutely disqualifying. Since the 1992 election, the public has learned far more about what is known, euphemistically, as the "character issue." The additional information abundantly confirms the *Spectator*'s judgment about the man in both his private and public lives and adds new charges to a list that is already lengthy. Yet, none of this appears to affect Clinton's popularity. It is difficult not to conclude that something about our moral perceptions and reactions has changed profoundly. If that change is permanent, the implications for our future are bleak.

It would be wrong, however, to make confident predictions about the future. American culture is highly complex, diverse, and resilient. To criticize the decadence and nihilism that are growing apace in America is not to deny that the nation still contains much that is good and healthy.

All that is true. I have been describing trends, not making an overall assessment of our culture, but it is also true that the trends have been running the wrong way, dramatically so in the past thirty years. It would be difficult to contend that, the end of racial segregation aside, American culture today is as healthy as the culture of the 1950s. Country singer and social philosopher Merle Haggard says that the decade of the Sixties "was just the evening of it all. I think we're into the dead of night now."[9] If the trends of modern liberalism continue, the dead of night still lies ahead.

If there are signs that we have become less concerned than we should be with virtue, there are also signs that many Americans are becoming restless under the tyrannies of egalitarianism and sick of the hedonistic individualism that has brought us to the suburbs of Gomorrah. But, for the immediate future, what we probably face is an increasingly vulgar, violent, chaotic, and politicized culture. Our hopes, our struggles, and our optimism must be for the long run. The first requisite is knowing what is happening to us. This book has tried to answer that, to show that decline runs across our entire culture and that it has a common cause, modern liberalism.

The second step is resistance to radical individualism and radical egalitarianism in every area of culture. It is pointless to ask, "What is the solution?" There is no single grand strategy. Just as the New Left abandoned an overarching program and became a series of like-minded groups advancing area by area, so it must be counterattacked area by area. Religion must be recaptured church by church; and education, university by university, school board by school board. Bureaucracies must be tamed. The judiciary must be criticized severely when it oversteps its legitimate authority, as it now regularly does. A few of the necessary actions must involve the government, as in capturing and punishing criminals, and, perhaps, in administering censorship of the vilest aspects of our popular culture; otherwise, government must be kept at a distance. When, for example, black churches try to save the youth of the inner city, the financial and moral support for that effort must be private. Government is largely responsible for making the inner cities what they are. Perhaps government can stop doing harm by reforming welfare, but it should leave to private institutions the task of redeeming the culture.

I end where I began, contemplating burnt books. Though I did not suspect it then, the charred law books on the sidewalk in New Haven were a metaphor, a symbol of the coming torching of America's intellectual and moral capital by the barbarians of modern liberalism. We have allowed that capital to be severely damaged, but perhaps not beyond repair. As we approach its desolate and sordid precincts, the pessimism of the intellect tells us that Gomorrah is our probable destination. What is left to us is a determination not to accept that fate and the courage to resist it—the optimism of the will.

Afterword:
The Olympians

The gods are just, and of our pleasant vices
Make instruments to plague us....

—WILLIAM SHAKESPEARE, *King Lear*

The slaughters of September 11, 2001, we are frequently told, changed America forever: a culture that had grown soft and hedonistic recovered its coherence and moral clarity. The attacks did provoke an outburst of patriotism, and the men of the New York City fire and police departments, putting duty before their own lives, behaved heroically. But the conclusion that our culture as a whole has recovered from its long decline is more dubious. Despite the threat from radical Islam, despite the patriotism of most Americans, America's culture faces a continuing assault from within. What long-run effects that will have upon our cohesion and morale remain to be seen.

Modern liberalism, which I have argued is the source of our cultural travails, is a state of mind and spirit aptly described by Kenneth Minogue: "We may call it Olympianism because it is the project of an intellectual elite that believes that it enjoys superior enlightenment and that its business is to spread this benefit to those living on the lower slopes of human achievement.... Olympianism burrowed like a parasite into the most powerful institution of the emerging knowledge economy—the universities."[1] Olympians are verbalists, distinguished less by their intellectual prowess than by the uniformity of their antibourgeois attitudes, utopian musings, and authoritarian temper. If those of us on the lower slopes do not recognize the superiority of the Olympians' attitudes, we must by coercion, hard or soft as the circumstances may warrant, be brought to their point of view.

This afterword discusses where modern liberalism (or Olympianism) has brought us in the seven years since this book was first published, with special attention to the areas of pornography and censorship, race relations, the homosexual movement, the incipient internationalization of our Constitution, and, throughout, the relentless erosion of American moral values. The American Supreme Court, it will be seen, is the chosen instrument of aggressive Olympianism. Tethered neither by the Constitution, nor by the desires of the American people, nor by understanding of the ways in which a society works, the Court has been, and for the foreseeable future seems certain to remain, the primary shaper of public policy about culture and morality. Because law inevitably has an educational effect, the Court reshapes public views of moral and cultural issues. Both the Court and the Olympian culture to which it responds are hostile to limits on hedonistic individualism, the expression of sexual morality through law, rewards according to achievement rather than group identity, and traditional Western religions.

CENSORSHIP: THE DISPARATE TREATMENT OF OBSCENITY, PORNOGRAPHY, VULGARITY, AND IDEAS

In chapter 8, I argued for a revival of censorship to suppress "the most violent and sexually explicit material now on offer, starting with the obscene prose and pictures available on the Internet, motion pictures that are mere rhapsodies to violence, and the more degenerate lyrics of rap music." That case, viewed in isolation, is even stronger now. Much of popular entertainment has sunk even lower. There is no need to rehearse once more the effects of such programming on our culture, or the near impossibility of watching many shows with any degree of comfort. If that were all censorship would reach, the case for it would seem conclusive. The difficulty, which complicates the case, is that censorship is being captured by the Left. One of the first and most important tactics of Olympians is to silence dissent. Pornography, obscenity, gratuitous depictions of carnage, and the grossest forms of vulgarity will not be censored, given today's Supreme Court, but conservative and traditional ideas and attitudes, which are anathema to modern liberals, may well be. That is taking place today, and it would be foolish to endorse a weapon that, at least in today's circumstances, will fail to curtail depravity but will be turned against conservative political and cultural expression.

The Supreme Court, in the name of the First Amendment, has made it abundantly clear that legislatures will not be permitted to ban pornography or even obscenity. In this area, the Court is not defining the limits of the "freedom of speech" so much as it is obliterating them.

The themes the Court has been developing reached a crescendo of sorts in *United States* v. *Playboy Entertainment Group, Inc.* (2000),[2] which held unconstitutional a congressional statute requiring cable television channels "primarily dedicated to sexually-oriented programming" to limit their transmission to hours when children are unlikely to be viewing. The Court majority found the law a restriction on the content of speech that was not justified because there appeared to be less restrictive methods of protecting children.

The Justices, once more equating sex and speech, said that "Basic speech principles are at stake in this case." That was a peculiar view, not to say an eccentric one, since *Playboy* advertised, as Justice Scalia pointed out in dissent, that its channel featured such inspiring materials as "female masturbation/external," "girl/girl sex," and "oral sex/cunnilingus." Most of the "speech" in such entertainments probably consisted of simulated moans of ecstasy, which the females are required to utter in order to excite viewers. The legislation focused on the danger that children would be exposed to erotic sounds or pictures. The Court, on the other hand, true to the tenets of radical individualism, gave little weight to the well-being of children and none to the interest of society in preserving some vestige of a moral tone, but was concerned only to protect the salacious pleasures of adults. "Where the designed benefit of a content-based speech restriction is to shield the sensibilities of listeners, the general rule is that the right of expression prevails, even where no less restrictive alternative exists. We are expected to protect our own sensibilities 'simply by averting [our] eyes.'" Many of the people around us will not avert their eyes, and that fact will certainly produce a moral and aesthetic environment which it is impossible to ignore. We are forced to live in an increasingly ugly society.

Indeed, the Court majority refuted its own avert-your-eyes solution by stressing the social value of even the most depraved versions of "speech": "It is through speech that our convictions and beliefs are influenced, expressed, and tested. It is through speech that we bring those beliefs to bear on Government and society. It is through speech that our personalities are formed and expressed." Try substituting "watching female masturbation/external" or "viewing oral sex/cunnilingus" for the word "speech" in that passage and see how persuasive it remains.

Apparently aware that this line of cases has been criticized, the majority opinion essayed a rebuttal:

> When a student first encounters our free speech jurisprudence, he or she might think it is influenced by the philosophy that one idea is as good as any other, and that in art and literature objective standards of style, taste, decorum, beauty, and esthetics are deemed by the Constitution to be inappropriate, indeed unattainable. Quite the opposite is true. The Constitution no more enforces a relativistic philosophy or moral nihilism than it does any other point of view. The Constitution exists precisely so that opinions and judgments, including esthetic and moral judgments about art and literature, can be formed, tested, and expressed. What the Constitution says is that these judgments are for the individual to make, not for the Government to decree, even with the mandate or approval of a majority.

In a word, what the Constitution says, as interpreted by today's Court, is that one idea is as good as another so far as the law is concerned; only the omnipotent individual may judge and then only for himself. A majority may not enact its belief, apparently self-evidently wrongheaded, that the production and consumption of obscenity and pornography inflict social harms. That is a relativistic philosophy if anything is. Moral nihilism is what, in the end, radical individualism comes to. And it is not the Constitution's philosophy; it is the Court's.

More recently, *Ashcroft* v. *The Free Speech Coalition* (2002)[3] held that Congress may not prohibit even "entertainment" that amounts to perversion: the depiction of children engaged in sexual acts. Actual children may not be used, but computer simulation (which is increasingly indistinguishable from the real thing) or the use of adults who look like children qualify as protected speech. Justice Kennedy's majority opinion described the Child Pornography Prevention Act of 1996 as "proscrib[ing] a significant universe of speech" that falls "within the First Amendment's vast and privileged sphere." Child pornography, we learned, qualifies as privileged. If so, it is hard to imagine what abominations lie outside the privileged sphere.

To anyone unfamiliar with the Court's extraordinarily permissive rulings in the past, it might seem, as it did to Congress, that any depiction of children in a variety of sexual acts could be, and certainly should be, prohibited. To the commonsense suggestion that child pornography might be used to lure children into sexual encounters or might tip over the line adults teetering on the verge of pedophilia, the Court responded, "The prospect of crime...by itself does not justify laws suppressing protected speech." The *Free Speech Coalition* decision typifies modern First Amendment decisions. The Court stated that its "precedents establish...that speech within the rights of adults to hear may not be silenced completely in an attempt to shield children from it." Grant that proposition. But why is pornography of this virulence within the rights of adults to hear and see? *Playboy Enterprises, Free Speech Coalition*, and *Planned Parenthood* v. *Casey*, discussed in chapter 6, raise the question whether there remains any vestige of the Court's distinction between pornography and obscenity. Obscenity, the Court said in *Miller* v. *California*, discussed in chapter 8, could be banned if three conditions were met: that the average person would find that the work appeals to prurient interest; that the work depicts or describes patently offensive material; and that the work as a whole lacks serious intellectual value. It has never been clear, of course, why the Court thought obscenity, so defined, lay outside First Amendment protection, but it was said to be vulnerable to regulation, nonetheless. Yet *Casey*, in its infamous "mystery-of-life" passage, said that only the individual could determine what gave meaning to his existence. It seems impossible to explain, moreover, why the materials protected by *Playboy Enterprises* and *Free Speech Coalition* were not obscene. The Court in those cases simply ignored *Miller's* tests, perhaps because obscenity is speech and thus "privileged" no matter what its content. Even *Miller's* puny and ineffective safeguards are now on the ash heap of jurisprudence.

To take another category of speech undeserving of the Court's solicitude, why are the rawest forms of profanity exempt from regulation? Cable television is saturated with words never before used in public, and the broadcast networks are racing to catch up. The *New York Times* reports that in the ESPN TV movie *A Season on the Brink,* the character playing Indiana basketball coach Bobby Knight "drops the F-word 15 times in the first 15 minutes," and that the characters in *South Park* used a "well-known word for excrement 162 times in 30 minutes." The industry response to criticism on this score is that such words give the programs authenticity; this is the way people talk. In reality, however, the arrow of causation probably points in the other direction. Perhaps people increasingly talk this way because they hear the words on television, and they hear the words on television because the Supreme Court's rulings have deprived the government of any effective sanctions for profanity. In justifying its decision in *Free Speech Coalition,* the Court actually said, "The right to think is the beginning of freedom, and speech must be protected from the government because speech is the beginning of thought." One might have supposed that thought preceded speech. And one might also wonder what thoughts valuable to freedom are triggered not only by portrayals of children being sexually used but by the language of the gutter. The point is not that the Court should outlaw such things; it has no authority to do so. But it ought not to deny society the power to curb speech or images of no social value and capable of debasing society and discourse.

Exhibitions like those protected by these decisions, far from enhancing thought, make thought irrelevant. The reduction of "speech" to a point well below the barracks-room level actively destroys thought of any complexity, subtlety, gradation, or nuance. What is protected, if it can be called speech at all, exists at the level of a grunt, which leads to thought at the same level. So long as this is the law, we must endure mental and emotional squalor. There is no reason for a future Court to accept such cases as binding precedents; it is not condoning judicial activism to urge that such precedents be overturned, that the First Amendment be restored to its proper scope and office. These cases were themselves departures from prior law. There is no constitutional justification for a ratchet effect that progressively and irreversibly liberates the worst in our natures. It is not too much to say that the pornography and suffocating vulgarity of popular culture is in significant measure the work of the Court. Though the Court did not create our moral smog, it has consistently outlawed attempts of communities to contain that pollution. When such law is declared unfit to survive, not only are sordid tastes freed, they are also validated.

That is the case for censorship: the right of the majority to live in an environment free of the worst insults to decency and of a popular culture that incites violence and sexual nihilism.

There is, unfortunately, also a case against censorship. It is not the usual blather heard in Hollywood, the press, and the universities, i.e., the right of the individual to find self-fulfillment in producing or consuming absolutely unrestricted expression. The case against censorship lies in the fact that censorship today has become more virulent and comprehensive, and that it has changed its nature: it now seeks to banish ideas and prohibit their expression. Much of this new censorship escapes the First Amendment, in part because it is imposed by nongovernmental actors, and in part because many courts are at least qualifiedly sympathetic to it.

The current rage for political correctness—the suppression of unwelcome language and idea—is one more bastard child of the 1960s. Though the political and cultural Right sporadically engages in attempts at suppression, usually unsuccessfully, it is far and away the specialty of the Left, which has abandoned devotion to free speech where conservative ideas are concerned. Political correctness is everywhere in our society, but it is especially malignant in universities, where it is usually overlooked, if not condoned or imposed, by administrators and faculties. The shouting down of invited conservative speakers, stealing of conservative campus newspapers, discipline for the expression of incorrect attitudes, monitoring of professors suspected of improper views, and coerced "sensitivity" training are all common.[4]

David Horowitz, a former radical turned conservative, found that some of his campus audiences were so hostile that he had the greatest difficulty speaking, even though he was an invited speaker. He had to hire bodyguards to ensure his physical safety.[5] Ward Connerly, a black member of the Board of Regents of the University of California and an opponent of racial preferences, receives similarly hostile receptions at universities, as have Jeane Kirkpatrick, Henry Kissinger, Dinesh D'Souza, and others.[6] All too often the university administrations make no effort to protect such speakers or guarantee them a hearing.

A FIRE (Foundation for Individual Rights in Education) survey that shows that three-quarters of America's well-known universities significantly restrict student speech. The University of North Carolina at Chapel Hill, for example, prohibits behavior that "destroys the environment of tolerance and mutual respect," while Shippensburg University, a state school in Pennsylvania, states in its student code of conduct that freedom from "emotional abuse" is a "primary right" that takes precedence over the secondary right to "express a personal belief system." In application, the attitudes underlying these seemingly moderate, if not insipid, injunctions often become flat-out attempts to demonize the person who speaks truth about facts that may not, consistently with political correctness, be admitted to exist.

Professor Lino Graglia, a professor of law at The University of Texas, was quoted in a newspaper, in a discussion of low minority test scores, as saying that in some minority communities academic failure is not regarded as a disgrace. Although that fact is a truism and has frequently been publicly reported, Graglia was subjected to a "public lynching." The chancellor and the president of the university called his remark "abhorrent." The NAACP accused him of "racial harassment," the state Hispanic caucus demanded his dismissal, fifty law professors signed a letter condemning his remarks, and Jesse Jackson, who had said much the same thing, told a student rally that Graglia should be treated as a "moral and social pariah" for his "racist, fascist, and offensive speech." There was more, including a march on the law school by a mob of students that caused university security officers to advise Graglia to cut short the class he was teaching at the time. The entire episode was attempted censorship by intimidation. Although Graglia was not intimidated, many others learn to remain silent on such matters or even to disavow not only what they know to be true but those who do speak the truth.

Columnist John Leo, invited to speak at Columbia University, arrived to discover that the event at which he was scheduled to appear with five other speakers on the topic "A Place at the Table: Conservative Ideas in Higher Education" was forced to move to an off-campus location. After supporters of race and gender preferences created a disturbance, the university, with aid of president George Rupp, tried to limit attendance to university members only—a move the event sponsors, Accuracy in Academia, rejected. The president of the Black Students Association said, "I thought it was great. They were entirely dislocated." Leo wrote: "This is mainstream opinion on campus these days: you show distaste for intellectual opponents by blocking speeches and stealing newspapers, not by debating with them. Freedom of speech has no value."[7]

When the *Daily Californian,* the student newspaper at the University of California at Berkeley, ran an ad offered by Horowitz headed "Ten Reasons Why Reparations for Slavery Is a Bad Idea—and Racist Too," Leo reports that "angry leftists stormed the offices of the student paper, thrashed about for a while, screaming and weeping and trying to intimidate staff. Then they fanned out around the campus to steal the remaining copies of the offending edition from their racks." The paper and its editor apologized for running the ad and the latter said the fee Horowitz paid might be turned over to black groups on campus. Horowitz sent the ad to thirty-five college papers, but at the time Leo wrote, only six had run it and two had apologized for doing so.

"The notion that free speech is a tool of the oppressor is now mainstream in the campus culture," Leo writes. "This is why campus newspapers with the wrong news keep getting stolen, posters for the wrong events keep getting torn down, and speakers with the wrong views keep getting disinvited or silenced."[8] Citing the tight monitoring of jokes, rumors, questions in class, comments by teachers, speech and behavior codes, zero-tolerance policies, heavy indoctrination at freshman orientation, and sexual harassment police, Leo concludes that "Students in high school and college face the most politically repressive atmosphere America has seen in almost 50 years."[9] That may be an understatement. Leo apparently refers to the McCarthy era. Although McCarthy was a thoroughly lamentable phenomenon, and although his recklessness severely damaged some reputations and careers, the atmosphere in high schools and colleges then was not as politically repressive as it is today. McCarthy was generally regarded on campuses as either potentially dangerous or a bad joke, but there was nothing resembling today's repression, coming as it does from inside the campus, from student activists, faculty, and administrators. Some speech codes at state universities have been held to be violative of the First Amendment, but the Constitution does not reach private universities, and even at state universities, like Berkeley, the courts are generally ineffective in controlling censorship by violence and intimidation.

Eli Lehrer, a senior editor of *American Enterprise* magazine, writes, "How did speech codes become so pervasive in our supposed cradles of open inquiry? Experts point to two trends: the rise of 1960s radicals to positions of power on college campuses, and an influx of academically under-prepared minority students as a result of affirmative action."[10] The 1960s radicals orated endlessly about freedom, but their authoritarian ambitions were always obvious and were realized when they reached positions of power and influence in the universities where freedom now means freedom to coerce others who have the wrong attitudes. Despite their rhetoric, it was never freedom the radicals sought, it was always power. That was what the culture war was about then, and it is what the culture war is about now: whose views of life and meaning or lack of meaning will dominate. Minorities, many of them placed in higher-echelon colleges than they were prepared for, banded together defensively, abetted by the '60s radicals in power, and achieved bans on politically inconvenient thoughts and arguments.

The effort to regiment thought and attitudes extends to primary and secondary schools. New York University's Diane Ravitch compiles a seemingly endless list of nonsensical deletions and alterations of passages from literature used in tests. As might be expected, these are freighted with political correctness. One publisher stated that everything written before 1970 was biased. Ravitch points out the ridiculous extent to which publishers have gone to avoid stereotyping: "Asian Americans should not be portrayed as academics; African Americans should not be portrayed as athletes; Caucasians should not be portrayed as businesspeople; men should not be portrayed as breadwinners; women should not be portrayed as wives and mothers. In the ideal world of education-think, women would be breadwinners; African Americans would be academics; Asian Americans would be athletes; and no one would be a wife or a mother."[11]

Attempts at censorship are not confined to liberals. Paleoconservatives object to references to dinosaurs or fossils because they imply evolution, but it is liberals who object to any mention of religion or religious holidays, including Thanksgiving.[12] What is left after the language and thought police have done their work are stories that have no geographical location or regional distinctiveness, in which older people are never ill, all conflicts are insignificant, men are fearful and women are brave, blind people and people with physical disabilities need no assistance from anyone, fantasy and magic are absent, and historical accuracy is ignored. "The result of all this relentless purging is dishonesty, a purposeful shielding of children from anything challenging, controversial, or just plain interesting. It is a process that drains literature of its life and blood, converts it into dreary reading materials, and grinds reading materials into pabulum."[13]

This is not, however, the worst of it. Ravitch notes with annoyance the tone of certainty in school textbooks, which "seem to share the same political orientation. Textbooks like Democratic presidents; textbooks don't like Republican presidents."[14] The industry appears to have been captured by the ethos of 1960s radicalism: the accomplishments of European and American civilization are downplayed or ignored so as not to be "Eurocentric," while the defects of other civilizations are glossed over. All cultures are equal, except, in some cases, where the history of the United States is portrayed as one of unrelieved oppression and ignorance. "Several texts lionize the upheavals of the 1960s; they present the counterculture and student rebels as avatars of social justice, with no balanced discussion of the negative phenomena of that era, such as bombings, harassment of dissident professors and speakers on campus, and a sustained assault on social mores. The texts treat the Black Panthers as a beneficent social service organization, with little or no reference to their tactics of intimidation and violence."[15]

There is, of course, resistance to censorship. FIRE presses universities to protect freedom of expression, using litigation where necessary. The Intercollegiate Studies Institute publishes a guide to universities which, along with much other information, discloses the political leanings of the instruction provided. ISI also publishes magazines and provides speakers to counter leftist ideological dominance. The Federalist Society encourages diversity of opinion in law schools by arranging debates and panel discussions that present diverse views, some of them unrepresented in the classrooms. But these are efforts to make headway against the dominant ultra-liberal ethos of most campuses, and so far left-liberal efforts at repression have the upper hand.

Nor is political expression, the core of the First Amendment's guarantee of freedom of speech, free from governmental suppression. Although this suppression is not explicitly ideological, it indicates the devaluing of political speech by state and federal legislatures and a worrisome attitude about such speech on the part of the Supreme Court. Repression here takes the form of laws regulating when such speech may occur in political campaigns, and how money may be contributed to candidates to enable them to reach mass audiences with their messages. The incentives for legislatures to enact such laws are obvious. Despite sanctimonious rhetoric about the need to purge politics of the corrupting influence of money and to avoid even the suspicion of corruption, it is clear that these laws are intended to, and do, have the effect of protecting incumbents from effective challenges at the polls. It is less clear, however, why the Supreme Court upholds such laws against First Amendment attacks when the reform's results are both to diminish political speech and to shift power among political speakers.

Buckley v. *Valeo* in 1976[16] upheld portions of the Federal Election Campaign Act, one of several misbegotten post-Watergate gestures toward purity, which severely limited individual contributions to political campaigns on the theory that large contributions may lead to the corruption of politics or may create a public impression of corruption. The public-impression rationale, though without any empirical support, was used to justify contribution limits far below any that could realistically be thought to raise any possibility of actual corruption. Had limits so severe been in effect at the time, they would have made it impossible for Eugene McCarthy to accept the large contributions necessary for his primary challenge that led Lyndon Johnson not to run for reelection in 1968.

Any hope that *Buckley* was an aberration that the fading of overwrought Watergate passions and the appointment of new justices would remedy was disappointed in 2000 by *Nixon v. Shrink Missouri Government PAC*.[17] A Missouri law set limits on campaign contributions for state elections that were considerably more severe than the limits set by federal law. The Supreme Court once more held that corruption or the possible appearance of corruption were adequate grounds to regulate contributions. Justice Stevens concurred, insisting on "one simple point. Money is property; it is not speech." That point, it may be suggested, was too simple. A soapbox is property, not speech, but the speech of an orator in Hyde Park would be much less effective without it. Television equipment, paid for by contributions, is property, but speech could not reach a mass electorate without it. A contributor provides the electronic soapbox for a candidate who shares the contributor's views on issues. The contribution makes it possible for both the candidate and the contributor to speak. The lower the contributions allowed, the more time and energy must be devoted to fundraising, and the less may be devoted to the development and delivery of the message.

Justice Breyer's concurrence, while conceding that money enables speech, argued that limiting the size of the largest contributions serves "to democratize the influence that money itself may bring to bear upon the electoral process." If the democratization rationale is sufficient to limit political participation through contributions, there seems no reason, in principle, why that argument would not justify limiting political expression by those who wield "disproportionate" influence by other means—journalists, union members and students who can canvass door to door, celebrities, and, of course, incumbent politicians. Regulating campaign contributions alone censors the expression of views by one segment of the public and shifts political influence from that group to others not similarly restrained.

The Court has turned the First Amendment inside out, freeing uninhibited pornography and obscenity from democratic control while allowing the suppression of some forms of political expression. It is perhaps not too speculative to think that laws enlarging penalties for crimes that appear to be "hate crimes" may be the forerunner of a movement of speech codes from American campuses into the public arena, and perhaps the more widespread use of compulsory "sensitivity training." Given the overwhelming likelihood that the Left would have more success in suppressing the expression of ideas and attitudes than would the rest of us in suppressing obscenity, it might, under present circumstances, be the part of wisdom not to endorse the concept of censorship.

THE CONTINUING DILEMMA OF RACE

The American situation with respect to race remains much as it was seven years ago. Positive signs in some areas are paired with negative signs in others. The major setback in race relations is the elites' continuing insistence upon racial preferences for some— which are, of course, simultaneously racial penalties for others. The results are entirely predictable. In the United States, as in all other countries where preferences of this sort have been awarded, the result is increased tribalism and social divisiveness.

The preeminent victory for the Olympians, and disaster for public policy, was, of course, the Supreme Court's decision in *Grutter* v. *Bollinger*,[18] backed by an opinion of transparent sophistry. The result was to be expected, however, since the Court is in thrall to Olympianism but cannot reason persuasively on this topic because all of the legal and prudential rationalizations for racial preferences were exploded some time ago.

Barbara Grutter, a white resident of Michigan, was denied admission to the university's law school despite having a grade point average (GPA) and a score on the law school aptitude test (LSAT) that would have guaranteed her admission had she been black, Hispanic, or Native American. She sued the law school and various university functionaries, alleging violation of the Equal Protection Clause of the Fourteenth Amendment and the 1964 Civil Rights Act. The law school responded by claiming that "diversity" is essential to its educational function as a first-class law school. Grutter lost, five to four, and the reasons given by the Court majority reveal the dishonesty of the "diversity" rationale that is now the favorite locution of intellectual Olympians in justifying antiwhite discrimination.

The established law was, but apparently is no more, that a racial classification could be justified only by a "compelling governmental interest," must be narrowly tailored to meet that interest, and limited in duration, and that courts must apply strict scrutiny to ensure that those conditions are met. None of these conditions was met in the program of racial discrimination the Court upheld. Justice O'Connor's opinion for the Court majority said, "We hold that the Law School has a compelling interest in attaining a diverse student body." The reason given was that "The Law School's educational judgment that such diversity is essential to its educational mission is one to which we defer." That is astounding. In no other case has the Court accepted the word of an institution that racial discrimination is essential to its performance. As described in chapter 8, when VMI, a military institute, argued that preserving an all-male student body was necessary to the kind of education and training it offered, the Court simply brushed the argument aside without a trace of deference. Deferring to the judgment of the discriminating institution that its discrimination serves a compelling interest is to eviscerate the test of strict scrutiny. The difference between *VMI* and *Grutter* cannot be explained on legal grounds. The explanation is political: a majority of the Court is dedicated to feminism and to affirmative action for blacks. If those political commitments require legally irreconcilable results in different cases, so be it.

The opinion attempted to disguise what the Court was doing in language that columnist Michael Kinsley aptly satirized: the law school "'engages in highly individualized, holistic review of each applicant's file.' It 'awards no mechanical, predetermined diversity "bonuses" based on race or ethnicity.' Instead, it makes 'a flexible assessment of applicants' talents, experiences, and potential...' blah, blah, blah."[19] If one were to assign real meaning to the school's vapid rhetoric, the impossibility of its claims is apparent. In the year 2000, there were 3,432 applicants. If we assume that fully half of them were automatic acceptances or rejections, that would leave 1,716 for "highly individualized, holistic" assessment in terms of each one's "talents, experiences, and potential." Or if two-thirds were automatically accepted or rejected, 1,144 would require that degree of attention. Even a three-quarters rate would leave 858 applicants for a "highly individualized holistic review." Anybody who has served on a law school admissions committee knows that is impossible. Each file contains not merely the applicant's GPA and LSAT score but a list of extracurricular activities, letters of recommendation, and his own essay on why he is a splendid candidate for admission, an essay that must be evaluated for content and style. Account must also be taken of the quality of the college the applicant attended and the difficulty of the courses taken in order to judge the weight to be given his GPA.

Individualized, holistic assessment, etc., etc., would require at least a staff of ten or twenty persons, which in turn would result in widely varying assessments of very similar individuals. To achieve any degree of consistency, the ten or twenty examiners would have to meet, discuss, and compare each of the 1,716 or 1,144, or 858 files. One can only conclude that the process described by the law school is a sham. Chief Justice Rehnquist applied that term to the school's further claim to be seeking a "critical mass" of each of the specified minority groups—blacks, Hispanics, and Native Americans. In fact, the figures show that blacks were preferred to Hispanics. Thus, in 2000 there were twelve black and twelve Hispanic applicants in the same range of GPAs and LSATs. Only two of the Hispanics were admitted but all twelve blacks were. Columnist Mark Steyn remarked that

> the court has dignified "diversity"—a flag of activist convenience, a wily obfuscation—as a compelling state interest, and on its promoters' terms. "Diversity" doesn't extend to, say, some dirt-poor fundamentalist white trash. Her presence wouldn't "enrich" anyone. "Diversity" means more blacks. That's why traditional African-American colleges are exempt from its strictures: as 100 percent black schools, they're already as diverse as you can get.[20]

The majority opinion even quoted Justice Lewis Powell, whose constitutionally incoherent *Bakke* concurrence introduced the diversity concept into constitutional law. He said that an admissions program that used race as a "plus" factor would weigh a white applicant's qualifications fairly and competitively so that "he would have no basis to complain of unequal treatment."[21] He would be rejected because his skin color did not qualify him for the "plus" factor, but he would have no reason to complain? For incoherence, that is on a par with the majority opinion in *Grutter:* since there are serious problems of justice when a race is preferred, "narrow tailoring, therefore, requires that a race-conscious admissions program not unduly harm members of any racial group." Apparently Grutter, excluded solely because of her race, was only duly harmed.[22]

Quoting Lewis Powell again, Justice O'Connor said, "'[S]ome attention to numbers,' without more, does not transform a flexible admissions system into a rigid quota." Quite right. The result is a soft quota, but a quota nonetheless. Why a soft quota passes constitutional muster but a rigid one does not remains a mystery. Nor is there any explanation of the school's assertion that diversity (racial, of course) is "essential to its educational mission." The Court simply defers to that judgment, an outright fabrication. There is no evidence that learning law is enhanced by the presence in the classroom of any particular racial group. If diversity of group identities were taken seriously as essential to a quality education, the Michigan law school should endeavor to construct classes containing whites, blacks, Hispanics, Native Americans, Asian Americans, Christians, Jews, Muslims, and secular rationalists. Probably students with differing socioeconomic backgrounds should be added to the mix. Not only is the diversity rationale impossible to implement honestly, it rests upon the vicious assumption that membership in a group so defined determines the individual's views—and that such membership is always an asset. Group membership may determine some individuals' views, but, we had always thought, it was the function of education to break or weaken that linkage. Only then can the individual be said to be educated; only then will there be a valuable intellectual diversity in the classroom. To the extent that law is an amalgam of history, economics, political theory, logic, and the close reading of texts, what counts is the quality of the intellectual discourse, not critical masses of any racial or ethnic groups.

The expert for Michigan's law school testified that without race consciousness the class that entered in 2000 would have had only 4 percent minorities rather than the actual figure of 14.5 percent. (There were, of course, more minorities, individuals with disparate and unique experiences in life, than that, but only favored groups count as minorities.) What would have happened to the 10.5 percent had they not been admitted to Michigan? The assumption seems to be that they would not succeed in life, an assumption that has been ridiculed as "Yale or jail." The fact is that those not preferentially admitted to Michigan would have gone to very good but less prestigious law schools—Wisconsin or Rutgers, say—where they would have competed more successfully. In turn, Wisconsin and Rutgers would have been relieved of their own internally generated pressure to recruit minorities not equipped to compete at that level. The minorities would have received good legal educations and gone on in the profession without the self-doubt and stigma that preferential policies impose.

Yet another difficulty with the "critical mass" argument is that it has not relieved minorities of the sense of isolation. Quite the opposite. Perhaps because many minority individuals feel themselves unequipped to compete at the law schools to which they have been preferentially admitted and suspect that some stigma attaches to them, they have tended to form exclusive groups in order to feel comfortable. Justice Scalia mentioned "those universities that talk the talk of multiculturalism but walk the walk of tribalism and racial segregation on their campuses—through minority-only student organizations, separate minority housing opportunities, separate minority student centers, even separate minority-only graduation ceremonies." This is to be expected whenever coerced "diversity" reigns. Peter Wood wrote that "all those diversities are, in the end, species of illusion. They pump life and energy into the assertion of the radical separateness of all the parts, and then childishly prate about the unity that is sure to follow." Commenting on Martha Nussbaum's defense of diversity doctrine by picturing today's campuses as places where faculty and students grapple with issues of human diversity, Wood says "The 'grappling' is her ennobling conceit for the festering discontents, censorship and fear; the gloating privilege; the rotting intellectual insecurity; and the regnant falsehoods that diversity has brought to most campuses."[23]

Shelby Steele, a research fellow at the Hoover Institution, explains such self-imposed segregation on campuses: "Because diversity works by group preferences, all the individuals in these beatific diverse environments must pursue a good part of their self-interest through their racial groups. The incentive is to make a tribe of one's race. You end up with a racialist diversity going more toward segregation than integration." The root of the policies the Supreme Court endorsed, he said, is a spurious moral authority rooted in "the summary indictment of America that emerged in the '60s from the convergence of so many social protest movements—civil rights, anti-war, feminism, farm workers, environmentalism, etc. The compound effect of all this protest was to cast America as a spiritually empty, greedy, racist and imperialistic nation—a malevolent force in the world." Anti-Americanism, he points out, is a formula for power because of its faux moral authority.[24] It is sad, in fact unnerving, that the Supreme Court has now endorsed this outlook.

Whatever else may be said of racial and ethnic preferences, it seems undeniable that they inflict injustices on both those who are excluded and those who are included because of their race or ethnicity. At least equally serious, the defense of the indefensible requires conspicuous intellectual dishonesty by the institutions that practice discrimination and by the courts that ratify that practice. As lies and half-truths become increasingly necessary to sustain the charade, there will inevitably occur the progressive loss of individual and institutional integrity. Finally, the effect of Grutter will not be confined to universities; the decision ratifies discrimination in the name of diversity (which is already the common practice) in government and private-sector employment and promotion. What is morally acceptable for higher education must be acceptable everywhere. Race relations will not be improved; probably they will be worsened, for which the cure will be more diversity and mandatory sensitivity training to change thoughts and attitudes as well as behavior. These are very high prices to pay for the empty moral posturing that lies at the root of the concept of diversity. But at least our Olympians will feel good about their virtue.

THE HOMOSEXUAL MOVEMENT

How should parents react when a son or daughter announces that he or she is "gay"? The Supreme Court has adopted a principle that, by its own logic, suggests that the parents should be indifferent, that the question of sexual "orientation" is nobody's business but the son's or daughter's, and that any contrary attitude is nothing more than bigotry. That answer is not only morally perplexing but has absolutely no plausible connection to the Constitution the Court claims to be interpreting. The Court's answer, however, has everything to do with the modern liberal attitude toward sexuality.

That answer was given in *Lawrence* v. *Texas*,[25] which effectually made homosexual sodomy a constitutional right by means of an argument that owes nothing to law but everything to a subsophomoric moral argument.

Viewed narrowly, what was at stake in *Lawrence* was the state's criminal statute prohibiting homosexual sodomy between men. Lawrence and Garner were seen engaged in sodomy in an apartment by a police officer who was lawfully on the premises. Fined $200, they took the case, ultimately, to the Supreme Court. The Court majority, in an opinion by Justice Kennedy, struck the statute down as a violation of the liberty said to be guaranteed by the due process clause of the Fourteenth Amendment.

The majority opinion continues the tradition of incoherence in these matters. Although it purported to apply a clause ratified in 1868 (and taken verbatim from the Fifth Amendment, ratified in 1791), the majority opinion said, "we think that our laws and traditions in the past half century are of most relevance here." In 1955, for example, the American Law Institute, an unofficial organization of lawyers, stated that its recommended Model Penal Code did not advocate or provide for "criminal penalties for consensual sexual relations conducted in private." In 1957, in the Wolfenden Report, a committee established by the British Parliament recommended repeal of laws punishing homosexual conduct, and ten years later Parliament complied. The puzzle is twofold. There is no explanation of why recent events of the last fifty years are relevant to the meaning of a constitutional amendment over one hundred and thirty years old, nor why recommendations about *legislation* in the United States and Britain should affect the meaning of the United States Constitution.

Even more puzzling was the Court's statement:

Of even more importance,...the European Court of Human Rights considered a case....[in which] [a]n adult male resident in Northern Ireland alleged that he was a practicing homosexual who desired to engage in homosexual conduct. The laws of

Northern Ireland forbade him that right....The court held that the laws proscribing the conduct were invalid under the European Convention on Human Rights.

This was said to show the falsity of the premise that the claim to a right to engage in homosexual conduct was insubstantial in Western civilization. Justice Kennedy also cited the trend in American states to decriminalize homosexual conduct.

None of this should be taken as serious constitutional analysis. Whatever the ALI and the Wolfenden Report said, however the Court of Human Rights sitting in Strasbourg decided under its law, and however many states decided to decriminalize homosexual sodomy, the fact remains that Texas had a right to make its own moral judgments unless something in the federal Constitution denied that right. And it is here, in the attempt to muster a *constitutional* rationale for its decision, that the Court majority opinion floundered most abysmally.

That effort began, amazingly, with a repetition of the same mystery-of-life passage from *Casey* mentioned earlier, as though it had some discernible meaning:

In explaining the respect the Constitution demands for the autonomy of the person in making these choices [about marriage, procreation, contraception, family relationships, child rearing, and education], we stated as follows:

These matters, involving the most intimate and personal choices a person may make in a lifetime, choices central to personal dignity and autonomy, are central to the liberty protected by the Fourteenth Amendment. At the heart of liberty is the right to define one's own concept of existence, of meaning, of the universe, and of the mystery of human life. Beliefs about these matters could not define the attributes of personhood were they formed under compulsion of the State.

Persons in a homosexual relationship may seek autonomy for these purposes, just as heterosexuals do.

These words defy explanation just as they defy any attempt to guess what the concept of constitutionally guaranteed liberty might cover. This passage, discussed in chapter 6, is at best a blank slate on which anything may be written at the pleasure of the justices. The wonder is that this empty incantation, despite having been endlessly ridiculed, should now be relied upon once more as the opening gambit in what purports to be a constitutional argument.

Justice Kennedy went on, with the approval of four colleagues, to quote *Romer's* conclusion that the provision of the Colorado constitution denying localities the right to make homosexuals a specially protected class, along with racial minorities, by claiming that "the provision was 'born of animosity toward the class of persons affected' and further that it had no rational relationship to a legitimate governmental purpose."[26] This denies the right of government to enact the judgment of its citizens that some behavior is immoral and harmful. That is not a proposition that can be applied across the board; moral judgments are the stuff of legislation.

The opinion went on to offer an utterly unpersuasive assurance. This case, the Court said, "does not involve whether the government must give formal recognition to any relationship that homosexual persons seek to enter." That means that *Lawrence* does not decide the question of same-sex marriage as a constitutional right. But, of course, it does. The principle of radical personal autonomy upon which the case rests necessarily means that the state may not deny homosexual couples a marriage license. We are entitled to suspect, indeed to be certain, that that is precisely what the Court majority is leading up to.

It is abundantly clear, then, that a majority of the Supreme Court no longer considers itself a constitutional court—one highly respected federal judge said to me that *Lawrence* v. *Texas* means that the Constitution is simply gone. Instead, the Court majority has made itself into a secular papacy, the final authority on matters of faith and morals. We may, therefore, assess its performance on those grounds as well.

One issue posed by the normalization of homosexuality, which *Lawrence* largely accomplishes—the only step remains is the creation of a constitutional right to homosexual marriage—is whether as a society we want a significant increase in the number of homosexuals. Other arguments are largely beside the point. Homosexuals argue that allowing them all the rights of heterosexuals, including the right to marry, is simply a question of justice, of the equal protection of the laws. That argument leaves out of account the effects of normalization on individuals and on society. It would have force only if there were no serious adverse effects from homosexual behavior. There are such effects, however, and we are entitled to consider them.

We may begin at the personal level. How many fathers and mothers are pleased or even indifferent to whether their sons and daughters grow up to spend their lives as practicing homosexuals? Very few, if any. They may love their child regardless, but they are not happy about the direction taken by the child's sexuality. There are excellent reasons for that unhappiness. Perhaps there is revulsion at the nature of homosexual acts, perhaps sadness that there will be no grandchildren, perhaps a well-founded fear of the dangers of a homosexual life, or perhaps the reasons for unhappiness about the child's homosexuality are never fully articulated in the minds of the parents. Still, there is, as Leon Kass said in opposition to human cloning, the "wisdom of repugnance."

The issues to be confronted, then, are whether complete acceptance of the normality of homosexual behavior would lead to an increase in the number of homosexuals and whether there are good reasons to resist any policy that leads to unqualified approval of homosexual behavior. I think the answer to both of these questions is yes. The subject for discussion is not a degree of tolerance, which seems to me appropriate and humane, but full acceptance, which is neither.

To address the first issue, if homosexual marriage completes the normalization of homosexuality that is now racing forward, there will be more homosexuals in the population, probably very significantly more. There is not a "gay gene," but there are very probably genetic factors, along with environmental influences in the womb or in early life, that create greater or lesser predispositions toward homosexual behavior. Like other predispositions, toward alcoholism, for example, the urge to homosexual conduct can often be resisted, and a significant number of homosexuals respond to therapy that enables them to live contentedly as heterosexuals. The willingness to resist or to seek therapy will certainly be affected by the degree of stigma attached to the behavior in question. If all traces of taint are removed, if homosexuality is made to seem completely normal, a matter of indifference to anyone else or to society, young men and women uncertain of their sexuality will be that much more likely to be drawn into a homosexual life. There will surely be some young men and women who will not be deterred from homosexuality by any degree of stigma, just as there will be some who are deflected by quite mild degrees of social disapproval. There could hardly be a stronger signal from society that homosexuality is perfectly normal and acceptable than the creation of a right to homosexual marriage.

The next question, therefore, is what would be so calamitous about removing all restraints on homosexual behavior? The answer is, a great many extremely unhappy consequences would follow.

The first of these is the severe distress inflicted upon many individuals who choose, or are led into, the homosexual way of life. Though many homosexuals would deny it, homosexual males are much more likely to lead unhappy lives than are heterosexuals. Homosexual males engage in substance abuse and suffer mood and anxiety disorders, and major depression, as well as considering and actually attempting suicide, at rates far greater than do heterosexual males. Homosexual apologists attempt to explain these facts by citing the pressures of discrimination. But the rates are similarly high in the Netherlands and New Zealand, two countries known as homosexual-friendly. Thus, in the Netherlands the prevalence of mood disorders among homosexuals was 39 percent and among nonhomosexuals 13.3 percent, a ratio of about three to one. For anxiety disorders, the numbers were 31.7 percent as opposed to 13.2 percent; and major depression, 39.3 and 10.9 percent.[27] A study in New Zealand found the numbers for homosexual and nonhomosexual thoughts of suicide to be 67.9 percent and 28 percent, while those for suicide attempts were 32.1 and 7.1 percent.[28]

Psychiatrist Jeffrey Satinover reports, "In spite of its superficial appeal and the activists' repeated claims, no studies support the hypothesis that the social disapproval of homosexuality is the prime cause of the high levels of internal distress evident in homosexual populations, even long before AIDS."[29] Richard Fitzgibbons, a clinical psychologist specializing in anger management, notes that a child's anger at felt betrayal by his peers or father is "one of the major reasons a notable element of sado-masochism is found in homosexual practices. When the extreme sadomasochistic behaviors engaged in by homosexual men are reported, most people are shocked....If the same type of behavior took place among heterosexuals, the identical acts would be con-sidered forms of abuse and evidence of a disorder, yet they are considered 'normal' among homosexual men."[30] Homosexuality, moreover, is an addictive disorder. As Dr. Fitzgibbons notes, "The first men diagnosed with AIDS reported an average of one thou-sand partners during their lives. Those who have researched the HIV-AIDS epidemic have noted that some homosexual males actually have five to ten sexual encounters in a single night." "The person has often attempted to fill the emptiness experienced in childhood or adolescence with numerous sexual encounters but it is an emptiness that is never satisfied sexually."[31] It is no wonder that he says, "Involvement in a homosexual lifestyle starts many young men down a clear path of self-destruction."

These manifestations of psychological distress that seem fre-quently accompany homosexual conduct make the use of the word "gay" absurdly inappropriate. Psychiatrist Joseph Nicolosi calls it "a self-deceptive identity" that has been "brilliantly marketed and bought without question by the most influential institutions—professional psychology and psychiatry, churches, educators, and the media—of American society."[32] The term "gay" makes homo-sexuality sound innocuous, if not appealing, but it hides the terrible reality that so many homosexuals experience.

It may be too soon for reliable studies of the effect upon chil-dren of adoption by homosexual couples. Common sense suggests, however, that apart from proselytizing and pedophilia, which it strains credulity to rule out, the adopted child of a homosexual couple is more likely than a child adopted by a heterosexual cou-ple to turn to homosexuality himself. If nothing else, that result seems likely because of the natural admiration of the child for its parents. It can hardly be supposed that a young boy whose fathers sleep with each other would not often come to see such an arrangement as natural and, indeed, to be emulated.

Facts such as these should be sufficient, standing alone, to jus-tify efforts to deter youths from engaging in homosexual behavior. But there is, of course, more: the ravages of disease that homosexuals suffer far more than do heterosexuals. The best known is AIDS. In addition to AIDS, however, active homosexuals have high rates of hepatitis, gastrointestinal infections, cancer, and tuberculosis. Women have higher rates of bacterial vaginosis and breast and ovarian cancer. The incidence of violence is also high within homosexual relationships.

But there is more than the personal tragedies of homosexuals and their families to the argument against the normalization of homosexuality. There are, for one thing, the harmful effects on the institutions of marriage and family of recognizing homosexual relationships as marriages. The location of the line that separates the moral from the immoral is always, to some degree, arbitrary in the sense that a narrow rationalist argument can be made for moving the line in one direction or the other. After all, shortsighted rationalists may and do argue, a stable, loving, sexual relationship between men is not different in principle between the same sort of relationship between a man and a woman. The mechanics of the sexual activity differ, to be sure, but the principle is the same. That is false. The moral line between heterosexuality and homosexuality has been drawn for good reason. For thousands of years civilizations have drawn that line, and it has all the legitimacy that tradition, religion, and concern for the persons directly involved and for the rearing of children can confer. There is no other line regarding sexuality as firmly rooted as this one. But once that line is breached, there is no other line, no fallback position, of any remotely comparable strength. William Bennett was entirely correct: "Say what they will, there are no principled grounds on which advocates of same-sex marriage can oppose the marriage of two consenting brothers. Nor can they (persuasively) explain why we ought to deny a marriage license to three men who want to marry. Or to a man who wants a consensual polygamous arrangement. Or to a father and his adult daughter."[33]

By the same token, Sen. Rick Santorum was correct when, in anticipation of the Supreme Court's decision in *Lawrence* v. *Texas*, he said that "if the Supreme Court says that you have the right to consensual (gay) sex within your home, then you have the right to bigamy, you have the right to polygamy, you have the right to incest, you have the right to adultery. You have the right to anything. All of those things are antithetical to a healthy, stable, traditional family." That statement was immediately denounced by Democratic senators, homosexual groups, and some Republicans as "shameful," and there were calls for Santorum's resignation as Republican conference chairman. Many came to Santorum's defense by pointing out that Justice Byron White's majority opinion in *Bowers* v. *Hardwick* (1986) stated that "It would be difficult, except by fiat, to limit the claimed right to homosexual conduct while leaving exposed to prosecution adultery, incest, and other sexual crimes even though they are committed in the home. We are unwilling to start down that road." There were no calls at the time for Justice White's resignation from the Supreme Court, nor should there have been. Santorum was right, just as White and Bennett were right. A line is being crossed, and there is no other line to separate moral and immoral consensual sex that will hold.

Many consider such fears laughable: it is said, for instance, that no one would ever advocate a right to polygamy. The fact is that some do. More instructive for present purposes is the erosion of the taboo against homosexual pedophilia. That taboo remains powerful in the general public—witness the outrage over the homosexual abuse of young boys and male adolescents by homosexual Catholic priests—but it is eroding among some homosexuals and cultural elites, an erosion that resembles the process by which homosexuality has been raised from obloquy to tolerance to a status close to normalization in the past few decades. I can do no better than to urge the reading of two articles by Mary Eberstadt, "Pedophilia Chic,"[34] and "'Pedophilia Chic' Reconsidered: The Taboo Against Sex with Children Continues to Erode."[35] Eberstadt writes in the first article: "In one corner, enraged parents from across the country screaming for help in protecting their children; in the other, desiccated salonistes who have taken to wondering languidly whether a taste for children's flesh is really so indefensible after all. And they wonder why there's a culture war." In the second, she makes it clear that the pedophilia in question is about boys, not girls, and "this 'question,' settled though it may be in the opinions and laws of the rest of the country, is demonstrably not yet settled within certain parts of the gay rights movement. The more that movement has entered the mainstream, the more this 'question' has bubbled forth from that previously distant realm into the public square."

"About pedophilia," Eberstadt concludes, "there remains one and only one proposition that commands public assent. It is this: *If the sexual abuse of minors isn't wrong, then nothing is.*" That same statement could have been made about homosexual conduct a few decades back. Perhaps it is not too far-fetched to imagine that some activist homosexuals, like the North American Man Boy Love Association (NAMBLA), will ultimately decrease resistance to homosexual pedophilia. Observe the punishments visited upon the Boy Scouts—denunciation, withdrawal of corporate support, etc.—for refusing to allow an active homosexual adult male to be a leader of young Scouts, and that despite the obvious fact that a general rule permitting such a role would undoubtedly lead to homosexual pedophilia in a number of cases. That many homosexuals roundly condemn pedophilia does not alter the fact that homosexual pedophilia is increasingly thinkable among many Olympians, and thus may become more common.

The point of this discussion is not that we are about to be overwhelmed by a tidal wave of pedophilia, but rather that the unimaginable becomes imaginable, and then actual, when some moral lines—call them taboos, if you will—weaken and become vulnerable.

It is in this sense that White, Santorum, and Bennett are dead right about there being no difference in principle between the legalization of homosexual sodomy and homosexual marriage and the other behaviors they cite. Indeed, the groundwork for permitting such behavior has already been laid in the ultralibertarian "mystery passage" of *Casey* and *Lawrence.* If abortion and homosexual sodomy are among "the most intimate and personal choices a person may make in a lifetime," if they are "choices central to personal dignity and autonomy," if they are "central to the liberty protected by the Fourteenth Amendment," and if, as the Court assured us, such practices are protected as "the right to define one's own concept of existence, of meaning, of the universe, and of the mystery of human life," then how can adultery, polygamy, the marriage of three men, or the marriage of a father and daughter be far behind? To exclude them would be indefensibly arbitrary, a manifestation of simple bigotry. By the mystery passage's logic, if that is the word, homosexual marriage is inevitably the next step.

That being the case, it should be obvious that the more homosexuality is accepted as one among other varieties of the normal, leading up to homosexual marriage, the more traditional hetero-sexual marriage is demeaned, becoming itself no more than one sexual arrangement among others. That in turn demeans the fam-ily's place as the central institution of stability and childrearing in society. Homosexual marriage cannot substitute for traditional marriage in these respects. Though there is a dispute about the statistics on the longevity of homosexual unions, there is no dis-pute that they are far briefer than heterosexual marriages. There is similarly no dispute that men in homosexual relationships have many more sexual encounters outside the relationship than do heterosexuals. There are, it appears, monogamous homosexual part-ners, but it is notorious that promiscuity is rampant in much of that culture. Richard Fitzgibbons notes that "the majority [of men in same-sex attractions] will have more than twenty sexual part-ners per year, and less than nine percent of those with same-sex attractions will have relationships that last three years."[36] Another study found that 95 percent of couples have an arrangement that allows the partners to have sexual activity with others.[37] These findings are not new. Other studies show the same pattern, although they are hardly necessary, since the centrality of promis-cuity in the homosexual culture is common knowledge.

It may be accounted odd that a sexual practice with such dire effects upon individuals and on society has become so widely accepted. But that it has is undeniable. The Episcopal Church has not only ordained homosexual priests but elevated a practicing homosexual to the post of bishop, and has made the celebration of homosexual unions in church a matter of local option. Quite soon it will be mandatory. More startling is the silent advance of homo-sexuality within the American Catholic Church. Official doctrine opposes homosexual acts, and the Pope has stated the unaccept-ability of homosexual marriage. There are, nevertheless, apparently significant numbers of homosexually active priests, and there is open pro-homosexual sentiment in the church.

Cardinal Francis Arinze, a Nigerian who presides over the Pontifical Council for Interreligious Dialogue at the Vatican, gave Georgetown University's commencement speech this year. In the section devoted to God's gift of the family, Arinze said, "In many parts of the world, the family is under siege. It is opposed by an anti-life mentality as is seen in contraception, abortion, infanticide and euthanasia. It is scorned and banalized by pornography, dese-crated by fornication and adultery, mocked by homosexuality, sab-otaged by irregular unions and cut in two by divorce." A professor of theology protested the reference to homosexuality by leaving the stage while Arinze was speaking, and a number of students walked out. A professor of American Studies at the university questioned why, at a commencement, the Cardinal "decided to do the pro-family thing" and called the prelates comments "un-Christian." A protest letter signed by about seventy faculty mem-bers was delivered to the dean of arts and sciences who had invited the Cardinal to speak.

This was an extraordinary performance, and an amazing illus-tration of the cachet homosexuality has achieved. A Catholic car-dinal, speaking at a Catholic university, utters orthodox Catholic doctrine, and provokes an uproar from Catholics. The event gives point to Robert Royal's remark that the Church is supposed to evangelize the culture but instead the culture is evangelizing the Church.

There are two possible routes to a judge-created right to homosexual marriage. One is a direct attack on state marriage laws in state or federal courts, followed by review in the Supreme Court. Though *Lawrence* v. *Texas* indicates that the homosexuals would win, there is the possibility that the prospect of an uproar by an enraged public would cause the Court to temporize. A more circuitous route may, therefore, commend itself to the lawyers for the homosexuals. This would involve an attack in state courts based on state constitutions (rulings involving only state law are not appealable to the Supreme Court). There is little doubt that the argument for homosexual marriage would prevail in a number of state courts, but it would take only one favorable ruling to set the process in motion. After a clear victory in a state court, homo-sexuals will come to that state, marry, and then claim the marital status in their home states under Article IV, section 1 of the United States Constitution: "Full faith and credit shall be given in each state to the public acts, records, and judicial proceedings of every other state. And the Congress may by general laws prescribe the manner in which such acts, records, and proceedings shall be proved and the effect thereof." Some states may refuse to accord homosexual marriages on the grounds of their public policy as well as upon the federal Defense of Marriage Act (DOMA), relying upon Congress's power given by the constitutional clause just quoted. DOMA provides that no state shall be required to give effect to the law of any other state with respect to a same-sex marriage. The homosexuals will then challenge DOMA as violative of the invented right of privacy, as well as the Equal Protection Clause. These rights were invented or enacted after Article IV and will be said to override it. Given the mood of the present Supreme Court majority, the activists will almost certainly succeed, full faith and credit will be ordered given to same-sex marriages, and the United States will have a right to homosexual marriage, spread by one state to the other forty-nine.

The only apparent way to avoid this result is by a constitutional amendment. Language such as the following is now being urged: "Marriage in the United States shall consist only of the union of a man and a woman. Neither this Constitution or the constitution of any state, nor state or federal law, shall be construed to require that marital status or the legal incidents thereof be conferred upon unmarried couples or groups." Though the amendment has gathered considerable support even at this early stage, it has, interestingly enough, received some opposition from both the Left and the Right. The ACLU claims that the second sentence of the amendment would prohibit legislation allowing civil unions and opposes the amendment on that ground; they read "construed" as if it meant "applied," thus misunderstanding a requirement that courts not read marital status or its incidents into laws not explicitly addressing these topics. Concerned Women for America, on the other hand, has declared opposition because civil unions would not be barred. It is clear that the amendment does not affect the legality of legislatively approved civil unions, and that, far from being a defect, is the amendment's virtue: it does not preclude democratic decisions on the subject.

The danger we face is from runaway courts, not elected legislatures, and it is that danger that the amendment seeks to avert. The second sentence uses the word "construed" rather than "applied" or some similar word to indicate that it is judicial invention that is barred, not the straightforward application of explicit law. That distinction will be made even plainer by the discussion of those who support the amendment. The legislative history will further lay to rest any fears on this score. The bona fides of those who oppose the amendment on the ground that it would bar democratically enacted provisions for civil unions may be doubted because they do not propose any word or group of words that would make the matter clearer. What they want is a right to same-sex marriage—a right that will not exist unless made up by courts —and that requires the defeat of this amendment.

The objections from the Right are no more persuasive. Whether or not it would be desirable to bar legislatures from authorizing civil unions, the attempt to do so would almost certainly assure the amendment's defeat; Americans are tolerant on that subject as they are not on the topic of same-sex marriages. Reaching too far would leave not only civil unions but same-sex marriage open to judicial creation of such rights. There is some conservative opposition to the amendment on the grounds that family law, including the law of marriage, is a matter for the states, not the federal government. That is an argument that might have had resonance in a different era; it has none now. The question of homosexual marriage is going to be decided at the national level; either there will be a constitutional right to such marriages, created out of whole cloth by judges, or there will be an amendment to block that development.

*   *   *

Each of the subjects discussed in this Afterword has been heavily influenced, if not determined, by courts, most prominently by the Supreme Court. In each case, the Court has departed from any plausible meaning of the Constitution or a statute. We have, then, national law with respect to our culture that has nothing to do with the Constitution or statute but everything to do with the captious ponderings of a majority of the Justices, led in turn by the latest visions of the self-anointed intellectual elite.

Matters are worse than this, however. Courts have become partisans in our culture war, just as the courts of other Western nations have become partisans in theirs. The culture war is transnational—the contending ideas are the same—and it is natural, though thoroughly illegitimate, that the various national courts, which side with intellectual class liberals, would begin to cooperate in forcing their respective cultures in the same direction. As Minogue wrote: "We may define Olympianism as a vision of human betterment to be achieved on a global scale by forging the peoples of the world into a single community based on the universal enjoyment of appropriate human rights. . . . Olympians instruct mortals, they do not obey them."[38]

We should not be surprised, then, to find the United States Supreme Court "interpreting" the American Constitution in accordance with foreign court decisions. In *Lawrence* v. *Texas,* as already noted, the Court cited a decision of the European Court of Human Rights to show that it was false to say that a claim of a right to engage in homosexual behavior was insubstantial in Western civilization. In *Grutter,* Justices Ginsburg and Breyer concurred to cite the International Convention on the Elimination of All Forms of Racial Discrimination. The internationalization of United States law continues apace,[39] so much so that the reporter covering the Court for the *New York Times*, citing the engagement of American Justices with foreign judges and constitution writing, could say with every indication of approval, "it is not surprising that the justices have begun to see themselves as participants in a worldwide constitutional conversation."[40] She could more accurately have said, "a worldwide constitutional convention."

There could hardly be a plainer demonstration that some Justices are leaving the text and history of the U.S. Constitution behind for a left-liberal international moral consensus among Olympians. It is bad enough that this is the rule of judges, not the rule of law, and that the Olympian version of morality is being imposed on majorities that do not want it. It is still worse if this internationalization of law is a major force in a movement toward more international government, which, as we see in the European Union, is likely to be authoritarian, if not ultimately tyrannical.

Endnotes

Introduction

1. Daniel Patrick Moynihan, "Defining Deviancy Down," *The American Scholar*, Winter 1993, p. 17.
2. *Ibid.*, pp. 17–20.
3. *Ibid.*, p. 19.
4. Charles Krauthammer, "Defining Deviancy Up," *The New Republic*, November 22, 1993, p. 20.
5. *Ibid.*
6. Christopher Lasch, *The Revolt of the Elites and the Betrayal of Democracy* (New York: W.W. Norton, 1995), pp. 233–4.
7. Lionel Trilling, *Sincerity and Authenticity: The Charles Eliot Norton Lectures, 1969–1970* (Cambridge, MA: Harvard University Press, 1974), p. 1.
8. *Ibid.*

Chapter 1

1. James Miller, *"Democracy Is in the Streets": From Port Huron to the Siege of Chicago* (Cambridge, MA: Harvard University Press, 1994), p. 305.
2. Philip Gourevitch, "Vietnam: The Bitter Truth," *New York Review of Books*, December 22, 1994, p. 55, reviewing Jade Ngoc Quang Huynh, *South Wind Changing* (St. Paul, MN: Graywolf Press, 1994).
3. Interview of Bui Tin conducted by Stephen Young, "How North Vietnam Won the War," *Wall Street Journal*, August 3, 1995, p. A8.
4. Christopher Jencks quoted by Todd Gitlin, *The Sixties: Years of Hope, Days of Rage* (New York: Bantam Books, 1993), p. 271.

5. José Ortega y Gasset, *The Revolt of the Masses* (New York: W.W. Norton, 1957), p. 50.

6. *Ibid.*, p. 51.

7. *Ibid.*, p. 53.

8. Seymour Martin Lipset, *Rebellion in the University* (New Brunswick, NJ: Transaction Publishers, 1993), pp. xxxix–xl.

9. Gitlin, p. 104.

10. Peter L. Berger and Richard John Neuhaus, *Movement and Revolution* (Garden City, NY: Doubleday, 1970), p. 60.

11. Gitlin, pp. 40–1.

12. *The Sixties*, ed. Gerald Howard (New York: Washington Square Press, 1982), p. 18.

13. Gitlin, p. 34.

14. Midge Decter, *Liberal Parents, Radical Children* (New York: Coward, McCann & Geoghegan, 1975).

15. James Q. Wilson, *The Moral Sense* (New York: The Free Press, 1993), p. 109.

16. Stanley Rothman and S. Robert Lichter, *Roots of Radicalism: Jews, Christians, and the New Left* (New York: Oxford University Press, 1982), p. 389.

17. Cited in Robert Lerner, Althea K. Nagai, and Stanley Rothman, *American Elites* (New Haven: Yale University Press, in press), chapter 8.

18. Helmut Schoeck, *Envy: A Theory of Social Behavior* (Indianapolis: Liberty Press, 1987).

19. *Ibid.*, pp. 337–8.

20. Peter Collier and David Horowitz, *Destructive Generation: Second Thoughts About the Sixties* (New York: Touchstone, 1990).

21. Quoted in Gitlin, pp. 109–10.

22. Reprinted in James Miller's *"Democracy Is in the the Streets": From Port Huron to the Siege of Chicago*, pp. 329–74.

23. Paul Johnson, *A History of Christianity* (New York: Simon & Schuster, 1976), p. 255.

24. *Ibid.*, p. 263.

25. *Ibid.*, p. 305.

26. Robert Nisbet, *Conservatism: Dream and Reality* (Minneapolis: University of Minnesota Press, 1991), p. 105.

27. Lionel Trilling, *Sincerity and Authenticity* (Cambridge, MA: Harvard University Press, 1974), pp. 93–4.

28. Collier and Horowitz, p. 96.

29. Terry H. Anderson, *The Movement and the Sixties: Protest in America from Greensboro to Wounded Knee* (New York: Oxford University Press, 1995), p. 65.

30. William L. O'Neill, *Coming Apart: An Informal History of America in the 1960s* (Chicago: Quadrangle Books, 1971), pp. 295–6.

31. Lipset, p. 3.

Chapter 2

1. Peter Collier and David Horowitz, *Destructive Generation: Second Thoughts About the Sixties* (New York: Touchstone, 1990), p. 14.

2. "In Praise of the Counterculture," *New York Times*, December 11, 1994, Sec. 4, p. 14.

3. Charles J. Sykes, *The Hollow Men: Politics and Corruption in Higher Education* (Washington, DC: Regnery Gateway, 1990), p. 145.

4. Joseph B. Treaster, "Brewster Doubts Fair Black Trials," *New York Times*, April 25, 1970, p. A1.

5. John Hersey, *A Letter to the Alumni* (New York: Bantam Books, 1971).

6. *Ibid.*, p. 114.

7. Many of the facts recited here and all of the quotes are taken from Allan P. Sindler's unpublished manuscript "The Cornell Crisis of 1969."

8. "Investigations; Kent State: Another View," *TIME*, October 26, 1970, p. 27.

9. *Ibid.*

10. Peter L. Berger and Richard John Neuhaus, *Movement and Revolution* (Garden City, NY: Doubleday, 1970), pp. 43–7.

11. *Ibid.*, pp. 46-7.

12. Walter Berns, "The New Left and Liberal Democracy," *How Democratic Is America? Responses to the New Left Challenge*, ed. Robert Goldwin (Chicago: Rand McNally, 1971), pp. 29–30.

13. Collier and Horowitz, p. 77.

14. Robert Nisbet, *Prejudices: A Philosophical Dictionary* (Cambridge, MA: Harvard University Press, 1982), p. 186.

15. "September 1, 1939," *The Collected Poetry of W. H. Auden* (New York: Random House, 1945).

16. Collier and Horowitz, pp. 294–5.

17. George Will, "Slamming the Doors," *Newsweek*, March 25, 1991, pp. 65–6.

18. Stanley Rothman and S. Robert Lichter, *Roots of Radicalism: Jews, Christians, and the New Left* (New York: Oxford University Press, 1982), pp. 392–4.

19. Terry H. Anderson, *The Movement and the Sixties: Protest in America from Greensboro to Wounded Knee* (New York: Oxford University Press, 1995), p. 413.

Chapter 3

1. Robert Nisbet, *The Quest for Community* (New York: Oxford University Press, 1953), p. 225.

2. *Ibid.*, pp. 225–7.

3. Gordon Wood, *The Radicalism of the American Revolution* (New York: Alfred A. Knopf, 1992), pp. 239–40.

4. John Stuart Mill, "On Liberty," *Three Essays* (Oxford, UK: Oxford University Press, 1975, 1978), p. 14.

5. Gertrude Himmelfarb, *On Liberty and Liberalism: The Case of John Stuart Mill* (New York: Alfred A. Knopf, 1974).

6. Gertrude Himmelfarb, *On Looking Into the Abyss: Untimely Thoughts on Culture and Society* (New York: Alfred A. Knopf, 1994), p. 103.

7. James Fitzjames Stephen, *Liberty, Equality, Fraternity*, ed. Stuart D. Warner (Indianapolis: Liberty Fund, 1993).

8. Himmelfarb, *On Liberty and Liberalism*, p. xx.

9. Himmelfarb, *On Looking into the Abyss*, pp. 77–8.

10. T. S. Eliot, *Christianity and Culture: The Idea of a Christian Society & Notes Towards the Definition of Culture* (New York: Harcourt, Brace & World, 1940, 1949), p. 12.

11. *Ibid.*

12. Pierre Manent, *An Intellectual History of Liberalism* (Princeton: Princeton University Press, 1994), pp. 62–3.

13. *Victorian and Edwardian Poets: Tennyson to Yeats*, eds. W. H. Auden and Norman Holmes Pearson (New York: Viking Press, 1950), p. xix.

14. Irving Kristol, "My Cold War," *The National Interest*, Spring 1993, pp. 141, 144.

15. Mill, p. 118.

16. Edmund Burke, "Speech at His Arrival at Bristol Before the Election in That City (1774)," *Speeches and Letters on American Affairs* (London: J. M. Dent, 1908, 1956), p. 66.

17. Edmund Burke, *Reflections on the Revolution in France and on the Proceedings in Certain Societies in London Relative to That Event* (London: Penguin Books, 1968), p. 91.

18. William J. Bennett, "The Children," *What to Do About . . .* , ed. Neal Kozodoy (New York: Regan Books/HarperCollins, 1995), p. 5.

Chapter 4

1. Gordon S. Wood, *The Radicalism of the American Revolution* (New York: Alfred A. Knopf, 1992), p. 234.

2. Christopher Lasch, *The Revolt of the Elites and the Betrayal of Democracy* (New York: W. W. Norton, 1995), p. 22.

3. Keith Bradsher, "Gap in Wealth In U.S. Called Widest in West," *New York Times*, April 17, 1995, p. 1.

4. Michael Novak, "What Wealth Gap?," *Wall Street Journal*, July 11, 1995, p. A16.

5. Irving Kristol, *Neoconservatism: the Autobiography of an Idea* (New York: The Free Press, 1995), p. 166.

6. The quotes in the subsequent five paragraphs are from Walter J. Blum and Harry Kalven, Jr., *The Uneasy Case for Progressive Taxation* (Chicago: University of Chicago Press, 1953, 1976).

7. James Q. Wilson, *The Moral Sense* (New York: The Free Press, 1993), pp. 55–78.

8. *Ibid.*, pp. 60–1.

9. *Ibid.*, p. 77.

10. James K. Glassman, "The Rich Already Pay Plenty," *Washington Post*, July 11, 1995, p. A17.

11. Helmut Schoeck, *Envy: A Theory of Social Behavior* (Indianapolis: Liberty Press, 1987), p. 179.

12. Bertrand de Jouvenel, *The Ethics of Redistribution* (Cambridge, UK: Cambridge University Press, 1952), pp. 79–81. (Footnote omitted)

13. Martin Malia, "A Fatal Logic," *The National Interest*, Spring 1993, pp. 80, 87.

14. Pierre Manent, *An Intellectual History of Liberalism* (Princeton: Princeton University Press, 1994), pp.107–8.

15. Kurt Vonnegut, "It Seemed Like Fiction," *Wall Street Journal*, July 29, 1994, p. A10.

16. William Manchester, *American Caesar: Douglas MacArthur 1880–1964* (Boston: Little, Brown, 1978), p. 7.

17. Schoeck, p. 329.

18. Wilson, *The Moral Sense*, p. 74.

19. Allan Bloom, "The Democratization of the University," *How Democratic Is America?: Responses to the New Left Challenge*, ed. Robert Goldwin (Chicago: Rand McNally, 1969), p. 114.

20. Karl Mannheim, *Man and Society* (London: Routledge & Kegan Paul, 1940, 1966), pp. 89–91.

21. *Ibid.*, p. 91.

22. John Rawls, *A Theory of Justice* (Cambridge, MA: The Belknap Press of Harvard University Press, 1971) and *Political Liberalism* (New York: Columbia University Press, 1993).

23. Rawls, *Political Liberalism*, p. 6.

24. Richard Grenier, "Equality of Intelligence," *Washington Times*, May 29, 1995, p. A21.

25. Jouvenel, p. 73.

26. Aaron Wildavsky, *The Rise of Radical Egalitarianism* (Washington, DC: American University Press, 1991), p. xxx.

27. Alexis de Touqueville, *Democracy in America* (New York: Vintage Books, 1945), vol. 2, p. 337.

28. *Ibid.*

29. *Ibid.*, p. 101.

30. Manent, p. 111.

31. Charles J. Sykes, *A Nation of Victims: The Decay of the American Character* (New York: St. Martin's Press, 1992).

32. Tocqueville, vol. 2, p. 352.

Chapter 5

1. Friedrich A. Hayek, *The Constitution of Liberty* (Chicago: University of Chicago Press, 1960), p. 2.

2. Joseph A. Schumpeter, *Capitalism, Socialism, and Democracy* (New York: Harper & Brothers, 1947), p. 147.

3. Max Weber, *The Sociology of Religion* (Boston: Beacon Press, 1963), pp. 124–5.

4. *Ibid.*, p. 135.

5. Richard Grenier, *Capturing the Culture: Film, Art, and Politics* (Washington, DC: Ethics and Public Policy Center, 1991), pp. xxxiv–xxxv.

6. Hillary D. Rodham, "Remarks on the Occasion of Wellesley's 91st Commencement," speech delivered May 31, 1969.

7. Release of the Office of the Press Secretary, the White House, "Remarks of the First Lady at Liz Carpenter's Lectureship Series," University of Texas, April 6, 1993.

8. Michael Kelly, "Saint Hillary," *New York Times Magazine*, May 23, 1993, pp. 22, 24.

9. *Ibid.*, p. 65.

10. Thomas Fields-Meyer, "This Year's Prophet," *New York Times Magazine*, June 27, 1993, p. 28.

11. Rabbi Michael Lerner, "Work: A Politics of Meaning Approach to Policy," *Tikkun*, May/June 1993, pp. 23, 25–6.

12. Robert Lerner, Althea K. Nagai, and Stanley Rothman, *American Elites* (New Haven: Yale University Press, in press).

13. *Ibid.*, chapter 7.

14. *Ibid.*, chapter 6.

15. *Ibid.*, chapter 9.

16. Paul Hollander, *Anti-Americanism: Critiques at Home and Abroad, 1965–1990* (New York: Oxford University Press, 1992), p. 149.

17. Jennifer Kaylin, "Bass, Yale, and Western Civ.," *Yale Alumni Magazine*, Summer 1995, p. 39.

18. Frederick Lewis Allen, *Only Yesterday: An Informal History of the 1920's* (New York: Harper & Row, 1964), p. 189–90.

19. Ken Ringle, "Political Correctness: Art's New Frontier," *Washington Post*, March 31, 1991, p. G1.

20. Hollander, p. 86.

21. Robert Alter, "The Persistence of Reading," *Partisan Review* Special Issue on "The Politics of Political Correctness" (1993), p. 512.

22. Schumpeter, p. 148.

23. *Ibid.*, pp. 148–9.

24. James Gardner, *Culture or Trash?: A Provocative View of Contemporary Painting, Sculpture, and Other Costly Commodities* (New York: Carol Publishing Group, 1993), p. 218.

25. Seymour Martin Lipset, *Rebellion in the University* (New Brunswick, NJ: Transaction Publishers, 1993), p. 200.

26. Helmut Schoeck, *Envy: A Theory of Social Behavior* (Indianapolis: Liberty Press, 1987), pp. 328–9.

27. *Ibid.*, p. 127.

28. James Q. Wilson, *On Character* (Washington, DC: The AEI Press, 1991), p. 39.

29. Myron Magnet, *The Dream and the Nightmare: The Sixties Legacy to the Underclass* (New York: William Morrow, 1993).

Chapter 6

1. Robert Nisbet, *Conservatism: Dream and Reality* (Minneapolis: University of Minnesota Press, 1986), p. 41.

2. William A. Donohue, *Twilight of Liberty: The Legacy of the ACLU* (New Brunswick, NJ: Transaction Publishers, 1994), p. 65. This and his other book, *The Politics of the American Civil Liberties Union* (New Brunswick, NJ: Transaction Publishers, 1985), are the definitive works on the ACLU.

3. Mary Ann Glendon, *Rights Talk: The Impoverishment of Political Discourse* (New York: The Free Press, 1991).

4. These matters are discussed in Robert H. Bork, "What to Do About the First Amendment," *Commentary*, February 1995, p. 23.

5. *Cohen* v. *California*, 403 U.S. 15 (1971).

6. *Ibid.*, at 25.

7. *Ibid.*

8. *Texas* v. *Johnson*, 491 U.S. 397 (1989).

9. *Ibid.*, at 414.

10. *Ibid.*, at 417.

11. Paul Greenberg, "Burning questions over the Stars and Stripes," *Washington Times*, July 6, 1995, p. A16.

12. Dissenting in *Street* v. *New York*, 394 U.S. 576 (1969). The majority did not reach the question.

13. Walter Berns, *The First Amendment and the Future of American Democracy* (New York: Basic Books, 1976), pp. 160–1.

14. *Brandenburg* v. *Ohio*, 395 U.S. 444 (1969).

15. *Lee* v. *Weisman*, 505 U.S. 577 (1992).

16. *Griswold* v. *Connecticut*, 381 U.S. 479 (1965).

17. *Eisenstadt* v. *Baird*, 405 U.S. 438 (1972).

18. *Roe* v. *Wade*, 410 U.S. 113 (1973).

19. See Robert H. Bork, *The Tempting of America: The Political Seduction of the Law* (New York: The Free Press, 1990).

20. *Planned Parenthood* v. *Casey*, 505 U.S. 833 (1992).

21. *Ibid.*, at 851.

22. *Bowers* v. *Hardwick*, 478 U.S. 186, 204 (1986).

23. *Ibid.*

24. *Ibid.*

25. *Brown* v. *Board of Education*, 347 U.S. 483 (1954).

26. Bork, *The Tempting of America*, pp. 74–83.

27. *Harper* v. *Virginia State Board of Elections*, 383 U.S. 663 (1966).

28 *Reynolds* v. *Sims*, 377 U.S. 533 (1964).

29. *United Steelworkers of America* v. *Weber*, 443 U.S. 193 (1979).

30. *Johnson* v. *Transportation Agency, Santa Clara County*, 480 U.S. 616 (1987).

31. *Metro Broadcasting, Inc.* v. *FCC*, 497 U.S. 547 (1990).

32. *Adarand Constructors, Inc.* v. *Pena*, 115 S.Ct. 2097 (1995).

33. *United States* v. *Virginia*, 116 S.Ct. 2263 (1996).

34. George F. Will, "VMI: Gone," *Washington Post*, June 30, 1996, p. C7.

35. *United States* v. *Virginia*, 116 S.Ct. at ___ (Scalia, J., dissenting).

36. *Compassion in Dying* v. *State of Washington*, 49 F.3d 586 (9th Cir. 1995).

37. 79 F.3d 790, 800 (9th Cir. 1995).

38. *Quill* v. *Vacco*, 80 F.3d 716 (2d Cir. 1996).

39. *Baehr* v. *Lewin*, 74 Haw. 530, 580; 852 P.2d 44, 67 (1993).

40. *Romer* v. *Evans*, 116 S.Ct. 1620 (1996).

41. *Ibid.*, at 1629.

42. *Ibid.*

43. Lino Graglia, "It's Not Constitutionalism, It's Judicial Activism," *Harvard Journal of Law & Public Policy,* Winter 1996, pp. 293, 298.

44. Don Van Natta, Jr., "Judges Defend A Colleague From Attacks," *New York Times,* March 29, 1996, p. B1.

45. Quoted in Gerald Gunther, *Learned Hand: The Man and the Judge* (New York: Alfred A. Knopf, 1994), pp. 247, 248.

46. *Ibid., p. 249.*

Chapter 7

1. Michael Bywater, "Never mind the width, feel the lack of quality," *The Spectator,* May 13, 1995, p. 44 (reviewing *The Faber Book of Pop,* London: Faber, 1995).

2. Robert Pattison, *The Triumph of Vulgarity: Rock Music in the Mirror of Romanticism* (Oxford, UK: Oxford University Press, 1987), pp. 122–3.

3. S. Robert Lichter, Linda S. Lichter, and Stanley Rothman, *Prime Time: How TV Portrays American Culture* (Washington, DC: Regnery Publishing, 1994), p. 416.

4. *Ibid.*, pp. 404–5.

5. Walter Goodman, "As TV Sows Outrage, Guess What It Reaps," *New York Times,* March 28, 1995, p. C26.

6. Paula Span, "Where Do They Find These People?," *Washington Post,* April 16, 1992, p. D1.

7. James Gardner, *Culture or Trash?: A Provocative View of Contemporary Painting, Sculpture, and Other Costly Commodities* (New York: Carol Publishing Group, 1993).

8. *Ibid.*, p. 183.

9. Roberta Smith, "A Show of Moderns Seeking to Shock," *New York Times,* November 23, 1995, p. C11.

10. Roger Kimball, "The heritage of Dada," *The Public Interest,* Fall 1994, p. 120.

11. *Ibid.*, p. 123.

12. John Leo, "The leading cultural polluter," *U.S. News & World Report,* March 27, 1995, p. 16.

13. All quotes not citing a periodical source are from "notes" taken by Pete Wehner at the May 18, 1995 meeting between William Bennett, DeLores Tucker, *et al.*, and Time Warner executives.

14. Howard Kurtz, "Time Warner, on the Defensive for the Offensive," *Washington Post,* June 2, 1995, pp. A1, A18.

15. *Ibid.*

16. Bernard Weinraub, "Filmmakers Discount Criticism by Dole," *New York Times,* June 2, 1995, p. A24.

17. "The New Global Popular Culture," American Enterprise Institute Conference, Washington, DC, March 10, 1992.

18. *Ibid.*

19. *Ibid.*

20. Martha Bayles, *Hole In Our Soul: The Loss of Beauty and Meaning in American Popular Music* (New York: The Free Press, 1994), p. 259.

21. *Ibid.*, p. 258.

22. John J. O'Connor, "Music as the Food of Hate: Rock for the Skinheads," *New York Times*, June 19, 1993, p. 47.

23. Simon Winchester, "An Electronic Sink of Depravity," *The Spectator*, February 4, 1995, p. 9.

24. *Ibid.*, p. 10.

25. *Ibid.*, p. 11.

26. Stephen Bates, "Alt.Many.Of.These.Newsgroups.Are.Repellent.," *The Weekly Standard*, October 30, 1995, p. 27.

27. Winchester, p. 11.

28. John R. Wilke, "A Publicly Held Firm Turns X-Rated Videos Into a Hot Business," *Wall Street Journal*, July 11, 1994, p. 1.

29. George Gilder, "Breaking the Box," *National Review*, August 15, 1994, p. 37.

30. Leo, p. 16.

31. Maggie Gallagher, *Enemies of Eros: How the Sexual Revolution Is Killing Family, Marriage, and Sex and What We Can Do About It* (Chicago: Bonus Books, 1989), p. 251.

32. *Ibid.*, p. 252.

Chapter 8

1. Stanley Brubaker, "In praise of censorship," *The Public Interest*, Winter 1994, p. 48.

2. Christopher Lasch, *The Revolt of the Elites and the Betrayal of Democracy* (New York: W.W. Norton, 1995), p. 85.

3. *Ibid.*, p. 86.

4. "Mr. Dole's Entertainment Guide," *New York Times*, June 2, 1995, p. A28.

5. George Will, "This Week With David Brinkley," *ABC News*, June 4, 1995.

6. Michael Medved, *Hollywood vs. America: Popular Culture and the War on Traditional Values* (New York: HarperCollins, 1992), pp. 239–252; Vincent Ryan Ruggiero, *WARNING: Nonsense Is Destroying America* (Nashville: Thomas Nelson Publishers, 1994), pp. 91–125.

7. Jane D. Brown and Jeanne R, Steele, "Sexuality and American Social Policy," p. 1. A report prepared for the Henry J. Kaiser Family Foundation and the American Enterprise Institute, presented September 29, 1995.

8. *Ibid.*, pp. 23–24.

9. S. Robert Lichter, Linda S. Lichter, and Stanley Rothman, *Prime Time: How TV Portrays American Culture* (Washington, DC: Regnery Publishing, 1994), pp. 425–31.

10. *Miller* v. *California*, 413 U.S. 15 (1973).

11. George Will, "America's Slide Into the Sewer," *Newsweek*, July 30, 1990, p. 64.

12. *Chaplinsky* v. *New Hampshire*, 315 U.S. 568, 571–2 (1942). (footnotes omitted)

13. Walter Berns, *The First Amendment and the Future of American Democracy* (New York: Basic Books, 1976), p. 221.

14. John R. Wilke, "A Publicly Held Firm Turns X-Rated Videos Into a Hot Business," *Wall Street Journal*, July 11, 1994, p. 8.

15. Michael Medved, "The Cultures of Hollywood," Bradley Lecture Series, American Enterprise Institute, January 12, 1993.

Chapter 9

1. The facts are set out in accessible form in Gertrude Himmelfarb, *The De-Moralization of Society: From Victorian Virtues to Modern Values* (New York: Alfred A. Knopf, 1995), pp. 222–37.

2. James Q. Wilson, *The Moral Sense*, (New York: The Free Press, 1993), p. 178.

3. Christine Bachrach, William Mosher, Susan Newcomer, and Stephanie Ventura, "What is Happening to Out-of-Wedlock Teen Childbearing?," paper presented at an American Enterprise Institute conference in Washington, DC, March 20, 1995.

4. James Alan Fox, dean of Northeastern University's College of Criminal Justice, as reported in the *Wall Street Journal*, April 21, 1995, p. B1.

5. Maggie Gallagher, *The Abolition of Marriage: How We Lost the Right to a Lasting Love* (Washington, DC: Regnery Publishing, 1995), pp. 31–2.

6. Charles Murray, "The Coming White Underclass," *Wall Street Journal*, October 29, 1993, p. A14.

7. Irving Kristol, "Welfare: The best of intentions, the worst of results," *Atlantic Monthly*, August 1971, p. 45.

8. See *Looking Before We Leap: Social Science and Welfare Reform,* eds. Kent R. Weaver and William T. Pickens (Washington, DC: Brookings Institution, 1995).

9. Myron Magnet, *The Dream and the Nightmare: The Sixties Legacy to the Underclass* (New York: William Morrow, 1993), pp. 141–2.

10. Douglas J. Besharov, "What About the Poor?: The Hope of a New Approach," *Washington Post*, December 3, 1995, p. C1.

11. Joseph Tierney, Jean Baldwin Grossman, with Nancy L. Resch, *Making a Difference: An Impact Study of Big Brothers/Big Sisters* (Philadelphia: Public/Private Ventures, 1995).

12. John J. DiIulio, Jr., "Violent Crime and Representative Government," Bradley Lecture Series, American Enterprise Institute, June 10, 1996.

13. "The State of Violent Crime in America," First Report of The Council on Crime in America, The New Citizenship Project, Washington, DC, January 1996.

14. Ben J. Wattenberg, *Values Matter Most: How Republicans or Democrats or a Third Party Can Win and Renew the American Way of Life* (New York: The Free Press, 1995), pp. 139–57.

15. Paul Johnson, "Crime: The People Want Revenge," *Wall Street Journal*, January 4, 1994, p. A10.

16. Robert Lerner, Althea K. Nagai, and Stanley Rothman, *American Elites* (New Haven: Yale University Press, in press), chapter 4.

17. "The State of Violent Crime in America," p. 17.

18. Daniel D. Polsby, "The False Promise of Gun Control," *Atlantic Monthly*, March 1994, p. 57.

19. *Ibid*.

20. John Carlson, "Go To The People," *The American Enterprise*, May/June 1995, pp. 39–40.

21. John J. DiIulio, Jr. and Anne M. Piehl, "Does Prison Pay? Revisited," *Brookings Review*, Winter 1995, pp. 21–95.

22. John J. DiIulio, "Let 'em Rot," *Wall Street Journal*, January 26, 1994, p. 14. Professor DiIulio promptly protested the savage title given his piece by some *Journal* headline writer.

23. "The State of Violent Crime in America," p. 55.

24. Murray, p. A14.

25. See James Dale Davidson and Lord William Rees-Mogg, *The Great Reckoning: How the World Will Change in the Depression of the 1990s* (New York: Summit Books, 1991). Their previous book was encouragingly entitled *Blood in the Streets*.

26. Murray, p. A14.

Chapter 10

1. Doris Gordon, "Abortion and Rights: Applying Libertarian Principles Correctly," *Studies in Prolife Feminism*, Spring 1995, pp. 121, 127.

2. James Q. Wilson, "On Abortion," *Commentary*, January 1994, p. 21.

3. *Ibid*.

4. Mary Ellen Bork, Letter to the Editor, *Commentary*, March 1994, pp. 7–8.

5. *Ibid*.

6. Peter Singer, "Killing Babies Isn't Always Wrong," *The Spectator*, September 16, 1995, p. 22.

7. Candace C. Crandall, "The Fetus Beat Us," *The Women's Quarterly*, Winter 1996, p. 1.

8. Naomi Wolf, "Our Bodies, Our Souls," *The New Republic*, October 16, 1995, p. 26.

9. Taken from Aida Torres and Jacqueline Darroch Forrest, "Why Do Women Have Abortions?," *Family Planning Perspectives*, July/August 1988, pp. 169-70.

10. *Ibid.*, p. 173.

11. Richard D. Glasow, "Statistics Show Abortion Being Used as Birth Control," *National Right to Life News*, May 9, 1994, p. 18.

12. "Anesthetized to truth," *World*, January 13, 1996, p. 17.

13. Diane M. Gianelli, "Shock-tactic ads target late-term abortion procedure," *American Medical News*, July 5, 1993, p. 3.

14. Diane M. Gianelli, "Outlawing abortion method," *American Medical News*, November 20, 1995, p. 3.

15. Richard John Neuhaus, "Don't Cross This Threshold," *Wall Street Journal*, October 27, 1994, p. A20.

16. "The Use of Anencephalic Neonates as Organ Donors," *Journal of the American Medical Association*, May 24/31, 1995, p. 1614.

17. *Ibid.*, p. 1615.

18. Charles Krauthammer, ". . . And a Troubling Development," *Washington Post*, June 9, 1995, p. A27.

19. Charles Krauthammer, "Traveling Executioner," *Washington Post*, December 3, 1993, p. A29.

20. Elizabeth Kristol, "Soothing Moral Shroud," *Washington Post*, December 3, 1993, p. A29.

21. *Compassion In Dying* v. *State of Washington*, 49 F.3d 586, 593-94 (9th Cir. 1995), quoting Report from the New York State Task Force on Life and the Law, "When Death Is Sought: Assisted Suicide and Euthanasia in the Medical Context," May 1994, p. 122.

22. Herbert Hendin, "Dying of Resentment," *New York Times*, March 21, 1996, p. A25.

23. Dr. Edmund D. Pellegrino, "Ethics," *Journal of the American Medical Association*, June 7, 1995, pp. 1674-5. The interior quote is from Derek Humphrey, "Letter to the Editor," *New York Times*, December 3, 1994, p. A22.

24. Michael Fumento, "What the Dutch can teach us about euthanasia," *Washington Times*, March 19, 1995, p. B3.

25. Carlos F. Gomez, "Managing the Unmanageable: The Case Against Euthanasia," in *Medicine Unbound: The Human Body and the Limits of Medical Intervention*, eds. Robert H. Blank and Andrea L. Bonnicksen (New York: Columbia University Press, 1994), pp. 228-41. See also Gomez, *Regulating Death: Euthanasia and the Case of the Netherlands* (New York: The Free Press, 1991) for an earlier and lengthier study, which confirms a very pessimistic view of the Dutch reality.

26. David C. Thomasma, "Euthanasia as Power and Empowerment," *Medicine Unbound: The Human Body and Limits of Medical Intervention*, eds. Robert H. Blank and Andrea L. Bonnicksen (New York: Columbia University Press, 1994), pp. 210-27.

27. *Ibid.*, p. 223.

28. Herbert Hendin, "Selling Death and Dignity," *Hastings Center Report*, May-June 1995, pp. 19-23.

29. *Ibid.*, p. 20.

Chapter 11

1. Sandra Harding of University of Delaware and Susan McClary, "who applies feminist theories to music," respectively. Quoted in John Leo, "PC: Almost dead. Still funny," *U.S. News & World Report*, December 5, 1994, p. 24.

2. See discussion in chapter 1.

3. Carol Iannone, "The Feminist Confusion," *Second Thoughts: Former Radicals Look Back at the Sixties* (Lanham, MD: Madison Books, 1989), p. 153.

4. Christina Hoff Sommers, *Who Stole Feminism?: How Women Have Betrayed Women* (New York: Simon & Schuster, 1994).

5. Midge Decter, "You're On Your Own, Baby," *The Women's Quarterly*, Winter 1996, p. 4.

6. Daphne Patai and Noretta Koertge, *Professing Feminism: Cautionary Tales from the Strange World of Women's Studies* (New York: Basic Books, 1994), p. 183. Other excellent works include Sommers, *Who Stole Feminism?* and a monograph by Dale O'Leary, "Gender Feminism: The Deconstruction of Women," Free Congress Foundation, August 1995.

7. Carol Iannone, "The Feminist Confusion," *Second Thoughts: Former Radicals Look Back at the Sixties*, eds. Peter Collier and David Horowitz (Lanham, MD: Madison Books, 1989), p. 149.

8. Bella Abzug, "A message from NGO women to UN member states, the Secretariat and the Commission on the Status of Women," New York, April 3, 1995.

9. James Q. Wilson, *The Moral Sense* (New York: The Free Press, 1993), pp. 165–6.

10. Melford E. Spiro, *Gender and Culture: kibbutz women revisited* (Durham, NC: Duke University Press, 1979), p. 106.

11. Barbara Crossette, "A Warrior, A Mother, A Scholar, A Mystery," *New York Times*, August 17, 1994, p. C1. Why the headline writer would call her "a mystery" is itself a mystery. Presumably it is because Dr. Kirkpatrick is a neo-conservative rather than a leftist.

12. Patai and Koertge, p. 112.

13. Rene Denfield, "Old Messages: Ecofeminism and the Alienation of Young People from Environmental Activism," p. 3. Paper presented at "The Flight from Science and Reason," New York, May 31–June 2, 1995.

14. *Profane Existence*, May/June 1992, p. 1.

15. Anne Wilson Schaef, *Women's Reality: An Emerging Female System in the White Male Society* (Minneapolis: Winston Press, 1981), p. 27.

16. Martha Nussbaum, "Justice for Women," *The New York Review of Books*, October 8, 1992, p. 43.

17. Interview with Simone de Beauvoir, "Sex, Society, and the Female Dilemma," *Saturday Review*, June 14, 1975, p. 18.

18. Shere Hite, *The Hite Report on the Family: Growing Up Under Patriarchy* (New York: Grove Press, 1994), pp. 352–60.

19. Dianne Knippers, "Building a Shrine in Beijing," *Heterodoxy*, October 1995, p. 7.

20. Susan Faludi, *Backlash: The Undeclared War Against American Women* (New York: Crown, 1991).

21. *Ibid.*, p. xxii.

22. Faludi's arguments have been exposed as false many times over. See, among others, Sommers, *Who Stole Feminism*, especially pp. 234–44; Mary Eberstadt, "Wake Up Little Susie," *American Spectator*, October 1992, p. 30; Gretchen Morgenson, "A Whiner's Bible," *Forbes*, March 16, 1992, p. 152; Maggie Gallagher, "Exit Stage Back," *National Review*, March 30, 1992, p. 41; and Charlotte Allen, "New Wave Feminism," *Commentary*, February 1992, p. 62.

23. As cited by Christina Hoff Sommers, "Feminist fatale," *The New Criterion*, October 1995, p. 64.

24. Susan Cheever, "An Accidental Symbol," (review of *I Am Roe* by Norma McCorvey with Andy Meisler), *New York Times Book Review,* July 3, 1994, p. 7.

25. Patai and Koertge, p. 116.

26. "Feminism Against Science," *National Review*, November 18, 1991, p. 30.

27. *Ibid.*

28. Carol Innerst, "Feminists remake college curriculums," *Washington Times*, June 21, 1993, p. A1.

29. George F. Will, "Literary Politics," *Newsweek,* April 22, 1991, p. 72.

30. "Blackboard Jungle," *The NEA Higher Education Journal*, Spring 1991, p. 15.

31. Joyce Price, "Lesbians get place at the table at women's studies conference," *Washington Times,* June 21, 1993, p. A8.

32. Michael Pack, "Campus Culture Wars," video distributed by Direct Cinema Limited, Santa Monica, CA, 1993.

33. Edmund Daniels and Michael David Weiss, "'Equality' over Quality," *Reason*, July 1991, p. 44.

34. Camille Paglia and Christian Hoff Sommers, "Has Feminism Gone Too Far?" *Think Tank with Ben Wattenberg,* Produced by New River Media, Washington, DC, November 4, 1994.

35. John Leo, "De-escalating the gender war," *U.S. News and World Report*, April 18, 1994, p. 24.

36. George Will, "A Kind of Compulsory Chapel," *Newsweek*, November 14, 1994, p. 84.

37. Letter from Robert Weissberg to *Measure*, August/September 1995, p. 4.

38. Pack, "Campus Culture Wars."

39. Sommers, *Who Stole Feminism?*, p. 91.

40. Robert Nisbet, *Prejudices: A Philosophical Dictionary* (Cambridge, MA: Harvard University Press, 1982), p. 245.

41. John Corry, "The Death of Kara Hultgreen," *The American Spectator*, June 1995, p. 40.

42. Robert J. Caldwell, "Navy files cast doubt on gender neutral," *San Diego Union-Tribune*, May 14, 1995, p. G1.

43. Corry, p. 40.

44. K. L. Billingsley, "Dancing with the Elephant," *Heterodoxy*, March/April 1995, p. 12.

45. Much of this material is taken from Billingsley, "Dancing with the Elephant" and K.L. Billingsley, "Feminist Forced March," *Heterodoxy,* June 1995, pp. 1, 13.

46. Cal Thomas, "Navy's thought police," *World*, June 17/24, 1995, p. 17.

47. *Ibid.*

48. David Horowitz, *The Feminist Assault on the Military*, Center for the Study of Popular Culture, Studio City, CA, 1992, pp. 21–3.

49. *Ibid.*, p. 16.

50. Billingsley, "Feminist Forced March," pp. 9–10.

51. Dana Priest, "Navy Punishes Two for Sex Aboard Ship," *Washington Post*, February 19, 1995, p. A13.

52. Horowitz, *The Feminist Assault on the Military*. Testimony before the Presidential Commission on the Assignment of Women in the Armed Forces also claimed that the military is desensitizing male soldiers to screams of women prisoners being tortured. "Major Mom," *World*, September 26, 1992, p. 7.

53. Maggie Gallagher, *Enemies of Eros: How the Sexual Revolution Is Killing Family, Marriage, and Sex and What We Can Do About It* (Chicago: Bonus Books, 1989), p. 270.

54. Spiro, p. 109.

55. Spiro, pp. 109–10.

56. Gallagher, p. 148.

Chapter 12

1. Glenn Loury, "Black Political Culture After the Sixties," *Second Thoughts: Former Radicals Look Back at the Sixties* (Lanham, MD: Madison Books, 1989), p. 143.

2. Shelby Steele, *The Content of Our Character: A New Vision of Race in America* (New York: St. Martin's Press, 1990), p. 27.

3. *Ibid.*, pp. 27–8.

4. Jason DeParle, "For Some Blacks, Social Ills Seem to Follow White Plans," *New York Times*, August 11, 1991, sec. 4, p. 5.

5. Paul Craig Roberts and Lawrence M. Stratton, *The New Color Line: How Quotas and Privilege Destroy Democracy* (Washington, DC: Regnery Publishing, 1995).

6. Thomas Sowell, *Preferential Policies: An International Perspective* (New York: William Morrow, 1990), pp. 15–6.

7. Terry Eastland, *Ending Affirmative Action: The Case for Colorblind Justice* (New York: Basic Books, 1996), p. 40.

8. *Ibid.*, pp. 143–158.

9. *Ibid.*, p. 179.

10. Albert S. Braverman and Brian Anziska, "Challenges to Science and Authority in Contemporary Medical Education," *Academic Questions*, Summer 1994, p. 14.

11. See generally Roberts and Stratton, *The New Color Line*.

12. *Ibid.*, p. 152.

13. Evidence cited in Roberts and Stratton, p. 89. See also Paul Craig Roberts and Lawrence M. Stratton, "Color Code," *National Review*, March 20, 1995, p. 36.

14. Sowell, p. 22.

15. See generally Gary Becker, *The Economics of Discrimination* (Chicago: University of Chicago Press, 1957).

16. Peter Brimelow and Leslie Spencer, "When quotas replace merit, everybody suffers," *Forbes*, February, 15, 1993, p. 102.

17. Steele, p. 115.

18. Christopher Lasch, *The Revolt of the Elites and the Betrayal of Democracy* (New York: W.W. Norton, 1995), pp. 84–5.

19. Quoted in Paul Craig Roberts and Lawrence M. Stratton, *In Defense of Liberalism* (forthcoming).

20. B. Drummond Ayres, Jr., "Conservatives Forge New Strategy To Challenge Affirmative Action," *New York Times*, February 16, 1995, p. A1.

21. "Campus Protest Against Slurs," *New York Times*, February 16, 1995, p. A22.

22. Mary Lefkowitz, *Not Out of Africa: How Afrocentrism Became An Excuse To Teach Myth As History* (New York: Basic Books, 1996), pp. 2–4. The following account and quotations are from this work.

23. "Remark Ends a Job Candidacy," *New York Times*, July 29, 1993, p. A21.

24. Michael Pack, "Campus Culture Wars," video distributed by Direct Cinema Limited, Santa Monica, CA, 1993.

25. Nino Langiulli, "When It Came to 'That' at the University of Cincinnati," *Measure*, March 1993, p. 3.

26. Dominic Lawson, "Taboo Or Not Taboo, That Is The Question," *The Spectator*, November 19, 1994, p. 9.

27. *Ibid.*

28. Paul Johnson, "Gone is the time when Americans led the world in saying what they thought," *The Spectator*, November 26, 1994, p. 31.

29. Lawson, p. 14.

30. *Ibid.*

31. Michael Brenson, "Is 'Quality' An Idea Whose Time Has Gone?" *New York Times*, July 22, 1990, Sec. 2, p. 1.

Chapter 13

1. Brigette Berger, "Multiculturalism and the Modern University," *The Politics of Political Correctness*, a special issue of *Partisan Review* (1993), pp. 516, 519. Gertrude Himmelfarb expresses a similar thought: "[T]here is an intimate, pervasive relationship between what happens in our schools and universities, in the intellectual and artistic communities, and what happens in society and the polity." *On Looking Into The Abyss: Untimely Thoughts on Culture and Society* (New York: Alfred A. Knopf, 1994), p. xii.

2. Richard Hofstadter, *Anti-intellectualism in American Life* (New York: Vintage Books, 1962), p. 51.

3. *Ibid.*, p. 23.

4. Joshua Meyrowitz, University of New Hampshire, quoted by John Leo, "Spicing up the (ho-hum) truth," *U.S. News & World Report*, March 8, 1993, p. 24.

5. *National Standards for United States History: Exploring the American Experience, Grades 5–12,* National Center for History in the Schools, University of California, Los Angeles, 1994.

6. *Ibid.*, p. 44.

7. *Ibid.*, p. 47.

8. *Ibid.*, p. 56.

9. Daniel J. Boorstin, *The Americans: The Colonial Experience* (New York: Random House, 1958), pp. 53–8.

10. Lynne V. Cheney, "The End of History," *Wall Street Journal*, October 20, 1994, p. A22.

11. Susan Olasky, "History Substandards," *World*, April 20, 1996, p. 18.

12. National Association of Scholars, *The Dissolution of General Education: 1914–1993* (Princeton: National Association of Scholars, 1996).

13. Robert J. Samuelson, "The Low State of Higher Ed," *Washington Post*, September 2, 1992, p. A21.

14. *The Dissolution*, p. 47.

15. Todd Gitlin, "Is America overdosing on entertainment?," *San Francisco Examiner*, August 23, 1994, Fourth Ed., p. C2.

16. Paul Hollander, "Political correctness is alive and well on campus near you," *Washington Times*, December 28, 1993, p. A19.

17. L. H. Gann and Peter Duignan, "The New Left and the Cultural Revolution of the 1960s: A Reevaluation," Hoover Institution, Stanford, CA, 1995, p. 43.

18. On this subject, see Carl Sagan, *The Demon-Haunted World: Science as a Candle in the Dark* (New York: Random House, 1995).

19. Marlise Simons, "Land of Descartes Under the Spell of Druids?," *New York Times,* April 30, 1996, p. A4.

20. John R. Searle, "Rationality and Realism, What is at Stake?," *Daedalus*, Fall 1993, p. 55.

21. Paul R. Gross and Norman Levitt, *Higher Superstition: The Academic Left and Its Quarrels with Science* (Baltimore: Johns Hopkins University Press, 1994).

22. *Ibid.*, p. 3.

23. *Ibid.*, p. 5.

24. *Ibid.*, pp. 223–4.

25. *Ibid.*, p. 24.

26. Richard J. Herrnstein and Charles Murray, *The Bell Curve: Intelligence and Class Structure in American Life* (New York: The Free Press, 1994).

27. Himmelfarb, *On Looking Into The Abyss*, p. 132.

28. David Lehman, *Signs of the Times: Deconstruction and the Fall of Paul deMan* (New York: Poseidon Press, 1991).

29. Robert H. Bork, *The Tempting of America: The Political Seduction of the Law* (New York: Free Press, 1990).

30. Alan D. Sokal, "Transgressing the Boundaries: Toward a Transformation Hermeneutics of Quantum Gravity," *Social Text*, Spring/Summer 1996, p. 217.

31. Alan D. Sokal, "A Physicist Experiments with Culture Studies," *Linguafranca*, May/June 1996, p. 62.

32. *Ibid.*, p. 63.

33. Malcolm W. Browne, "Scientists Deplore Flight From Reason," *New York Times*, June 6, 1995, p. C1.

34. *Ibid.*

Chapter 14

1. Alexis de Tocqueville, *Democracy In America*, ed. Phillips Bradley (New York: Vintage Books, 1945), vol. 1, pp. 315–8.

2. *Ibid.*, vol. 2, pp. 25–33.

3. James Q. Wilson, *On Character* (Washington, DC: The AEI Press, 1995), p. 28.

4. Christopher Lasch, *The Revolt of the Elites and the Betrayal of Democracy* (New York: W.W. Norton, 1995), p. 215.

5. Richard John Neuhaus, *The Naked Public Square: Religion and Democracy in America* (Grand Rapids, MI: William B. Eerdmans Publishing, 1984).

6. C. S. Lewis, "On Ethics," *The Seeing Eye and Other Selected Essays From Christian Reflections*, ed. Walter Hooper (New York: Ballentine Books, 1992), pp. 74–5.

7. Wilson, p. 28.

8. James Q. Wilson, *The Moral Sense* (New York: The Free Press, 1993), p. 9.

9. Irving Kristol, "The Cultural Revolution and the Capitalist Future," *Neoconservatism: The Autobiography of an Idea* (New York: The Free Press, 1995), pp. 132–3.

10. Letter to the Editor, *Wall Street Journal*, February 26, 1993, p. A15.

11. C. S. Lewis, p. 61.

12. *Ibid.*, p. 63.

13. José Ortega y Gassett, *Revolt of the Masses* (New York: W.W. Norton, 1957), pp. 135–6.

14. Recent sociological surveys are summarized in Kenneth L. Woodward, "The Rites of Americans," *Newsweek*, November 29, 1993, p. 80.

15. Stanley K. Henshaw and Jane Silverman, "The Characteristics and Prior Contraceptive Use of U.S. Abortion Patients," *Family Planning Perspectives*, July/August 1988, pp. 158, 162.

16. James Hitchcock, "Conservative Bishops, Liberal Results," *Catholic World Report*, May 1995, p. 22.

17. Frederic Lewis Allen, *Only Yesterday: An Informal History of the 1920's* (New York: Harper & Row, 1959), p. 164.

18. Charles J. Sykes, *A Nation of Victims: The Decay of the American Character* (New York: St. Martin's Press, 1992), p. 51.

19. See Herbert Schlossberg, *Idols for Destruction: Christian Faith and Its Confrontation with American Society* (Washington, DC: Regnery Gateway, 1990), chapter 4.

20. See, for example, George Gilder, "The Materialist Superstition," *The Intercollegiate Review*, Spring 1996, p. 6.

21. L.H. Gann and Peter Duignan, "The New Left and the Cultural Revolution of the 1960s: A Reevaluation," Hoover Institution, Stanford, CA, 1995, p. 30.

22. K. L. Billingsley, *From Mainline To Sideline: The Social Witness of the National Council of Churches* (Washington, DC: Ethics and Public Policy Center, 1990), p. 180.

23. Ernest W. Lefever, *Nairobi to Vancouver: The World Council of Churches and the World, 1975–87* (Washington, DC: Ethics and Public Policy Center, 1987), pp. 4–5, 56. Dr. Lefever's previous book on the WCC was *Amsterdam to Nairobi:*

The World Council of Churches and the Third World (1979). The WCC was formed at Amsterdam and the Assembly before Vancouver met in Nairobi.

24. "Petition Campaign Advances," Institute on Religion and Democracy, *Presbyterian Action Briefing*, Winter 1996.

25. "Episcopal Women's Unit Co-Sponsors Radical Feminist Conference," Institute on Religion and Democracy, *Episcopal Action Briefing*, Winter 1996.

26. "UM Board Backs Puerto Rican Terrorists," Institute on Religion and Democracy, *UM Action Briefing*, Winter 1996.

27. "Global Ministries Bashes Republicans, Praises UN Women's Summit," Institute on Religion and Democracy, *UM Action Briefing*, Winter 1996.

28. Frederick P. Jones, Dana Preusch, and Lonni Jackson, "Documenting the Oldline/Ecumenical Anti-War Movement: Consistent Themes, Faulty Premises" (Washington, DC: Institute on Religion and Democracy, June 1991), p. 5.

29. Alan Wisdom, "An Open Circle of Conversation," *Mainstream*, Fall 1992, p. 1.

30. "Religion in America," *The Public Perspective*, March/April 1993, p. 6.

31. Larry Witham, "Protestant Churches Unite, Push Tolerance," *Washington Times*, July 31, 1993, p. C4.

32. Arthur M. Matthews, "Religion Watch," *World*, July 27, 1991, p. 19.

33. Joyce Little, *The Church and the Culture War: Secular Anarchy or Sacred Order* (San Francisco: Ignatius Press, 1995), p. 75.

34. William Oddie, *What Will Happen to God?: Feminism and the Reconstruction of Christian Belief* (San Francisco: Ignatius Press, 1988), p. 143.

35. Robert Sokolowski, "Splitting the Faithful: Inclusive Language Is Wrong Biblically, Pastorally, and Doctrinally," *Crisis*, March 1993, p. 25.

36. Paul Mankowski, "When Words Become Weapons: Voices of Wrath," *Crisis*, December 1992, p. 25.

37. Donna Steichen, *UNGoDLY RaGE* (San Francisco: Ignatius Press, 1992), p. 23.

38. See Robert H. Bork, "What To Do About the First Amendment," *Commentary*, February, 1995, p. 23. For lengthier discussions of the historical evidence, see Walter Berns, *The First Amendment and the Future of American Democracy* (Chicago: Gateway Editions, 1985); Robert Cord, *Separation of Church and State* (Grand Rapids, MI: Baker Book House, 1988); and C. Antieau, A. Downey, and E. Roberts, *Freedom from Federal Establishment: Formation and Early History of the First Amendment Religion Clauses* (Milwaukee: Bruce Publishing, 1964).

39. *Abington School District* v. *Schempp*, 374 U.S. 203, 313 (1963).

40. Fred Barnes, "Faithful Bigots," *Forbes Media Critic*, vol. 1, no. 2, 1994, p. 10.

41. David Brooks, "The Naked Public Cave," *Weekly Standard*, April 22, 1996, p. 14.

42. Joe Maxwell, "A Caveman With Convictions," *World*, April 20, 1996, p. 12.

43. Jason Goodwin, "Where Heretics Fought and Lost," *New York Times*, April 14, 1996, p. 13.

44. Hitchcock, p. 26.

45. Joe Maxwell, "Promise Keepers' Parachurch Paradigm," *World*, March 2, 1996, p. 13.

46. James Fitzjames Stephen, *Liberty, Equality, Fraternity*, ed. Stuart D. Warner (Indianapolis: Liberty Fund, 1993), p. 3.

47. Michael J. Behe, *Darwin's Black Box: The Biochemical Challenge to Evolution* (New York: The Free Press, 1996).

48. Patrick Glynn, "Beyond the Death of God," *National Review*, May 6, 1996, p. 28. See also John Gribben and Martin Rees, *Cosmic Coincidences: Dark Matter, Mankind, and Anthropic Cosmology* (New York: Bantam Books, 1989).

49. Paul Johnson, *A History of Christianity* (New York: Simon & Schuster, 1976), p. 517.

Chapter 15

1. John Gray, *Post-liberalism: Studies in political thought* (London: Routledge, 1993), p. 45.

2. Steven Emerson, "The Other Fundamentalists," *The New Republic*, June 12, 1995, p. 22.

3. Arthur Schlesinger, Jr., *The Disuniting of America: Reflections on a Multicultural Society* (New York: W.W. Norton, 1992), p. 41.

4. See, generally, *The Failure of Bilingual Education*, ed. Jorge Amselle (Washington, DC: Center for Equal Opportunity, 1996).

5. Richard Bernstein, *Dictatorship of Virtue: Multiculturalism and the Battle for America's Future* (New York: Alfred A. Knopf, 1994), p. 244. The interior quotation is from Jim Cummins, *Empowering Minority Students*, California Association for Bilingual Education, Sacramento, 1989, p. ix.

6. *Ibid.*, p. 244.

7. *Ibid.*, pp. 245–6. The interior quotation is from *A Curriculum of Inclusion: Report of the Commissioner's Task Force on Minorities: Equity and Excellence* (Albany, July 1989).

8. Bernstein, pp. 6–7, 9.

9. Lynne V. Cheney, *Telling the Truth: Why Our Culture and Our Country Have Stopped Making Sense — and What We Can Do About It* (New York: Simon & Schuster, 1995), p. 29.

10. Bernstein, p. 58.

11. *Ibid.*

12. David O. Sacks and Peter A. Thiel, *The Diversity Myth: "Multiculturalism" and the Politics of Intolerance at Stanford* (Oakland: The Independent Institute, 1995), p. 18, note 5.

13. John Leo, *Two Steps Ahead of the Thought Police* (New York: Simon & Schuster, 1994), p. 307.

14. Schlesinger, p. 68.

15. Bernstein, p. 37.

16. Nick Felten, "Enforcing Diversity at DePaul," *Campus: America's Student Newspaper*, Fall 1995, pp. 13, 19.

17. Peter Berger, *A Far Glory: The Quest for Faith in an Age of Credulity* (New York: The Free Press, 1992), p. 85.

18. Katherine J. Mayberry, "White Feminists Who Study Black Writers," *The Chronicle of Higher Education*, October 12, 1994, p. A48.

19. José Ortega y Gasset, *The Revolt of the Masses* (New York: W.W. Norton, 1957), p. 134.

20. Schlesinger, p. 18.

21. Ortega y Gasset, p. 76.

Chapter 16

1. Sir Henry Sumner Maine, *Popular Government* (London: 1886), p. 1.

2. *Ibid.*, p. 2.

3. *Ibid.*, p. 5.

4. Francis Fukuyama, *The End of History and the Last Man* (New York: Avon Books, 1992).

5. Lino Graglia, "It's Not Constitutionalism, It's Judicial Activism," *Harvard Journal of Law & Public Policy*, Winter 1996, pp. 298–9.

6. John Gray, *Post-Liberalism: Studies in Political Thought* (London: Routledge, 1993), p. 45.

7. Randall Jarrell, *Pictures from an Institution* (New York: Alfred A. Knopf, 1954), p. 221.

8. James K. Glassman, "Jobs: The (Woe Is) Me Generation," *Washington Post*, March 19, 1996, p. A17.

9. David Riesman, *The Lonely Crowd: A Study of the Changing American Character* (New Haven: Yale University Press, 1961), abr. ed., pp. 225–35.

10. The quotes in this and the subsequent four paragraphs are from Robert Lerner, Althea K. Nagai, and Stanley Rothman, *American Elites* (New Haven: Yale University Press, in press), chapter 4.

11. *Ibid.*

12. *Ibid.*

13. Robert Nisbet, *Twilight of Authority* (New York: Oxford University Press, 1975), pp. 223–9.

14. Martin Mayer, *Today and Tomorrow in America* (New York: Harper & Row, Publishers, 1976), p. 4.

15. Peter L. Berger and Richard John Neuhaus, *To Empower People: From State to Civil Society*, 2nd ed. (Washington, DC: The AEI Press, 1996).

16. Stanley Rothman, "The Decline of Bourgeois America," *Society*, Jan/Feb 1996, p. 13.

Chapter 17

1. Friedrich A. Hayek, "Postscript: Why I Am Not a Conservative," *The Constitution of Liberty* (Chicago: The University of Chicago Press, 1960), p. 398.

2. Paul Hollander, "Reassessing the Adversary Culture," *Academic Questions*, Spring 1996, p. 37.

3. Thomas Cahill, *How the Irish Saved Civilization: The Untold Story of Ireland's Heroic Role from the Fall of Rome to the Rise of Medieval Europe* (New York: Nan A. Talese, 1995), p. 4.

4. Paul Johnson, *A History of Christianity* (New York: Atheneum, 1980), p. 143.

5. Richard John Neuhaus, "Second Thoughts," *Second Thoughts: Former Radicals Look Back At The Sixties*, eds. Peter Collier and David Horowitz (Lanham, MD: Madison Books, 1989), p. 9.

6. Roger Scruton, "Godless Conservatism," *Wall Street Journal*, April 5, 1996, p. A8.

7. James Q. Wilson, *The Moral Sense* (New York: The Free Press, 1993), p. 9.

8. "Virtue Unrewarded," *The Spectator*, November 7, 1992, p.5.

9. Jason DeParle, "Merle Haggard; Under the Growl, a Crooner," *New York Times*, July 29, 1993, p. C1.

Afterword

1. Kenneth Minogue, "'Christophobia' and the west," *The New Criterion*, June 2003, pp. 1, 9.

2. 529 U.S. 803.

3. 152 L Ed 2d 403.

4. See David Horowitz, *Uncivil Wars: The Controversy Over Reparations for Slavery* (San Francisco: Encounter Books, 2002).

5. Horowitz, *Uncivil Wars*.

6. *Ibid., passim.*

7. John Leo, "Diarist: 'Academic Freedom,'" *City Journal*, Winter 1999, p. 116.

8. John Leo, "Free speech as a tool of oppressors," *San Diego Union Tribune*, "Section: Opinion," March 10, 2001.

9. John Leo, "Lovely monsters," *U.S. News & World Report*, March 5, 2001, p. 14.

10. Eli Lehrer, "Another result of racial politics on campus: Speech," *The American Enterprise*, April/May 2003, pp. 40, 42.

11. Diane Ravitch, *The Language Police* (New York: Alfred A. Knopf, 2003), p. 27.

12. *Ibid.*, p. 22.

13. *Ibid.*, pp. 29–30.

14. *Ibid.*, p. 149.

15. *Ibid.*, p. 155.

16. 424 U.S. 1.

17. 528 U.S. 377.

18. *Grutter* v. *Bollinger*, 123 S. Ct. 2325 (2003).

19. Michael Kinsley, "Want diversity? Think fuzzy," *Washington Post*, June 25, 2003, p. A23.

20. Mark Steyn, "Counting on diversity in court," *Washington Times*, June 29, 2003, p. B3.

21. Powell, J., concurring in *Regents of Univ. of Cal.* v. *Bakke*, 438 U.S. 265 (1978).

22. The opinion is replete with such gibberish. "To be narrowly tailored, a race-conscious admissions program cannot use a quota system—it cannot 'insulat[e] each category of applicants with certain desired qualifications from competition with all other applicants' [citing Justice Powell in *Bakke*]. A uni-

versity may consider race or ethnicity only as a 'plus' for a particular applicant, without 'insulat[ing] the individual from competition with all other candidates for the available seats.'... [A]n admissions program must be 'flexible enough to consider all pertinent elements of diversity in light of the particular qualifications of each applicant, and to place them on the same footing for consideration, although not necessarily according them the same weight.'" If that means anything, it is that black applicants get a "plus" that insulates them from competition with otherwise equally or better qualified white or Asian applicants.

23. Peter Wood, *Diversity: The Invention of a Concept* (San Francisco: Encounter Books, 2003), pp. 98, 246.

24. Shelby Steele, "A victory for white guilt," *Wall Street Journal,* June 26, 2003, p. A16.

25. No. 02-102 Slip Op. (2003).

26. *Romer* v. *Evans,* 517 U.S. 620 (1996).

27. Stanford *et al., Arch. Gen. Psychiatry,* Vol. 58 (2001).

28. Fergusson *et al., Arch. Gen. Psychiatry* (2000).

29. Jeffrey Satinover, "The biology of homosexuality: Science or politics?," *Homosexuality and American Public Life,* ed. Christopher Wolfe (Dallas: Spence Publishing Co., 1999), p. 22.

30. Richard Fitzgibbons, "The origins and therapy of same-sex attraction disorder," *Ibid.,* p. 92.

31. *Ibid.,* p. 95.

32. Joseph Nicolosi, "The gay deception," *ibid.,* p. 98.

33. William Bennett, *The Broken Hearth: Reversing the Moral Collapse of the American Family* (New York: Doubleday, 2001), p. 113.

34. Mary Eberstadt, "Pedophilia chic," *The Weekly Standard,* June 17, 1996, p. 28.

35. Mary Eberstadt, "'Pedophilia chic' reconsidered," *The Weekly Standard,* January 1/January 8, 2001, p. 19.

36. Fitzgibbons, *Ibid.,* p. 85.

37. Amy Fagan, "Study finds gay unions brief," *Washington Times,* July 11, 2003.

38. Minogue, "'Christophobia' and the west," pp. 9–10.

39. Robert Bork, *Coercing Virtue: The Worldwide Rule of Judges* (Washington, D.C.: AEI Press, 2003).

40. Linda Greenhouse, "Heartfelt Words from the Rehnquist Court," *New York Times,* July 6, 2003, p. 3.

Index

hedonism, 8, 11, 34, 51, 281
Hefner, Hugh, 138
Heilbrun, Carolyn, 208
Hendin, Herbert, 188, 191
Heritage Foundation, 221
Herrnstein, Richard, 267–68
Hersey, John, 43
Hickey, Adm. Robert, 219–20
Higher Superstition (Gross and Levitt), 265
Hills, Carla, 200
Himmelfarb, Gertrude, 59, 60, 268
Hippies, 50
Hiroshima, atomic bombing of, 90
Hispanics, 107, 212, 299
    bilingual education for, 301
    multiculturalism and, 302, 304, 309
    preferential treatment of, 236, 239–41
Hispanic studies, 208
Hitchcock, James, 280, 292
Hite, Shere, 204–5
Hitler, Adolf, 102, 191
Ho Chi Minh, 19
Hofstadter, Richard, 251, 265
Hollander, Paul, 89, 262, 333
Hollywood, *see* movies
Holmes, Oliver Wendell, Jr., 101–2, 334
home-schooling movement, 334
homicide, *see* murder
homosexuality, 53, 55, 103–4, 112–14, 298, 325, 363–77
    and AIDS, 229
    and feminism, 197
    and multiculturalism, 304, 309, 311
    and popular culture, 127, 129
    and religion, 286, 288
    sensitivity training about, 216
Horowitz, David, 25, 221
Hot, Sexy and Safer Products, 159
House of Representatives, U.S., 206, 289
Housing and Urban Development, U.S. Department of, 200
Howard, Gerald, 23–24
Hultgreen, Lt. Kara, 219–20

humanism, secular, 276, 295
Humphrey, Hubert, 231
Hussein, Saddam, 91

Iannone, Carol, 196
Ice-T, 125
identity politics, 195
Ideologies of Desire (book series), 212–13
illegitimacy, 3, 143, 154–64, 170, 276, 340
immigration, 296–302, 311
    illegal, 243, 299
inclusive language, 287–89
income tax, progressive, 70–73
Indians, 90, 212, 254, 255, 323
    affirmative action for, 223
    multiculturalism and, 302, 304, 306–7, 309
individualism, radical, 5–6, 8, 11, 30, 88, 154, 331–32
    abortion and, 183
    and decline of intellect, 253, 256, 259, 267
    historical sources of, 56–65
    judicial, 98–105, 110–14, 140
    popular culture and, 129, 133, 134, 152
    religion and, 273, 281, 292
    resistance to, 342
Indonesia, 300
Inevitability of Patriarchy, The (Goldberg), 211
infanticide, 178, 182, 183
Institute on Religion and Democracy, 206, 284
intellect, decline of, 250–71
intellectual class, 10, 52, 83–95, 321, 328, 334
    British, 97
    Equal Rights Amendment favored by, 324
    and multiculturalism, 303
    and popular culture, 133, 134
    and religion, 277, 282, 289, 294
Internet, 135–38, 140, 147